FORBIDDEN MUSIC

FORBIDDEN MUSIC
THE JEWISH COMPOSERS BANNED BY THE NAZIS

MICHAEL HAAS

YALE UNIVERSITY PRESS
NEW HAVEN AND LONDON

2013

JUL

For information about this and other Yale University Press publications please contact:
U.S. Office: sales.press@yale.edu   yalebooks.com
Europe Office: sales@yaleup.co.uk   www.yalebooks.co.uk

Set in Minion Pro by IDSUK (DataConnection) Ltd
Printed in Great Britain by TJ International Ltd, Padstow, Cornwall

Library of Congress Control Number 2013934408

ISBN 978-0-300-15430-6

A catalogue record for this book is available from the British Library.

10 9 8 7 6 5 4 3 2 1

MIX
Paper from
responsible sources
FSC® C013056

The book is dedicated to the two men in my life who made it possible: My father Benjamin Leopold Haas who provided me with the roots necessary to keep asking the right questions; and my partner Kevin Bell whose patience and support made it possible for me to take the necessary time away from the recording studio to write.

Contents

Preface

'Should what's German and true be forgot, its memory be the Master's lot' (*Was deutsch und echt wüßt keiner mehr, lebt's nicht in deutscher Meister Ehr*) is Hans Sachs's final admonition at the end of Wagner's *Die Meistersinger von Nürnberg* and could have been understood as a veiled warning from the anti-Semitic Wagner to non-Jewish Germans on the cusp of Jewish emancipation. But Sachs's lines spoke just as strongly, perhaps even more resonantly, to Jews eager to contribute to what they had long perceived as a shared cultural heritage. In only 65 years, such intentions would be shattered and the loss would be felt by more than just the German nation.

As the producer for the recording series entitled 'Entartete Musik' released by London/Decca, I found myself confronting works by composers who had inexplicably vanished from the repertoire since their banning in 1933. My first encounter with some of this material took place in the mid-1980s when I began producing recordings of early orchestral works by Alexander Zemlinsky with Riccardo Chailly and the Berlin Radio Symphony Orchestra (now the Deutsches Symphonie-Orchester Berlin). That Zemlinsky was considered at all was thanks to the advocacy of the orchestra manager, Peter Ruzicka. When I was first shown the scores, I was slightly baffled. Chailly and Ruzicka were at the time both inquisitive musical progressives and the works they were considering reminded me more of Dvořák than their usual enthusiasms for more visionary twentieth-century composers. The fact that Zemlinsky was Schoenberg's teacher and brother-in-law offered an acceptable rationale and the recordings were surprisingly well received and were followed by Schoenberg's *Gurrelieder*. Then, as co-productions with *DeutschlandRadio*, (or RIAS, as it was then known), there came projects with Ute Lemper and John Mauceri, intended as the beginning of a series of the complete stage works of Kurt Weill. Disagreements with the Kurt Weill Foundation in New

York led to the idea being dropped and rather than return the designated budget to London/Decca, I pleaded that we should use it explore other composers whose names I kept encountering while researching Weill. I had begun to suspect that Weill was only the tip of a potentially large iceberg. I put this proposal to the president of the label, Roland Kommerell, who was not only German, but also a nephew of the literary historian Max Kommerell, former secretary to the poet Stefan George and later a close associate of the philosopher Martin Heidegger. For whatever reasons, Roland Kommerell clearly appreciated that money put into this particular large-scale recovery would be well spent. I remain grateful to him for his trust and faith in both the idea and my work. Assisting me with advice and scholarly support was the ever helpful and indefatigable Albrecht Dümling, who remains one of the first and foremost German academics to have dealt fearlessly and objectively with this period of cultural history. The composer Berthold Goldschmidt, with whom I would subsequently work very closely, not only took me through his scores bar by bar, but was able to offer sobering accounts of life in Germany before 1935 and later as an émigré in England. The integrity of the recording series would have been unthinkable without him. Additional support came from Thomas Gayda and others, some of whom came from Peter Petersen's 'Music Exile Project' at Hamburg University while others came from within London/Decca itself.

Though we were not the only label examining repertoire banned by the Third Reich, we were the first with international distribution and the financial wherewithal to record large-scale operatic and orchestral works. The series ran for nearly 10 years resulting in a total of 30 different projects and won many awards. The conductors Lothar Zagrosek, John Mauceri, Riccardo Chailly and Charles Dutoit along with the singers Ute Lemper, François le Roux and Matthias Goerne, and the instrumentalists Yo Yo Ma, Sabine Meyer and Chantal Juillet brought not only idiomatic authority but also a good deal of much-needed prestige. Sadly, all the recognition the series received could not save it from the turbulence of the recording industry during the final years of the last century. With the sale of Polygram to Universal Music, the series was cancelled and we went our separate ways.

I was subsequently approached by the Director of the Jewish Museum of Vienna to advise on a large exhibition being curated by Leon Botstein on the subject of Vienna as a city of music and Jews entitled 'Quasi una fantasia'. This was followed by my appointment as Music Curator, resulting in a number of exhibitions on various Viennese composers and allowing me the opportunity to do more than skim biographies and worklists in search of the most appropriate pieces to record. For the first time, I was able to explore the lives of individual composers, and the events that shaped them. This would not have been possible without an army of experts who assisted on each exhibition. These included the families of Hans Gál, Erich Korngold, Erich Zeisl and Egon Wellesz; Reinhold Kubik of the International Gustav Mahler Society in Vienna; Hannes Heher and Hartmut Krones of the Wellesz Foundation and the Austrian Hanns Eisler Society; Karin Wagner who co-curated the Erich Zeisl exhibition; Christopher Hailey, who is not only the leading authority on Franz Schreker but also an expert on the musical environment of prewar Vienna and Berlin; Brendan Carroll, whose Korngold biography finally gave us a scholarly reference that dealt with the composer as more than just a Hollywood phenomenon. Special thanks must go to the American relatives and friends who provided support and information: Gladys Krenek, Kathrin Korngold and her mother Helen; Barbara Zeisl-Schoenberg and the entire Schoenberg family, with particular gratitude to E. Randol Schoenberg the grandson of both Arnold Schoenberg and Erich Zeisl; the Los Angeles composer and critic Walter Arlen; and the grandson of Ernst Toch, Lawrence Weschler, as well as the grandson of Karl Weigl, Karl C. Weigl, along with Juliane Brand.

The Jewish Museum in Vienna is a centre of excellence and its curators could hardly have been bettered. They have all achieved wide recognition in their various fields: Michaele Feurstein, Werner Hanak, Wiebke Krohn, Marcus Patka, along with the extraordinary senior curator Felicitas Heimann and the museum's director, Karl Albrecht-Weinberger, whose support gave the institution, and its exhibitions and the accompanying catalogues, intellectual authority. The designer Thomas Geisler and his team created large-scale, multi-media, presentations so that the exhibitions were interactive, didactic and even theatrical. Perhaps most importantly, the museum's finance director Georg Haber made sure it could all be paid for. This resulted in critical praise and extraordinary visitor numbers. With the departure of Dr Albrecht-Weinberger, Georg Haber and Dr Heimann, along with much of their team, I moved to new opportunities. I am grateful to Gerold Gruber at Vienna's Music University, where together we head Exilarte, an organisation devoted to the recovery of Austria's composers lost after 1938.

Without the support of many organisations throughout Europe and America, the job of cultural restitution would hardly be possible. These include London's Jewish Music Institute and its indomitable director Geraldine Auerbach, who invited me to continue the work started at Decca as soon as she heard of the cancellation of the recording series. She helped assemble a committee that has remained a constant support and information resource. In addition, we all became close and mutually supportive friends. Together we make up the International Centre for Suppressed Music based at SOAS

(London University): Martin Anderson, Betty Collick; Erik Levi and Lloyd Moore (who both provided invaluable editorial assistance for this volume, with Erik Levi helping to locate important documentation and Lloyd Moore reading and commenting on each chapter), Malcolm Miller, Gavin Plumley, Jutta Raab-Hansen and Peter Tregear. Additional thanks must also go to the historian Philipp Blom. In America, further support has come from the OREL Foundation, thanks to the conductor James Conlon and the Foundation's Director Robert Elias who also contributed invaluable editorial advice and guidance. Finally, Malcolm Gerratt from Yale University Press who provided the much needed impulse to put e-pen to e-paper and most of all, my editor Nigel Simeone, who helped sharpen the narrative and focus the arguments in each chapter. All of them, and many others too numerous to mention, have helped to made this book possible, and I am deeply grateful to every one of them.

Translations are my own unless otherwise stated.

Introduction

This a magic cauldron be,
Wherein we find bewitching forces;
If you place your head inside
You'll witness all your future courses

A German future here to see
Within this fetid sink;
Yet don't be sickened by the scum,
Or its penetrating stink

With a smile, she bade me hither,
I quickly hid my fear
I hurried towards her, ever eager
To see what held this sphere

What I saw, I shall not say
To silence I am vowed
Indeed I hardly dare describe
The stench-enfolding cloud

With reluctance I recall
That dreadful, cursed smell
It seemed a mix of unwashed masses:
Ovens from a tannery in hell

Hideous the stench! Oh God help!
That still continued to rise
The fanning of dung it seemed to me
Of three-dozen fields in size.

Of Saint-Just's words, I know quite well
Once uttered on charitable boards
That sore afflictions, with rose-oil and musk
Won't work to cure the hoards

This rancid reek of a German future
Overwhelmed the senses
My nose had never inhaled the like
It shattered my defences.

Heinrich Heine, *Germany: A Winter's Tale*, from Caput 26, 1844

As this excerpt shows, German Jews had a complex relationship with their sense of national identity. Heine's epic poem from 1844, *Germany: A Winter's Tale*, offers a chilling prediction of the disastrous direction in which the German nation would move. In an apparent contradiction, Heine states in his introduction that his sense of patriotism consisted of dreaming of a world that one day would be entirely German.[1] Heine was simply personifying the conflict that resulted from his respect for German culture, above all its language, with his wariness about a national identity that saw itself as so exceptional as to be exclusive. As a Jew, he understood the notion of exclusion. At the same time, his response to German cultural exceptionalism was to reshape German culture through his own work: Heine was the poet for whom the Romantic German composers showed the greatest enthusiasm.

This book is about the Jewish composers who were banned by the Third Reich. Most of those directly affected were born within a decade of Heine's centenary in 1897. The mixture of exuberance and apprehension expressed by Heine had ripened by then into a sense of national entitlement. Jews were able to counter threats of exclusion from German culture by reacting as Heine, and reshaping it through their own creativity. Thus, by banning Jewish composers, Hitler's Reich amputated an essential limb from the body of German cultural continuity. Jews born within Germany or Austria had only recently been allowed to count themselves as full participants in their nations. In Austria, Jewish emancipation came about in 1867 with the creation of the new state of Austria-Hungary, while in Germany it started with the proclamation of the German Empire in 1871. Once Jews became active participants in what they viewed as the most cultivated and liberal society in Europe, they embraced all things German with a creative enthusiasm that came close to mania. As with Heine, years of looking into German Culture from the outside resulted in works of untold inventiveness. It was a creative intoxication so intense that many did not notice the numerous non-Jews who dismissed out of hand any notion of Jewish cultural entitlement. The more vehemently Jewish claims of cultural or national equality were rejected by anti-Semites, the more Jews proved that they were bringing creative elements to bear that resulted in the country's artistic life becoming more, not less German.

A fascinating example of this dynamic playing itself out in its many unappealing aspects was the slanging match between two Leipzig critics, Adolf Aber and Alfred Heuß, in the 1920s. It had been ignited by divided opinions surrounding Franz Schreker's opera *Der Schatzgräber*.[2] Schreker was widely regarded as Jewish though he had been brought up as Roman Catholic by his mother, a member of Austria's impoverished aristocracy. Heuß greeted the premiere of *Der Schatzgräber* in Leipzig on 23 October 1921 with an incendiary article implying that Schreker's popularity was manufactured, supported by the press with its principal cheerleader being the influential Jewish journalist Paul Bekker, who in 1919 had proclaimed Schreker as 'successor' to Richard Wagner.

Heuß's vile and paranoid article is not explicitly anti-Semitic, but its rant against 'the press' and Bekker (referred to as 'Plague-breath') would have been understood by anyone reading it. He denounces his fellow Leipzig critic Adolf Aber as a 'Bekker-poodle' and Schreker's operas as 'sexually charged kitsch'.[3] Such a toxic attack could not go unanswered and Aber wrote a short essay entitled *The Heuß Case* which he had privately published and sent to interested parties – one of whom happened to be Heuß.[4] Heuß reacted by dismissing Aber as 'Leipzig vermin,' but what disturbed Heuß most was Aber's reaction to the implication that Schreker, Bekker and Aber were somehow not sufficiently 'German'. Aber wondered how a Swiss such as Heuß could wrap himself in the flag of German nationalism while questioning Aber's own national allegiance. Aber reminds his Swiss colleague, that he – Aber – had not only fought in the recently ended war (in which Switzerland had remained neutral), but had been an officer in the Prussian Army. This was clearly a sore point for Heuß, and his retort tells us a good deal about the attitudes of the time: he wonders how Aber, as a Jew, can dare to question Heuß's German credentials. The assumption, which would have been understood by everyone following this row, was that a Prussian Jew (or even half-Jew, such as Bekker and Schreker), was far less 'German' than a Swiss-German.

In an attempt to put disputes such as the Heuß–Aber row into context, this book sets the scene from before the emergence of the German nation into its two political states. It considers the historical and cultural significance of Jewish composers who have been 'lost', and examines the obstacle-strewn path towards musical assimilation that they were made to take. From the first half of the nineteenth century, Jewish composers who did not emigrate to France (as Meyerbeer and Offenbach had done) appear to have been almost stiflingly conventional in order to underpin their German cultural credentials. Wagner even dismissed the brilliance of Mendelssohn, declaring that he, too, was merely the product of Jewish over-compensation.

Such views were a reflection of the hostile environment in which nineteenth-century Jewish composers found themselves rather than an objective assessment of their talent. This sheds light on the sobering fact that few of these composers – Mendelssohn excepted – have much to say to us today. Yet the cautious emergence of Jewish musicians evolved into a position of near dominance within German and Austrian musical life over the course of a mere half-century. Such was the situation that in 1938 the Nazis mounted an exhibition, 'Entartete Musik' ('Degenerate Music') in Düsseldorf to demonstrate the supposed 'degenerate' influence on German musical life by what they called 'Jewish Cultural Bolshevism'.

This is not a book about Nazis but about the composers who were lost, and the musical trends they established before being banned, murdered and exiled. It also examines the tragic postwar developments that kept them on the margins long after the fall of Hitler's Reich. As such, this book lays out how Jews saw themselves, and how they were seen by non-Jews. It tries to contextualise the discrepancy that often emerges from these different perceptions and to evaluate the music written by Jewish composers, much of which remains unjustly neglected.

In dealing with how Jews saw themselves and the world around them, I have used two main sources: Vienna's newspaper the *Neue Freie Presse*, which, since its earliest days, was seen as one of the great European papers and a voice of social and economic Liberalism. Its daily essays, called 'feuilletons', offered an exceptional forum for intellectual discourse. The paper was written and produced largely by secular Jewish journalists for a largely Liberal readership, many of whom were also secular and Jewish. The Viennese Jewish polemicist Karl Kraus in his own publication, *Die Fackel*, defines the journalism of the day by relentlessly attacking it. He saves his most lethal darts for all writers of feuilletons, especially those writing for the *Neue Freie Presse*. To Kraus, feuilletons were an unhealthy and unwelcome mix of fact and personal creativity. Kraus's ethical and intellectual standards have, I suspect, made many historians reluctant to use feuilletons as a source for understanding the thinking of the time. His views on creative journalism turned out to be fully justified. Still, to ignore feuilletons that appeared in the Viennese press is to ignore the manner in which some of the age's brightest and most articulate writers viewed and responded to the world around them. I take the view that feuilletons (*pace* Karl Kraus) are not journalism in the pure sense of reporting events, but a literary genre that grew out of people's reaction to the world in which they lived. With photography and moving pictures still in their infancy, they offer some of the most captivating images of the past. Nobody would dare to challenge the ethical might of Karl Kraus, but I believe the world has moved on, and his rants against opinion-based journalism can – for our purposes – be respected, but passed over.

My other key source comes from the journal *Musikblätter des Anbruch*, later called simply *Anbruch*. It was launched in 1919 by Universal Edition (UE), the Viennese publisher of many of the composers who would find themselves banned in Germany after 1933. *Anbruch* was run by secular Jews and aimed at a progressive readership. With the highly regarded Eduard Hanslick serving since 1864 as principal critic for the *Neue Freie Presse*, and his successor Julius Korngold, along with Guido Adler who was the 'éminence grise' of *Anbruch*, we gain a very clear idea of how Jews participated in musical life until 1933 in Germany, and 1938 in Austria. Both publications represented authoritative forums for cultural, musical and intellectual discourse: they were progressive, secular and resoundingly aware of their own Germanic culture in the international context of musical trends and developments.

The 2003 exhibition at Vienna's Jewish Museum took the title 'Quasi una fantasia' to express the cultural delusion that grew out of Jewish political and social emancipation. The implication was that assimilation was a mirage that had beguiled Jewish composers into writing works that affirmed their entitlement to German culture, only then to be ejected from their natural home by Hitler. This implied delusion meant that even when they enjoyed great popularity among non-Jewish audiences, these composers remained very far from obtaining true equality and acceptance.

Yet it wasn't only a delusion. To leave it at that would be to chalk up a victory to the anti-Semitism that culminated in the Third Reich. By banning Jewish artists, musicians and writers the Nazis had not removed delusional fantasists but, instead, broken fundamental links in the chain that made up German musical continuity.

In an eerie fulfilment of Hugo Bettauer's satirical novel from 1922 *The City without Jews* or *Die Stadt ohne Juden*, Germany and Austria, rendered virtually *Judenfrei* after 1945, have struggled in the decades following, to regain their prominence as leaders of musical development. After centuries of determining how music interacted within society, these two German nations found themselves overtaken by the very countries that had given refuge to their émigrés. Yet even these host countries largely mishandled their opportunities. Few composers could establish themselves in their new homelands without either appealing to new and unknown audiences or relying on the support of fellow émigrés who ran many of the musical institutions in America and elsewhere for quarter of a century after the war.

There may be no qualitative difference in the music composed by Weill on Broadway, or Korngold in Hollywood or even Joseph Kosma in Paris with his now iconic French chansons, but one thing is beyond dispute: their development as composers, despite new-found success, was disrupted. With many others, it was stopped altogether. It was perhaps only the most talented, opportunistic or resourceful who could continue to remain creative in their new environments.

This is an epic story that starts with the Congress of Vienna in 1815 and ends with the new definitions of music and society in the 1960s. Such an expanse of history squeezed into a single volume means that significant people and events are sometimes merely signposted, in the hope that interested readers will investigate further for themselves. This book also tries to avoid the inevitable 'what if' questions, offering instead an account of what happened and exploring what shaped the decisions that an important lost generation of composers was forced to make.

CHAPTER 1

German and Jewish

And as I reached the country's border,
I felt an inner tremble growing
It moved within my deepest breast
And wet with tears my eyes were glowing

Yet when I heard the German tongue
A strange mood overtook my soul
It seemed as if my very heart
Though bleeding, filled with joy, was whole

Heinrich Heine, *A Winter's Tale*, Caput 1

Isak Schrecker, the Jewish father of the composer Franz Schreker, had been court photographer in Budapest to Franz Joseph, King of Hungary and Emperor of Austria, as well as to his son and heir Crown Prince Rudolf, since obtaining the royal seal of approval in 1871. In 1874, he divorced his Jewish wife, converted to Protestantism and changed his name to Ignácz Ferenz Schrecker before placing an advertisement in the paper in search of a new, presumably non-Jewish, wife. The success of this venture must have startled even him: with his marriage to the penniless god-daughter of Princess Eleonore Maria Windisch-Graetz, his new wife, Eleonore von Clossmann, was related to the families Thurn und Taxis, Fürstenberg, Lobkowitz and Waldstein, Austria's most blue-blooded aristocrats. Only a decade earlier, such a union would have been unthinkable, and seen in the context of the time, the marriage demonstrated the speed and degree of acceptance of Jewish assimilation.

Isak had been born in 1834 in Bohemia, which at the time was Austrian. Typical of Jews during these early days of Liberalism, he had become an early

adopter of new technologies and by the late 1860s had based himself in
Budapest where, in addition to royalty, he accumulated an impressive list of
celebrity clients.

Equally characteristic of this new age of social emancipation was the fact
that in 1912 Wilhelm Pickl von Witkenberg, the son of Eleonore von
Clossmann's older sister, would compile a notorious directory of aristocratic
families who had intermarried with Jews: *Weimarer historisch-genealogen
Taschenbuch des gesamten Adels jehudäischen Ursprungs* – or simply known as
the *Semigotha*.

As we shall see later, Franz Schreker,[1] born to Eleonore and Ignácz in 1878
during a family sojourn in Monaco, would be the object of virulent anti-
Semitic attacks in the immediate lead-up to Hitler. Schreker, whose works are
only today returning to opera houses and concert halls, was a central figure in
pre-Nazi musical life; the number of performances of his operas came close to
those of Richard Strauss and, in the early 1920s, frequently overtook them. He
was thus one of Germany's most performed living composers in addition to
being a highly regarded conductor who had given the premieres of many
important works, including Schoenberg's *Gurrelieder* in 1913. He was accorded
the ultimate German accolade when in 1919 one of Frankfurt's most influential critics, Paul Bekker, announced that Schreker – among a number of other
prestigious German opera composers including Richard Strauss – was the only
credible successor to Richard Wagner. In 1920 Schreker left Vienna to take up
the directorship of Berlin's Music Academy. In 1932, he joined his friend and
colleague Arnold Schoenberg at the Prussian Academy of Arts, where he held
a composition master class. The names of Schreker's pupils, both in Vienna
and Berlin, represent a roll-call of central European musical life during the
1920s and 1930s. He was unquestionably one of Germany's cultural giants.

Schreker had nevertheless been the object of frequent anti-Semitic vilifica-
tion even before the Nazi dictatorship of 1933, forcing his move from Berlin's
Music Academy to the Prussian Academy of Arts. With Hitler's arrival, there
followed a ban on Schreker as conductor and teacher along with a performance ban on his works. His complete removal from public life, his inability to
emigrate and a vindictive cancellation of his promised pension resulted in a
stroke that proved fatal only a few days short of his 56th birthday in 1934. He
thus became Hitler's first high-profile musical victim.

Schreker, whose father Ignácz had died when Franz was still a boy of nine,
most likely never set foot in a synagogue. With a Christian mother, he was by
Jewish law not even a Jew. His musical education had been paid for by
Princess Windisch-Graetz, and as a young man he had played the organ in his
local parish church in Vienna. When in 1933 he stood accused of 'racially'

being a Jew under Nazi law, his admittedly feeble defence was that his cousin had written the *Semigotha*. Yet when he completed his most popular opera, *Der Schatzgräber*,[2] on 12 November 1918, the day that Austria, now bereft of its former empire, proclaimed itself a republic, he scribbled on the bottom of the final page of his manuscript that his most fervent hope was that his homeland would soon be annexed by Germany. It was a hope that would be fulfilled with tragic consequences only 20 years later.

Jews on a Journey

In the preface to the 1937 edition of his 1927 essay *Juden auf Wanderschaft*,[3] the writer Joseph Roth, living in Paris, could conceivably have had both Isak Schrečker and Franz Schreker in mind while writing his attack on assimilated and inter-married German Jews – an attack that underlined the delusionary aspects of what they believed to be fulfilled aspirations:

> The German Jew is absolutely not an Eastern European Jew. He's forgotten how to suffer, pray and up-root himself. He's only good at working – and even this is now denied him. . . . In any event, these émigré German Jews [in reference to the influx of German Jews in Paris after 1933] constitute a new nation: they've forgotten how to be Jews and must laboriously re-learn Jewishness. On the other hand, they're equally incapable of forgetting that they're German and cannot escape their fundamental Germanness. They're like snails cursed to carry two shells on their backs. They can't deny either their Germanness or their Jewishness since they can't lie. Ghastly how the outside-world thinks in lazy worn-out pigeonholes and stereotypes! It demands to know where the traveller is moving *from* rather than where he's moving *to*. However, for the traveller himself, the goal is far more important than the point of departure.[4]

The main body of this essay, originally written in 1927, dealt with Roth's view of what he saw as the unwholesome eagerness with which Jews acquired 'Germanness' and its ensuing delusions: 'When Jews finally arrive, they do not, as they are so often accused, assimilate too slowly, but sadly, rather too quickly. . . . They become diplomats and journalists, mayors, nobles, police detectives, and bank directors, and other assorted pillars of a solid and decent society. Only very few become revolutionaries.'[5] And again, 'The impoverished Jew is the most conservative of all impoverished creatures. He is a guarantor for the safeguarding of social order. The Jews by and large form a class of solid citizens albeit with their own racial, national and religious idiosyncrasies.'[6]

The misapprehension of being considered totally German despite having a single Jewish parent, as was the case with Schreker, is anticipated by the music critic Eduard Hanslick 40 years earlier in his memoirs from 1894. Hanslick would be the object of some of Wagner's most unpleasant anti-Semitic attacks. He faces them head on:

> That Wagner managed to smuggle me into his pamphlet *Jewishness in Music* disturbed me less. Wagner didn't like Jews and therefore assumed everyone who didn't like him must logically be Jewish. I would have felt myself flattered to be burned at the stake alongside the likes of Meyerbeer and Mendelssohn by Pater Arbuez Wagner;[7] sadly this privilege would have to remain denied to me as my father and all of his ancestors, at least as far back as I can trace them, were the sons of staunch Catholic farmers. In addition, they came from an area where the only Jews they would have encountered would have been tinkers plying their trade door-to-door.[8]

These comments demand more clarification. Hanslick specifically mentions his father but not his mother, Karoline Kisch, who was the daughter of wealthy Jewish merchants. Under Jewish law, this would have actually made him Jewish, should he have wished to count himself as such

As Heinrich Heine and Felix Mendelssohn demonstrated, the choice facing German-speaking Jews at the beginning of the nineteenth century appeared to be one between full participation in German cultural life or continued religious adherence and exclusion. Wagner was only the first to articulate his paranoia that with conversions, assimilation and inter-marriage, Jews had masterminded an insidious deceit of racial camouflage that would eventually undermine German identity and its innate moral character.

German

How Jews in German-speaking Europe would become such enthusiastic chauvinists in the cause of German culture, particularly when seen through the prism of the Holocaust, demands a good deal of explanation. Jews would only achieve social and political emancipation with the creation of Europe's two German-speaking States: the German Reich (Empire), headed by the Prussian King in 1871, and the dual monarchy of Austria-Hungary, headed by the Austrian Emperor in 1867. Emancipation was a result of guarantees made by the freshly drawn-up constitutions of both. It corresponded to the prevalent mood that Europe's many diverse people, with their various languages

and religious confessions, were allowed self-determination within the structures of a uniquely individual nation state, such as the newly created German
Reich. In Austria-Hungary, rights were accorded so that no cultural or ethnic
community within the multi-cultural dual monarchy could gain an advantage
over any of the others. Thus the German Reich along with Austria-Hungary
guaranteed the rights of confessional diversity, and their new constitutions
meant that Jews, long denied the rights accorded to other German-speakers,
could finally become fully active participants in the culture, language and
music of the German-speaking people. To Jews, who had lived among
Germans for two thousand years, it was the long-awaited entry into the most
élite, educated and cultivated 'club' on earth. Membership was an honour
bestowed on only a few; after millennia of being kept outside, they embraced
their new identity with an enthusiasm that frequently resulted in an exuberant
rejection of their Jewishness. To sceptical anti-Semites, such exuberance
appeared not only vulgar but potentially oppressive. Reactionary forces, along
with the Roman Catholic Church, meant that rights guaranteed by the constitution would still need to be fought through the Austrian Parliament indi-
vidually. For example, a Parliamentary rejection of an imposed concordat
between Rome and Vienna in 1868 allowed Jews access to education and
access to teaching positions, while the intermarriage between Jews and non-
Jews in Austria was not made legal until 1869.[9] Yet Parliament and the
Habsburgs stood firm in their support, and once these essential rights were
won, there were no theoretical barriers to Jews integrating into every part of
Austrian society.

Why 'German' does not mean 'from Germany'

In the English-speaking, post-Hitler world, we see what we assume to be a
clearly defined state called Germany populated by a collection of Europeans
calling themselves 'Germans'. We speak of 'the Germans' as we speak of 'the
French' or 'the English' and never assume that the confluence of state, culture
and people should ever have been a subject of debate or misunderstanding. In
today's transient and global society, we shrug our shoulders and assume that
if one is born within the geographical borders of a country called Germany or
France and speaks the language reflected in the name of the country, then one
is obviously German or French. But 'Germany' as a place and, more importantly, 'German' as an adjective *were* different, and it was the insecurity
surrounding what it was to *be* German that culminated in many of the horrors
of the twentieth century. Only after the defeat of Hitler in 1945 has 'German'
come to mean 'from Germany'.

What's more, when we speak or write of 'German' achievement, it is usually assumed that it took place somewhere within the regions of today's Germany. It probably never occurs to us that disparate German thinkers, musicians, writers, adventurers, politicians and artists should come from anywhere else. That such 'German' cultural and intellectual icons as Immanuel Kant and E. T. A. Hoffmann should hail from present-day Russia, or Sigmund Freud, Franz Kafka and Gustav Mahler from the Czech Republic; Arthur Schopenhauer, Günter Grass or the physicist Max Born from Poland; Theodor Herzl, the founder of Zionism, from Hungary or Walter von der Vogelweide from Italy, seems contradictory – or even contrary. Why would such prominent individuals call themselves 'German' when all of them quite obviously hail from countries with very impressive cultural legacies of their own?

The Germany we know today is a very different country from the Germany of the nineteenth century and bears little resemblance to the Germany of earlier times. Today, it is a neatly defined country that covers the bit of central Europe occupied by those German speakers not in Switzerland and Austria. Until the latter part of the nineteenth century, however, Germanic Europe was not a single unified country but a network of independent fiefdoms, principalities, bishoprics and kingdoms, often reaching far into neighbouring regions. Nor was Austria the tidy German-speaking Alpine Republic of today, but a sprawling empire consisting of Slavs, Italians and Hungarians ruled by the German-speaking House of Habsburg. Austria's German-speakers were a volatile minority; German was the official language throughout most of the Empire and Austria's Germans, known as German-Austrians, saw themselves as being part of the greater German nation. Most of Austria's assimilated Jews, whether living in Hungary or in the Slavic regions, spoke German as a first language.

For centuries, the view was maintained that as long as the principal European nation states (France, the tsarist Russian Empire and Britain) could keep the Germans in their checkerboard of competing microstates, the status quo of a thousand years was maintained and the European balance of power was forever guaranteed. It meant that the largest single linguistic unit on the continent could join together or break apart as the situations and interests of the major nation states demanded. As an arrangement, it suited nearly everybody except the vast majority of German-speaking Europeans. Urgency was added to the need for German unification following the Napoleonic wars and a perception that only by living together in a single country could Germans provide a reliable defence against future foreign incursions. Despite a bewildering array of competing interests, Prince von Bismarck completed a partial unification in 1871 placing most, but not all, of Europe's German states under the Prussian king. For reasons that are explained later, it excluded the German-speaking holdings of the Austrian emperor.

Bismarck's Prussian Germany nonetheless provided more than a bulwark against future marauding French. Indeed, the realisation that the new country would be condemned to defend borders on nearly all sides began to add a degree of paranoia which itself turned aggressive. By 1914, it seemed to be aching for a fight so that it could confirm its geopolitical position as the most important country in Europe. With enormous wealth and a population that was the same as the United States, there was no reason to suppose that Germany couldn't become the leading country in the world.

After the First World War, the French understandably saw great advantages in trying to return to the pre-Bismarck network of competing German states. France had little enthusiasm for its robust neighbour that had been cobbled into a single political unit within the living memory of most of France's ruling élite. By the end of the war in 1918, the German-speaking people of Europe were still divided between the two principal states of Austria and Germany. The French intended that the occupied Rhineland would break away and become yet another separate German-speaking republic. With Austria's empire wiped off the map, there was concern about what might happen should its remaining rump of German speakers be folded into its much larger neighbour to the north. That such moves towards unification were thwarted by the French and Americans was deplored not only by the composer Franz Schreker, but also by millions of Austrians like him – Jews and non-Jews alike. To many Europeans, it was illogical to support national self-determination, while not merging these two unequal German republics. Indeed, it was seen by German speakers as vengeful, 'victors' justice' imposed through the Treaty of Versailles, which ended the war with Germany, and Saint-Germain, a separate treaty settled with Austria. The conditions of these treaties were harsh and harboured the unspoken French desire that inflation and economic chaos would result in many of the constituent parts of Bismarck's project splitting up. They nearly did.

Twenty years later, most Europeans, non-Germans and Germans alike, were resigned to the view that Austria's annexation by Nazi Germany in 1938 was simply fulfilling an inevitable cultural and national destiny. Within a decade after the Anschluß Austria and a large chunk of Eastern Germany under Soviet control returned to the status quo of separate German states. In the case of Austria, its much longed-for fusion with Germany had proved a disastrous union that only underlined the degree to which history had fundamentally determined separate European destinies for these two very different German-speaking nations. After 1918, however, many Austrians seeking

German cultural identity within a distinctively German nation state felt betrayed by history and insurmountable political forces. It created a sense of being German that often exceeded anything found in Germany itself. One of the most obvious exponents of this malaise among disaffected Austrians was Adolf Hitler – but quite a few others were the children and grandchildren of recently assimilated Jews.

The Congress of Vienna

The beginnings of this complex story go back a century, and bring us to the years following the final defeat of Napoleon. In 1814, Prince von Metternich, Austria's Foreign Minister, invited representatives from all of Europe's 200 sovereign States to convene at what became known as the Congress of Vienna. Despite the large numbers represented, the only significant negotiators at the Congress remained the principal European powers: Austria, Prussia, Russia, Great Britain and the restored monarchy of France. The Congress, which met over a period of two years, did not so much attempt to re-establish the pre-Napoleonic status quo as to divide the post-Napoleonic spoils of war.

In 1806, Napoleon had created or changed the status of a number of German states along France's eastern frontier by joining several of them together to form new kingdoms or duchies. Each new state was accorded a higher status than previously held so that their new rulers would become dependable allies against the Habsburgs. This so-called 'Rhine Federation' was not just a military alliance, but also brought with it the 'Code Napoleon', which resulted in a remodelling and liberalisation of both social and legal systems. Thus, the expectations of these states at the Congress of Vienna were high. The advantages they had gained could not simply be declared null and void. For the aristocratic old order, however, the aim was a return to the near-feudal system of pre-Napoleon times.

In order to understand how Europe organised itself, it is important to register the difference between a 'state' and a 'nation': a 'nation' is what in German is called 'Volk' or a people. A nation is perceived as homogenous and normally shares a common language from which springs a common culture and, often, a common religious faith. A 'state' is the political structure that is mounted on top of either a single nation or group of nations. It is the political unit we call today 'a country'. A 'nation state' is the convergence of a single nation into its dedicated state. European leaders at the time of Prince Metternich's Vienna Congress saw no apparent contradiction in political states being imposed upon any number of diverse nations. For this reason, Metternich and his fellow reactionary aristocratic rulers opposed the dreams of single-nation statehood which was growing more attractive as an idea among the many smaller nations spread throughout various historic, pre-existing states. In Metternich's view, a Europe of numerous nation states could not guarantee any meaningful balance of power. It may have been historically inevitable for France, tsarist Russia and England to be nation states, but it was an arrangement that was felt could never work for German-speaking central Europe.

For Metternich and the old order, it was far better to continue having subjects rallying around something inclusive, such as an emperor, rather than citizens rallying around something as exclusive as a state. After all, the French Revolution had shown how badly things could go when the nation gained control of the state.

Prussia, Austria and the Rhine Federation

By the end of the Congress of Vienna, German-ruled Europe had settled into three fundamental geopolitical units: Prussia and Austria constituted two of these and stretched respectively from the Slavic north-east and south-east towards the third unit which consisted of the cluster of states that previously formed Napoleon's Rhine-Federation. From 1815, they all regrouped as the German Federation with its proto-parliament called the Bundestag, a two-house assembly in Frankfurt which met at the palace of Thurn and Taxis. In truth it was hardly more than a talking shop of querulous fiefdoms and mini-states all pushing and shoving for advantage with the biggest players, Austria and Prussia, in the upper 'Presidium' making the major decisions.

The Bundestag representatives weren't elected and it was very far from being 'democratic' in the modern sense. As unlikely as it may seem today, these various states, including Prussia, muddled along under the respected but distant Austrian emperor who historically had been the inclusive figure-head of all the German-speaking people of Europe. Napoleon's defeat of the Austrian Emperor Franz II and the dissolution of the Habsburg Holy Roman Empire in 1806 still left the Austrian Emperor with an historic entitlement unmatched by other German rulers. The Holy Roman Empire had existed since 962 and had maintained its seat in Vienna since the sixteenth century, though it had long ceased to be either 'holy' or 'Roman'. Even by 1806, it was an anachronism.

One bit of diplomatic horse-trading to come out of the Congress of Vienna was a foretaste of what a unification of the German mini-states under Prussia might become: it was agreed to hand the Rhineland to Prussia as a sop for agreeing to let Russia take Warsaw. Significantly, this included the Ruhrgebiet, an area rich in mining and industry that guaranteed Prussia great wealth and allowed it in the coming decades to rise above rival German states. The result of this decision, added to the other regions that already made up the patchwork of Prussia, was the near encirclement of the independent states of the northern and central German Federation. As a purely German State, Prussia, despite its smaller share of Slavic holdings in the north-east, now far exceeded Austria, whose realm reached into Italy, Hungary, and deep into the Slavic East.

Biedermeier Life and the Revolution of 1848

The years 1815 to March 1848 are often referred to as the 'Biedermeier Age', portrayed usually as a period of comfortable bourgeois self-satisfaction. Indeed, the very name of 'Biedermeier' was concocted by the satirist Ludwig Eichrodt as a composite of two smug figures named 'Biedermann' and 'Bummelmeier' ('Bieder' in German means 'conventional and stuffy'). Nevertheless, the Biedermeier years were anything but stolid and comfortable. The period immediately following the Congress of Vienna often evokes cosy images of 'Hausmusik' and intimate performances of Schubert Lieder and chamber works; yet Hausmusik, or musical evenings in private homes, were about the largest assemblies allowed by Metternich's secret police. Schubert himself was not as innocuous as one might believe. He occasionally used coded metaphors to spice up the texts of some of his best-known Lieder.[10] Eduard Hanslick, Wagner's subsequent *bête noir*, moved to Vienna from Prague in 1846 and recalled the two years before the revolution of March 1848 as offering only a diet of empty virtuoso recitals; intellectual and artistic life had stagnated. The secret police made political discussion impossible and censorship of all publications became obsessive. Metternich's suppression of national ambitions by keeping all debate under tight surveillance was a wilful misunderstanding of the aspirations of the growing middle classes and it inflamed rather than controlled the national mood. Yet powerful voices were being heard. The genteel age, peopled by genteel 'Biedermeier-Burgers' who were themselves mindful of recent revolutions in France and the Netherlands, were heading inevitably towards a very un-genteel revolution.

As revolutions go, the Revolution of 1848 was a peculiar affair. Though bloody and by appearances initially successful, it was ultimately unable to achieve its primary objectives of liberalising either society or the economy. It also largely failed in its most important ambition, which was the unification of the German Federation into a single German state, under a constitutional monarch. At its conclusion, exhausted revolutionaries managed at least the abdication of the feeble-minded Emperor Ferdinand I, Metternich's pawn for the past dozen years, and had him replaced by his 18-year-old nephew, 'Franzl'. Metternich fled to London, though three years later, with most of the important revolutionary leaders executed or imprisoned and the others compliantly subsumed within various local assemblies, he returned to Vienna as advisor to Austria's fresh-faced 21-year-old Emperor, now known as Franz Joseph I.

A short-lived but important achievement to grow out of the revolution was the freely-elected National Assembly or Nationalversammlung that met from March 1848 until its dissolution in May/June 1849. Like the 'Bundestag', it also met in Frankfurt, but at the Paulskirche (St Paul's Church). It was an elected assembly of lawyers, professors, intellectuals and idealists, and provided a forum in which the shape and nature of a united German State could be debated.

The complexities of the debate should not be underestimated. The notion that disparate German states and far-flung German enclaves in Russia, Poland, Hungary, Romania and other corners of Europe could somehow join together to become a single state was fraught with conflict. Though the rise of France under Napoleon had made it obvious to everyone except the dele-gates at the Congress of Vienna that a united German state was a necessary survival tactic, the diplomacy needed to create this was more than even the *bien-pensant* members of the Paulskirche Assembly could achieve. Germany was simply not the tidy country then that it appears today. In the nineteenth century, the concept of 'German' was quite literally everywhere in Europe that wasn't Slavic or Latinate. The English king was represented in the German Bundestag by the House of Hanover, as were countless other non-German holdings which historically had ended up under the rule of various German heads. This extremely wide concept of 'German' extended beyond Britain and into the Netherlands and Scandinavia.

Unification debates in the Paulskirche led to discussion of the pros and cons of a 'Greater' or 'Lesser' German solution. The 'Greater' solution included Austria and its many non-German holdings; the 'Lesser' solution excluded Austria altogether, which meant losing Vienna, the seat of the Habsburg Emperor and until then, the figurehead of all that was German. Defenders of the 'Greater' solution, who simply could not envisage a unified German state without such central players as Bohemia and Austria, toyed with the idea of subsuming non-German Austrian and Prussian holdings as satellites of a Greater Germany. Ultimately, however, it was clear that only with Austria excluded could the resulting enterprise be purely German. The price to pay would be high, so another solution was put forward to hive off Austria's German holdings, and allow them to join the united German state while excluding the non-German holdings altogether. This was not an arrangement that the Habsburgs were prepared to accept.

Thus the Lesser German Solution eventually won through, and with Austria excluded from the newly mapped out German State, the National Assembly offered the Imperial German crown to the Prussian King, Friedrich Wilhelm IV, in April 1849. He refused, since he did not see it as a gift that was the people's to give. He would only accept the title if offered by other ruling families within the German Federation. As he is apocryphally reported to have put it, the offer 'should come from God rather than the gutter'.

With the king's refusal and plans for a unified Germany in disarray, the Paulskirche National Assembly, without an army to enforce its will, was powerless. Friedrich Wilhelm unilaterally called a Prussian Parliament into being (backed by the Prussian army), and the National Assembly was dissolved in late spring of 1849.

In 1848, the playwright Franz Grillparzer, a patriotic Austrian, wrote the following verses: 'Oh God, please come and see / That the Germans are set free / That their bellyaching ceases to be.'[11] More chilling was his rhyming prediction that 'The path our latest lessons shows that Humanity / Moves along towards Nationality / Into bestiality.'[12] This may have been seen at the time as a reactionary and typically Austrian point of view, but Grillparzer nonetheless identified that nationalism had the ugly tendency to define itself not so much by who could be part of a nation, but more crucially, by who would need to be left out.

The Legacy of the Revolution

Metternich's return to Vienna in 1851 only underlines how wrong it would be to assume that the Emperor Franz Joseph was in any way more sympathetic to the idea of self-determination expressed by the many nations under Habsburg control. The nominal head of the German-speaking people of Europe was also ruler over numerous Slavs, Hungarians and Italians, as well as Jews, who were perceived as just another nation which, though living in Europe, was not considered fully European. The concept of any state, even Austria, as a unified body was not an idea that Franz Joseph would even begin to entertain. Indeed, whenever he could, he removed the word Austria from official documents and replaced it with his own name. In his view, and that of Metternich, it was easier to rally support around a ruler supposedly appointed by God rather than around a mere man-made state. In addition, too many Germans were Protestant for Franz Joseph's liking. Austria thus represented a Catholic German Universalism that had little room for the secular nation state in the modern sense.

A German Showdown between Austria and Prussia

The third quarter of the nineteenth century is riddled with wars and tensions that were meant to establish a meaningful balance within Europe's powerful dynasties. The only tangible achievement of the 1848 Revolution was a number of liberalising concessions that allowed the greater German economy to boom, thus further expanding the influence of the middle-classes. At the same time, German-speaking Europe spent the ensuing 20 years fighting a number of extremely illiberal wars involving a dizzying combination of various alliances and enemies.

The 'Holy Alliance' between Austria, Prussia and Russia which had once defeated Napoleon was maintained after the Congress of Vienna. Until the Crimean War of 1853, Russia's absolutist influences within Austria and Prussia were not only a guarantor of Europe's feudal order – helping to restore the forces of reaction following the revolution – but also a staying hand on Prussian expansionism.

Austria joined the French and British in the Crimean War ostensibly to defend the decrepit Ottoman Empire against Russian expansionism, but in reality it was to remove Russian influence from Western Europe.

Another war in 1859 between Austria and France provided the basis for Italian unification with Austria's loss of Lombardy. Italian unification, which served as a model for German unification a few years later, was completed when the Italians sided with Prussia in the Seven Week War ending in Königgrätz in 1866. Austria (referred to by Italian freedom fighters as 'German rulers') was thus ejected from the rest of the peninsula apart from the port of Trieste.

Despite the importance of these wars in the formation of a single German identity within a unified state, it is the conflict over entitlement to rule this state that concerns us here. It was being fought not just on the battlefield, but also on philosophical and psychological fronts. It had become clear even after the debacle of the Paulskirche Assembly that a unified Germany could have no room for multi-national Austria, and the only philosophical matter to ponder was that posed by Robert Blum, a prominent republican member of the National Assembly in Frankfurt, who became the Revolution's most famous political martyr. Before his execution by the Austrians, Blum asked a fundamental question concerning Germany's European destiny: would Prussia ultimately dissolve into a united Germany or would a united Germany dissolve into Prussia?

Fifteen years later, in a letter from 24 December 1863 to Count Robert von der Goltz, Otto von Bismarck bracingly explained that he clearly held the latter view:

Chasing after popularity among the German states has cost us dearly over the last 40 years, both among the German states and Europe. . . . One reads in the press and hears in public debates, signs of developments that may help us in pursuit of hegemony; I think of all those things as radical nonsense: our policies are not made by the press and such talking-shops, but by the weaponry that comes with being a World Power. . . . Events will inform us as to when and how we separate from Austria.[13]

More significant was Bismarck's speech made a year earlier to the Prussian Parliament:

It is not to Prussia's Liberalism that [the Kingdoms of] Bavaria, Württemberg and Baden look, but to its power. They may choose to indulge the Liberal movement, but Prussia must gather its strength and prepare for its most propitious opportunity – something that has already been missed on countless occasions: Prussia's borders following the Viennese agreements are not compatible with its survival as a state. It will not be speeches or royal decrees that address the great questions of the day – that was the mistake of 1848 and 1849 – rather, these questions will be answered by *blood and iron*.

Königgrätz

The Austrian defeat at Königgrätz was a conveniently concocted conflict over the administration of the North German province of Holstein which allowed Bismarck to rid the German Federation of Austria's presence for good. Defeat was guaranteed not only by superior Prussian weaponry, but also by an alliance with Italy that split Austrian forces on two fronts. This single battle changed the face of Europe and determined the direction of history for the next century. However, the Habsburgs had centuries of perfecting the art of survival and self-reinvention; within a year Vienna had finalised an arrangement with Austria's least reliable ally and neighbour, Hungary. By exchanging its former power-base within German-Europe for a dual monarchy with Hungary, Austria had by 1867 turned disaster into opportunity, but at the cost of isolating and further frustrating its minority German-speaking subjects.

This arrangement was called the 'Ausgleich', meaning an equalisation of ruling status between Austria and Hungary. It gave the Magyars, historically inclined to sympathise with Austria's enemies, partnership in a new multicultural Empire. Just as the Germans were a minority in Austria's half of the Empire, so the Magyars were a minority in Hungary's. The German-Austrians and Magyars were thus united by the mutual suspicion of those over whom they ruled.[14] The alternative was breaking Austria's remaining possessions into a loose federation that would have allowed Slavs to dominate – something that neither the German nationalists of Austria nor the equally nationalistic Magyars wanted.

The Franco-Prussian War of 1870/71 was the most important of Bismarck's opportunistically organised conflicts. This one was over perceived slights to the house of Hohenzollern concerning the future king of Spain. By this point, Napoleon III had reached such a state of narcissistic delusion that Bismarck hardly needed encouragement. Defeat of the French ended with Napoleon III's exile, several months of the Paris Commune's workers' revolution, and the country's eventual return to a republic. It also left a festering diplomatic sore with Alsace-Lorraine conceded to Germany.

By 1871, these conflicts had redrawn the map of Europe. Prussian victories had directly led to the unification of Germany, the re-formation of the House of Habsburg as the dual monarchy of Austria-Hungary, the restoration of the French Republic, and the unification of Italy. Bismarck's united Germany was proclaimed an 'empire' in 1871. The Prussian King, Wilhelm I, became German Emperor and was now on a par with the Austrian Emperor who reigned over an impressive land-mass stretching through central Europe, along the Danube and into the Ukraine. Both Austria-Hungary and the newly united German states had similar populations of around 40 million.

Bismarck's 'blood and iron' unification had achieved what the short-lived, democratically elected Paulskirche National Assembly had attempted without losing a single drop of blood. History suggests that this was a Prussian precedent that would inform Germany's European relations for the next 75 years. Bismarck's achievements resulted in a national and political monoculture. Königgrätz's ultimate legacy was less a unification of the German peoples than a fusion of 'German' and 'Prussian'. It was a development that the Austrian composer and prominent Schreker pupil Ernst Krenek later referred to in his memoirs as the 'ultimate Austrian tragedy'. Indeed, he also saw it as a German, and thus a European tragedy.[15]

Conclusions and Constitutions

Today, Prussia as a political state doesn't exist at all, having been removed from the European map in 1947, and Austria has been reduced to a small Alpine republic with only its spectacular imperial capital, once the sixth largest city in the world, as a reminder of its former importance in global affairs. Between the Congress of Vienna and today's Germany and Austria lay 130 years of wars, battles and diplomatic jostling. The result was not only to destroy the known European order and leave millions dead, but inevitably to have a profound impact on music, art and literature.

For a variety of complex, interconnecting reasons, the way in which the arts in general, and music in particular, changed has a relevance to what the Third Reich would do to music 70 years later. Language is the first and most obvious element that identifies a nation, followed by its religion and culture. Within the broader topic of 'culture', hardly any discipline defines a nation more innately than its music. The distant dream of German unification had finally come to pass, but excluded the passionately chauvinistic German-Austrians, who had decidedly mixed feelings about being left out of the newly formed German nation state, while being fobbed off with what many perceived to be the less desirable multi-cultural dual monarchy of Austria-Hungary. Where was German cultural identity to be found if not in a common German state? To many of these German-Austrians, exclusion made absolutely no sense. The more the Habsburgs tried to gloss over the differences of its 'many nations', the more the 'nations' themselves began to accentuate them, first by seeing themselves as different peoples, and later by referring to themselves as different 'races'.

The German-Austrians would become the political shuttlecock between politicians of both left and right, and between those who saw as inevitable the incorporation of Austria's German-speakers into the new Germany, and those who saw Austrians as a totally different and independent nation. These patriotic, largely aristocratic and haut-bourgeois Austrians held nostalgically to their own particularity as representatives of a predominantly Catholic German nation. For them, Austria was divinely chartered, whereas the pragmatic unification of German states was created by lowly Prussian Protestants. Returning to the turbulent years of 1867–71, during which a reorganised Austria-Hungary and a united Germany sought to establish new national visions, it became necessary to yield to an unavoidable act of social liberalism: a modest extension of enfranchisement coupled with the granting of civil rights to nearly all male citizens, including previously disenfranchised Jews. In Catholic Austria, Jews were recognised as a European people and offered what Franz Joseph needed most in his multinational, multi-confessional state: another recognised nation to add to the many others so that none should prevail. If unity was achievable, it was through the sort of diversity that kept each of the individual ethnic groups in check. For that, diversity needed to be recognised, accepted and even promoted.[16] Jews, who for years had been persecuted by German Christian churches, were finally recognised as equal, albeit exotic, Austrians, often referred to as 'Orientals' or even 'Israelis'. Jews were allowed to live and travel where they liked, vote within the limitations of the constitution, study, and in the following years with the parliamentary rejection of the Catholic concordat in questions of education and marriage, marry whom they wished and teach at universities.[17]

This act of Liberal emancipation took place in Austria and Hungary with the so-called Constitution of 21 December 1867.[18] Similar acts soon followed in the North German Federation in 1869 and finally throughout the German Empire in 1871.

The Austrian Emperor Franz Joseph would be seen by his Jewish subjects as being actively philo-Semitic, a view borne out when some thirty years later he distanced himself from any association with Vienna's devoutly Roman Catholic, anti-Semitic mayor Karl Lueger.[19] The German Emperor, Wilhelm I, managed a contained tolerance towards Jews; his eventual successor, Wilhelm II, was happy to accept invitations from the Jewish shipping magnate Albert Ballin to use his many ships and yachts, while at the same time remaining enthralled by the paranoid anti-Semitic writings of Richard Wagner's English son-in-law, Houston Stewart Chamberlain.

The ambivalent positions held by the Austrian and German Emperors were reflected throughout society. The assimilation of Jews was a develop- ment that would cause great social and cultural changes in the coming decades. Cosima Wagner, Richard Wagner's wife and daughter of Franz Liszt, wrote the following in her diary on 22 November 1878: 'R. said yesterday: if I were to write again about the Jews [in reference to his anti-Semitic tract *Judenthum in der Musik*] I would write that I haven't anything against them, only that they have become Germans far too early. We simply aren't sturdy enough to take in such elements.'[20]

A few days later, on 1 December, she goes on to relate that Wagner believes that Jews are about 50 years too early in their attempts to 'amalgamate'. He believed that Germany needed time to find its own identity following unifica- tion before allowing such 'foreign' influences free rein. 'Now, the damage done is terrible', she recounts him as saying.[21] Indeed, Wagner's view – not that different from issues Karl Marx was grappling with – was that Jews were avari- cious capitalists and that giving them the same rights as Germans would not allow the new state to develop into the anti-capitalist society he envisaged, and for which he had fought on the Dresden barricades in 1848. As Cosima writes again on 17 June 1879, 'the ultimate results of the emancipation of the Jews was explained to the children today as ending with the subjugation of the middle- and the corruption of the lower-classes. The Revolution may have broken feudalism, but it has now been replaced by Mammonism [capitalism].'[22]

The effect emancipation would have on musical life would soon become obvious. Gustav Mahler was born in 1860, as was the music critic Julius Korngold, soon to be Mahler's principal cheerleader in the press, and father to the prodigy Erich Wolfgang Korngold. Mahler's childhood friend Guido Adler, the father of modern musicology, was born in 1855. The musicologist, Robert Hirschfeld, Julius Korngold's fellow critic and *bête noir*, was born in 1857; Alexander Zemlinsky was born in 1871 and his future brother-in-law, Arnold Schoenberg, in 1874. Together, they represented the first generation of prominent Jewish musicians to come of age during Austria's so-called years of 'Liberalism'.

Assimilation

Ideas and ideals circulating during the period of European Enlightenment in the late 18th century were adapted by a number of Jewish Ashkenazi leaders seeking to promote secular studies and the speaking of German as a means of gaining greater political and social mobility within wider non-Jewish communities. This movement is generally referred to as the *Haskalah*. To enlightened Jews, the Ghetto was something to escape from, not something to be cultivated as a refuge against an unfriendly Christian world. Such ideas had been mooted as early as the seventeenth century when the Jewish philosopher Baruch Spinoza promoted the idea of secular identities for Jews. A hundred years following the death of Spinoza, Moses Mendelssohn (the grandfather of composers Felix and Fanny Mendelssohn) was seen as the father of a movement of Jewish Enlightenment that ideally would unite Jews to the world around them by building linguistic bridges between the liturgical language of Hebrew and the secular language of German, while marginalising Yiddish, the common language spoken by most German Jews at the time. Ideally, it was seen as a movement that ultimately would result in Jews entering the wider community as fellow citizens while allowing them to maintain their religious traditions. It thus demanded tolerance and acceptance from the surrounding non-Jewish environment, yet recognised that acceptance could only be achieved with a demystification of Jewish identity. This process could only be initiated from the Jewish communities themselves, who needed to reach out and master the local vernacular rather than hide away in Yiddish enclaves. In other words, if Jews started to build bridges towards the outside world, the outside world would respond positively with its own acts of bridge-building.

Various local acts of liberalisation allowed Jews greater opportunities since the Revolution of 1848, but it was the Constitution of 21 December, printed in full in the *Neue Freie Presse* on 23 December 1867, which finally offered a full guarantee of personal freedom for Jews.[23] Articles 14 and 15 of the Second Statute deal with citizenship, religion and personal conviction, and lifted the last remaining restrictions on all Austrian Jews. At no point does the actual word 'Jew' appear, but the tenor of the article is so clearly inclusive that it could not be misinterpreted: no beliefs or religious adherence would be a hindrance to securing employment, education or a right of abode. As these had specifically been some of the most repressive measures used against Jews, it was a major act of emancipation and removed the remaining hurdles to assimilation. But as we shall see, full integration would remain for most an unachievable goal.

For many Jews, musical assimilation, as opposed to social assimilation, became a tale of double- or even cross-assimilation, by which the Jewish musician or composer was accepted as a full citizen and, from there, could become an active proponent of German culture. The German nation, however, had split into two States, with the consolidated monoglot country on one side and a polyglot one on the other. Did German culture look inwards or outwards, and what was the effect of enfranchising Jews in Austria while, at the same time, denying all Austrian German speakers, Jews included, the 'right' of citizenship in a uniquely German state? A partial answer as to how this issue developed over the next half century can be found in the titles of two books written by the Jewish violin virtuoso from Austria's Polish district of Galicia, Bronislav Huberman, who addressed such dilemmas first in *My Path as a Pan-European*, published in 1925, and *Fatherland Europe*, written in 1932, just as the full force of German nationalist terror was to be unleashed.

The word 'German' as an adjective remained viable in the dual monarchy, yet there is confusion even to this day as to what constituted 'Austro-German' as opposed to the Prussian-tainted 'Reich-German'. So numerous were the Slav-Austrians, that 'German-Austrians' (*Deutschösterreicher*) became the official definition accorded to all Austrian German speakers. It must also be recalled that German remained the official language of the Austrian half of the monarchy. Austrian Jews from the non-German-speaking eastern regions faced a double process of assimilation: the first was that of becoming Austrians, followed by the process by which they became German-Austrians.

Ernst Krenek refers to this point on several occasions in his memoirs, though in a manner that many have taken, wrongly, to imply a personal distaste for Jews. In fact, Krenek is merely making the point that he found German Jews assimilated to such an extent that it was nearly impossible to tell who was Jewish and who wasn't, while in Austria he found they were far more redolent of the *shtetl* (Eastern European Jewish communities). And little wonder: Jews in the Rhineland had lived in the area since Roman times and inter-married with non-Jews, thus looking and sounding totally 'German', with no trace of the accent of the East-European closed communities. Czech, Alpine and even Hungarian Jews were also largely German-Austrian in manner, customs and speech. Austria also had more Jews than Germany from its eastern non-German provinces such as the Bukovina and Galicia, not to mention the Balkans and Hungary.

Some of the Yiddish-speaking Galician Jews such as Joseph Roth, Soma Morgenstern, Manès Sperber and Paul Celan from Romanian Bukovina would count themselves among the most elegant of twentieth-century German writers, along with the Bulgarian born Elias Canetti (for whom German was his third, if not fourth, language) and the Hungarian-born Arthur Koestler. Krenek mentions that his fellow Schreker pupil, Karol Rathaus, had been a childhood friend of Roth and Morgenstern, and took his Germanisation with the hyper-perfection typical of Galician Jews who had learned the language at a provincial German *Gymnasium* and was thus equipped with a command of the language that was far superior to many native speakers.[24]

The rapid migration to Vienna produced a near hundredfold increase in the city's Jewish population, from 2,617 in 1857 to over 200,000 by 1920. This move from the Empire's provincial ghettos and *shtetls* was accompanied by a liberating rush of assimilation that saw artists and musicians becoming fully enfranchised participants in Austrian intellectual life and players within the greater German cultural arena. Such rapid assimilation brought with it two extraordinary and seemingly contradictory effects: the first was that it provided the freshness that nearly always comes with the arrival of new blood, and the second was that this new blood arrived with a respect for German culture that had grown out of a near mystic reverence for the past and a profound comprehension of the enlightened values that this past had produced.

The Language of Assimilation: *Die Neue Freie Presse*

In his memoirs, Julius Korngold, the music critic of Vienna's leading news-paper, *Die Neue Freie Presse*, and successor to Eduard Hanslick, mentions his good fortune at being born during the 'age of Liberalism'. On 20 December 1927, the same year that the writer and journalist Joseph Roth wrote his extended essay entitled *Juden auf Wanderschaft*, the *Neue Freie Presse* ran a front-page article celebrating '60 years of Liberalism'. In it, we find not only a concise and lucid exposition of the historic and political processes that resulted in one of the most inclusive and wide-ranging European constitu-tions of the age, we also sense, as with Roth's essay, the reactionary powers gathering steam in the years running up to National Socialism. *Juden auf Wanderschaft* tries to come to terms with what Roth saw as an inevitable development; the leader-writers of the *Neue Freie Presse* may have even sensed the same with their salute to 60 years of Liberalism aimed at a still undeclared but clearly present enemy.[25] This was hardly surprising since the paper had been founded in 1864 by the Jewish journalists Max Friedländer and Adolf Werthner, and was published and edited from 1879 by two other Jews, Eduard Bacher and Moritz Benedikt. Benedikt was the only journalist whom the Austrian Emperor Franz Joseph would meet. The *Neue Freie Presse* became the primary German-language paper offering a secular and politically liberal perspective and, with its flotation on the Viennese stock exchange in 1871, it was established as one of the leading papers published in the German language. The founder of modern Zionism, Theodor Herzl, was its cultural editor, and Richard Wagner's favourite 'Jewish' hate-figure, Eduard Hanslick, Professor of Aesthetics at Vienna's University, was its principal music critic. With regular articles and features by Peter Altenberg, Hugo von Hofmannsthal, Max Nordau, Felix Salten, Arthur Schnitzler, Stefan Zweig and even Karl Marx, it was the paper of the liberal, educated bourgeoisie, a demographic in which Jews were becoming ever more prominent. Stefan Zweig in *The World of Yesterday* sums it up nicely by referring to the paper as 'a Temple of Progress' and goes on to write, 'With its distinguished exposition on events, its cultural authority and its political prestige, it came to represent for the entire Austro-Hungarian monarchy the same as *The Times* for the English speaking world.'[26]

Though life had become progressively better for Jews since the 1848 Revolution and the emancipation of 1867, the rise of Jewish scholars and intellectuals to the top of the professional classes – and even to the nobility – took place in less than a generation. Such rapid progress would not go without resentment. The ideals of the Austro-Hungarian Constitution of 1867 and Germany's Constitution of 1871 were directly responsible for creating the dynamic cultural environments in both German states prior to the rise of Nazism. It could be argued, as the 1927 article in the *Neue Freie Presse* makes clear, that the wide-ranging liberalism of these constitutions also allowed the emergence of a pan-German, exclusionist nationalism.[27] To try to understand the dysfunctional relationship between Jews and non-Jews, we need to turn to Wagner, in many ways the father of German anti-Semitism based on 'race' rather than religious adherence, and as a composer, a central figure within this story.

CHAPTER 2

Wagner and German Jewish Composers in the Nineteenth Century

Stern tells us the latest joke: H. is busy imitating his adored Wagner as
composer; he's written an operatic trilogy: 'The Ring of the
Never-Last-Long': 1) Unfreed; 2) The Wantons; 3) Twilight of the Ghetto

Als neuesten Witz erzählte Stern: H. eifere seinem Liebling Wagner als
Componist nach; er habe eine Operntrilogie geschaffen: Der nie gelungene
Ring: 1. Niefried. 2. Die Willkür. 3. Ghettodämmerung.

Viktor Klemperer, *Diaries*, 27 March 1937

Wagner's *Judaism in Music*

In Richard Wagner's 1850 polemic *Das Judenthum in der Musik (Judaism in Music)*[1], several features demand special attention. Not only can the document be seen as a template for what was still to come, but it also offers a reflection of the period in which Wagner lived and wrote. The impulse to produce the pamphlet grew out of a casual reference to a work possessing a 'Hebrew flavour' that was made by Wagner's friend Theodor Uhlig in the *Neue Zeitschrift für Musik*. The gusto with which Wagner addresses this point becomes apparent within the first paragraph. It is equally clear that he is addressing a subject that already enjoys common currency. As with most demagogues, he writes as if addressing 'Everyman' and expressing an opinion that all are thinking but none dare say. It is the tabloid approach, but using language that is at once lofty and condescending, while making frequent self-regarding references to 'the people' in the safe assumption that his readers believe that Jews are hardly the same species. He published the work twice: under the pseudonym of 'K. Freigedank' (K. Freethinker) in 1850, and under his own name in 1869.

One of the most fascinating contemporary résumés of Wagner's tract comes from his nemesis at the *Neue Freie Presse*, Eduard Hanslick, who finds himself the object of attack in Wagner's 1869 revision. In the 9 March issue of the same year, Hanslick tells us perhaps all we need to know about the tract itself and offers a marvellous depiction of the way that both sides viewed this debate:

Richard Wagner has augmented his usual practice of self-glorification over the years with an increasingly industrious sideline in pamphleteering. Most recently, we have been treated to something called *Judaism in Music*. Jews are apparently 'the most abhorrent beings of all creation' – and a Jew happens to be any- and everyone who doesn't choose to worship at the shrine of Richard Wagner ... [Wagner] sets forth with the accusation of enmity in the press, and 'not just in Germany but also France and England'. Behind this finely woven web of animosity stands, according to Wagner, 'a cabal of Jewish intrigue' directed specifically against him. Ever since his tract *Judaism in Music* appeared in a Leipzig music periodical in 1850, everyone who spurns the eating of ham and pork also spurns the works of Richard Wagner and never misses an opportunity to avenge themselves. Wagner further informs us that his tract was widely read and caused enormous offence, though astonishingly enough the essay was published not under his own name but that of a certain Mr Freethinker [*Freigedank*]. [. . .] Of course it fits Wagner's sense of self-importance that the entire cultural establish-ment, along with all of its journalistic partners, carries around a grudge acquired from an anonymous article published some 19 years ago in Leipzig. [. . .] I have to admit that I found myself only aware of Wagner's illustrious pamphlet of 1850 with the publication of its present up-date. [. . .] Indeed, [according to Wagner] the rot would appear to have started with the publica-tion [of my book] *On Musical Beauty*. '[Hanslick] won his reputation as an aestheticist in order to acquire a position in a leading paper where he could declare all of my work as null and void.' Further, my 'Nimbus' is such that all papers, the world over, have taken up this tone. [. . .] [Wagner further writes] Leipzig has 'been musically baptised into Jewry' thanks to its long associa-tion with Mendelssohn. Leipzig is now 'the undisputed capital of Jew-music'. The brochure continues in this obnoxious and hateful manner. [. . .] It was in the 'Jew-Music capital' that the plot 'that Wagner should henceforth be ignored' was hatched: 'More than just ignored, he should be punished in all of his musical and literary efforts.'[. . .]

After his attack on journalism, he moves rapidly to theatre directors. As he puts it [. . .] 'You have no doubt wondered why following the rapid success in all German theatres of my early works, these very same theatres have reacted with lazy indifference to my later ones; my works were popular before the start of the Jew-agitation and it was quite impossible to halt their success.' [. . .]

Not every theatre in the land can match the Court Opera of Munich as a pre-natal clinic for Richard Wagner's musical offspring. Wagner even allows his passions to lead him to the impertinent accusation that correspondence with directors of the court operas in Berlin and Vienna convinces him that not only was it their intention that [his] operas not play in their own theatres, but that they would do what they could 'to stop performances anywhere'. [. . .]

The biggest lie, my apparent Jewishness, I put down to a man deranged by anger, not unlike the Rabbi in Heine's *Disputation* who went everywhere with an open knife in order to circumcise harmless and unsuspecting Christians. [. . .][2]

Wagner [finally] stumbles over the name of Robert Schumann about whom he has to say something hateful [. . .] 'Compare the two periods of Schumann's output: the one full of plastic creativity, the other flat bombast'. And what could the cause of this change be? Could it be, as we have always assumed, the nervous condition under which he tragically suffered and died? Of course not! Wagner informs us that the reason lies in the exposure of Schumann to Jews! If Wagner's pamphlet had until now only seemed ridiculous, it now appears to be deeply repellent. With this, we slam shut this tiny booklet that will win the author few friends and most likely not add appreciably to his Jewish enemies. Wagner's characteristics can only be of psychiatric interest. This most hopeless case of self-idolatry has reached such an unimagined height that there is simply no oxygen left for normal brain functions. One can only recall Wagner's Old Testament predecessor, King Nebuchadnezzar, who for so long believed himself to be a god that over time he turned into an ordinary ox, eating grass – and eventually found himself turned into an opera by Verdi.[3]

Mendeslssohn's Shadow

Before the emancipations of 1867 and 1871 in Austria and Germany, many Jewish composers – prominent among them, Jacob Liebermann Beer, better known as Giacomo Meyerbeer, and Jacob (Jacques) Offenbach – left for France. Felix Mendelssohn, who since his family's conversion to Christianity had taken on the additional name of Bartholdy, was the exception, having found more acclaim in Britain. With works such as *Lobgesang* and the oratorios *Paulus* and *Elijah*, and with his revival of Bach's *St Matthew Passion*, Mendelssohn showed a reverence for tradition that would become a feature of German and Austrian Jewish musical assimilation.

Wagner aims many of his most barbed attacks at those Jews whose financial circumstances allowed them the luxury of both artistic and social confidence, but who, despite these advantages, continued to seek comfort in the past rather than the future. He interprets as racially shallow the precarious social position obtained by recently assimilated Jewish musicians. To Wagner, their over-caution when composing resulted in blandness, which they compensated for by their use of dazzling technique. Their music, in his view, resides on the outer shell of virtuosity rather than within the inner spirit. By plumbing spiritual depths, something of which he believed Jews were intellectually and culturally incapable, composers communicated at a deeper level that propelled music towards the future. In the writings of both Richard Wagner and the diaries of his wife Cosima, Mendelssohn is mentioned on hundreds of occasions.[4] Wagner suggests, for example, that Mendelssohn was incapable of writing something as complex and self-revealing as an opera, while ignoring the vast number of popular operas written by utterly forget-table non-Jewish composers.[5] He praises Mendelssohn for his talent, cultiva-tion and sensitivity, while at the same time turning these attributes into barriers to deeper spiritual communication. He accuses Mendelssohn of taking his musical models, such as Bach, from the past while remaining singularly incapable of transmitting the deeper meaning of Bach's works. According to Wagner, Mendelssohn only touches us when he 'lets us notice his spiritual impotence'.[6]

Throughout this entire tirade, he never ceases to damn Mendelssohn by praising him as the perfect student, only pleasing to us if we are in need of simple 'entertainment with perfect structures, sequences, dazzling and tweaking out the most perfect arabesques'.[7] He also goes on to condemn Mendelssohn as an interpreter of past German masters for preferring fast, superficial, tempos. Later he accuses the Mendelssohn 'school' of 'avoiding emotion' and not employing 'expressive effects'.[8] He describes Mendelssohn's performances of Bach as so 'effect-free' that he felt himself transported to a 'Hellenic synagogue' and needed thereafter to seek musical solace from Liszt in order to restore his faith.[9]

Wagner's very personal experiences bring him to the conclusion that Jews are physically so different from other European races that they could never be used to represent heroes or romantic leads in the theatre: 'If the outward appearance of the Jew is inappropriate for transmitting artistic ideas of this or that dramatic character, should one not question if the Jew's inner being is incapable of artistic expression?'[10] He also damns their use of language. One of his many contentious points is the view that every non-Jew is viscerally repulsed by Jews. He mentions this reaction as being 'psychological' and 'instinctive'; for a tract deriving from the middle of the nineteenth century, Wagner is quite free with the use of 'scientific' terms that compensate for his lack of hard evidence. He cites Jewish liturgical music as proof that the Jew does not live in today's world, but languishes in a petrified past. He states that the majority of music-lovers are interested in music's future and couldn't care less about its past. As we come to the last part of the tract, it becomes clear that Wagner is settling grudges and perceived slights. He proceeds to denigrate as thoroughly as possible both Mendelssohn, whom he names, and Meyerbeer, who remains anonymous. Mendelssohn's early death in 1847, which Wagner describes as 'the death that Mendelssohn's guardian angel sealed at the right time by closing his eyes permanently,'[11] presumably made him an easier target than Meyerbeer, though there is also the very faint chance that Wagner may have recalled his youthful debt to Meyerbeer. The chances of this are slim, since there is absolutely no mistaking his target, and the language is not pleasant.

In Wagner's opinion, German music would for ever remain a foreign tongue to Jewish composers, implying that the cultural assimilation they were seeking could never end in full integration. These views are ageless and one need only recall in recent times the huge influx of Chinese, Korean and Japanese performers of Western classical music who have been objects of the same prejudice; the opinion that newly assimilated minorities must dazzle in order to impress is obviously not new. That Wagner could smash the existing mould of music-theatre and altogether change how music was perceived goes equally without saying. That he could do so more easily than Mendelssohn, unhampered by the grudging anti-Semitic bigotry of the cultural environment in which he worked, is fundamental to understanding how music developed in German society. As it happened, the conditions that coloured the reception of Wagner and Mendelssohn earlier in the nineteenth century continued throughout the later assimilation phases: forward thrusts by one group are balanced – or impeded – by an obsessive clinging to the conventional by more cautious new arrivals.

It is fascinating to compare Wagner's views of Mendelssohn as being facile and superficial with those of the Jewish poet Heinrich Heine. Heine saw Mendelssohn as representing the essence of German *gravitas*. He spills a good deal of ink on the subject of Judaism and Christianity, while being remarkably candid about his own conversion. In *Lutetia*, Heine speculates on why Mendelssohn remained unpopular in France. In a direct comparison between Rossini's *Stabat Mater* and Mendelssohn's oratorio *Paulus*, he writes:

> Heaven preserve me from speaking ill of so worthy a master as the creator of *Paulus*, nor would it remotely occur to [me] to doubt the deep underlying Christianity of the oratorio because Felix Mendelssohn-Bartholdy happens by birth to be a Jew. But I simply cannot suppress the observation that by the time Mendelssohn had converted to Christianity at the age of thirteen ..., Rossini had already left it and given himself entirely to the worldly delights of opera. [With the *Stabat Mater*] he has now dreamt his way back into the Catholicism of his youth. ... One seems to proffer the view that in order to be sincere, Christianity (in art and music) must be both bloodless and pale. ... No, it is not the outer dryness that makes for true Christianity, but an inner ebullience that can neither be baptised into nor learned. ... As such, I find Rossini's *Stabat Mater* far more Christian than Mendelssohn's *Paulus*, despite Rossini's enemies who praise the latter as the very essence of the faith.[12]

When assessing Wagner's hostility towards Mendelssohn, it is worth remembering that he was attacking a man who had died at the tragically early age of 38 (not far off Wagner's own age at the time he was firing off polemics from the relative safety of Zurich having fled from Germany in 1849). He had yet to compose the *Ring*, *Tristan*, *Meistersinger* or *Parsifal*.

Wagner and the Jews, the Jews and Wagner

By the mid-1850s, Wagner's obsession with Mendelssohn seems to have lessened somewhat; and by 1872, he is happily corresponding with the Jewish conductor Hermann Levi, whom he regularly addresses as 'honoured friend' and even later, 'most valued friend'. Levi went on to conduct the premiere of Wagner's most ardently Christian work, *Parsifal*, while politely declining Wagner's (or more likely Cosima's[13]) entreaties to convert. Levi wrote to his father on 13 April 1884: 'Even his fight against that which he calls "The Jewish elements" in music and modern literature comes from the most honourable motives. That it does not betray the small-minded hostility of, say, the landed-gentry or self-righteous Protestantism is proven in his treatment of me, Joseph Rubenstein and his earlier close relationship with Tausig, to whom he showed the deepest affection. The most wonderful thing to happen in my life has been the privilege of being near such a human being. For this, I thank God daily.'[14] Levi is certainly correct in his assessment of

Wagner's relationship with Tausig, who had apparently reassured Wagner in correspondence that 'all Jews were reconciled' with him. In answer to this, Wagner wrote back that Jews would in fact be well advised to read his *Judaism in Music* pamphlet.[15]

Wagner was also outwardly grateful to Moritz Szeps, the Jewish proprietor of Vienna's *Wiener Tagblatt*, which was the more progressive counterweight to the rabidly anti-Wagnerian *Neue Freie Presse*.[16] The *Wiener Tagblatt* was the more widely read of the two papers at the time, and it was rumoured to be the mouthpiece of the heir to the Austrian throne, Archduke Rudolf. Another apparent softening in his attitude to Jews came in 1880, when Wagner refused to sign Bernhard Förster's anti-Semitic petition demanding that Bismarck retract the rights accorded to Jews in the constitution. However, Wagner's essay from 1881, *Erkenne Dich selbst (Know yourself)*, goes well beyond any of his previous anti-Semitic writings. He denounces as ludicrous the laws that allow Jews to see themselves as Germans – 'it's like the law in Mexico authorising all Negroes to see themselves as white'.[17]

This rambling tract expresses outrage at the tolerance shown by Christian clergy in accepting the emancipation of Jews, and at their view that Germans are Germans regardless of religious confession. Wagner argues that being a 'German Jew' is not the same as being a Protestant or a Catholic German. Surprisingly, he pronounces the death of the pure German race following the Thirty Years War; Jews, however, have remained the 'purest of all races and it matters not with whom they mix: the Jewish race always dominates'. He fumes that the new political orders, be they democratic, socialist or social-democrat, all rely on Jewish usury to finance their wars. To Wagner, the emancipation of Jews is the emancipation of Jewish capital. In this unseemly context, he confirms the hitherto presumed anti-Semitism of the *Ring*: 'The cursed Nibelungs' ring understood as a portfolio of stock market investments confronts us with the alarming reality of invidious world-domination.'[18]

Dietrich Mack mentions in the introduction to Cosima Wagner's diaries that Wagner was a child of his time and thus maintained a deeply persecuted view of himself. He had an irrational fear of Jews achieving the same civil and legal rights as Christians. Yet Jens Malte Fischer draws a more chilling conclusion when analysing the final moments of *Parsifal*, sung by the concluding chorus, 'Höchsten Heiles Wunder: Erlösung dem Erlöser!'/ 'Highest healing miracle: redemption of the Redeemer!' By the time Nietzsche had broken with Wagner, he had despaired of Wagner's obsession with 'redemption'.[19] In every opera, redemption is obtained through either self-annihilation, as with Senta in *The Flying Dutchman* and Brünnhilde in *Götterdämmerung*, or divine transfiguration denoted by the protagonist 'falling lifelessly to the ground': Elsa in *Lohengrin*, Kundry in *Parsifal*, Tannhäuser, Isolde, and so on. The apotheosis of Wagner's redemption-obsession comes when Parsifal appears to redeem the Redeemer himself. From what the Redeemer could possibly require redemption is not clear until Malte Fischer refers us back to Cosima Wagner's diary entry for 25 July 1878: Wagner had been reading aloud from the third part of his tract *Publikum und Popularität* (*The Public and Popularity*) in which he presents the view that Jesus, the Redeemer, as a Jew is anathema, and places him in a state that must demand atonement. Cosima, upon hearing this, quotes back to Wagner the final chorus of *Parsifal* and Wagner confirms that she has understood correctly. *Parsifal* represents Wagner's solution to what he viewed as Christianity's most complex metaphysical contradiction. In the shadow of such intellectual ruthlessness, talent and transcendental creativity, it was intimidatingly difficult to be another composer; if Jewish, it was unimaginable.[20]

Jewish Composers at the Time of Wagner

Giacomo Meyerbeer and Ignaz Moscheles are fascinating case studies of just such composers born during the early years of post-revolutionary Enlightenment. Both had ambitious, wealthy parents, and precociousness and virtuosity were considered 'fast tracks' into respectable non-Jewish society.[21] It was believed that such assimilation was best achieved, as demonstrated by the many Jewish literary and music salons, by the dissemination of culture itself. If Heine, who was nearly the same age as Meyerbeer and Moscheles, converted in order to obtain his apocryphal 'entrée billet to European culture', Meyerbeer and Moscheles gained access via their prowess as performers. Moscheles would go on to become the teacher of both Felix and Fanny Mendelssohn, though at the time he had already settled in England. It was Moscheles's contacts in London that paved the way for Felix and his subsequent musical successes with Queen Victoria, Prince Albert and the British public. Though England was more tolerant than most of the German states, including Moscheles's native Bohemia, he found it 'convenient' to have his children baptised Anglican, while remaining Jewish himself. He returned to Leipzig to teach in the conservatory founded by Mendelssohn in 1843 and became its director following Mendelssohn's death in 1847.

Mendelssohn's popularity in England meant that the conservatory in Leipzig would later attract such British luminaries as Arthur Sullivan, Charles Stanford and Ethel Smyth, among many others. Both Mendelssohn and

Moscheles believed that music must aspire to the classical purity of a past age. When Wagner's arch-enemy Eduard Hanslick became a professor of music and aesthetics (in effect the precursor of musicology) at Vienna's university, and published his manifesto *Vom Musikalisch-Schönen* (*Of Musical Beauty*) in 1854, it became clear to Wagner that Jews were camouflaging their lack of innovation and individuality by wrapping themselves in a mantle of reverence for the past.

This could hardly have been less true of Meyerbeer, who was happy to pursue as much new theatrical 'effect' as possible. His innovation and mastery of musical theatre would influence Wagner far more than the latter cared to admit. To shroud any suspicion that this might have been the case, his attacks of Meyerbeer were relentless. The hundreds of Wagner's references to Mendelssohn pale beside those he makes of Meyerbeer.[22] Where Meyerbeer differs from his younger compatriot Jacques Offenbach was his fundamental sense of German identity. Both Meyerbeer and Offenbach were Prussians, though Offenbach's family became Prussian through Prussia's acquisition of the Rhineland in 1815, whereas Meyerbeer's family came from the long-held Prussian region of Brandenburg. Like Meyerbeer, Offenbach was groomed by his ambitious father as a virtuoso and, until 1849, he appeared as a noted cellist accompanied by the likes of Franz Liszt, Anton Rubinstein and Felix Mendelssohn. With the success of *Orphée aux enfers* in 1858, his reputation as a composer was secure. For Wagner, Offenbach's works were the embodiment of all that was superficial and fatuous: gratuitous music by a Jewish composer that only charmed and flattered without exciting any deeper resonance. In Wagner's anti-Semitic tracts, Offenbach is so beneath contempt that he hardly merits a mention, yet references in letters and memoirs make it clear that Offenbach was to Wagner the very epitome of the facile musical Jew: able to appeal to a large public and merely interested in making money. The only Jewish composer who escapes condemnation is Jacques Fromental Halévy, though he too, according to Wagner's *Autobiographical Sketches* of 1842, was 'like all Parisian composers, interested only in having at least one big success, then lying back and enjoying the resulting income'.[23] Halévy was not German and he comes into Wagner's line of fire more for being French than for being a Jew, though he faces the same charge of being disinterested in music but obsessed with financial reward.

If we take Schumann, Chopin and Berlioz, and place them in direct comparison with Moscheles, Mendelssohn and Meyerbeer, it is possible to understand some of Wagner's musical arguments while disagreeing with his conclusions. The question is not so much in regard to the quality of their music, but to the conditions that allowed their works any kind of lasting place in the repertoire. Moscheles, Mendelssohn, Meyerbeer and Offenbach had started as virtuoso performers. Had they not, it is doubtful that circumstances would have allowed them to make their subsequent mark as composers. It can be taken as understood that a Jewish Berlioz or Wagner would never have entered the musical mainstream since neither was a virtuoso instrumentalist. Wagner's view that Mendelssohn's compositions consisted of facile note-spinning blithely overlooks the same quality in many of the works by his father-in-law, Franz Liszt, or the demonic violinist, Niccolò Paganini. Mendelssohn's aspiration to Mozartian purity, free of artifice and devoid of effect, was not far from Rossini's ideals and had philosophical origins in the Enlightenment idea of music as not just an art, but as a natural science. These Kantian views would have been seen by many at the time as logical and the result of empirical analysis; but to Wagner and Liszt, such values were already old-fashioned and in conflict with their understanding of Schopenhauer's metaphysical philosophy of the will that disparaged the rational thinking of the past and embraced the more impassioned mood at the root of Romanticism.

The European Enlightenment saw music as trans-national and translinguistic in its discourse, sharing many of the same scientific qualities as mathematics. John Locke's view that all men were born fundamentally equal, and with an equal potential for rational growth, was an underlying belief of the period that defined Mozart's reception as a child prodigy. Mozart, whose background offered no obvious access to the aristocratic society he reached as a *Wunderkind*, appeared to confirm to Jews that assimilation and acceptance within the highest circles of society was achievable for them as well. The reasoning of the age was that childhood was simply the first stage in the development of rational and equal citizens in a democratic and egalitarian world. As such, Mozart became a symbol not only for the ambitious who lived on the margins of society, but as a demonstration that every child harboured enormous potential. Music as a natural science had laws, but the brilliance of Mozart, and later Mendelssohn, showed how these laws themselves could be used to expand the non-verbal discourse that was the fundamental nature of music.[24] The extraordinary originality of both Mozart and Mendelssohn lay in their dazzling application of existing models, not by reinventing them. The virtuoso composers Moscheles, Mendelssohn, Ferdinand Hiller and Meyerbeer all came from wealthy Jewish families from German cities. As such, they were greatly influenced by the Jewish Enlightenment, the *Haskalah*, which made them well aware of the artistic and aesthetic value (as well as the social advantage) that came from assimilation.

The view later propagated by Wagner that national character was the absolute determinant of musical expression came long after Mozart's death and followed the rise of post-1848 Romanticism and its frequently obnoxious elder relative born during the French Revolution, Nationalism. This idea is expounded in its own chapter from Wagner's 1850 manifesto *Das Kunstwerk der Zukunft* (*The Art-work of the Future*). To Wagner, music was the logical expression of nationhood and since Jews were only pseudo-Germans, their attempts to compose German music were doomed to failure. They did not possess the true Germanic soul.[25] The more defined these ideas became, the more bombastic the debates were between Wagner and his contemporaries regarding national character and how music should develop. Towards the end of the century, the camps were well delineated, with Brahms representing the 'old' school of German music and Wagner and his followers representing the 'new'. The 'old' school, despite some bourgeois anti-Semitism from the likes of Robert and Clara Schumann, became a by-word for philo-Semitism. It was this that led German nationalists and supporters of Wagner's new-German School to aim blatantly anti-Semitic attacks at non-Jewish composers such as Brahms and Bruch.

Wagner's Political and Cultural Legacy

The 'new' school of Wagner and his father-in-law Liszt was largely opposed by the musical establishment in Leipzig – paradoxically, Wagner's native city. It was where Mendelssohn had triumphed at the Gewandhaus and the city came to represent the antithesis of Wagnerian 'Art-of-the-Future' ideals. It is fascinating to read how this process came about in the memoirs of Alfred Richter, a composer and teacher (and son of the Thomaskirche Kantor Ernst Richter) who became a scrupulous chronicler of Leipzig's 'golden age'. This important document remained unpublished until its chance discovery in the municipal museum in 2004. Richter recalls working with Mendelssohn, Schumann, Wagner, Lortzing and others, and he offers an account of the local reception of Wagner's *Das Judenthum in der Musik*:

> Wagner's *Judenthum in der Musik* written under a pseudonym and published in the *Neue Zeitschrift für Musik*, a journal originally edited by Schumann and then by Franz Brendel, exploded like a bomb. The indignation among the faculty of the Leipzig conservatory was enormous; it even resulted in demands on Director Schleinitz for Brendel's dismissal, though who led this attack, I can't actually say. Schleinitz, whose own opinions of Mendelssohn bordered on idolatry, wisely rejected these demands. This was certainly

sensible and justified; although the pamphlet was not especially complimentary to the Jewish race and its influence on German music, it had not actually libelled Mendelssohn in any way. It only proved again how dangerous it
is for the arts when they become too factional. No doubt it would have been
better had the article remained unwritten. Wagner's music and ideas would
have still managed to make their mark and he would have been spared a
number of bitter enemies. One also accused him of ingratitude to Meyerbeer,
who was often a great help to Wagner – something he even admitted himself.
Wagner later claimed that his personal animosities and feelings were not
involved while writing the pamphlet. Perhaps he even believed this, but we
can't know what inner urge motivated him.[26]

Wagner's views undoubtedly helped to shape the nineteenth century and,
by extension, the twentieth. The American historian Peter Viereck in an
essay from 1941 picks up on a concept communicated to Wagner by an
admirer, Constantin Frantz. He called Wagner's political visions 'metapo-
litical', in other words, having the same relationship to normal politics
as metaphysics to physics. Viereck uses the concept of 'metapolitics' to
explain the evolution of Wagnerian thought into full-blooded National
Socialism and by so doing, he deals with the very nature of the nineteenth
century's *Zeitgeist*. This is a complex evolution that begins with the
Enlightenment and continues through the French Revolution, Napoleon and
the resulting philosophy of the sovereignty of the individual. Starting
from this point, Wagner's own political development moves him through
the barricades in Dresden with his anarchist comrade Mikhail Bakunin, and
ends in Swiss exile. It is along this route that he replaces Hegel with
Schopenhauer and finally Feuerbach and, by doing so, evolves from the
'Latinate' view of the autonomous individual to the concept of the individual
as an element within the collective. This epiphany concerning Wagner's
adherence to the German 'people' or 'nation' had already come as a defining
experience with his return from France in 1843. Along with his new-found
devotion to the German people or '*Volk*', he abhors the French and the superficial financial motivation of French composers. Indeed, the leitmotif in
Wagner's life is the idea of money (Gold) and its power to individualise by
creating disparities within an autonomous nation. It fits neatly as the cornerstone into what would soon emerge as a uniquely anti-Semitic variant of
German nationalism.

    In fact, as Viereck goes on to explain, the Romantic notions of 'nation',
'nationhood' and 'the people' (*Volk* or 'folk') were the basis for a rejection of
the Enlightenment and therefore required that reason be conquered by

instinct, that law be conquered by passion, form by content, and scientific truth by collective mythology – ultimately, that the 'dynamic' conquer the 'static'.[27] It culminated in the Romantic view that 'life was its own law'. With such dynamic forces of Germanic self-identification at work, it ultimately seems ironic that the French aristocrat Count Gobineau, with his *Essai sur l'inégalité des races humaines*, and Wagner's own son-in-law, the English philosopher Houston Stewart Chamberlain, would have the greatest influence in shaping and propagating Wagner's racist views. Even more potent may have been Wagner's own lingering doubts as to whether his father might have been his mother's second husband, the actor Ludwig Geyer, who had lived as a lodger in the Wagner household before the death of Wagner's father. More disturbing for Wagner was the possibility that Geyer was Jewish. Nietzsche claimed he was, but without any proof, and it has never been ascertained whether Geyer was in fact Wagner's father. There were also continuing doubts about the parentage of Cosima Wagner. Her grandmother was the daughter of the Frankfurt banker Simon Moritz Bethmann, whose name and profession may suggest Jewish origins, though these, too, have never been proven. Yet regardless of the exact physical and psychological origins of Wagner's anti-Semitism, Viereck shows how Hitler was able to quote, almost word for word, much of Wagner's musings as being the foundation of his own political ideas. Indeed, Wagner was cited by Hitler as being his favourite 'political' writer.

More relevant to music itself was Wagner's specific condemnation of Giacomo Meyerbeer, a composer whose operas dominated the stage during the nineteenth century. His *Robert der Teufel*, better known as *Robert le Diable*, was, from the moment of its Viennese premiere in 1833, the single most frequently performed work in the city until a combination of costs, casting difficulties and, above all, Wagner's attacks had so undermined the composer's credibility that by the turn of the century the opera had lost all support. A hint of its former glory is to be found in Erich Wolfgang Korngold's own opera *Die tote Stadt* (1920), in which *Robert le Diable* features in the storyline. Korngold took it for granted that the public would understand the symbolism of his character Marietta being a dancer who portrayed the spirit of a long-dead satanic nun in *Robert le Diable*.

Meyerbeer was the most prominent and original composer to disappear predominantly as a result of Wagner's directed attacks. Yet such was the cult around Wagner that by 1900, Teutonic Romanticism's belief that change grew out of a disruptive surge produced by a shared national spirit resulted in a voluntary shift away from most nineteenth-century Jewish composers, with Mendelssohn being virtually the only survivor. This change of priority would presage musical developments throughout the twentieth century, where 'new' was preferable to the familiar. Jewish nineteenth-century composers were willingly forgotten because they were, supposedly, largely conventional. Wagner had re-interpreted the concept of 'conventional' as meaning at best 'safe' and at worst 'inadequate'. Wagnerian idolatry grew, and in Vienna it eventually split into Jewish and non-Jewish adherents. Guido Adler, the father of modern musicology and childhood friend of Mahler, would be prominent in the Jewish Wagnerian Society which viewed Wagner as the prototype of the artist-as-catalyst, a view that would be shared first by Mahler and later by Schoenberg, both of whom would themselves become catalysts during the course of the twentieth century.

Hitler, however, turned Wagner's view of the 'dynamic versus the static' onto its head and by 1935 had ushered in a period of stifling conventionalism. Furthermore, the Nazis' racist conclusions, extrapolated from selectively chosen anti-Semitic polemics by Wagner, resulted in banning the very composers, who though Jewish, had regularly reflected the conviction that German music was predestined in its unique superiority – the very view held by Wagner himself. Decades before the rise of Nazism, Jewish Wagnerians, in their capacities as performers, writers and musicologists, were leading the fight for the musical dynamism that they believed to be uniquely German. They rejected what they saw as the static conformity of the past. Thus, nineteenth-century Jewish composers were removed by Jewish programmers not because they were Jewish but because they were deemed to represent the conventional. With Hitler's arrival, composers were suppressed not because they were conventional but because they were Jewish.

With the exceptions of Mendelssohn and Offenbach, prominent Jewish composers of the nineteenth century have largely disappeared from today's concert halls and opera houses. To Meyerbeer and Moscheles, one could add also the once popular Jacques Fromental Halévy (1799–1862), Ferdinand Hiller (1811–85), Ferdinand David (1810–73), Charles-Valentin Alkan (1813–88), Anton Rubinstein (1829–94), Friedrich Gernsheim (1839–1916), Karl Goldmark (1830–1915) and Camille Erlanger (1863–1919). To these should be added the virtuoso performing-composers: Moritz Moszkowski (1854–1925), Karl Davidov (1838–89), Louis Moreau Gottschalk (1829–69), Henryk Wieniawski (1835–80), Józef Wieniawski (1837–1912), Joseph Joachim (1831–1907), David Popper (1843–1913) and Ignaz Brüll (1846–1907). Most of these musicians had a closer sympathy with Brahms than with Wagner. Why these composers have virtually disappeared from the repertoire, and what influence, if any, they might have had on a musical legacy not conditioned by Wagnerian anti-Semitism followed by 12 years of National Socialism, asks more questions than answers can provide. Wagner's anti-Semitism is something to which we shall often return. Not only did he represent the view of a particular time and place, but his writings, more than those of almost anyone else, contributed to shaping Hitler's opinions. Yet, when we place his rambling polemics in context, what emerges most strikingly is the anger, resentment and, above all, the jealousy that Wagner felt at having to share his natural musical inheritance with people he saw as interlopers in German culture.

CHAPTER 3

An Age of Liberalism, Brahms and the Chronicler Hanslick

... this was carried out by a Viennese lawyer [Hanslick], who was a great music enthusiast and expert of Hegelian dialectics, who by virtue of his Jewish origins, which he kept elegantly hidden, wrote much that was easily accessible. [...] He went on to author a pamphlet on the subject of 'Musical Beauty' in which he cleverly proceeds to propagate Jewish musical ambitions.

... dies ward durch einen Wiener Juristen erreicht [Hanslick], welcher großer Musikfreund und Kenner der Hegel'schen Dialektik war, außerdem aber durch seine, wenn auch zierlich verdeckte jüdische Abkunft besonders zugänglich befunden wurde. [...]

Dieser schrieb nun ein Libell über das 'Musikalisch-Schöne', in welchem er für den allgemeinen Zweck des Musikjudenthums mit außerordentlichem Geschick verfuhr.

Letter from Wagner to Frau Muchanoff, née Countess Nesselrode, Tribschen bei Luzern, 1869

The Political Movement of Liberalism

The years 1867 to 1897 were defined by the central role played by the Austrian Liberal Party and matched almost precisely the period that Brahms was resident in Vienna (1868–97). Economically, these years of Liberalism financed the burgeoning Industrial Revolution and promoted open markets, unregulated trade, a liberal economy, and easy access to finance. It shunned institutions that put barriers in place and inevitably began showing tendencies of anti-clericalism and anti-nationalism, both seen as impediments to unhampered capital growth. Its emergence, following the creation of the Austro-Hungarian dual Monarchy in 1867, picked up where the missed political opportunities of the Revolution of 1848 had left off. The Revolution had at least been followed by a boom in Moravia, Bohemia and Austria, and demanded an economic environment in which it could continue to flourish. This was only possible with the arrival of a political class sympathetic to widening wealth-creation. Until the Vienna stock market crash of May 1873, Liberalism, with its values placed more highly on the individual than on the broader social community, had created the basis for a strengthened, confident, yet still emerging, middle class that was demanding greater participation in affairs. With the crash of 1873, a general disenchantment with the capitalist model demanded concessions from the ruling party, leading to enfranchisement being increased to approximately 6 per cent of all Austrian males, followed by several further reforms until 1907, when all men over the age of 24 were eligible to vote. This right was extended to women in 1919. The December Constitution of 1867, which opened the way for full Jewish emancipation, along with progressive extensions of enfranchisement, gave increasing opportunities to an ever expanding Jewish middle class.

This newly assimilated bourgeoisie came to enjoy prominence far beyond their actual numbers within the general population, especially in the liberal professions of law, academia and medicine, though the Habsburg institutions of the civil service and military continued to remain resistant to full Jewish integration. Franz Joseph himself was seen by Jewish professionals as someone who represented their interests. In the long term, however, it was the inability of Liberals to deal with the effects of policies resulting in social disparities between the middle and lower orders that eventually caused their downfall: a benevolent, albeit not fully democratic, paternalism had been blind to the deprivation beyond their immediate class. One of the last reports of Brahms's political discussions was an account of his agitation at the election in 1895 of the populist, anti-Semitic Christian-Social mayor of Vienna, Karl Lueger, as something that he had foreseen and about which he had repeatedly warned his fellow Liberals. As Stefan Zweig relates in his memoirs, *Die Welt von Gestern*,[1] it was only with the fall of Liberalism that 'one became aware of how thin yet noble its veneer had been. With its passing, the conciliation found in public life was lost and divergent interests collided. From this point on, it would become a fight.'[2] Elsewhere, Zweig eloquently explains how the wealthy aristocracy, which under normal circumstances would have been the target of 'the little man's' social outrage, gave support to Lueger's stridently anti-Semitic Christian Social Party so that Jews, rather than aristocrats, would be seen as the wealthy exploiters of the labouring poor.[3]

Brahms and the Liberal Party

Until the fall of Liberalism in 1897, a confident Viennese bourgeoisie became increasingly culturally ambitious, valuing music and opera more than appeared to be the case in Paris, London or Berlin. What seems surprising from today's perspective is the apparent contradiction between Liberalism's progressive economic policies and its conservative cultural agenda throughout the 1870s and 1880s. It would be another ten years before this started to change in Vienna. With the still recent emergence of an educated middle class, it was inevitable that their cultural ambitions would affirm their social position. In art and architecture, this resulted in a wave of neo-classical paintings and buildings, the best of which still remain grand and impressive, radiating confidence in bourgeois stability. That such a movement would appeal to Austria's minuscule Protestant minority – including the Hanseatic Brahms – and to newly enfranchised Jewish professionals is hardly surprising. That it would become anathema to Pan-German nationalists, who worked themselves up into waves of mass conversions to Protestantism over the following decades in order to distance themselves from Catholic (seen as non-German) Austria, is perhaps less obvious.

Yet German nationalism was mixed with many other ideals and theories. At one extreme, it was socially inclusive, even Socialist, and could point to the Liberal Party's neglect of the proletariat, the agricultural labourers and the unemployed, who had no social standing, nor any prospect of improving circumstances. The nationalism that grew out of the 1848 Revolution was progressive in that it was middle-class revolutionaries who saw a state, laboriously hewn out of a nation, as an instrument for everyone, regardless of class or position. It must be remembered that the aristocracy was largely supranational, with little sympathy for the people who made up the nations they administered. German academia, however, was overwhelmingly nationalist, and student unrest, in the modern sense, found its equivalent in the fiercely sectarian *Burschenschaften* (academic fraternities). Thus Brahms's own sense of 'German-ness' can be compared to that of millions of assimilated Jews, though works such as the *Triumphlied* and his *Academic Festival Overture* exude a sense of national pride that would have amounted to more than mere patriotism during the later years of the nineteenth century in Vienna.

The number of Viennese (predominantly from the servant classes) who spoke Czech as a first language was significant enough to lead to proposals for the city to become officially bi-lingual in the manner of Prague, with a minimal demand that at least all municipal documents and forms should be available in both languages. Even this tiny, yet practical concession resulted in

German nationalists virtually taking to the barricades and the proposal was dropped. One of Brahms's closest friends, the noted surgeon Theodor Billroth, was not only a prominent Liberal, but also an unashamed apologist for German as the official first language throughout the Empire. Despite Brahms's admiration for Bismarck, he was not an obvious supporter of any of the pan-German movements. Like many Liberals, he felt that unrestricted capital would eventually allow those at the bottom of the social ladder to join in the general prosperity of the age. Brahms's philo-Semitism has entered into legend, with the journalist Daniel Spitzer even joking that it was his friendship with the composer that had led to speculation that Brahms himself was a Jew.[4] He was clearly fond of socialising with Vienna's *haute-bourgeoisie*, which was largely made up of banking and industrial families. This was itself a philo-Semitic environment and included such prominent Jewish families as the Mautners, Gutmanns and Todescos, as well as the non-Jewish brothers von Miller zu Aichholz. The Jewish pianists Julius Epstein and Ignaz Brüll were among Brahms's closest friends, and, of course, he had a long friendship with Joseph Joachim; his private physician was Robert Breuer, one of the principal specialists at Vienna's Jewish Hospital. He was the son of Josef Breuer, one of the first doctors to treat neurosis, whose work was eventually developed by his young colleague Sigmund Freud. Other prominent non-Jewish friends and supporters included the surgeon Billroth, the critic and writer Max Kalbeck, and the composer and archivist at Vienna's Gesellschaft der Musikfreunde, Eusebius Mandyczewski. All of them shared Brahms's religious scepticism, and supported the Liberal Party and its policies of social tolerance.

Arthur Schnitzler describes the kind of society in which Brahms moved in his novel *Der Weg ins Freie*.[5] It tells the story of a non-Jewish composer (though Brahms is definitely not the model) who moved in Vienna's circles of wealthy Jewish families. In one revealing passage, the father of one of the protagonists in defending his Zionist position makes the observation that it was the Jews who had founded the Liberal Party, only to be betrayed by non-Jewish Liberals; and it was the Jews who had supported pan-German nationalism, only to be betrayed by non-Jewish nationalists. He goes on to say that one could expect the same to be true of the Social Democratic and the Communist Parties in the fullness of time. It was a prescient observation in what Schnitzler saw as a social drama from the late 1890s, though the book was not published until 1908.[6]

Brahms's Musical World and Jews

If Brahms was accused of philo-Semitism in the German nationalist press, it was more because he stood in opposition to Wagner and Bruckner rather than because of the company he kept. In his diaries, the composer and journalist Richard Heuberger recalls Brahms both despairing of Viennese anti-Semitism and at the same time suggesting it was time to call a halt to the influx of Jews from the East. Since most such arrivals were members of the poor, devout kaftan-wearing community, similar observations were made by middle-class Jews as well; it was more a question of class than of race

Brahms's notoriously curmudgeonly nature most likely extended to everyone, regardless of race and religion. One recalls his remark to a hostess upon departing for the evening: 'My apologies to any of the guests whom I may have forgotten to offend.'[7] The composer Karl Goldmark relates in his memoirs an unpleasant encounter in which Brahms addressed him in an anti-Semitic tone when he discovered that Goldmark had set a text by Luther that Brahms had intended for himself. But just as well documented is Brahms's angry outburst at the election of the anti-Semitic mayor of Vienna, Dr Karl Lueger. In short, Brahms was a North German Hanseatic Protestant in South German Catholic Austria, and was seen as the sober antithesis to the Romantic Movement's tribal German nationalism. Despite his own Teutonic pride, or even the nationalist tone struck in his *Academic Festival Overture*, he fundamentally had little sympathy for the ideas of 'German soul' and 'German spirit' that were often violently disseminated by German *Burschenschaften*, making middle-class Jews, who failed to understand why *Burschenschaften* did not see them as German, feel both nervous and exposed.

The Romantic view of spirit, soul and nation was, on one level, a visceral identification with a geographical place and culture, while on another it was a thinly disguised lever with which to remove those perceived as not belonging. To recently enfranchised Jews, there was no contradiction in being both Jewish and German. Romantics, however, saw the individual blessed by the Almighty with a unique 'racial' identity founded on nationhood, using the more emotive description of 'blood'. To them, to be Jewish and German was not only a contradiction but a physical impossibility. While some Jews were swept away by the fervid nationalism represented by Wagner, others were intoxicated by Wagner's music alone. Meanwhile, many non-Jews were drawn to the more soberly ordered world of Brahms. Thus the perception of Brahms and Wagner as polar opposites led to Brahms being thought to hold particular positions merely because they were not held by Wagner.

Brahms's Liberal sympathies and his circle of friends and colleagues brought many important representatives of Jewish assimilation into his orbit. These included both patrons and musicians. Within this circle was the first generation of Jews who were able to participate in musical life without restriction. It is fascinating to differentiate between those who helped shape the age, and those who merely tried to fit in. There are two principal sources associated with Brahms that facilitated or documented Jewish entry into German and Austrian musical life. One is the musical movement that grew out of Mendelssohn's Music Academy in Leipzig and which became the bastion of the so-called 'Old German School', as opposed to the 'New German School' deriving from Liszt and Wagner in nearby Weimar. The other source is from the writings and reviews of Brahms's friend and principal apologist, Eduard Hanslick. The following short excerpt by Hanslick from his obituary of the composer Robert Franz in the *Neue Freie Presse* on 1 November 1892 joins these two sources together in a single and succinct résumé:

> With the death of Robert Franz, the last of the glorious circle has now departed which in youthful enthusiasm rallied around the banner of Romanticism unfurled by Mendelssohn and Schumann. These two masters have long since left us, but following them were [Ferdinand] David, Moritz Hauptmann, [Julius] Rietz, [Robert] Volkmann, [Sterndale] Bennett, [Ferdinand] Hiller and latterly, [Niels] Gade. Only Clara Schumann remains as the Madonna of the Davidsbündler – and God grant her a long life! The last fading lights are now extinguishing from Leipzig's golden age. Robert Franz was one of the most appreciated and talented of this circle.[8]

As with the visual arts, architecture and literature that grew from the dominant, liberal middle classes, much of the music was stolid, respectable and often quite derivative. Today, re-acquaintance with the works of some of these minor composers offers frustratingly limited rewards. Yet the conventionality of much of this music tells its own intriguing tale and sets the tone for developments that would come later in the following century.

Hanslick's Musical World

Hanslick was the centre of Brahms's circle and although he was raised Christian, his mother had been born into the Kisch family, who were prominent Jewish merchants by royal appointment in Prague. Hanslick reported in his memoirs how his father was the only parent from whom he received an education, avoiding any in-depth mention of his mother's family apart from confirming that her parents were originally Viennese. He circumnavigates the issue of his Jewish ancestry by devoting an entire chapter to his mother in his autobiography where he maintains that it was through her and her parents that he developed a love of French literature. This at least indicated, if only vicariously, the enlightened, outward-looking model of those rational ideals and beliefs typical of the age of Liberalism. He was dismissive of many of the emotive, as opposed to expressive, qualities that were beginning to define music in the latter half of the nineteenth century. His rigidly Rationalist view of art and music made him suspicious of showmanship and empty virtuosity, which, as we know from Wagner, was in itself often seen as a near diversionary tactic of Jewish instrumentalists. Hanslick's ideals harkened back to the purity of the age of classicism and had no time for the portentous matters of nation and spirit being crow-barred into music or, indeed, into opera. His book, a Hegelian aesthetic thesis from 1854 entitled *Vom Musikalisch-Schönen*,[9] underwent numerous reprints and, with a doctorate of law in his pocket, he was able to begin lecturing on music history and aesthetics in 1861 with a piano at his side and an auditorium full of curious students from all disciplines. As pointed out by Hanslick's English translator Henry Pleasants, it probably constituted the very first 'music appreciation' course.[10] It, along with his *Geschichte des Concertwesens in Wien*[11] from 1870, became prime documents for drawing intellectual battle-lines between the Wagnerian Romantics of the so-called 'New German School' on the one side and the 'Old German School' Romantics, represented by Brahms and the Conservatory in Leipzig, on the other. That Brahms was a full generation younger than Wagner only heightens the tone of the dialectic that was bandied about: the younger composer represented the old, the older composer represented the new.

Hanslick reserves special condemnation for triviality in music, the banal and the picturesque. He does not spare Jewish composers, and his acidic reviews attacking bland conventionalism highlight that he was always aware of 'empty worthiness' as an ever-present danger. His reviews of Wagner and Liszt are notoriously partisan, often written in a way that shamelessly basks in his own highly enjoyable and immensely readable vituperation. Yet, taking a selection of reviews from his decades of writing on music, we can discern the lines he drew between progressive and conservative, conventional and original, and often, by extension, between the assimilating Jew and the establishment Gentile.

His review of Liszt's tone poems, and specifically *Les Préludes* from 1857, is a directory of musical values with which he challenges the very basis of the New German School. The extraneous burdens imposed on music to provide a programmatic narrative leave him particularly piqued.[12] In later reviews, he hands Liszt a back-handed compliment by praising his orchestration of a Schubert march – Schubert being as incapable of orchestrating in the manner of Liszt as Liszt is of coming up with ideas as original as Schubert.[13] Elsewhere, he voices a suspicion that the 'Gretchen' movement of Liszt's *Faust Symphonie* was included in a Philharmonic concert as it was the only bit of the work worth hearing.[14] To Hanslick, Liszt was of a fundamentally unproductive nature. Hanslick's review of Liszt's *Des Bohémiens et de leur musique en Hongrie*, published in the *Neue Freie Presse* on 22 November 1881, tells us as much about the critic as it does about Liszt. The book was originally published in 1859, but Hanslick is profoundly disturbed to find ten pages brimming with anti-Semitism added to the new edition. Hanslick quickly locates a pamphlet originally printed in [Buda]Pest called 'Franz Liszt on the Jews' written under the pseudonym of Sagittarius, in all probability the name of *Pester Lloyd*'s music critic Max Schütz.[15] Armed with Liszt's previous statements regarding Jews, Hanslick offers him enough rope to hang himself and quotes copiously from the most offensive passages of *Des Bohéhmiens*. He is outraged at Liszt's character assassinations of Mendelssohn and Meyerbeer, for whom Hanslick recalls Liszt having earlier expressed the highest admiration. Most of Liszt's polemic is rehashed Wagner on the same subject, though Liszt adds the quite hair-raising practical suggestion of ridding Europe of all Jews, by force if necessary, and shipping them to Palestine. 'Is this Wagner's influence or has the Abbé simply been spending too much time in Rome?' Hanslick quips. He ends this review more in sadness than anger while expressing alarm at the prominent platform Liszt's writings offer for such mindless bigotry.[16]

The final irony however comes with Hanslick's obituary of Liszt printed in the *Neue Freie Presse* on 8 August 1886. He reminds us that Liszt was born in the German-speaking border regions of Hungary and never spoke a word of Hungarian. 'Furthermore, he preferred to write and speak French, even when conversing with Germans.' He cites Liszt's formative years in Paris, where he was a supporter of equality and freedom during the 'July Revolution', while remaining a devotee of the aristocracy and a lover of beautiful women. Ultimately, according to Hanslick, Liszt grew to be too cosmopolitan, 'at home everywhere and nowhere, a characteristic that ultimately undermined the profundity of his music'.[17] It is quite startling how Hanslick unwittingly uses almost the same vocabulary to describe Liszt's music as that employed by Hitler's National Socialists to describe Jewish composers some fifty years later.

It is only when Wagner's music appears on a concert programme that Hanslick is prepared to liken Liszt's 'Gretchen' movement to the transcendental heights of Mozart. The Prelude to *Tristan and Isolde* is compared to listening to the beginnings of sentences without ever being able to hear their conclusions. He complains of the constant repetition of chromatic motifs, meaningless seventh chords, and orchestration that is meant to inject sensuality but instead, 'jangles nerves'.[18] '*Mild und leise*' (the 'Liebestod') is denounced as the scrupulous translation into music of Wagner's bombastic libretto, while the trombones at the beginning of Hans Sachs's second act aria, 'Jerum! Jerum! Hallahalohe!' from *die Meistersinger* 'sound like cannibals who have bitten into a piece of human flesh that is still too hot to eat'.[19] In short, Wagner's near perfect depiction of the erotic in music is something that offends and unsettles Hanslick's rational sensibilities; his references to nerves being 'jangled', 'confused' or 'disturbed' are a pejorative swipe at Wagner's ability to wrench control over the listener's emotional reactions.

Jewish composers hardly fare any better. Anton Rubinstein is warned against trying to inject too much originality into every bar, creating what Hanslick calls a 'Baroque and unmusical' effect. He is also cautioned against writing too much music too quickly. Hanslick noted that Rubinstein had already composed 'half-a-hundred' works, many of which weren't significant. Later, when reviewing Rubinstein's *Ocean* Symphony, he criticises what he calls Rubinstein's inability to maintain his originality.[20] Hanslick writes that he cannot recall a single work by Rubinstein, including his first two operas, in which quality was sustained throughout, or where it even improved as the work progressed. Reviews such as this, along with reviews of countless piano recitals, indicate that Vienna was hearing a lot of Rubinstein, both as performer and composer. His performances of Mendelssohn and Schumann are praised as sublime re-creations: Hanslick uses the word 'nachdichten', meaning to re-compose as a poet. An indication of Jewish musical assimilation can be inferred from the 1871 appointment of Anton Rubinstein as artistic director of Vienna's Musikverein, or 'Society of Music Friends'. His successor from 1872 was Brahms.

It is worth recalling that Hanslick was reviewing Wagner before he began reviewing Brahms – indeed, reviewing Wagner positively. Yet as Hanslick commented in 1862, 'Brahms is already a significant personality, possibly the most interesting among our contemporary composers.'[21] It is fascinating that the first thing Hanslick praises in the young Brahms is his individuality and his finely organised musical nature. This highlighting of 'organised' is telling. He praises Brahms in his D major Serenade for avoiding sumptuous orchestral effects. His respect for Brahms is seemingly boundless, bearing in mind that Hanslick is the older of the two (Hanslick was eight years older than Brahms and twelve years younger than Wagner). Taking the position of the senior statesman, he still managed to criticise Brahms in several important works such as the G major Sextet, describing parts of it as abstract music-making and complaining of headaches, caused by its restless mixing and brooding. He found no sensual beauty, rhythmic life or melodic pliancy and thought the finale reminded him of Schumann's staler, later works.[22]

Moving from Brahms to his immediate circle, however, we gain an even clearer understanding of Hanslick's ideals. Hanslick's reaction to the young Goldmark's overture *Sakuntala* reveals a number of points that shed light on Hanslick's values: the work is 'fresh and characteristic in inventiveness'; 'clearly structured and with the finest details'. Only a few places remind him of Goldmark's 'earlier sentimentality' and 'dissonance'.[23] Of Joseph Joachim, Hanslick writes that 'even in the enviable position of being the most important violinist of our day, he plays with the embodiment of transfigured virtuosity'. He goes on to say that the appreciation of Joachim's musical insight only reminds one later of his staggering technical command. 'How easy and sweet it is to enjoy this utter perfection, yet how difficult it is to describe.'[24] He also loves Joachim's 'purity and discipline of style'. The recital reviewed here must have been an exceptional experience as Joachim was accompanied by none other than Brahms. They played Schubert's Fantasy in C major and Beethoven's A major Sonata in addition to solo works by Tartini and Bach. 'No third person stood either between them or beside them. Bound together by artistic closeness and close friendship, here were two artists, whom Germany must joyously count among its noblest!'[25] Hanslick regrets that no works of Brahms were played and despairs of Brahms's own reluctance to shine as a virtuoso. He then goes on to suggest that Rubinstein is the better pianist of the two. Joachim as a composer leaves Hanslick unimpressed: his music is too reflective, 'his creative flow is neither swift nor rich; his inventive powers are honourable, but lacking in sensuality and elementary strength.'[26]

For Brahms's close friend, the Jewish pianist-composer Ignaz Brüll, Hanslick has few words of encouragement, despite the popularity his operas enjoyed at the time, mounted with the best casts that the Imperial Opera could provide. In his review of Brüll's opera *Bianca*, Hanslick mentions that the music remains as unoriginal as Brüll's previous works:

> It remains wedded to the pleasant-sounding without ever setting its sights any higher; it delivers what a harmless, attractive and agreeable small opera has to deliver. [. . .] If one is familiar with the music of his opera *Das goldene Kreuz*, which has even made its way to America, or his now [ubiquitous] *Landfriede*, one knows the music of *Bianca* as well. We are the least of those who should wish to criticise Herr Brüll in any manner, but didn't we pointlessly martyr our brains trying to think of something to say that we have not already said about *Landfriede* and *Das goldene Kreuz*? We can only mention the same good and bad points with perhaps more emphasis on the latter than the former. Indeed, even the wish that Brüll could be more self-critical

can be read in earlier reviews. In *Bianca*, we see a facile hand able to turn out what an unimaginative muse has not only produced but pronounced as satisfactory. [. . .] The composer works with only two key elements: his talent and his art. The former is inborn, the latter acquired, and they not only enhance or support each other, but rather the one takes up where the other lets off.[27]

Towards the end of this blistering appraisal, Hanslick outlines the dilemma of reviewing Viennese composers. Readers would certainly have been aware that Brüll was a friend of Brahms and therefore part of Hanslick's own musical circle:

The conscientious critic finds himself placed in a difficult position when dealing with local composers. He owes the talents of the city a certain consideration while at the same time needing to be forthright. He should not deflate the expectations that come with the enormous amount of work that has been invested, but neither should he lose the confidence of his public by heaping empty praise. In the case of Brüll, this dilemma is marvellously solved by the observation that we can be quite sure that in future, the composer will deliver us something far better than *Bianca*.[28]

Another major figure that moved in orbits around Mendelssohn, Schumann and Brahms was the Jewish pianist and composer Ferdinand Hiller, largely forgotten today. Hanslick has enormous affection for Hiller and mentions him frequently in his autobiography, an endorsement not reciprocated by Hiller, who makes just one passing reference to Hanslick in his own memoirs. Despite respect bordering on reverence, Hanslick refuses to offer empty praise. In his memoirs, he recounts Hiller's jovial comment that Hanslick was inclined to review his writings more favourably than his compositions. Hanslick gleefully acknowledges this – he did not undervalue Hiller's gifts as a composer, but thought his books far better.[29] On 18 and 19 August 1885, only three months after Hiller's death, Hanslick devotes six pages to him, using the correspondence between Hiller's librettist and friend Moritz Hartmann as the basis for an extended obituary. This is all the more exceptional as Hanslick makes the point that Hiller wanted to make his mark as an opera composer, though this was a task for which he was unsuited (along with other unnamed German pianist-composers, presumably Brüll or Rubinstein). The correspondence between Hartmann and Hiller centres on finding an appropriate operatic subject to follow his successful oratorios *Saul* and *Die Zerstörung Jerusalems*.[30] The resulting opera, *Die Katakomben*,[31] was finally produced in Wiesbaden ('a place better known for curing gout rather than important operatic premieres') and eventually made it to Hanover, Karlsruhe and Rotterdam. Hanslick mentions dryly that it was 'the most successful' of Hiller's many operas. Fundamentally, he finds Hiller's music lacking in originality, a trait Hanslick believes that Hiller recognised in himself when writing to Hartmann of his natural tendencies towards consensus, 'perhaps a tendency that was also reflected in his music'. Schumann, who thought very highly of Hiller's compositions (as did Mendelssohn), eventually came to the conclusion that Hiller's music was like a basket of ripe und unripe fruit thrown together. It could produce no true pleasure, since alongside the inspired was the trivial and contrived. This was an opinion that Hanslick shared. The rest of the article is devoted to praising Hiller's gifts as a writer.[32]

At no point does Hanslick consider the religion or cultural background of the composers whose works he reviews as pertinent. However, his feuilletons for the *Neue Freie Presse* provide a fascinating documentation of where Jewish composers were heading culturally, and although these were composers towards whom Hanslick may have been favourably disposed from a purely aesthetic point of view, most of them were fundamentally cautious and conventional. A hint of an exception is felt in Hanslick's review of Mahler's completion of Weber's opera *Die Drei Pintos*. He finds the work itself unexceptional, though it might have been better had Weber lived to complete it. Of Mahler, he writes that he is competent at matching Weber's instrumentation, though he grows weary of continuous passages of rushing semi-quavers, punctuated by trombones and bass drum: 'Mr Mahler is orchestrating for today's public not the public of the 1820s.' Hanslick goes on to praise Mahler's composition of the entr'acte before the second act, which he says offers an anticipation of Richard Wagner's sound world.[33]

Hanslick is equally impatient with the works of countless non-Jewish composers of the same period: for example, Josef Fuchs's 1889 opera *Die Königsbraut* ('a composer who instinctively knows his limitations'),[34] Johannes Hager's *Marffa*, performed in 1886 ('it would be nice if his melodies did not leave one feeling that they had passed through a number of other hands first'),[35] Victor Ernst Nessler's *Der Trompeter von Säkkingen* from 1884 ('the most remarkable thing about this work is its success'),[36] Karl Gramman's *Andreasfest* from 1885 ('his work is neither better nor worse than that which we regularly encounter within contemporary German opera; however, that standard itself is depressingly low at the moment'),[37] and Josef Hellmesberger's *Fata Morgana* from 1886 ('I put the work's weaknesses down to the fact that he composed it in only 3 months').[38]

One Jewish composer who came in for favourable treatment from Hanslick was the British musician Frederic Hymen Cowen, whose *Scandinavian* Symphony he reviewed in January 1882:

It isn't often that the English compose symphonies and even less often that they do it with success. Such a rarity was presented by Hans Richter in his most recent Philharmonic concert: both the symphony and its accompanying English composer. [. . .] His *Scandinavian* Symphony is large, and into the last detail a well-crafted work. Cowen has long ceased to be a beginner and has for some considerable time possessed the necessary skills of writing for all the techniques of the modern orchestra. In his newest work – the only one of his we know – he presents himself more as poet and land-scape artist than an independent and inventive musician. For that reason, the thematic material and counterpoint come less to the fore than his pallet of colours.[39]

With Cowen, who studied in Leipzig, we encounter the other centre around which newly assimilated Jewish composers could frequently be found. In some cases, they had direct, regular and friendly contact with Brahms, such as Friedrich Gernsheim. Cowen met Brahms during his Viennese sojourn, while others, such as Salomon Jadassohn (one of Cowen's professors at Leipzig), were obviously influenced by Brahms.

Hanslick's writings on Wagner and Liszt are far more nuanced than legend would have it. His moving obituary of Wagner published on 20 February 1883 opens with the line: 'The news of Wagner's sudden death painfully shocked and stunned our musical circle.' He can only acknowledge Wagner's impor-tance within the stagnant pool of German opera. He goes on to say that Wagner had no enemies who were simply mean-spirited and partisan (presumably referring to himself), while restating his belief that Wagner set music on a destructive course. Hanslick feigns admiration for Wagner's ability to have done this single-handedly, and cites the enormous vacuum left by his passing: 'He created a new art-form, for which we remove our hats, without for a moment dishonouring those practitioners of the "old" art such as Mozart, Beethoven and Weber.' He then goes on to declare that he was never in opposition to Wagner himself, but rather to the Wagnerians. Following Wagner's death, Hanslick's doubts about Wagner's music have all but disap-peared. He ends with a quotation from Grillparzer: 'Death is like a bolt of lightning: it transfigures that which it has destroyed.'[40] Yet it is revealing that with the death of Verdi 18 years later, *Die Neue Freie Presse* not only offers Hanslick's fulsome tribute, far longer than his Wagner obituary, but makes it their lead story, according Verdi the celebrity status of departed royalty, prime-ministers and generals.

Most of the Jewish composers Hanslick reviews, with the obvious exceptions of Mendelssohn and Meyerbeer, are condemned as conventional. But his affectionate obituary of Offenbach from 10 October 1880 finds him praising another innovative voice: 'Offenbach was a true original. His music was recognisable as Offenbach within a matter of only a few bars.' He mentions that in Offenbach's style, the language of Auber and Adam dominates, but Mozart and Weber are also apparent. After two full pages of praise, and documenting Offenbach's many successes and fewer failures in Vienna, Hanslick goes on with a certain benevolent cattiness to mention that 'less brilliant than his melodic and rhythmic genius was his harmonic artistry; and his contrapuntal skills came to zero. But his power to amuse has no musical equal [. . .] and as a final point [. . .] he was a master of form and structure. Whatever one may criticise him for, he was a musician of great brilliance and a genius of the theatre.'[41]

Karl Goldmark, Hanslick and Brahms: a Musical Triumvirate

Hanslick had praised Brahms as early as 1862 and he had been made aware of Goldmark's talent from as early as 1857, when Goldmark requested that Hanslick appraise a score in order to encourage support for his first concert. Hanslick's response was 'talent, but not ready.'[42] Later, when Hanslick headed a scholarship committee initiated by the Ministry of Education in 1863, he noted that his fellow committee member, the poet and playwright Franz Grillparzer, lamented that there were no more composers like Schubert: 'In those days, we had the talent, but no means of aiding it. Today we have the means, but no talent!' Hanslick then goes on to say that despite Grillparzer's misgivings, they in fact managed to promote a large number of promising youngsters, including Eusebius Mandyczewski, Richard Heuberger [. . .] and above all, Antonín Dvořák and Karl Goldmark. In due course, Goldmark and Brahms would both join Hanslick as scholarship adjudicators.[43]

Goldmark relates his first encounter with Brahms as taking place around 1860 or 1861 when he was the viola player in a Viennese quartet which met at the Café Čech, just off of the Graben (Vienna's most central square) near St Stephen's Cathedral. Brahms eventually offered the ensemble 'a string quintet in an early version which was latterly much reworked.'[44] Goldmark thought it was Brahms's self-belief that had initially so impressed Hanslick. In his memoirs, Goldmark notes that Brahms had admitted that Hanslick often turned to him for musical advice. He found Hanslick's deference to Brahms tiresome and even went so far as to say that Hanslick probably didn't understand Brahms at all. Elaborating on the one anti-Semitic remark Brahms made to him, Goldmark tells how Brahms discovered that Goldmark had set a text of Luther's that he had wanted to use himself, and informed Hanslick that it was not by Luther, but by someone else. When the work was performed, he was amused to read that Hanslick had simply repeated this bit of misinformation, planted by Brahms. It was during a later encounter, when Brahms spotted Goldmark in a restaurant, that he bellowed in front of other diners that he couldn't understand why a Jew would even wish to set a text by Luther.

At his seventieth birthday celebration, hosted by the family of Viktor von Miller zu Aichholz, Hanslick remarked that nothing made him happier during all the years he had spent writing music criticism than 'writing reviews that gave great joy to those who read of others being torn to shreds'. Brahms, according to Goldmark, was visibly unsettled by the comment, but went up to Hanslick afterwards and thanked him for his years of devoted support.[45] Goldmark and Brahms were on close terms and met frequently, but Goldmark admitted that Brahms thought only Goldmark's *Ländliche Hochzeit*[46] any good. Brahms had apparently told Brüll that he didn't really find much in Goldmark's music to appreciate, but that he valued both him and Brüll 'for their proficiency'. Further, he didn't really get on with the theatre, so wouldn't wish to comment on opera. Despite this, he did write to Hanslick of his enthusiasm for Goldmark's opera *Merlin*.

Goldmark was often thought to be a Wagner epigone, thus resulting in some ambivalence when Hanslick came to review his works, particularly as the two men moved in the same circle. In writing a *Laudatio* in honour of Goldmark's seventieth birthday, Hanslick reviewed the extraordinary success of his operas – most especially *Die Königin von Saba*[47] – and quoted extensively from a letter Goldmark had written, begging him to intercede with the powers at the Imperial Opera. Hanslick goes on to write, with some relief, that his intercession was unnecessary, as the work had already been accepted for performance. His reviews of Goldmark are carefully worded, but his views of *Königin von Saba* would today be construed as verging on the anti-Semitic, while giving us a strong indication of the sensibilities of the period – it was acceptable to be Jewish, but not to be too fulsome about it:

Goldmark's score offers us an impressive work, which often highlights a strong and individual talent. The strength is shown most in the passion, explosion of feeling, not to say the pure sheen of the musical colours which offer the distinctive peculiarities of the Jewish Orient. [. . .] Occasionally

Goldmark drives the passion to its outer limits, with voice registers at the top of the range, the chromatic storm in the orchestra with its thundering timpani and trombones, and racing bolts of lightning in the violins. The most noticeable feature of Goldmark's individuality is the musical translit-eration of Jewish Orientalism. [This] could be noted even in his earlier works such as his *Sakuntala Overture*, an interesting, rather strange yet arti-ficial work. As the story of *the Königin von Saba* is so profoundly Jewish, he allows this particular attribute full reign. Perhaps it's my own blinkered view, but I can only tolerate this sort of music in small doses: as a stimulus, but not as regular nourishment. With brilliant determination, Goldmark has wrapped himself in a display of oriental exotica, with all of its plaintive melisma, its augmented 4ths and diminished 6ths, its shunting between major and minor, its heavy thudding basses above which one hears the flick-ering and darting of countless dissonant harmonies and slivers of tones. The abundant use, one could say *abuse* [my italics], of accidentals, syncopations and dissonance are recognisable features of the modern German school. But to be able to carry them through with such positive results is something that eludes most of Goldmark's colleagues. [. . .] Where orientalist exoticism is called for, Goldmark gives everything he has. This works particularly well in the religious scenes and also in the ballet music and other dance scenes, which happen to be the highlights of the work. However, this tiresomely exotic manner grows wearisome after a while. It's even used when general human feelings are called for rather than anything specifically Jewish. How strange the 'song without words' sounds with which Astaroth tempts Assad to come to the queen. This is music that calls devout Jews to prayer, not lovers to a rendezvous! This is [Solomon] Sulzer written in the treble clef![48]

Hanslick's review of *Merlin* is equally revealing as he compares it with *Königin von Saba*. He is not impressed by Siegfried von Lipiner's text (credited to 'Lipiner von Immermann'), and believes that it tends to undermine the opera:

In *Merlin* we encounter, without any shadow of doubt, the composer of *Die Königin von Saba* but discover that his strengths have grown and become clearer. We are particularly delighted to notice the absence of the deter-mining feature of *Die Königin von Saba*, which was its fussy Jewish wailing which frankly threatened to derail this otherwise beautiful work. Nevertheless, the story of *Die Königin von Saba* at least justified the Oriental colouring without making it any more agreeable to listen to. But could one conceivably claim that this original feature was perhaps more characteristically 'goldmarkian' than what we have with *Merlin*? It would be possible to presume so and not without reason: the colourful embers of the Orient, with its restless heaviness and exalted religiosity, were not so much a unique characteristic of *Die Königin von Saba* as they were of its composer who grew up exposed to double doses of Orientalism, namely the Jewish and Hungarian varieties! Our slight preference for *Merlin*, however, does not counter the fact that *Die Königin von Saba* in its second finale reaches a climax [...] that offers no equivalent in effectiveness in *Merlin*.

For all of the musical independence that Goldmark has now acquired, it's apparent that in *Merlin* he still stands under the influence of Meyerbeer and even more obviously, Wagner. [...] His musical expression is impregnated with Wagnerian essences, though Goldmark captures different perfumes from the ones that have been floating about for the last 30 years. Occasionally, though, he inhales too deeply. King Arthur reminds one with his spongy sentimentality of König Heinrich and the Landgraf Hermann. [...] The love-duet is inconceivable without the templates of *Lohengrin* and *Tristan*. One is further reminded of Wagner with his unnatural emphasis on the dramatic, the restless chromatic breaks, and the flooding enharmonic modulations. ... Yet the means by which the work is composed is quite different from Wagner. With Goldmark, the sung melody remains at the centre, despite the fact that it doesn't exactly flow in generous quantities, but at least it isn't allowed to dry into stammering declamation, which swings back and forth over a melody being spun out endlessly in the orchestra. Where there is need of a lyrical oasis, Goldmark places these within the architectural forms which became the jewels of opera in the days before Wagner: choruses with knights and elves and women; even strophic songs, marches, and a well-organised ballet are offered.[49]

Mahler's admiration for Goldmark becomes understandable. Siegfried von Lipiner, librettist for *Merlin*, was a friend from pre-Alma days, and Goldmark's self-confidence as a Jew would have spoken deeply to Mahler's own creative spirit, as we shall see in the following chapter. He went on to conduct three of Goldmark's operas: *Das Heimchen am Herd* (1896), *Die Kriegsgefangene* (1899) and a new production of *Königin von Saba*. Indeed, Goldmark stayed as a regular feature of Vienna's opera season until Hitler's German henchmen persuaded compliant Austrians to have him removed two years before the Anschluss.

Brahms's death is chronicled by Hanslick, not by an obituary, but by an hour-by-hour account of his last days. A typically Hanslickian touch is recalling Brahms's last visit to a Philharmonic concert in which they performed his Fourth Symphony: 'The maestro, though ill, was brought from the back of his box at the end of each movement by stormy applause [. . .] and this despite the fact that the E minor symphony is not his most popular – with its utter lack of charm, it never will be.' It would be another two months before Hanslick could bring himself to write another article for the *Neue Freie Presse*. His reappearance as feuilletonist would consist of thirteen pages of memories and letters devoted to Brahms.[50]

Ultimately, Brahms represented the artistic expression of Liberalism, a political environment that would soon produce Jewish composers who were no longer cautiously moving into the glare of daylight, as chronicled by Hanslick, but basking in dazzling brightness. What remained from the years of Liberalism and Brahms's support was the belief in the aesthetic purity of music as part of German cultural identity. The younger generation of Jewish composers from the early twentieth century no longer felt Hanslick's conflicts. Indeed, as Julius Korngold, Hanslick's successor at the *Neue Freie Presse* and a notorious antagonist of atonal music, makes clear at the Hanslick centenary celebrations at the International Society for Contemporary Music in Venice in 1925:

The tonality traitors know well why they're against expression. They have to make a virtue out of necessity. Atonal cacophony negates sensual, melodic, emotional sensibility. We read in Alfred Einstein's *Dictionary of Modern Music* that 'The atonal melody is fundamentally a purely mechanical product and presents us with a *contradictio in adjecto* – an absurdity, since the comprehending spirit is incapable of finding any coherent relationship between the individual notes. One cannot write music based purely on a negative principal.' Hence the flight into linear contrapuntal writing that *lucus a non lucendo* – cannot be correctly voiced – causing a flight from all relationships into the tonality death-zone: the Twelve-Tone Row; this in turn results in objective, soulless attempts at messing about with material; the psychological effects of pitch and tone themselves being raised as the postulate of 'new music'. And on whom do they so desperately call as their spiritual Godfather? One hardly can credit it: Eduard Hanslick! This is because the composers of the younger generation, even the ones who still compose tonal music, have taken up Hanslick's arguments against Wagner and attempt to find in them their own aesthetic justification.[51]

In his memoirs, Julius Korngold sees Hanslick's aesthetic battles in the more measured tones of his own youthful development: 'It was not a question of Brahms or Wagner, but rather, Brahms *and* Wagner.'[52] They evolved an amalgam of values in which both the purity of art and the purity of German musical traditions merged. Few would wish to stray from these particular absolutes, which most, including Schoenberg, felt to be immutable.

CHAPTER 4

Mahler and His Chronicler
Julius Korngold

Mahler's Jewishness is not to be found within his use of the folkloristic, but rather expresses itself through all conduits as cerebral and restrained, while ultimately remaining tangible in its entirety.

Was jüdisch ist an Mahler, partizipiert nicht unmittelbar an Volkstümlichem, sondern spricht durch alle Vermittlungen hindurch als ein Geistiges, Unsinnliches, gleichwohl an der Totalität Fühlbares sich aus.

Theodor Adorno, *Der lange Blick*, 1963

It is a historic coincidence that Mahler should arrive at the Imperial Opera in Vienna in the same year that Brahms died. The significance of this intersection of musical biographies is highlighted by a lecture and interview given by the Anglo-Austrian composer and musicologist Egon Wellesz. Recordings of the lecture and interview reveal that they were given at two different times and in two different languages: German and English. The English interview is from a 1962 BBC broadcast with Deryck Cooke and comes from Wellesz's period as lecturer (retired) at Lincoln College, Oxford, a position he took up after fleeing Austria in 1938. The German lecture comes from the 100th anniversary of Mahler's birth given at the Vienna Staatsoper in 1960. Both deal with musical life in fin de siècle Vienna. In the English interview, Wellesz mentions the crucial figure that conditioned musical life as Johannes Brahms, whereas in the German lecture, it's Gustav Mahler.[1]

Mahler was the musical personality who would provide hundreds of twentieth-century Jewish composers – whether religious or not – with the means to do more than just assimilate into Austro-German musical life. He broke down the barriers that subsequently allowed younger Jewish composers to surge forward with their own ideas and agendas. They no longer had to accept the conditions tacitly demanded by the unwelcoming environment of the nineteenth century. By the time of his death in 1911, Mahler had demonstrated that he, as a Jewish composer, had not only broken with previous conventions, but had, with his highly individual approach to the Austro-Germanic symphonic tradition, placed himself in the pantheon of German Masters, uniting the disparate 'old' and 'new' German schools. The significance of this is summarised by the Jewish critic and writer Adolf Weissmann: 'Mahler lived from the very beginning in a state of high-voltage creativity, though it was racially coloured: he was born a Jew, but as one of the most noble of his race he was elevated to sainthood.'[2]

In Arnold Schoenberg's lecture on Mahler from 1912 (which Dika Newlin translated into English in the early 1940s), he writes: 'I believe firmly and steadfastly that Gustav Mahler was one of the great men and artists. For there are only two possibilities of convincing someone of an artist's greatness: the first and better way is to perform his work; the second, which I am forced to use, is to transmit my belief in this work to others.'[3]

Schoenberg then proceeds to counter much of the anti-Semitic criticism of Mahler without once referring to the fact that Mahler was Jewish. Schoenberg's translation would have come from a period when he was more than ever aware of his own Jewishness, but this is not allowed to intrude on his original lecture from 1912, in which he takes issue with the usually unspoken but implied anti-Semitic charges of Mahler's banality, emptiness and sentimentality, or his 'lack of inventiveness'.[4] In 1912, Schoenberg did not need to use the word 'Jewish' to make his position clear.

Jewish Vienna at the Time of Mahler

By 1897, Mahler's call to the Imperial Opera in Vienna may have required him to convert to Catholicism, but by this time, anti-Semitism was less the domain of the aristocrats making the appointment than of the aspiring non-Jewish middle classes. Indeed, Karl Goldmark was already an established grandee by this time and is likely to have been involved in discussions with Chancellery Director Eduard Wlassack, who was responsible for Mahler's appointment.

By the turn of the century, the scene was firmly set. Assimilation had guaranteed a wealthy, culturally hungry Jewish bourgeoisie that enriched Viennese life not only by supporting local musical life, but also by commissioning paintings from Klimt's Secessionists and filling their homes with objects designed by Joseph Hoffmann's handicraft counterpart, the Wiener Werkstätte.

Their cultural forum became the quintessentially Jewish phenomenon of the 'Salon', with its origins in the early nineteenth century when wealthy Jews reacted to their exclusion from aristocratic houses by holding alternative 'courts', reserved for the intellectual aristocracy of artists, writers and anyone who was stimulating and open to intelligent debate and conversation.

Berta Zuckerkandl was the most prominent of Vienna's many salonnières, and it was her close relationship to Klimt and his relationship to the artist Carl Moll – step-father of Alma Schindler – which eventually resulted in Gustav Mahler meeting his future wife at one of Zuckerkandl's weekly 'at homes'. The visual arts were one of the few cultural fields that allowed social interaction between Jews and non-Jews. Almost all of the important Viennese artists from the end of the nineteenth century were not Jewish, whereas most of their patrons and supporters were. Berta Zuckerkandl, in addition to being one of Vienna's best-known hostesses, was also a prominent art critic and journalist. It was in her salon that the Secessionist movement was founded, as indeed, she would later be midwife to Hugo von Hofmannsthal and Max Reinhardt's idea of a performing arts festival in Salzburg. Alma Schindler's immediate family was notoriously fraught with contradictions regarding the Jews and non-Jews within the Zuckerkandl circle. Alma was an unreformed anti-Semite who seemed to display a near fetish-like preference for Jewish men, while her step-father Carl Moll, whose gallery and patrons were nearly all Jewish, would become a passionate follower of National Socialism and committed suicide in 1945 when it became apparent that Hitler would not triumph.

The result of bourgeois Jewish enthusiasm for the arts was that wealthy non-Jews appeared to lose interest, meaning that cultural events nearly ceased being the common meeting ground between well-off Jews and non-Jews. Alma Mahler, in her journals, hints at the distaste felt by non-Jewish Viennese towards the city's Jewish public by describing important premieres and openings disparagingly as having 'all of Israel in attendance', an expression that is repeated word-for-word by other chroniclers of the time.[5]

No matter how wealthy and important they were, Jews would discover that even conversion to Christianity was not sufficient to offer easy entrance into mainstream society. The journals kept by the daughters of the wealthy Viennese Gallia family, patrons of the Secessionists and of the architect Josef Hoffmann as well as commissioners of one of Klimt's best portraits, indicate how rarely members of even the minor aristocracy moved within their circles. Former Jews whose parents or even grandparents had converted (as in the case with the Gallias) appeared unable to move outside the circles of other wealthy converts and Jewish professionals, academics and industrialists.[6]

It was therefore no surprise that Jews and former Jews were bound by circumstance to keep to their own clubs, cafés and circles. The limitations imposed by Viennese society were more than compensated for by their presence within the media: newspapers from across the political spectrum such as *Das neue Wiener Tagblatt*, *Die Wiener Allgemeine Zeitung* and *Die Arbeiter Zeitung* were all Jewish-owned and run. But as we have already seen, it was the powerful *Neue Freie Presse* that ultimately dominated. It represented a paper with balanced, objective and fair reportage that was produced, published and largely written by secular Jews and read by nearly everyone within the educated classes and the highest reaches of government. The *Neue Freie Presse* predictably became a target not only for anti-Semites, but also for ultra-conservatives on the right and for Social Democrats and Communists on the left. It was respectful of the monarchy, but unsentimental as soon as it was replaced by a republic. During the years that Theodor Herzl was editor of its cultural pages, it never once allowed any coverage of Zionism. With Julius Korngold its primary music critic from 1904, it became Mahler's most important supporter and the voice of a younger, self-confident, Jewish musical élite.

The biographical parallels between Gustav Mahler and Julius Korngold are quite surprising: both were German-speaking Jewish Moravians born in 1860, in what is today part of the Czech Republic. Both grew up in aspirational families where the father's income was earned from the sale of spirits. This allowed money and opportunities for the children that the parents were unable to enjoy. In his memoirs, Korngold mentions on more than one occasion the good fortune of growing up during the years of Liberalism. Like Mahler, he spent time studying with Bruckner while a student in Vienna, which brought him closer to understanding Wagner. Korngold makes little direct reference to his own Jewish origins, but anecdotal accounts from his grandchildren Ernst and George (sons of the composer Erich Wolfgang Korngold) give the impression that though Jewish under Nazi racial law (and perceived as Jewish), the Korngolds could hardly have been more secular. This was noticeably different from Mahler's family.

The Austrian musician and musicologist Michael Haber in *Das Jüdische bei Gustav Mahler* offers a very clear picture of Mahler's religious background.[7] We already know that Mahler's great-grandfather Abraham Mahler (1720–1800) was a cantor who would have observed strict religious laws. Haber even offers circumstantial evidence suggesting that he may have been Hassidic. Abraham's grandson Bernard (Baruch) Mahler was Gustav's father.[8] Though probably fully assimilated, as can be deduced from accounts and photographs of the time, there is reason to believe that Bernard was by no means secular. He and Gustav participated in Jewish holy services, and Bernard was even elected to the educational committee of the Jewish community – not something that would have been possible for a secular Jew in the relatively rural community of Iglau in 1878. Bernard was also close to the local cantor who stood as godparent to Gustav's sister Justine. This historic background offers enough circumstantial evidence to suggest that Gustav probably celebrated his *Bar Mitzvah* in common with other boys from traditional Jewish families when he was 13. Preparation for that would have required intensive study of liturgical Hebrew and sacred texts.

There is nothing in Julius Korngold's memoirs to suggest that he enjoyed a similar religious upbringing, though the customs of the time may have dictated a minimal adherence. Such adherence would most likely have been a good deal less in the Moravian capital city of Brünn than in rural communities such as Iglau. Haber goes on to quote correspondence between the young Mahler and his family indicating his consciousness as a Jew. As late as 1886, he writes to his sister Justine that she shouldn't worry about him taking a conducting post in Leipzig as even there 'one could find synagogues'.[9] Later, Gustav and his siblings would show considerable diligence at putting cultural space between their adult lives and their provincial, religious upbringing while nevertheless making casual references to 'the holidays' which could only have been in reference to traditional Jewish festivals. The Mahlers were obviously from the provinces, but they were not unsophisticated and they certainly did not belong to one of the communities of bearded, kaftan-wearing Jews of Eastern Europe. Indeed, the pull to German culture probably motivated Bernard to move to German-speaking Iglau in Moravia from Czech-speaking Kalischt in Bohemia (where Gustav was born) as soon as the 'October Diploma' of 1860 lifted restrictions on the movements of Jews within these two provinces. Later, Alma Mahler makes it clear that her husband never tried to hide his Jewish origins – she was often irritated that he appeared to go out of his way to draw attention to them.

Julius Korngold, on the other hand, moved seamlessly within the circles of law and journalism where religious confession played no role and he was beholden to no appointing aristocrat. Along with countless other prominent Jews of his generation, including Mahler, he saw no contradiction in being both a Moravian Jew and a German Nationalist, and his earliest articles and reviews were published in the Pan-German Czech paper, *Der treue Eckart*. Eduard Hanslick was alerted to Julius Korngold by Brahms, who had read a Korngold review in the Moravian press. Initial meetings led to a formal invitation to join the *Neue Freie Presse* from the cultural editor Theodor Herzl in 1901.

Die Neue Freie Presse

This anti-feudal, capitalistic and secular-liberal newspaper had been founded in 1848 as *Die Presse*. In 1861 Karl Marx was its London correspondent. In 1864 the editorial staff set up a new paper that was purchased by Max Friedländer and Michael Etienne, and henceforth called *Die Neue Freie Presse*. The paper benefited from the slow but steady trend of Liberalism that began by defining the separation of administrative powers and haltingly allowed a trickle of widening enfranchisement. One of the most important of these acts was the so-called 'February Patent' of 1861, which replaced the 'October Diploma' of 1860. Both reforms would come to fruition in the biggest victory of all championed by the paper: the December Constitution of 1867, which began the process of wider emancipation of Jews and brought about a more balanced exercise of powers between Emperor and Parliament.[10] The paper suffered a loss of prestige with the role it played in the disastrous stock-market crash of 1873, but under the stewardship of Eduard Bacher and Moritz Benedikt (both of whom were also German-speaking Jews from Moravia) it became the German-language equivalent of the London *Times* and one of the dominant newspapers in Europe. Benedikt eventually was able to buy out Bacher, and his son Ernst took command of the paper in 1920. At the turn of the century it employed 80 to 100 foreign correspondents and the maxim of the day was that it was 'impossible to rule the country against the will of the *Neue Freie Presse*'.[11] The coup of an interview with Bismarck, which appeared in the paper in 1892, elevated it beyond all other German-language media, and Benedikt was the only journalist the Emperor Franz Joseph would deign to meet.

The influence that the *Neue Freie Presse* and its editor wielded can be further inferred from the attacks by the brilliant Viennese satirist Karl Kraus. In his epic 'tragedy in five acts with prologue and epilogue' *Die Letzten Tage der Menschheit*,[12] Kraus refers to Benedikt as 'Lord of the Hyenas' and ruthlessly parodies both Julius Korngold and his son, the prodigy Erich Wolfgang. In Kraus's periodical *Die Fackel*[13] he continuously attacked both paper and editor, once writing that for Benedikt 'there was no wickedness that he would not represent for money and no value that out of idealism he would not betray'.[14] Kraus's response to an offer made by the *Neue Freie Presse* to become one of its principal feuilletonists in 1899 was printed in *Die Fackel*: 'there are two marvellous things in this world: either to be part of the *Neue Freie Presse*, or to loathe it. I never for a moment doubted which I would choose.'[15]

The paper boasted a starry array of contributing politicians and essayists. David Lloyd George wrote an article for the paper in 1914 arguing against armaments, and after 1918 he continued right through the 1920s as a regular contributor.[16] Winston Churchill is quoted in an article published by the paper in 1913 also denouncing current armament policies and, incredibly, Churchill himself wrote an article published during the war in October 1917. He was a frequent contributor until 1938.[17] Julius Korngold, with his doctorate in law and as a fiercely secular Jew, was a perfect fit for the environment of *Die Neue Freie Presse*. He remained its principal writer on musical matters until Ernst Benedikt was forced to sell his shares in 1934 to the Austro-Fascist government that had ruled Austria since March 1933. In 1938 after the Anschluss and owing to its largely Jewish staff, the Nazis had the paper closed down. By the time of Korngold's departure in 1934, he had long ceased to be the defender of Mahler's brand of Modernism and had been denounced by the President of the International Society of Contemporary Music, Edward Dent, as modern music's most 'formidable enemy', a quote Korngold gleefully includes in his memoirs.[18]

The Metropolis Vienna: City of Music, City of Jews

By the first decade of the twentieth century, about one third of those studying violin and piano at Vienna's conservatory were Jewish. Even allowing for the fact that many of these students came from the outer reaches of the Empire (in Vienna the Jewish population never exceeded 8 per cent), it remains a remarkable statistic. Indeed, it was such a common occurrence for Jews to make their way to the conservatories of the major cities that Alexander Moszkowski (brother of the composer Moritz) wrote an amusing Berlin-based satire entitled *A Genius* that appeared in the *Neue Freie Presse* on 12 February 1892.[19] Yet in nineteenth-century Viennese society, the social structures were inherently open to Jewish musical assimilation, and membership of institutions and music societies provided an entry point for social and political integration that was not available within other guilds or fraternities. The very fact that Anton Rubinstein, a Russian Jew, could in 1871 be made head of Vienna's Gesellschaft der Musikfreunde is a remarkable demonstration of the speed of cultural integration. Its building, the Musikverein, which opened in 1870, not only was the city's most prestigious concert venue, but also housed a conservatory and an archive.

The extent to which the social and cultural climate had improved for Jews by 1900 is related by the American conductor and scholar Leon Botstein. He cites a memorial concert for the Jewish liturgical composer Salomon Sulzer held in Vienna's Musikverein in 1900 as a key moment that symbolised this transition. Sulzer had been a reformer and principal cantor of Vienna's main synagogue, the Stadttempel. He had arrived from Western Austria's Hohenems in 1825 – during the lifetimes of Beethoven and Schubert; he was in contact with both. The collection of liturgical works composed by Sulzer under the title *Shir Zion*,[20] first published in 1840 and reprinted in 1868, shows a marked influence of the secular music of the period, making Sulzer one of the earliest modernisers of music in the synagogue. In addition, he was also a respected teacher at Vienna's music conservatory. The musicians participating in the memorial concert included Sulzer's son, Joseph, born in Vienna and not only the solo cellist of the Vienna Philharmonic, but also the former cellist of the Hellmesberger and Prill Quartets, two of the leading ensembles of the day. He was accompanied on the piano by Heinrich Schenker, the renowned music theorist. The memorial speech was given by Adolf Ritter von Sonnenthal, Vienna's most famous actor and one of the city's principal celebrities. He was one of the first Jews to be ennobled by the Emperor following the enactment of the December Constitution and he would, incidentally, become the future grandfather-in-law of the composer Erich Wolfgang Korngold. Botstein's fascinating point is that each of these musicians represented a different stage of Jewish participation and assimilation in Vienna's musical life. Salomon Sulzer was influenced by the non-Jewish secular music of Biedermeier Vienna. His son, born just after the Revolution of 1848, had progressed to the position of star soloist with the Vienna Philharmonic; Sonnenthal was the city's leading actor, *bon vivant* and social lion within Vienna's most exclusive circles setting the tone in matters of fashion, taste and style. Schenker, who had studied with Bruckner, became the music theorist who most characterised the Brahmsian values of the 'Old German School' that we examined in the previous chapter. Botstein goes on to point out that Schenker published his own book on harmony in 1906, five years before Schoenberg.[21]

Inquisitiveness and a fascination with the past have already been mentioned as being the target of Wagner's attacks on Jews, whom he saw as reaching back into history in order to compensate for a lack of originality. Yet it was also the steady dominance of Jewish musicologists and thinkers that would further divide the Austro-German house between musical progressives and conservatives. On the one side, there was Eduard Hanslick and Heinrich Schenker, who held to the ideals of classical sobriety and balance, along with the scholar Guido Adler, who chose to classify Wagner as a conservative, in stark contrast to the prevalent view of the time. The critic Robert Hirschfeld, a virtual contemporary of Adler, was seen by many as the leader of Vienna's anti-Mahler press. Nevertheless, Hirschfeld singled out Bruckner, rather than Brahms, as the culmination of abstract musical purity. It was the pupils and followers of these scholars and writers who would not only solidify Jewish support for musical tradition, but also provide a basis for progressive thinking. With Karl Goldmark, Robert Hirschfeld, Guido Adler and Julius Korngold, we see the dogmatic lines held by Hanslick rendered meaningless, as a new generation of Jews see in Wagner a composer who was not predominantly an anti-Semite but rather an artist who redefined the purpose of music. This conflict was made poignantly clear in the creation of two Wagner Societies in Vienna: the Vienna Academic Wagner Society co-founded by Guido Adler, and a competing Wagner Society, of which Anton Bruckner was made honorary president, that explicitly excluded Jews. It was in this spirit of music renewing its very purpose that Karl Weigl, Alexander Zemlinsky and Arnold Schoenberg founded the Society of Creative Musicians (*Vereinigung schaffender Tonkünstler*) in 1904, with Mahler as honorary president. In 1907, Mahler would defend Schoenberg against hisses and boos at the premiere of the latter's First String Quartet in the Bösendorfersaal, while admitting privately that he was not sure what the music meant.

Guido Adler, a childhood friend of Mahler, succeeded Eduard Hanslick at the University of Vienna. With his essay from 1885 *Umfang, Methode und Ziel der Musikwissenschaft*,[22] along with the collection of *Denkmäler der Tonkunst in Österreich*[23] that he edited, Adler became the father of modern, systematic musicology. His pupils included several Schoenberg students such as Anton Webern and Paul Pisk. They also included two other composers who came to represent the Viennese musical traditions that grew from Brahms and Mahler: Hans Gál and the Schoenberg pupil, Egon Wellesz.

The *Neue Freie Presse* offers a fascinating series of essays analysing the nature of anti-Semitism by Theodor Haase during April of 1887.[24] Anatole France wrote again on the subject on 3 April 1904.[25] Yet the Vienna of 1900 was a city where it was possible for Jews to live and work relatively openly within most circles of society. But Vienna, with the second largest Jewish population of any European city after Warsaw, also had to contend with a deeply held, ubiquitous anti-Semitism. The story that Mahler rejected Humperdinck's pupil Leo Blech as a potential assistant at the opera tells us a good deal. Mahler felt that the institution would not tolerate a second Jew, even a converted one.

In fact it was not only in Vienna, but throughout Europe that anti-Semitism was shaping the social environment, as the Dreyfus Affair in France demonstrated. But in music, Wagner had unleashed a beast that was particularly mendacious. Vienna, with music as its cultural centre of gravity and its large Jewish population, was vulnerable. The writer Rudolf Louis published

Contemporary German Music in 1909. It was an enormous success as it was the first work to deal with Austro-German composers after Wagner. After informing his readers that he had no time for anti-Semitism, he laid into Mahler with particular venom: 'What I find so fundamentally repellent about Mahler's music is its axiomatic Jewish nature. If Mahler's music spoke Jewish, I perhaps wouldn't understand it, but what is disgusting is that it speaks German with the Jewish accent – the all too Jewish accent that comes to us from the East.'[26]

It is worth reading an extract from Julius Korngold's review of the second edition of Louis's book, printed in 1914. Korngold is outraged that the reprint fails to deal with Mahler's Eighth Symphony, premiered in Munich in 1910, but finds the omission even more disturbing given the number of institutions that had sprung up throughout Germany and Austria with the resources to mount performances of such 'maximalist' works. [27] Korngold's feuilleton dealing with Louis's book starts with a reference to Franz Schreker, founding director and conductor of the Vienna Philharmonic Chorus, who followed up his highly successful premiere of Schoenberg's *Gurrelieder* in 1913 with a performance of Mahler's Eighth. Much of Korngold's irritation concerns how little Louis has to say about Mahler in general – and what he does write is objectionable:

It seems quite remarkable that in a book that purports to pass judgement on current German music, even after the death of Mahler and the success throughout the German nation of his Eighth Symphony, he omits it with the belief that 'the music of Mahler is German music with an accent, the oriental cadence and above all, the gesture of the eastern, indeed, the extreme eastern European Jew [. . .] so that his music makes the same effect as a clown from the [Jewish cabaret ensemble] Budapest 'Orpheum' reciting Schiller's poetry. [. . .] Mahler has no idea how grotesque he appears wearing the mask of the German Master, which highlights the inner contradictions that make his music fundamentally dishonest.' And so he goes on and on. Mr Rudolf Louis, author of *German Music of Today*, hails from Munich, that citadel of the arts and the city in which the questionably German premiere of Mahler's Eighth Symphony took place. Its unparalleled success reflected if anything a huge demonstration of Mahler-admiration, a true apotheosis in view of the premature death of the artist. According to Mr Louis, however, 'whoever has a positive opinion about Mahler has forfeited his credibility of being taken seriously in an appraisal of western music, culture and the occidental races, and blind to the unbridgeable abyss that exists between them and Mahler's music'. Mengelberg [and others] should take note!

Both [the public] composer and private individual Karl Goldmark must be informed by Mr Louis that 'artistically and culturally he lacks all instincts for German culture which must remain strange and alien, as it is to any foreigner who lives his entire life in Germany'. So, there you are: both Goldmark and Rubinstein are through their provenance strangers to German culture. Mendelssohn's spiritual compositions were already dismissed in the first edition of his book as 'decidedly slick and inwardly shallow'. He's had a slight reprieve in the newer edition as now he's only labelled 'slick and inwardly mushy'. As such, one is inclined to suggest that Mr Louis is somewhat outwardly slick himself. I was further amused to note that in the new edition, the dismissive remark has been removed that made reference to Richard Strauss being born in the year that Meyerbeer died. In compensation, he manages a sleight-of-hand by hardly dealing with Arnold Schoenberg at all – remarkable for a composer who, regardless of what one thinks of him, obsessively occupies the entire musical world in furious discussion and debate. He's quite content to reject his sextet *Verklärte Nacht* as trivial and makes the point regarding his later works that 'one is either dealing with a madman or a criminal'. It can be seen as a blessing that such musical tendencies (*pace* Wagner) are only rarely expressed these days in Germany and enjoy limited resonance – indeed, are usually countered. Mr Louis's book doesn't really gain much even with a second printing. There are many omissions. Its pretentiously styled subjectivity, hasty conclusions and cranky dismissals only appear all the more lurid. Let's simply agree to put this new edition – not really improved – quietly to one side.[28]

Mahler and Korngold

Julius Korngold and Mahler were on friendly terms, but not necessarily close friends. A fair representation of the relationship is offered by Julius's son Erich in a letter to Arnold Rosé written on 3 January 1918: 'That the friendship between Director Mahler and father was true and based on mutual respect and understanding is something I have known since childhood.'[29] Apart from the odd individual letter in various European archives, their correspondence remains a mystery. The International Gustav Mahler Society in Vienna has a single photocopy of a letter from Mahler to Korngold that appears to indicate that it was one of 113.[30] Julius Korngold's memoirs quote copiously from letters he must have had in front of him at the time, but what happened to these after the ransacking of Korngold's home by the Nazis in 1938 remains unknown. Not only is this valuable correspondence missing, but also items from the musical estate of Eduard Hanslick which were entrusted to Korngold. Mahler's regard for Julius's son Erich is well known, as is his recommendation that he be taken away from Robert Fuchs, his own teacher at the academy, and be taught instead by Alexander Zemlinsky.[31] Julius was suspicious of this recommendation initially because of Zemlinsky's closeness to Schoenberg. But what Korngold's writings (such as his review of Louis) make clear is that though he disagreed with Schoenberg's ideas, he held him in high esteem, influenced, no doubt, by Schoenberg's closeness to Mahler (to whom Schoenberg dedicated his *Harmonielehre*). Considering Edward Dent's description of Julius quoted earlier, it is ironic that both Korngold and Schoenberg became close in Californian exile. Schoenberg's letter of condolence to Erich following Julius's death gives us a hint of the power of Mahler to bring together what had previously seemed irreconcilable.

Julius Korngold's understanding of Mahler's music is unique. Their relationship was professional rather than personal, but it was a genuine friendship with a collegial closeness that was useful to both. Mahler knew when to feed Julius information for his own ends and Julius was more than happy to comply. Mahler leaked his intention of leaving the Vienna Opera, an astute move that resulted in a three-page blast against Mahler's detractors in the paper on 4 June 1907.[32] Later, Mahler passed on his opinion of his successor Felix Weingartner as 'at best only a dim-witted conservatory student', a view he knew Korngold would use. He duly did, and ultimately had Weingartner driven from the post to which he only returned once Korngold was retired.[33]

In his memoirs, Julius sees Weingartner's support of his son Erich as nothing more than the machinations of a clever opportunist currying favour with an influential father. Erich's dilemma was palpable. As an attempt to calm the situation, the fifteen-year-old prodigy dedicated his *Sinfonietta* Op. 5 to Weingartner, who conducted its premiere in 1914. Mahler's dismissive remarks about Weingartner amounted to a well-placed cuckoo's egg, and his high regard for Bruno Walter (who lived on the next floor below Korngold in Vienna's Theobaldgasse) guaranteed that he remained Julius's musician of choice. When Richard Strauss, as director of the Opera after the First World War, had gone so far as to engage Erich as a conductor to gain relief for himself and Franz Schalk from the huge burden of nightly performances, Julius saw only plots and intrigues. His steadfast loyalty to Mahler remained, despite the fact that he had been dead for years. *De facto*, Julius found no subsequent opera director worthy of comparison, and if they showed a genuine interest in his son's works, he was convinced it was only a ruse.

Richard Strauss, who was ordinarily not given to bouts of anti-Semitism, was sufficiently piqued by Julius Korngold's unremitting attacks to call in Erich for a dressing down, accusing Julius of wishing to remove him so that a 'fellow Israelite', meaning Bruno Walter, could take over. The popular view, as expressed in an article by the piano professor Richard Robert in the *Wiener Sonn- und Montags Zeitung*, was that Julius was giving good reviews to those who promoted Erich's work and poor reviews to those who did not.[34] To outsiders, it was starting to look suspiciously like a cabal. From Erich's perspective, his father's loyalty to Mahler meant that some of the finest performers refused to take up his works for fear of attacks in the *Neue Freie Presse*. This impossible situation prevailed until he trumped Julius by changing direction and began updating and arranging popular operettas by Johann Strauss, Leo Fall and Offenbach, a move that gave him greater financial independence as well as an ersatz father-figure in the stage director and impresario Max Reinhardt.

Julius Korngold's passion for Mahler was a dilemma for his son. Far from taking Mahler as his model, Erich preferred Puccini and Richard Strauss. Recordings of Julius and Erich speaking are revealing. Julius speaks the immaculately articulated German of Vienna's leading opinion makers: he had honed a style of delivery that was originally meant to be heard in Vienna's law-courts (and his brother, Eduard Kornau, was a well-known actor). By contrast, Erich spoke with a Viennese cadence much coloured by an accent of Jewish Czech-German; it lacked any hint of pretension or self-importance.

Julius wrote extensively about each of Mahler's symphonies (it was he who nick-named the Sixth Symphony the 'Hammerschlag'[35]), and what he has to say about each is revealing. We can assume from reading Julius's memoirs that they reflect conversations with Mahler. Surprisingly, they are not always uncritical. But his article on Mahler's Third Symphony published in the *Neue Freie Presse* on 17 December 1904 gives us one of the most deeply sympathetic treatments of the man and his music. It reveals not only Korngold's innate understanding of the music but also his personal closeness with the composer. It opens by describing a painting at an exhibition at Vienna's Secessionist Gallery: 'A piano with its lid raised shows us waves rolling evenly into the background. A horrifying sea monster with its front paws extended threateningly rises out of them: it is half sphinx and half water-snake. Above the painting hangs its title *The Symphony*. One can but smile at the thought of the sympathetic visitor adding *The Mahler Symphony* as a welcome clarification.'

Korngold also considers the Strauss–Mahler duopoly in Austria and Germany at the turn of the century. Strauss was born in 1864 and was thus a few years younger than Mahler. At the time, the two were viewed as the musical Janus faces of the age, and during Mahler's lifetime they enjoyed a kind of friendly rivalry far more pronounced than generally perceived today. What adds piquancy to our reading of Korngold's comparison is that the full extent of Strauss's unblushing opportunism would not have been known to him at the time. Korngold would have been unaware of Strauss's playing on Cosima Wagner's anti-Semitism to keep Mahler out of Bayreuth. With Mahler long dead – and blacklisted from 1933 – Strauss was able to reign more or less supreme in Nazi Germany as their grand old man of music. With hindsight, Korngold's article looks far more balanced than it might have been had it been written thirty years later:

Why does Mahler have it more difficult than Strauss? One places the two composers often enough side by side as the apex of modern musical genius. Strauss, however, has until now not only been modern, but also modish. Isn't Mahler also a brilliant technician, virtuoso orchestrator, in possession of a gloriously deep musical spirit? Of course he is; but he is all of these things in a very different way from Strauss. One could say that Mahler is both more conservative, and more advanced than Strauss. Strauss on the other hand is the more potent 'new German' musician. He strides through paths that were trodden fifty years earlier by Wagner and Liszt. The symphonic poem, which takes its very existence with the introduction of extra-musical content, was called into being and placed next to the symphony. Mahler has not broken completely with the formal conventions of symphonic architecture. He simply believes that new art, through its combination of widely varying means of expression, must heighten the subjective musical response [of the listener]. To this is added minutely detailed realism within the framework of the multi-movement symphony. In the middle of structures that the great masters have [already] made familiar, we hear the most daringly modern musical-poetic vocabulary and it is this that primarily alienates – indeed, that *needs* to alienate. This battle between old and new appears to be fought on sacred ground.

We must inevitably turn to two other composers who are central in helping us understand Mahler: Berlioz and Bruckner. Their symphonic styles also wrestle in a similar way with the infiltration of poetic ideals. Mahler studied with Bruckner, and thus one hears not only the foundation of solemn religiosity which intensifies into insistent speculation, but also a child-like naivety in certain passages – all of this is present in addition to quite obvious compositional similarities. Nevertheless, Mahler's true progenitor is Berlioz, with whom his similarities simply mount up. As with Berlioz, we find with Mahler the tendencies to resort to representational means; the casual adding to the number of symphonic movements; the consolidation of vocal and instrumental elements; the far-flung sound fantasies; the mixture of the bizarre with the exalted and the primitive: 'the sulphuric bolts of irony' as Heine called them, all interspersed with voyages that bound between heaven and hell. Mahler belongs to the tribe of Berlioz, just as Strauss belongs to the tribe of Liszt. And the harder one looks, the higher one sees the walls growing between these two musical dynasties. Mahler looks for broad subjects that he melodically varies and spins out; Strauss works with motifs and minuscule motif particles that he combines in complex polyphonic escapades. Diatonic thinking remains at Mahler's core, while with Strauss it's chromatic. If Strauss sounds cacophonic by cleverness and contrariness, Mahler sounds cacophonic by conviction. And while Strauss remains firmly committed to 'the artistic'; Mahler's need is for naivety, naturalness, in fact nature itself and the folkloric. The preference of this composer for the poetry of the folksong has been a feature of his music for far too long for it to be thought a mere affectation.[36]

This observation gives Korngold the perfect lead into a discussion of the Third Symphony:

Mahler rejoices in nature awakening. The sun caresses the composer's hyper-receptive sensitivity, he bends over to smell the gentle scent of the flowers and to listen to the tales told by the animals of the forest: 'like a sound from Nature', writes Mahler again and again in his score; a natural sound is sought also in his reflections, his extravagancies, his search for the exceptional that he manages to wrestle out of his music. It would appear that with Mahler's arrival, 'Modern Music' attempts to free itself from the entanglements of debased compositional techniques, high-flown artiness and overladen sound-fixations. And the most telling element is to be found in his 5th and latest symphony: Mahler jettisons the very principals of 'new music' by discarding the poetic programme. Premonitions of this development could be noted even earlier. Yet if Mahler employed symphonic programmes before, it was so that he could dispense with them later. And so it is with his Third Symphony. Goodness! He virtually immerses himself in all that drips out of these leaking symphonic riddles; indeed, we find ourselves playing the equivalent of Symphony Charades. There are secretive mysterious entries everywhere for which we have no keys; sound-painting and horrifyingly realistic passages that can only make sense if they *mean* [my italics] something as music. And then we have the unexpected appearances of vocal movements, which clear paths that allow the purely symphonic movements to stumble along behind. For example, in the Fourth Symphony we have the final movement's folksong of 'Heavenly Joy'. In a manner of speaking, one was led through three dark rooms towards the flicker of a tiny candle. If we are to set the Hamlet of programme music across from a compliant Polonius, then at least he should tell us if he wishes the fog of music to be understood as a weasel or an elephant. Mahler doesn't wish to tell us in his Third Symphony, though especially in the third movement there is no shortage of weasels and any number of other creatures. At one point it was once called 'What the animals of the Forest tell me' and had, along with the rest of the symphony, a poetic concept. Indeed, the entire symphony was once called 'A Summer Morning's Dream'. The first movement would have been entitled 'The Arrival of Pan'; the second, 'What the Flowers tell me'. In the third, we're able to hear what the animals have to say. The rounds of Zarathustra from the 'Drunken Song' offer 'What Man tells me'. The fifth movement enters with the chorus singing a text taken from the *Knaben Wunderhorn*: 'Three tiny angels sang'. This movement once carried the heading 'What the angels tell me', and finally the last movement which was formerly headed 'What love tells me'. Yet, what does the music of the Symphony tell us? Perhaps at first it's worth noting that the composer Mahler is not able to be understood completely without also understanding the characters of the brilliant conductor and ingenious opera director who inhabit the same person. [With the Third Symphony] we are confronted with an extraordinary apparatus: in addition to the huge orchestra which is augmented by every kind of percussion, glockenspiel, tuned bells, we have Flugelhorn and a side drum off-stage along with solo voices, women's chorus, and a boys' choir up in the gallery. And in addition, the score abounds with performance instructions which do not solely apply to dynamic and meter, but also expression and even how one should play the instruments. And all of this interacts ceaselessly at just the right time, right spot, usually upon an invisible set: it offers the appearance of being expressive even if this is not immediately apparent from the musical notes themselves. Thus it is the creative conductor, the modern, expressive conductor who speaks out of his own conception of the music; in point of fact, certain sequences and musical gestures seem to come from the very indications he makes when conducting. All of this is bound up inextricably with the musician as a master of stagecraft.

Julius embarks in a more detailed breakdown of the symphony and at the end of his article returns to Berlioz's influence, concluding with the pronouncement that the Third Symphony, *pace* Berlioz, should be entitled, 'Episodes from the Musical Life of a Composing Fabulist'.[37]

There is much here that speaks from the time and process of assimilation. Quite apart from the association of the German soul with nature and the forest, the most telling sentence refers to Mahler's preference for the use of folk material having been a feature for too long to be taken as 'mere affectation'. The philosopher Hannah Arendt makes the point that Jews often saw nature and art as being socially and politically neutral, impervious to the obstacles they encountered elsewhere and thereby offering an easier path to assimilation.[38] Korngold's observation is to be understood in this context, but Mahler's love of nature was genuine and innate, not an attempt to 'fit in'.

Max Brod and Theodor Adorno, among others, have written about the 'Jewishness' of Mahler's music. How 'Jewish' it might be is less important than how liberating it was for the following generation. Nevertheless, the inner fights of Mahler with his Jewish destiny are illuminated by Natalie Bauer-Lechner, Mahler's *confidante* from 1890 to 1902. She gives an account in her unedited journals of Mahler relating a nightmare he had as an eight-year-old, in which Ahasver, the 'Wandering Jew', tries to force his walking stick into the hands of the terrified young Gustav. The symbolism speaks for itself.[39] Mahler's nervousness about his Jewishness has been much debated. In addition to rejecting Leo Blech for fear of taking on a second Jew at the opera, we have the instances in which he told Bruno Walter at various times to change his surname from Schlesinger, to convert and to serve in the military as a means of deflecting the mendacity of anti-Semites. Far from accentuating his Jewishness, as Alma claimed, he was well aware of having to keep it under wraps when necessary. He shuddered at the sight of kaftan-wearing, bearded Jews from Eastern Europe and refused to identify with them. Yet as Korngold rhetorically asked regarding the Third Symphony: 'What does the music tell us?'

Richard Taruskin is of the opinion that after Mahler, Germany and Austria handed the symphony as a musical ideal to the Slavs, Anglo-Americans and Scandinavians.[40] As we shall see, exiled Austro-German composers did return to the symphony, but mostly with limited success. Mahler, however, had cleared a path that was wide enough for the next generation of Jewish composers to explore. Having the way opened to follow him, it was no longer necessary to imitate him.

If Mahler, like Heine before him, saw conversion as his *billet d'entrée* to opportunity, Schoenberg would, with his reconversion to the religion of his birth, declare the opposite. Though Hitler provided Schoenberg with an immediate motivation, Mahler provided an inheritance of such undeniably great and original music that reconversion to Judaism could be understood as an act of defiance. This was one of Mahler's most remarkable, and as yet unsung, accomplishments.

CHAPTER 5

The Jugendstil School of Schoenberg, Schreker, Zemlinsky and Weigl

Art is individualism and individualism is a destructive and corrupting power. It is in this fact that we discover its monstrous significance. What it's attempting to destroy and corrupt is the pathetic monotony of conventionality, the enslavement of habit, the tyranny of decorum and the degradation of man to 'machine'. . . . Ideas about art are understandably taken from what we have known of art up to the present, whereas a new work is beautiful specifically because it represents something never witnessed before. . . .

Die Kunst ist Individualismus und der Individualismus ist eine zerstörende, zersetzende Kraft. Darin liegt seine ungeheure Bedeutung. Denn was er zerstören, zu zersetzen sucht, ist die armselige Eintönigkeit des Typus, die Sklaverei der Gewohnheit, die Tyrannei der Sitte und die Erniedrigung der Menschen auf 'Maschine'. . . . Denn die Ideen über die Kunst sind doch naturgemäß aus dem genommen, was die Kunst eben bis zu diesem Augenblick gewesen ist, während das neue Kunstwerk eben dadurch schön ist, daß es ist, was die Kunst bis dahin nie gewesen ist. . . .

Peter Altenberg, unpublished manuscript

Fin de siècle

According to Bertha Zuckerkandl, the popular cultural philosopher and historian Egon Friedell 'had both the misfortune and good luck to be an Austrian. Misfortune because Austrian genius has rarely, if ever, succeeded in obtaining domestic recognition, and good luck because Austria, as no other place, provided a unique hotbed of creativity that allowed uninhibited growth of vision, originality and individuality.'[1] Zuckerkandl could have been referring to any of the Viennese composers in the title of this chapter, particularly Arnold Schoenberg.

Describing the Vienna of 1901, the year in which Schoenberg left the city to work at Ernst von Wohlzogen's *Überbrettl* cabaret in Berlin, William Johnston, in *The Austrian Mind*, mentioned the prevalent atmosphere as one of 'therapeutic nihilism',[2] a medical term that refers to a state in which the patient retained a debilitating condition out of fear of applying any treatment. Fear of change was so traumatising that it was preferable to dwell on the inevitably fatal outcome if change did not take place; stagnation, however, was not a survival option. The music critic Paul Stefan, the artist Oskar Kokoschka and the poet Peter Altenberg were just a few of the chroniclers of the period who despaired of Vienna's inability to accept the change that they and many other Viennese were busy trying to bring about.[3]

Glimpses of 'therapeutic nihilism' can be found in the Viennese press at the turn of the century. On 6 May 1890, in a feuilleton (signed by a triangle of asterisks), we encounter an early mention of the term 'fin de siècle' in the *Neue Freie Presse*:

The nineteenth century is old and tired and draws towards its end. Some may note a certain lightness of the old lady and claim that despite the gravity of the war budget and the eternal issues surrounding the problems of the working classes, she's dancing merrily into her grave. Whether celebrating or complaining, the final foot-steps of the approaching end can be clearly heard; the last decade is upon us and soon even this will have flowed past unnoticed with only the pages of the calendar left in a heap on the floor. Inevitably such a transition from one age to another is anticipated as a major world-changing event, though in fact, it isn't that at all. The hands of the clock move at a hardly perceptible rate. Time won't stop for even a second until reaching midnight 1899 with the mighty voice of Actus dropping the curtain at the end of the play, only to draw it up again offering us a new scene. [. . .] Among the feelings of remorse for the dying century, we also sense the anticipation of the century to come. When the year 1900 is finally upon us [. . .] a suspended harmony resonates inside our being, mixing the tones of impending death along with those of a heightened urge to live.

To define this spiritual state, the Parisians have come up with a term that appeared several years ago and now [. . .] can be heard in every street and by-way. There is no paper, no novel, no play, in which one thing or another is not praised or condemned as 'fin de siècle'. This new concept, cobbled together by three words, can be used for either gracing or disgracing its object. It's not possible to translate and nobody is prepared to venture what it actually means. If someone were to mention that a person or a thing was thoroughly 'fin de siècle', then it apparently implies that said person or thing is capable of sensing the end of the century, or already senses what is to come afterwards. One thinks of the bloom of fresh life shining from beneath the pallor of death. But can't one find a single word for this concept? The best way to understand what is meant by the expression 'fin de siècle' is to examine how the Parisians themselves use it: Whatever is more modern than modern, whatever is taller than tall and whatever trumps the very newest, the most inconspicuous along with the biggest – all of these various things are referred to as 'fin de siècle'.[4]

Subsequent articles in the *Neue Freie Presse* published in 1899[5] and 1900 deal with both of these aspects: the decadence of the dying century and the invigorating dynamism of the new. Indeed, the (anonymous) article from 30 December 1900 was meant to be an obituary for the very phrase 'fin de siècle', which had been so over-used since 1890, that the feuilletonist couldn't wait for the emergence of the new century when it would no longer be applied.[6]

Contemporary discussions and debates on modernism from this period provide scant preparation for what went into creating Schoenberg's musical world. An example of what was understood by the concept of 'modern' comes in an article from the *Neue Freie Presse* for 19 and 20 November 1900 in which the former director of Vienna's Burgtheater, Max Burckhard, writes on modern art. He introduces Darwinian elements and attempts to show that modern art is an organic and logical progression that fits neatly into the laws of natural selection. He pits artistic realism – which offered unvarnished portrayals of life among the lower orders – against the art of the aesthetes appreciated solely for its innate loveliness. He sees modern developments moving towards something he calls 'neo-idealistic', a movement that maintains the portrayal of brutal realism while remaining sensitive to aesthetic beauty.[7] If this is a description of the emerging cultural landscape at the turn of the century, it hardly encompasses the spirit that would erupt in a work such as Schoenberg's 1909 melodrama *Erwartung*.

In 1896, the *Neue Freie Presse* continues its examination of 'modern' art with an extensive survey of the concept of 'Socialist art'.[8] By the turn of the century, we have articles entitled, variously, 'Insanity on the stage'[9] and 'Sick Art'[10], yet in none do we have the slightest premonition of the abandonment of accepted artistic conventions that characterised the Schoenbergian revolution. Indeed, 'modern' art meant reacting against the Aestheticism that had gone before, by showing sometimes awful and repugnant visions of real life. Yet these visions continued to be expressed – whether in painting, drama or music – in language that was familiar to all. An example of the sort of musical 'modernism' debated in feuilletons during the early years of the century can be found in Eugen d'Albert's opera *Tiefland* (first performed in 1903). This offered a level of sexual frisson and social realism that was very different from, say, the Pre-Raphaelite beauty of Debussy's *Pelléas et Mélisande* of 1902, though Debussy's score was far more daring than d'Albert's re-working of *verismo* for the German public. Even Stravinsky, eight years younger than Schoenberg, was not yet composing music that gave any indication of where Schoenberg was leading: compare Stravinsky's *Fireworks* with Schoenberg's *Erwartung*, both first performed in 1909. Arguably Richard Strauss's *Elektra*, also given its premiere in 1909, comes close – more so than anything by Debussy, Reger, Mahler, or even Bartók and Stravinsky at the time. Nothing up to this point had prepared the world for Schoenberg's violent rejection of traditional tonality.

Ethics and the End of Time

Only from Berta Zuckerkandl in 1902, when she states in a casual reference to the Flemish painter George Minne that 'artists are builders of our ethical properties',[11] do we get a hint of the thinking behind the impending musical upheaval and begin to sense a Schoenbergian view of art as something that must reflect as disturbing, an inner truth, whatever the consequences.

This ethical element emerging in the arts would take hold and resonate clearly in Vienna at the time. The notorious *Sex and Character*, published in 1903 by the Jewish philosopher Otto Weininger, followed by his spectacular suicide at the age of 23, was a demonstration of ethical perversion, though much admired at the time for its sheer audacity. Both the young Ludwig Wittgenstein and Hitler admired Weininger for taking the 'ethical' consequences of the spectacularly nihilistic conclusions of his dissertation: Hitler because of Weiniger's unbridled anti-Semitism and Wittgenstein because suicide seemed the only ethical response to an imperfect world.

A more realistic representation of Weininger's hold on early twentieth-century thinking can be found in the autobiographical novel *Die Flucht ins Mittelmäßige*[12] by the Bavarian political exile Oskar Maria Graf, in which he reproduces a fictional exchange on the subject of Weininger among a group of middle-aged exiles in a 1950s New York cocktail party. A former Austrian refugee comments:

When I was a student at the University in Vienna, Otto Weininger was en vogue. [. . .] It followed therefore that every seriously intellectual Jew must also be an anti-Semite, since Weininger's own anti-Semitism was absolutely iron-clad! Reading him today, one wonders how the Nazis never chanced upon him. I even heard that he was also homosexual, which explains his hatred of women: in fact, by and large, his book gives us nothing more than a gruesome mix of varying degrees and types of hatred. To Weininger, Jews and women were simply less than human. [. . .] Yet in the middle of this pseudoscientific nonsense one finds amazing shafts of blazing truth.[13]

Needless to say, Karl Kraus, the quintessential anti-Semitic Jewish intellectual, found much to admire in *Sex and Character*; both Weininger and Kraus were perfect embodiments of Johnston's 'therapeutic nihilism'.

Another important example of the overpowering ethical force that drove creative thinking in Vienna's fin de siècle was the 1908 essay *Ornament and Crime* by the architect Adolf Loos. It was to become a manifesto against the inorganic and non-functional use of the merely decorative in design prevalent in Habsburg Vienna. Propulsion of these ethical forces was provided by Karl Kraus's satirical periodical *Die Fackel* – launched in 1899 – which attacked the hypocrisy of the day in all of its numerous and often contradictory manifestations.

Ultimately, the position of ethics within the intellectual and artistic dialogue of the day was hammered home by Ludwig Wittgenstein in his *Tractatus Logico-Philosophicus*, conceived during his time at the Front during World War One and completed in 1918. In Sentence No. 6,421 of the *Tractatus* we read that 'Ethics and aesthetics are the same'. Schoenberg's *Harmonielehre* from 1911 grows out of the unyielding ethical positions already taken by Kraus, Loos and even Weininger. The inner truth it demands went far beyond the outer truths represented by the Naturalists or social realists. The nature of this particular ethical element being applied to art was a relatively new dimension. With Kraus, Schoenberg and Wittgenstein coming from families representing varying degrees of Jewish assimilation, it can be argued that ethics was part of their intellectual baggage. An inner sensibility attuned to a deep awareness of justice, combined with a clear understanding of right and wrong, is hardly a surprising attribute to be found among people who were marginalised for so many centuries. Even Wittgenstein, though brought up a Christian, gives us the much quoted dictum 'whereof one cannot speak, therefore one must remain silent',[14] an apparent resonance with the Jewish prohibition on naming God. This ethical fortitude also had a profound Talmudic, and thus cultural echo for Austro-German Jews. It would inevitably shape much of the work of even non-religious artists, musicians and writers who came from Jewish backgrounds, and it would also influence many who did not.

The need to create art that could tell an inner and inevitably unsettling truth, and serve as a warning against the consequences of 'therapeutic nihilism', began to churn beneath the subsoil of Austria and Germany in the early years of the twentieth century. In the run-up to the First World War, progressive artists began to resemble mad prophets shouting in the desert about the complacency of a society that only craved easy, immediately appealing and affirming music, literature and art. This ethical conviction went well beyond the empathy with the underprivileged that was the hallmark of 'Socialist', Naturalist or 'Veristic' art. Artistic ethical judgments were not to be understood as acts of kindness, but as brutal wake-up calls.

Egon Wellesz relates in his memoirs how his musicology professor Guido Adler was fascinated by the younger generation of his students who stated that they composed music which was moving away from tonality not because they wanted to, but because they felt compelled to.[15] The apocalyptic premonitions of the age were felt by many, Jew and non-Jew, but it was Schoenberg who gave them their most coherent and powerful voice.

The Old Testament tone regarding ethical duty can be sensed in Schoenberg's 1911 *Harmonielehre*:

> The view that today, one 'can write any- and everything' is depressing as it keeps young people from learning the essentials, understanding the great masters and acquiring broader cultivation. In fact it was always possible to write 'any- and everything' even in earlier times as well, but it simply wasn't any good. Only the truly great are not allowed to write 'any- and everything'. Instead, they do what they must in order to carry out their work. They prepare for this duty with industriousness, labouring under a thousand doubts wondering if a thousand scruples suffice – questioning if one truly understands what is being assigned by a higher power. This is reserved only for those who have the courage and the passion to bear the consequences as well as the strength to carry that which has been bestowed upon them, even if it is against their will. This is quite different from striking wantonly out on one's own – and it's also much braver.[16]

Further on, Schoenberg grows almost messianic:

> Once one is cured of the insane delusion that artists are only in the service of beauty, and is aware of the fact that it is the compulsion to create that results in what in the future will perhaps be found beautiful, only then does

it start to become clear that the artist has no need of bringing conventional coherency to his work – rather he must feel compelled to offer those elements for which his listener is hungering. [. . .] It is especially those who have a heightened sense of aesthetic beauty who shield themselves with what they find appealing against that which is new and aspires to beauty. [. . .] Who is right, the aesthete or the artist? History leaves us in no doubt that right resides with the creator – even if it isn't beautiful. [. . .] Music has, in addition to its central message, [. . .] one further element that it can call upon: it is the simultaneous sounding of the imperative. Perhaps this is why music communicates more widely than other art forms. Nevertheless, thus viewed, the value of this accomplishment gives today's music something that distinguishes it and makes it quite independent of conventional trends and tastes. [. . .] I value originality without overvaluing it – primarily a fault amongst those who lack it entirely. Originality is a symptom always present in the greatest works but also occurring in lesser ones: as such, it can never be used as a unit with which to pass judgement. Having said this, I believe in the new and believe that it is good and beautiful. I believe that we aspire to it as we aspire to the future. It is a future that contains an as yet hidden, yet glorious fulfilment, towards which all of our hopes are aimed. Perhaps it is the future that promises a higher level of our development that makes us long for that which gives us no peace during the present. Perhaps it's only a longing for death: or perhaps it's the certainty of a more elevated life afterwards. With the Future comes the new and perhaps it is for this reason that the future is rightly seen as being identical with beauty and goodness. . . . The laws of nature that determine genius are the laws of future mankind.[17]

If Mahler had provided the portal through which younger Jewish composers could walk, embracing their uniqueness as artists, it comes as no surprise to discover that much of this uniqueness stemmed from their ethical projections onto music – by no means a uniquely Jewish prerogative. Beethoven's *Fidelio* and his setting of Schiller's *An die Freude* in the Ninth Symphony are unambiguous in their ethical, humanist views. But, as the conductor Leon Botstein points out, Schoenberg was also attempting to move away from irrational nineteenth-century Romanticism and return to the values of the Enlightenment.[18] Projecting an innate purity in music on the one hand, while expressing an inner ethical voice on the other, was for Schoenberg a musical *Haskalah*, a point of artistic departure that finds few equivalents among his non-Jewish contemporaries such as Stravinsky but is found among his non-Jewish disciples.[19] Schoenberg opens his *Harmonielehre* by declaring that it could only have been written thanks to what he has learned from his pupils. Wellesz believed that it was Schoenberg's pupil Webern who encouraged him to ever greater artistic audacity, with Schoenberg's relationship with Webern such that ideas flowed in both directions.[20]

In 1920 Wellesz published the first biography of Schoenberg, just preceding the period of dodecaphonic (twelve tone) composition. Wellesz deals specifically with Schoenberg's motivation to explore beyond the confines of traditional tonality and quotes from a programme note by Schoenberg on the *Book of the Hanging Gardens* Op. 15 in which we learn that Schoenberg considered this to be the first of his works that fulfilled the musical vision that he had been attempting to realise for a long time. He admits that this is likely to provoke possible rejection, even from sympathetic listeners (thus anticipating his words in the *Harmonielehre*). Wellesz goes on to cite the important influence of painting in Schoenberg's quest to give expression to this inner voice.[21] He tactfully ignores the affair between Schoenberg's wife Mathilde and the painter Richard Gerstl. Nor could Wellesz have known that Gerstl would be one of the first painters to define Expressionism as an artistic movement, a development in Gerstl's work documented by his few surviving paintings, which move abruptly from figurative to jagged lines and slashes of colour, often obscuring everything but the most basic form.

That Gerstl, as a painter and friend, then a rival in love, would also be an important artistic influence was not something Wellesz felt able to discuss following the painter's suicide in 1908. Coincidentally this was the year in which Schoenberg 'found' his inner voice. Wellesz explains in his own memoirs how Schoenberg demonstrated in the *Harmonielehre* that on each degree of the scale, chords could be constructed which were constrained to maintain a relationship to the tonic-root. Using this as his starting point, Schoenberg began expanding harmonic relationships until arriving at a style that had departed from tonality as previously understood, allowing each tone in effect to become its own tonic. Wellesz also tells us that Schoenberg rejected the term 'a-tonal' in favour of 'a-tonic'.[22]

What remains most redolent of an Old Testament prophet is Schoenberg's view that beauty and truth are not the same. The 'inner' truth that he was compelled to reveal was meant to be destabilising. Viewed in retrospect, this was not the futuristic music of a distant utopia, but a chilling prophecy of horrors to come. Over the next ten years, less talented composers and apostles would solemnly believe that they were playing a part in bringing about a Schoenbergian visionary future of a world still to come, while others, such as Alban Berg with his *Three Orchestral Pieces*, written just before 1914, found resonance with Schoenberg's sense of the impending apocalypse. Adorno's comment that there could be no poetry after Auschwitz is unintentionally clarified by Schoenberg's pupil, Hanns Eisler, speaking at the International Congress of Composers and Music Critics in Prague in May 1948: 'Long before airplanes were invented he anticipated the horror of bombing attacks on people taking refuge in air raid shelters. He is the lyric composer of Auschwitz's gas chambers, of the concentration camp Dachau, of the total despair of the common man crushed under the heel of fascism. That is his humanity. It is proof of Schoenberg's genius and nature that he expressed all these emotions at a time when the world seemed safe. Whatever is said against him, he never lied.'[23] Eisler continues his argument that Schoenberg antici-pated the horrors of Hitler and even acknowledged this in his *Five Orchestral Pieces* Op. 16 from 1909, the first of which is called 'Vorgefühl' – 'Premonition'.[24]

Schoenberg's musical revelations – true, alarming, not beautiful – provided the poetry that warned of Auschwitz. Eisler goes on to mention that one of the most important things he learned from Schoenberg was *Redlichkeit in der Musik* – a term that can be translated as 'musical integrity' or simply 'ethics'.[25]

It is a paradox that Schoenberg's best-known followers were by and large not Jewish. Indeed, Schoenberg remains the ultimate paradox: he rejected the talk of 'soul' that characterised Romanticism, while insisting that he was responding to an 'inner voice'; he was a modernist who set great store by the new and unknown, while remaining unconvinced by what was merely 'modern'. Eisler wrote an entire essay on this apparent contradiction, concluding with the observation that Schoenberg 'unleashed a revolution in order to become a reactionary'.[26]

A Society of Creative Musicians

Despite the prophetic power of Schoenberg's mature music, before 1908 he was only one of many independent voices in a generation of Viennese composers with Jewish antecedents. These early developments are described by Wellesz in his Schoenberg biography, where he offers an account of the formation in 1904 of the *Vereinigung schaffender Tonkünstler*,[27] whose members were Alexander Zemlinsky, Rudolf Stephan Hoffmann, Oskar Karl Posa, Josef von Wöss, Bruno Walter, Arnold Schoenberg and Karl Weigl. Mahler was Honorary President. All of its members, with the exception of Wöss (remembered for his piano transcriptions of Bruckner and Mahler), were Jewish. Hoffmann would become a well-known writer on contemporary musicians; Posa was a composer who taught at Vienna's Music Academy. The major figures in the Vereinigung were Zemlinsky, Weigl, and Schoenberg – a very different composer in 1904 from the one he would soon become.

The Vereinigung represented a musical response to Jugendstil, a decorative style in the arts and crafts, painting, architecture and design. This was a reaction to the heavy historic style that dominated much of Vienna's outward appearance. Jugendstil was the principal artistic development within the Central European Aesthetic movement, adapting cleaner lines, and taking exotic inspiration from ancient Egypt and the Far East. The painters Gustav Klimt, Koloman Moser and Max Kurzweil, along with the architects Josef Hoffmann, Joseph Maria Olbrich and Otto Wagner, formed a group that rebelled against Vienna's traditionalist Association of Artists, and declared themselves Secessionists with the founding of the Union of Austrian Artists in 1897.

Though the formation of the Vereinigung suggests a musical equivalent of the Union of Austrian Artists, its composers were all considerably younger. Musically, they were influenced by French Impressionism, combining melismatic passages with eastern modal sequences suggesting the Orient. The Wagner of *Tristan* was constantly apparent, with the use of frequent chromatic modulations and complex polyphony, all striving towards music with a sensual outer glow. Though it lasted for just one season, the Vereinigung resulted in a number of important concerts: not only the premieres of Zemlinsky's *Die Seejungfrau* (based on Hans Christian Anderson's *The Little Mermaid*) and Schoenberg's *Pelleas und Melisande*, but also works by Mahler, Strauss and the unlikely figure of Siegmund von Hausegger, who would later be fêted by the Third Reich.

It is a paradox that Franz Schreker, the most representative of the 'Jugendstil' composers, did not belong to the Vereinigung despite his close associations with its members. However, with Zemlinsky born in 1871, Schoenberg in 1874, Schreker in 1878 and Karl Weigl in 1881, we have a decade of composers who wrote sensual, elaborate works that seemed to translate the modernist spirit of fin de siècle Vienna into sound. It was Schoenberg who later caught the dynamic of the age with his Second String Quartet Op. 10 from 1907–8, in which he sets poems by Stefan George. To quote from George's text, all of the Vereinigung's composers 'felt the air of another planet' and, taken collectively, were indeed musical 'Secessionists'.

Zemlinsky and Schoenberg

Following a Prague performance of Mahler's Eighth Symphony in March 1912, a photograph was taken of Schreker, Zemlinsky and Schoenberg standing in front of the assembled Vienna Philharmonic Chorus. The photograph invites a comparison between these three pillars of Austro-German Modernism. If Schreker continued to compose in a style abandoned by Schoenberg, Schoenberg departed from a style that he also absorbed from his brother-in-law and principal teacher Zemlinsky. It is in Zemlinsky's early works that we encounter a fusion of Brahms and Wagner, mediated through Mahler, who chose to present Zemlinsky's *Es war einmal*[28] at the Vienna Opera in 1900, which was met with guarded comments by Eduard Hanslick. Mahler flummoxed Julius Korngold when he advised him to take Erich's musical instruction away from Robert Fuchs – Mahler's own composition teacher – and to place him with Zemlinsky where 'in freely organised lessons, the boy will learn everything he needs'.[29]

This must have caused a good deal of anxiety for Julius Korngold, as one of the first things he had to review upon taking his position at the *Neue freie Presse* was a revival of Zemlinsky's *Es war einmal*, resulting in an assessment that reads as if Korngold was over-eager to score points with his mentor. He takes Hanslick's review from the previous year and quotes copiously from it, giving vent to what he presumed Hanslick would have enjoyed reading. In his own article on the work's premiere, Hanslick regretted that 'the voice instead of being allowed to sing from its entire soul is consigned to the significance of the second violins'. This is ruthlessly re-cycled by the cub-feuilletonist in a review that is even more hostile than Hanslick's.[30] In his memoirs, Korngold admits that he had to overcome a good deal of scepticism in order to follow Mahler's advice about what was best for his son's musical education.

Worse was to come: on 3 February 1905 Korngold reviewed the Vereinigung concert which included the premieres of Schoenberg's symphonic poem based on Maeterlinck's *Pelléas et Mélisande* and Zemlinsky's symphonic fantasy after Hans Christian Andersen, *Die Seejungfrau*, both conducted by their respective composers:

'Curious' is Maeterlinck's favourite word. Curious is also the effect elicited by Schoenberg's symphonic poem *Pelleas und Melisande*. We were able to make its acquaintance recently at the second orchestral concert of the Vereinigung schaffender Tonkünstler, during which one could only nervously smile while casting flirtatious glances towards the doors marked 'Exit'. How delightful the role of the critic is these days! We would, no doubt, find ourselves in the best of company, should we choose to join in the timid giggling and subsequent indignation before dashing out of the hall at the earliest opportunity. But we critics can neither allow nor even wish our lives to be so easy – after all, young composers don't take these things easily either. The sense of duty, honour and conviction that speaks to us from their work demands our serious appraisal.[31]

Korngold goes on to discuss the merits of the string sextet *Verklärte Nacht* of 1899 and regrets the development from that piece to the new orchestral work. He complains that Schoenberg's vision of *Pelleas* lasts nearly 45 minutes and, after giving us the plot, complains that Schoenberg is only creating 'atmosphere made by joining together chords and melisma. This is atmospheric Impressionism and it's the latest watchword of modern music, which is today where literature was several years ago. And as with literature, this latest musical development comes to us from France.'[32] Korngold dismisses Debussy as a mingler of pretty sounds which 'dethrone the melodic element to the benefit of the harmonic and cast music into a pit of dim, misty shapelessness'. He ends with another Maeterlinck quote: '"It cannot be said with certainty that disease is not actually the most authentic and diverse poetry of the flesh." Similarly it seems with our young composers, that it cannot be said with certainty that dissonance is not to be savoured as music's most diverse and authentic beauty.'[33]

Korngold finishes by calling the work an 'impenetrable musical fog', while hoping that 'the undisputed talent of the composer will eventually lift the mists and let in some sunlight'.[34] When he comes to review *Pelleas* again on 5 June 1920, Korngold refers to it as a 'kind of wordless melodrama'. He sees the problems as more pronounced than ever, yet by now he views Schoenberg as a major figure on the world stage of new music.[35]

Korngold writes on Zemlinsky's *Die Seejungfrau*:

Far less subversive [than Schoenberg's work] is Alexander v. Zemlinsky's orchestral Fantasy. Zemlinsky is presently the great hope of Young Vienna. To us, his original recommendation by Brahms was far more important than his subsequent development. His first songs, followed by a remarkable [string] quartet [Op.4], are perhaps preferable to his later banquets of [. . .] orchestral offerings, not to mention the thundering success of his opera *Es war einmal*. With this, his latest orchestral work, we are accorded yet another fairy-tale. It's by [Hans Christian] Andersen and called *The Little Mermaid*, which Zemlinsky has duly adorned into music. Saint-Saëns, Dvořák and Rimsky-Korsakov have all told us musical fairy-tales in similar fashion, probably with more melodic substance and spirit. The work is constructed in three not necessarily contrasting parts. There is no indication in the course of the work where we find ourselves within the narrative of the story.

Modern orchestral composers clearly require a well-prepared audience, which means that adults as well as children need to arrive with the fairy-tale imbedded into their memories. It starts off with the deep throbbing tone that once plunged us to the bottom of the Rhine, but now takes us to the bottom of the ocean. Its principal motif, however, is not quite that deep.[36]

Korngold then explains the programmatic treatment of the work and finishes off with the observation that Andersen's fairy-tale ends with 'the mermaid turned into foam on the surface of the ocean, which is perhaps the appropriate manner to view Zemlinsky's music, in which lapses of expressiveness and creativity are augmented by virtue of beautiful sounds thanks to his orchestration.'[37]

Needless to say, Korngold's opinions started to change once his son Erich was placed in Zemlinsky's musical care: his reviews of the operas *Kleider machen Leute* (1910),[38] *Eine florentinische Tragödie* (1917),[39] and *Der Zwerg* (1923)[40] are far more favourable, though in his review of *Der Zwerg* he turns the very points he criticised in *Die Seejungfrau* into attributes which, he suggests, elevate this one-act opera above anything by Schreker – a composer with whom Korngold had very different and very particular problems.

Karl Weigl

The third principal composer in the Vereinigung schaffender Tonkünstler was Karl Weigl. Like Schoenberg, he was a pupil of Zemlinsky and, like Webern and Wellesz, he studied musicology with Adler. In common with Mahler, Wolf, Schreker, Franz Schmidt and many of the most significant Viennese composers of the day, his composition teacher was Robert Fuchs. In 1904, Mahler appointed Weigl as principal coach at the Hofoper and during these years Weigl focused on composing Lieder. After the First World War, he taught harmony at Vienna's Conservatory, and in June 1928 he was awarded the honorific title of 'Professor', though by then, he had left formal teaching for full-time composing. In 1930, he returned to teaching and took over the position at the University previously held by Hans Gál, who by 1929 had left to head the Music Academy in Mainz. Among Weigl's students were Erich Korngold, Hanns Eisler, Kurt Roger and Erich Zeisl. He joined Schoenberg, Zemlinsky, Berg, Bartók, Janáček and Schreker in the catalogue of Universal Edition, and his works were taken up by the likes of Georg Szell, Wilhelm Furtwängler, Paul Wittgenstein, and the Busch and Kolisch Quartets. While Weigl was a member of the Vereinigung, he was certainly one of

Vienna's most adventurous young composers. Over time he would remain on the same stylistic path, rejecting the subsequent developments of Schoenberg and Zemlinsky. In criticising Weigl's *Symphonic Fantasy* in 1910, Julius Korngold refers to the now forgotten composer Franz Gut, who featured on the same programme. Korngold writes that Franz Gut was guilty of repeating a mistake that was 'typical among modern composers today'. He went on to add that Weigl's error was greater, 'succumbing to mistakes typical among the composers of yesterday'.[41] Korngold then goes on to explain:

> Symphonic music today [...] is in danger of falling for false attractions offered by the 'one-movement work'. Such a single, broadly spun-out movement as Weigl's *Symphonic Fantasy* demands a particular construction and an energetic rejection of the soupy a-rhythmic nature [of] post-Wagnerian orchestral music. [...] When Weigl attempts to tackle an orchestral work, he gives the impression of a sweet-natured gentleman being forced to bellow and bark. One knows of better works by this talented young composer and we expect finer things of his E major symphony [No.1].[42]

Later, when reviewing a Vienna performance of this same symphony on 5 June 1920 under Georg Szell, Korngold dismisses it as too old-fashioned:

> The first movement aspires towards the gentle charms of a serenade. The finale, which sounds as if it has been crow-barred on, maintains itself if only thanks to its Tchaikovsky-like bullish rhythmic energy. The most rewarding movement is the Adagio, which is lyrically Brahmsian in feel while maintaining the instrumental glow of Austria's younger composers. One finds (in this now familiar work) both cultivation and craftsmanship, but perhaps not entirely the full symphonic weight required; at least, not according to today's standards. The contemporary path has turned sharply away from the medium of the Romantic Symphony. Today, a work must plumb the depths and ascend to the heights while not forgetting to reflect a 'world-vision'. But, one hastens to add, to achieve all of this, one needs also to be in possession of the correct 'musical-vision'.[43]

Weigl's more natural voice is found in his songs and chamber works. Only in a number of shorter orchestral works such as his *Phantastisches Intermezzo* and his concertos for cello, for violin, and his two for piano (one of which was written for Paul Wittgenstein) can we hear what Julius Korngold called the 'glow of Austria's young composers'. His Violin Concerto of 1928, given its premiere by Josef Wolfsthal (a Carl Flesch pupil), is an example of a Viennese composition that maintains the sensual warmth that Schreker, Schoenberg and Zemlinsky had by then abandoned. At this point, all three composers had relocated to Berlin, a city with an insatiable demand for the new. By the late 1920s, the apocalypse of the First World War had gone and the shimmering sound-world of fin de siècle Vienna seemed hopelessly out of date. A work such as Ernst Krenek's opera *Jonny spielt auf* (1927) had proved that the New World, with its African-American jazz musicians, was capable of over-whelming the smugness of old-world culture. If the works of Schreker, Zemlinsky and Schoenberg show a sharpening of musical contours following their arrival in the edgier environment of Weimar Republic Berlin, Weigl represented a musical aesthetic that remained safely ensconced in Vienna. Yet to the Viennese masters now living and working in Berlin, Weigl still counted as a formidable voice of the age.

In 1938, with more than a hint of nostalgia, Schoenberg wrote the following recommendation of Weigl, who had been forced, like Schoenberg, to flee his homeland: 'I know Dr Weigl since more than forty years, when we both were quite young. He was at this time studying with Alexander Zemlinsky and gradu-ated both in piano and composition at the renown [sic] Vienna Conservatory. I always considered him as one of the best composers of this older generation, one of those who continued the dignified Viennese tradition of the Porporas, Fuxes, Albrechtsbergers and Sechters. He truly preserves this old culture of a musical spirit which is one of the best parts of Viennese culture.'[44]

Franz Schreker

Today, revivals of Schreker's music have started to fill out our knowledge of a composer who was marginalised for too long. As his biographer Christopher Hailey points out, the postwar declaration by musical modernists that it was music's destiny to move away from tonality overshadowed alterna-tive views that music was capable of moving forward by other means. Schoenberg's forebodings created such a sense of radical departure that other developments found themselves eclipsed. Schoenberg prophesied a murderous age – as such he was hailed as a musical Messiah: in effect, the messenger became the message. Anyone who represented an alternative aesthetic was seen as detracting from Schoenbergian truth and was, in effect, representing a false gospel.

Judging from the statements of fellow musicians, Schreker must have been a perplexing and infuriating man. Very few of the composers and performers who moved in Vienna and Berlin's progressive musical circles have a good word to say about him. The memoirs of Ernst Krenek, Artur Schnabel, Bruno

Walter and Carl Flesch dismiss him either as a joke or as a nostalgic musical dinosaur; yet the remorseless denunciation of such a major figure demands closer inspection. Reminiscences written long after Schreker's untimely death in 1934 (aged 55) must be viewed in the context of postwar cultural politics. Schreker was, by all accounts, an easy target. From his correspondence, we sense a man who is trustingly naïve and clearly eager to please. He belied the stereotype of the tortured genius and was benevolent and generous to students and colleagues. To some, he appeared ingratiating. One of his star pupils, Ernst Krenek, writes that he was reminded on first meeting him of a suburban Jewish photographer and was surprised to discover 'that this was in fact what Schreker's father had been'.[45] As a budding young composer, Schreker dropped the 'c', presumably to avoid the easy critical target of being dismissed as 'schrecklich' ('dreadful'). It was probably a wise move, though the inverse was no great help to the composer Franz Gut ('Good'), mentioned above. However, only when he developed an infatuation with the attractive Jewish socialite Grete Jonasz did he admit in a letter to her in 1907 that he in fact was half Jewish himself, thus deflecting her accusations of anti-Semitism. Krenek disliked his overbearing friendliness, his unctuous manner and, in short, everything about him that he considered 'typically Jewish'.

Most of all, however, Schreker's detractors resented his success. Given his professional and personal closeness to Schoenberg, this was perceived by Schoenberg's followers as near treachery. Indeed, Schreker enjoyed the kind of popular recognition that Schoenberg could only dream of, and, to make matters worse, it was thanks to his continued use of a musical language that Schoenberg had abandoned for ethical and artistic reasons. The lifelong mutual admiration of Schreker and Schoenberg is well documented, but Schreker's early death and Schoenberg's eventual stylistic victory left Schreker, one of the most significant figures in early twentieth-century music, forgotten by history.

Reading the reviews by Hanslick and Korngold, it is easy to sense the despair of young artists in Vienna over the city's unwillingness to provide a worthy forum for discussing their work. In his dismissive review of Schreker's opera *Das Spielwerk und die Prinzessin* from 18 March 1913, Korngold actually offers a rather acute description of Schreker the composer. As is often the case when re-reading reviews by both critics, we discover that the very characteristics that are now recognised as a composer's unique musical voice were precisely the points that came in for the harshest criticism. It could be argued that Schreker set himself up for a fall by writing, as always, his own libretto for *Das Spielwerk*. Pot-shots abound in Korngold's withering critique of an opera he feels is far too close to Gerhard Hauptmann's play *Und Pippa Tanzt!* Korngold writes:

It is difficult to understand Schreker the musician without taking a look at his development as a composer. Schreker started off tame – indeed, tamer than tame. His choral and orchestral compositions kept to the models of old masters and travelled the well-worn paths of worthy mediocrity. Any individuality or even an unexpected youthful indiscretion was as inconceivable as any possible element of surprise that might have slipped in – even in the unlikely event that such a surprise might have been a prickly one. But one day, he suddenly decided that prickly surprises and indiscretions were perhaps not such a bad thing after all and he became a *Modernist*, he '*secessionised*' himself; did things 'differently', especially in that particular area where mixing and matching musical effects can be placed snuggly against inspiration: creating new musical-sounds. New harmonies and colouristic developments are of course all the rage today; an entire generation of modern composers reach out for new sounds that are, no matter how one looks at such things, only deliberate chord-bending achieved with orchestral experimentation. This being the case, we suddenly find Schreker along with the rest in curious pursuit of as many new sounds as can be worked into his songs and orchestral compositions. It is no coincidence that the title of his first opera is taken from the ideal of the hero-musician [. . .] in search of *A Distant Sound* [*Der ferne Klang*]. All of the strange noises in this opera, in common with [*Das Spielwerk und die Prinzessin*] seem not so 'distant' if one starts to peer at the composer's obvious models. The mixture of reality and fantasy-Romanticism in *Der ferne Klang* is also found in Charpentier's *Louise*, in which we already encountered the idea that from the noise of daily life, the confusing cacophony of the big city, it is possible to construct a sound-kaleidoscope: [Schreker extracts] noises from the formless, driven to the limits until something similar to music is squeezed out. [. . .] Beyond the obvious Charpentier influence, one finds also the Impressionism of Debussy and Delius; yes, and even the introduction of futuristic principals that dare to offer up a heterophony of shrill, loud, simultaneous and disparate noises, sounds and sequences. Schreker has plunged his hands deep into the modernist filing cabinet and offers up the music of 'Angst', the subconscious, while digging into the deeper layers of neurosis in common with *Salome*, *Elektra* or Mahler's works or Pfitzner's *Rose vom Liebesgarten*, but above all in Dukas's *Ariane et Barbe-bleue*. Indeed, it is the Dukas work, much too little known in Germany and Austria, that holds the most perfect representation of this mysterious 'Sound-Music' that the composer of *Das Spielwerk und die Prinzessin* seems to love so much.

In addition, we find a bit of not very impressionistic post-Wagnerian phraseology und leitmotifs such as the use of spoken-song. With the above account, one basically has the elements of Schreker's operatic language rolled up together: style is less important than the creation of something new. The motivic and melodic substance – we wish to say this very clearly – is sparse, with the few promising plastic motifs only lasting over the course of a few bars. All emphasis is placed on the harmonies and orchestral weaving of voices [. . .] passages of sheer beauty, which naturally we were delighted to encounter, are less frequent than the kaleidoscopic secessionist noise-confusion of piercing, shrieking sounds that remind one of seeing a painting that has had the subject removed and is left only with its colours on display.[46]

Wellesz is far more generous towards Schreker, whom he recalls meeting during a visit at Schoenberg's home in 1908. He recounts Schreker's successes and his early dance works for the Wiesenthal sisters (Grete, Bertha and Else), who brought 'Ausdruckstanz' in the manner of Isadora Duncan to Vienna. Grete and Else had made a name for themselves in performances of Gluck's *Iphigenie auf Aulis* under Mahler and his designer Alfred Roller in 1907. Their collaboration with Schreker on *Der Geburtstag der Infantin*,[47] a 'dance-pantomime' based on Oscar Wilde, was conceived for Klimt's 1908 Kunstschau (Art Show), an event mounted as part of the celebrations for the diamond jubilee of the Emperor Franz Joseph. Wellesz called the Kunstschau a 'secession from the Secessionists', referring to the group of younger artists who joined Klimt and Carl Moll in leaving the Secession in 1905.[48] Wellesz goes on to give an appreciative description of Schreker, though he takes a jab at the self-written libretti. He recounts that the first thing he noticed when presented with a vocal score of Schreker's opera *Der ferne Klang* in 1911 was that Alban Berg had made the piano reduction.[49] Wellesz goes on to write: 'Today, I'm of the opinion that much of the material from *Wozzeck* and *Lulu* can be explained by [Berg's] intensive work with Schreker's music, indeed it was his work on this extraordinarily passionate opera [*Der ferne Klang*] with its orgiastic climaxes in the second act that preconditioned much of *Lulu* and determined the ultimate formation of Berg as a composer with dramatic genius.'[50] Wellesz goes on to describe Schreker's creation of the Vienna Philharmonic Chorus and his conducting of Schoenberg's *Gurrelieder* in 1913, mentioning that Berg had been commissioned to prepare the piano reduction for this work as well. Wellesz recalls Schoenberg telling him that, with *Wozzeck*, Berg had created something that he himself was ill-equipped for: composing an opera.[51] By putting this comment in his chapter on Schreker, Wellesz implies an acknowledgment by Schoenberg of Schreker's influence on Berg.

Wellesz singles out Schreker's *Die Gezeichneten*[52] as his greatest achievement, with its dramatic power and brilliant orchestration. Composed in 1913–15, it demonstrated that the diatonic language Schoenberg believed to be exhausted could be given an impressive new lease of life by Schreker. However, to most of the earnest young revolutionaries who followed Schoenberg, Schreker seemed a good-natured buffoon and an easy target, despite Schoenberg's enduring respect for him. But like Wagner before him, Schoenberg could not control the damage that his disciples might inflict.

It's easy to sense Wellesz's slight discomfort in defending a composer who would be so reviled by the Nazis and then by his own former colleagues and pupils. It is fascinating to read how the Nazi definition of Schreker as 'the Magnus Hirschfeld of Music for whom no sexual perversion could not be set to music'[53] chimes with the philosopher Theodor Adorno, who referred to Schreker as a musical pornographer.[54] Adorno's extensive essay on Schreker in *Quasi una fantasia* (1963) recalls Julius Korngold in elaborating the very elements of Schreker's originality in order to denigrate him. Yet *Quasi una fantasia* remains one of the most revealing of all postwar essays on Schreker, as Adorno's ultimate condemnation follows a fair analysis which underlines Schreker's influence within the Schoenberg circle. Adorno even praises such works as Schreker's *Chamber Symphony* and the prelude to *Die Gezeichneten*. It is in his magisterial but malevolent summary of Schreker as a composer of music 'still stuck in puberty' where Adorno succeeds in perpetuating the Nazi denigration of this scintillating musical personality.[55]

What Schoenberg's young revolutionaries could not know was that the apocalypse had not been fulfilled by the collapse of Europe's decrepit old order in 1918. 'The war to end all wars' was followed by what General Foch called 'an armistice of twenty years'. The earthquake of World War I would be followed by Hitler's equally destructive tsunami. The cautious mood at the end of the war in 1918 would start to produce new creative drives towards what a younger generation hoped might become a musical utopia that would rise from the ashes of the old-world order. But the 'twenty-year armistice' was frequently jolted by aftershocks. The epicentre of this 'Dance on the Volcano' was no longer post-imperial Vienna, but dynamic and *modern* Berlin.

CHAPTER 6

A Musical Migration

How much must Austrian tedium weigh for Austria itself to emigrate! Can the body survive if its blood is simply rechanneled? [. . .] That the Danube now flows via Passau towards Berlin and spills into the North Sea is a situation that must be of no small concern to the Danube itself.

Wie groß muß der Überdruß am Österreichischen sein, wenn auch schon Österreich auswandert! Lebt der Körper noch, der die Umzapfung seines Blutes klaglos erträgt? [. . . .] Daß die Donau jetzt über Passau nach Berlin fließt und in die Nordsee mündet, ist eine Angelegenheit, die der Donau nahegehen müßte.

Karl Kraus, *The Wall of China*, 1910, republished 1918

World War I

In 1900, Germany, the United States and Austria-Hungary had populations of around 40 million each. By 1919, Austria was reduced to just 6,420,000, including hundreds of thousands of immigrants from former Habsburg territories who flooded into the remaining 'rump-state' of Austria. This now consisted of Vienna – the sixth largest city in the world as recently as 1910[1] – a few German-speaking holdings, and a narrow neck of mountains running to Switzerland which prevented Germany from having a border with Italy. The disappearance of the Austrian Empire as a geographical entity was unprecedented in modern European history, with the possible exception of the demise of the Ottoman Empire. The removal of the dual monarchy of Austria-Hungary from the European map left the imperial capital of Vienna and a staggeringly well-equipped civil service with no empire to run. Worse still, the assassination of the heir to the throne at Sarajevo, which triggered the war, was an act of such audacity that the Habsburgs were seen by nearly everyone as being justified in declaring war on the terrorists' training ground of Serbia. Archduke Franz Ferdinand and his wife Sophie were assassinated at the end of June 1914, but already by 21 July newspaper articles were asking how to prevent an impending 'World War', clearly seeing the dangers of an entirely new type of conflict.[2] The satirist Karl Kraus, upon hearing the news of Franz Ferdinand's assassination in Sarajevo, speculated that Austria-Hungary had become the 'testing-station for the Apocalypse'.[3]

From a practical perspective, the German-Austrians were signing up to avenge what they saw as the shameless assassination of the heir to the Austro-Hungarian throne, though in truth the Hungarians themselves were not particularly sorry about their supposed loss. The Slavic citizens of the Habsburg-held territories were perhaps even more ambivalent, despite the fact that Franz Ferdinand had been making plans that would have left at least the South-Slavs in a more equitable position within the dual monarchy. Nevertheless, patriotism in this war wasn't based on the hostility of one nation state against another, but of empire against empire. Patriots fought for their ruling houses, not their political states.

Bismarck had spent the years since the Franco-Prussian War of 1871 entangling Germany and Europe in an ever more complex network of treaties intended to maintain the balance of power and save Europe from further warfare. He saw this work as a post-Metternich attempt to keep Russians, Austrians, the French and the British in a permanent state of political paralysis. By doing so, it could be argued that he kept a World War at bay for a period of 43 years. Nevertheless, when the war finally arrived, the treaties, some of which Bismarck's successor Bernhard von Bülow had not bothered to renew, were spun on their heads in order to tickle out the many sub-clauses and exceptions that would eventually result in Europe splitting into two camps, each gazing down gun-barrels aimed towards the other. For all Bismarck's machinations, the only treaties that counted were the axis between Prussian Germany and Austria on one side, and the Triple Entente between Britain, France and Russia on the other.

From the start of the conflict in 1914, things grew slightly more complicated. The Italians were bribed with promises to join the Entente, and the Bulgarians were bribed to join Germany and Austria – in any case, the Italians hated the Austrians, whom they simply saw as 'Germans', felt culturally closer to the French, and wished to secure Adriatic hegemony and 'clarify their borders'[4]; the French and British were bound by treaty with Russia, though, for the British, dynastic ties lay mainly with the Germans and to a lesser extent with the Russians. Despite international sympathy for the Austrians, the rest of Europe felt the Habsburg dual monarchy had largely become an anachronism, excluded from the larger German nation state, yet trying to compensate by imposing its Austro-Magyar will on Czechs, Poles, Slovaks, Ukrainians, the few Italians around their port at Trieste, and various Yugoslavians and Romanians right through the Balkans. As with the Turkish Ottomans, it was a trans-national empire that dominated its multi-cultural neighbours in an age of nation state aspirations. A popular aphorism of the day stated that Habsburg Austro-Hungary could only last as long as Ottoman Turkey.

But there was more at stake: Germany wanted to build on its territorial acquisitions, which had not expanded significantly since 1871, though 'Lebensraum' was not ever given as an official reason for going to war. If Germany had expansionist eyes, they most likely looked East towards what it called the 'Near Orient' as it set about building a railway line all the way to Baghdad in anticipation of opening up commerce beyond the Balkans. Austria wished to consolidate its foothold in the Balkans, which Bismarck (dead since 1898) had infamously described as not worth the bones of a Pomeranian grenadier – indeed, he had predicted that if there were to be a future war in Europe, it would be over something pointless 'like the Balkans'. Yet it would be wrong to assume that Austria was eager to acquire yet more Slavic nations. Such an enlargement would have seriously upset the status quo and made further devolution to the Slavs unavoidable – something the Magyars would never have accepted, though this was precisely the ambition that Franz Ferdinand harboured.

Austria was thus left to sort out its rights and wrongs with Serbia, while the Germans reacted to the declaration of war by turning their attention to the more advantageous opportunities they saw arising from the ensuing free-for-all. As Russian forces began mobilising on its western borders, the Germans decided to forestall a double-fronted war and knock out potential trouble from the French, attempting to render France neutral for the remainder of the conflict. This would allow German forces to concentrate on fighting Russia, which was perceived as being a far greater threat to its 'Near Orient' ambitions. The French were still smarting from the war of 1870 and the loss of Alsace-Lorraine, and dearly wished to see Germany back to where it was before Bismarck's 'blood and iron' unification. The Kaiser had built a huge navy, as a challenge to Britain and hopefully allowing the Germans a toe-hold in the colonial acquisitions that the British had more or less monopolised. If the Saxe-Coburg and Gotha cousins (soon to call themselves 'Windsor') in England could acquire an Empire with the help of a navy, so could their half-English first cousin, Germany's Wilhelm II. This, at least, is what he and Admiral Tirpitz believed. As it happened, the German navy hardly left port

for the duration of the conflict, and German naval warfare resorted to ethically questionable U-boat assaults on ships carrying civilians – ships which
the Americans and the British had used for the equally questionable transport
of military supplies. As the conflict was not between states, but between the
symbols of power represented by monarchs, it became a fight that was meant
either to strengthen the legitimacy of the established order, or to destroy it.
Attempts to avert war through negotiation were arrogantly dismissed.

Why everyone wished to go to battle remains a mystery to this day:
Germany had not yet officially considered expansion; Germany, France and
Britain were friendly trading partners and nobody, least of all the French,
wanted to see the influence of the Romanovs encroaching further into
Western Europe despite France's treaty with Russia. Austria had a bone to pick
with the Serbs, but did not wish to acquire further Slavic territories. Britain
wanted to stay out of the conflict altogether, but joined it once neutral
Belgium was attacked in Germany's move to knock out the French before the
Russians could mobilise. As tensions mounted, it would seem that only the
French had a concrete goal: the reacquisition of Alsace-Lorraine. Everyone
saw themselves as being the innocent party under attack: the Germans, as the
Russians mobilised; the Serbs; the French. Everyone also saw themselves as
being in the right, and God was evidently on everybody's side. Any goals that
were to be achieved during the war were thought up after it had started. It
would be the last conflict in which feudal values of honour were called upon
to trump patient diplomacy and negotiation. It would end with catastrophic
loss of life for the British, the Germans, the Austro-Hungarians and the
Russians. With the exception of the British, all of the other combatants
(including Turkey, which had fought on the Austro-German side) would lose
their royal heads of state and re-emerge as republics.

The casualties were unimaginable: France, Germany and Russia each lost
one and three-quarter million men. Austria lost one million, two hundred
thousand; and the British lost almost a million. These figures do not include
the outbreak of the Spanish flu in 1917 that went on to claim three per cent of
the world's population. At the end of the conflict, it was not clear who the
winners and losers were: the 'War to end all Wars' had ended with everyone
in a state of utter exhaustion.

The Musical Legacy of the War

In the *Neue Freie Presse* on 2 July 1917, Guido Adler wrote an article on music
and war. Unsurprisingly, he speaks of Austria as the country that has the most
music residing in its soul, though he includes Germany in his more general

discourse. He makes claims for 'predestined' superiority within 'musical culture', pointing out how absurd it would be for the French and British to boycott Beethoven, Mozart and Schubert. There follow, however, some fascinating observations:

> Until now, wars have had little effect on a nation's musical output. If economies were disrupted, it meant that performers couldn't be paid, but musical creativity was not disrupted. If, however, things should turn out differently in this particular conflict, then it would provide the opportunity to reform music from the very roots upwards.

In an echo of Wagner, Adler sees the German people needing to rediscover their natural musical talents and he hopes that postwar developments will guarantee musical opportunities throughout all social classes. He is careful to distance himself from 'Socialism', but uses the word 'social' freely to call for cultural renewal and accessibility throughout all levels of society. He calls for a new type of politics that views music as the ultimate catalyst of social reform.[5]

More startling to modern readers is Adler's vocabulary. He uses the term 'entartet' (degenerate) to denounce what he perceives as negative developments. Continuing with the same language employed by malevolent politicians twenty years later, he calls for 'musical boils to be lanced' so that 'degeneration' should not spread and thus infect the culture-starved masses. This plea, however, is directed less at Schoenberg and his followers than towards light music and operetta. His prediction that music should help in widening social enfranchisement is more interesting.[6] Hanslick's belief in music as an autonomous art that had no intrinsic means of confronting social issues or addressing non-musical questions still enjoyed wide currency at this time, yet what Adler was propagating was an ethical dimension similar to that proposed by Schoenberg, and an idea that had now taken root. From Mahler onwards, assimilated Austrian Jewish musicians saw their art as a tool that could help shape a more just, enlightened and unified society. That this view owed at least something to Wagner's anti-Semitic reactions to the half-Jewish Hanslick showed how far Jewish cultural integration had come.

The Immediate Legacy of War and a Mass Migration

The War and the Spanish flu epidemic were devastating. Jews saw the systems that had decreed and enforced their emancipation collapse. At the same time, many recognised the positive opportunities presented by the postwar secular republics that had sprung up in the wake of Austria's own *ancien régime*. This had steadfastly maintained the institutional anti-Semitism of the Catholic Church in spite of Franz Joseph's perceived philo-Semitism. Many Austrians and Germans believed that Jews preferred defeat in the war in the belief that memories of the ghetto could now be consigned to a closed chapter on feudal Europe. This ignored the far more generally held view among middle-class Jews that the Emperor was the only guarantor of equality. The Galician journalist and writer Joseph Roth, author of the novel *Radetzky March*, provided the most articulate voice for this position, and it was also the declared belief of Schoenberg and Wellesz. This generation of Jews (and former Jews) believed that the monarchy provided stability and protected minorities through its unquestioned authority. Democratic republics gave the people – potentially an unruly mob – too much influence and Jews were well aware that the unruly mob was, by and large, anti-Semitic. The need for work, for social housing, and for educational opportunities for everyone was becoming increasingly urgent, especially among the proletarian masses, which were joining the Christian Social Party, with its overt anti-Semitic bias opportunistically propagated by the party's founder and populist former mayor of Vienna, Karl Lueger.

Jews therefore filled the ranks of both the Communist and the Social Democratic parties. The Communist Party was attractive because it was international – the working man has no nation, according to the Communist Manifesto. Jews who had spent the decades after emancipation being told how they couldn't truly be counted as German, French or British, had an active interest in seeing such barriers to integration eliminated. With the Emperor no longer the rallying point, the 'International', as the Communist Party was then called, was perceived as an attractive alternative. For most liberal, educated Jews, however, the Social Democratic Party was the only practical political choice. Other parties represented land-owning and farming constituencies, which would only include a small number of livestock-trading Jews. Right of Centre parties as well as the populist Christian Social Party were closely affiliated with the church's open anti-Semitism. The once powerful Liberal Party of the 1860s was now insignificant and in any case it was seen as being partially responsible for the gulf between the prosperity of the middle classes and the wretchedness of the workers during the final decades of the nineteenth century. The policies of individualistic capitalism formerly represented by the Liberals had little attraction for soldiers coming home to the devastated economies of Germany and Austria.

War has a democratising effect. It may be fought over issues between potentates, but it must be fought by the people. They had to be persuaded, cajoled and bribed into fighting enemies who represented no threat to their personal interests. There was a limit to how much could be accepted by the masses before they demanded the right to join in the decision-making processes.

The 1919 peace treaties concerning Germany at Versailles and Austria at Saint-Germain were devastating for both. Nobody wanted to pick up the bill for the disaster. The most expedient solution was to declare Germany and Austria as sole aggressors, thus lumbering them with the full costs of all reparations. As Germany and Austria were not invited to the negotiations until the deal was settled, they had little choice but to accept, not without bewilderment since they had believed the war had ended in stalemate. Had not Serbian aggression against Austria started it? France had no desire to see a strong, united German state, or a return of the dual Monarchy of Austria-Hungary, and convinced the allies to recognise the autonomy of the self-declared independent states that had formerly made up the monarchy's constituent parts, reducing Austria to its German-speaking core around Vienna and along the Alps.

Berta Zuckerkandl, related by marriage to the French Prime Minister Georges Clemenceau (her sister Sophie was married to Georges's brother Paul), wrote of the anger Clemenceau felt against Austria and his desire to see its empire wiped off of the face of the earth. Zuckerkandl's attempts through family connections to negotiate a separate peace between Austria and France during the war came to nothing. In addition, the French were determined that Austrian German speakers should not be allowed to fold themselves into the larger German republic. Indeed, undermining German unification was their major, though largely unspoken, priority. Occupation of the Rhineland, which the allies hoped might become an independent republic, and economic pandemonium created by eye-popping war reparations, started a process in which some of the constituent German states temporarily declared independence in order to take control of local finances.

Postwar Austria was in ruins. It lost its agricultural holdings to Hungary, its port to Italy, and its industrial belt to Czechoslovakia. It was left with the Alps and a crescent-shaped stretch of the Danube, while conceding much of Tyrol to the Italians. Vienna looked like a faintly ridiculous duchess whose wig had suddenly blown away in a gale. If one thing united most Austrians, it was the wish in 1919 to be absorbed into Germany. With only the Alps and some farming along the Danube as natural resources, Balkan poverty would extend throughout Austria, with most of her rural population barely able to eke out a living.

On 3 September 1918, the *Neue Freie Presse* ran a moving account of Austrian soldiers on the wrong side of the front trying to return home. It was its last outwardly patriotic feuilleton. It refers specifically to Austrians rather than Germans, and describes in loving detail everything that made this homeland special to its young men and women.[7] Two months later, and a year before the Republic of Austria was declared, the paper carried news on 13 November 1918 of the Austrian parliament's decision to unite with Germany:

> At one time it was said that the German people [in the multi-national conglomeration of the Austro-Hungarian Empire] were the manure that allowed the other nations to grow. Well, the Austro-Germans are tired of being manure. The only harvest they have reaped has been the hatred and aggravation of foreign races. It too now wishes to be in a position of widening its horizons. The last war demonstrated how important it was that a state be able to feed and finance itself independently. This fact is no less true in times of peace.[8]

As if confirming the view that the Austrian Emperor was the only guarantor of Jewish freedom and safety, Lemberg, formerly part of Austrian Poland (today Lviv in the Ukraine), witnessed a monstrous pogrom only days after independence. On 16 March, the paper reported on Woodrow Wilson's decision to consider whether Austrian-German unification was in keeping with his 'Fourteen Points', which had become the basis of the Armistice in November 1918.[9] To the shock of the Austro-Germans who had believed that the 'Fourteen Points' guaranteed self-determination of Europe's many national identities, it didn't, and on 12 November, the Republic of Austria was declared. It was the day on which Franz Schreker completed his opera *Der Schatzgräber*, which by 1922 would become the most frequently performed opera by a living composer in the German-speaking world. At the bottom of the last page of the score he inscribed a disappointed note that acknowledged the founding of the Austrian Republic and called for immediate unification with Germany. As Zweig writes in *The World of Yesterday*, it must have been the first time in European history that a country offered independence, demanded instead absorption by a neighbouring state.[10] By the following year, however, at the invitation of the Jewish, Hungarian-born Leo Kestenberg, advisor to the Prussian Minister of Culture, Schreker had abandoned Vienna to take up the directorship of Berlin's Academy of Music and had taken his entire Viennese composition class with him: Max Brand, Walter Gmeindl, Alois Hába, Jascha Horenstein, Ernst Krenek, Alexander Lippay, Alois Melichar, Felix Petyrek, Karol Rathaus and Josef Rosenstock.

Meanwhile in Vienna, Elfriede Friedländer, her husband Paul Friedländer and brother Gerhart Eisler, established in 1918 the first Communist Party outside Russia. Elfriede and Gerhart were the elder siblings of the composer Hanns Eisler. The three Eislers, children of the noted Jewish philosopher and lexicographer Rudolf Eisler, had been antiwar activists in 1914, resulting in house searches and enforced conscription of both Gerhart and Hanns. Gerhart returned a decorated hero, whereas Hanns's service-record was more modest. Both had landed in non-German-speaking units so that they could not proselytise fellow conscripts with their Marxist beliefs.

With civil war still raging in Russia, political chaos was obstructing developments in both postwar Germany and Austria. With the Bolshevik Béla Kun on the rampage in Hungary and a 'Soviet Republic' declared in Bavaria, it was a miracle that Austria did not succumb to revolution. Nevertheless, the Communists moved in quickly. Elfriede Friedländer, following a jail sentence for initiating an armed occupation of the offices of the *Neue Freie Presse* in 1919, also joined the great migration to Berlin. Taking the name of her mother (her parents had not been married at the time of her birth) and her middle name, she became known (and later, notorious) as Ruth Fischer. At the invitation of local Berlin party activist Willi Münzenberg, she was soon leading the Communist Party, where many saw her as successor to Rosa Luxemburg, the Polish-born co-leader of the Spartacus League who had been murdered in January 1919.

Between the political extremes of the Marxist activist Ruth Fischer and the composer Franz Schreker were legions of politicians, intellectuals, artists and performers joining in a mass exodus from Vienna to Berlin: Hanns Eisler, Erich Kleiber, Fritz Kreisler, Fritz Lang, Lotte Lenya, Edmund Meisel (the composer for Sergei Eisenstein's 1925 film *Battleship Potemkin*), Georg Pabst, Max Reinhardt, Artur Schnabel, Arnold Schoenberg, Misha Spoliansky, Josef von Sternberg, Erich von Stroheim (though he first settled in the United States before moving to Berlin); Ernst Toch, Billy Wilder, and Alexander Zemlinsky. All saw Vienna as an impoverished city with no future. Many, like Meisel, Schnabel and Kreisler had relocated to Berlin much earlier. Others like Gál and Toch took up prominent positions in other German cities, though Toch moved to Berlin in 1929. Berg, Erich Korngold and Wellesz, along with the writers Karl Kraus and Hugo von Hofmannsthal, would simply commute. Berlin as a global centre was, according to Zweig, a fairly new concept, unencumbered by the traditions that weighed down Vienna.[11] Anton Kuh, self-confessed professional scrounger, cabaret artist and literary adversary to Karl Kraus, relocated to Berlin because he preferred being among other Viennese rather than the 'Kremsers' – citizens of the Lower Austrian town of Krems – whom Kuh holds up as the provincials who now blighted Vienna.[12]

The Musical Consequences of Change: Expressionism

Expressionism was the artistic movement that primarily defined the age before the war, but continued to be a potent force during and afterwards as well. Raoul Auernheimer, nephew of Theodor Herzl, wrote a useful explanation as well as a sarcastic brush-off of Expressionism in the *Neue Freie Presse* exactly 20 years before a notorious event took place that became known as the 'Expressionism Debate'. This debate carried out in the quasi-public forum of Communist émigré publications in German was primarily between the philosophers Ernst Bloch and Georg Lukás, but also involved the writers Bertolt Brecht and Alfred Kurella, as well as the composer Hanns Eisler. It was initiated following the support declared by the writer Gottfried Benn for Nazi criticism of Expressionism in 1933, and took place in 1937–8, at a time when Expressionism had already been overtaken by other modernist movements such as New Objectivity (discussed later in this chapter). The tone and length of the 'dialogue' in the Moscow-based émigré journal *Das Wort*[13] demonstrated not only the continued influence of Expressionism as a movement, but also its hold on artistic and intellectual circles. In the course of the increasingly doctrinaire and heated exchange, it paved the way to establishing a philosophical justification for what was becoming 'Socialist Realism'.

But Auernheimer's attack dated from 4 July 1918, a decade after Schoenberg's *Book of the Hanging Gardens* (1907) and *Erwartung* (1909), and six years after the most quintessentially Expressionist of musical works, *Pierrot Lunaire* (1912). It also came long after the 1908 suicide of the Expressionist artist Richard Gerstl. Nor is consideration given to the Expressionist movement *Der blaue Reiter*, founded by the painter Vassily Kandinsky in 1911, which was a continuation of Dresden's proto-Expressionist movement from 1905 called *Die Brücke*. If one takes 1905 as a starting point and the Lukás–Bloch debate in 1937–8 as its last gasp, Expressionism, no matter how it was understood, dominated the European cultural environment for nearly 35 years before flaring up again in numerous postwar exile compositions. That music should latch on to this movement before literature and theatre is a result of the painter Gerstl's direct influence on Schoenberg.

To understand how it was seen at the time, it is worth looking at extracts from Auernheimer's article. He begins as follows:

> There are quite a few myths being circulated about Expressionism these days – not only from this movement's literary and artistic leaders, but also from its most indoctrinated followers, not to mention the large number of camp followers who all hope that they won't find themselves left out. Yet nobody

really knows what to make of this dark, violent sounding word 'Expressionism' other than noting that it seemed to enter the German language around the same time as 'Bolshevism'.

An explanation of what Expressionism might mean was offered in a lecture given in Berlin by one of the movement's most fervent followers, the writer Kasimir Edschmid. It is about this lecture that Auernheimer writes, quoting Edschmid, that 'stagnation has been the state of things since Romanticism'.[14] Auernheimer deplores this generalisation and asks what happened to four generations of developments that included 'Naturalism', which the Expressionists call 'Impressionism'. He then goes on to write:

The young artists of today don't want to represent the world in the manner of artists in 1890. Instead, they would rather impose their own 'vision' created by emotion. They try and differentiate themselves from earlier exponents by insisting that 'the world is out there already and it would be pointless to repro- duce it'. They propose instead that the poet focus on 'creating something eternal'. Naturally, there is nothing to disagree with here, though they shouldn't argue that this idea only appeared as recently as December 1917. [. . .] What Edschmid calls the 'relationship with eternity' was already referred to in Goethe's day and then, a bit later, we came to recognise such ambitions as simply being part of 'human nature'. [. . .] From Edschmid's general intro- duction follow the specifics. Names are named and called out with the blissful partisanship that Expressionists see as their own rather endearing entitle- ment, as indeed it ever was with all youthful movements. Heinrich Mann leads in this particular dance; he's seen as some sort of 'head boy' within the Expressionist school, which is fairly amusing if one recalls that Heinrich Mann [. . .] is already 40 years old. For the Expressionists, however, he has reached the outer realms of human existence with one foot practically in the grave.[15]

Auernheimer goes on to name the authors on Edschmid's list of Expressionists: '[Frank] Wedekind, [René] Schickele, [Walter] Hasenclever, [Paul] Kornfeld, [Fritz] Unruh, [Alfred] Döblin, Georg Heym, [Franz] Werfel and [Georg] Trakl.'[16] All are significant German writers and he follows with intriguing observations regarding literature following art and the actual position of Expressionism vis-à-vis Impressionism:

Only music has not been touched by Expressionism, perhaps because music was always expressionist. But what the devil *is* Expressionism? Literally

translated, it is 'The Art that grows out of Expression'. Translating less literally, it appears to mean that it is that art which within expression seeks and
finds its own Ends. 'Feeling' is back to being the basis for everything, just like
in the days of the Romantics, and the youngsters today couldn't give a fig if
the worldly weight that they lug around within themselves has anything to
do with reality or not. The call of life doesn't register with them; rather they
harken only to the sound of their own warbling and twittering. They also
feel, not without some validation, that naturalistic art cannot be true to itself,
since it can only represent what nature has by chance placed together and
thus, the only thing that can be represented are objects without meaning.
Art, according to them, should not concern itself with the outward appearance which is constantly changing but the eternal inner truths which they
alone are able to translate. If left un-fashioned into art, these inner truths
remain mere philosophy. [. . .] The Expressionist is less concerned with
painting a person than *representing* a person and painting them 'as if they
wore their heart on the outer side of their breast'.[17]

The rest of the article dismembers the assumed uniqueness of the
Expressionist agenda ('wasn't *Sturm und Drang* just Expressionism in the
eighteenth century?') and its 'fatuous negation' of Naturalism-Impressionism,
a movement that Auernheimer defends using both Émile Zola and Gerhart
Hauptmann. Auernheimer concludes that artists have always tried to connect
to basic human emotions – it was ever thus: 'Goethe in conversation with
[Johann Peter] Eckermann once said, "Young people today seem to think that
alongside the black round centre of a target, there must be another that they
should aim for instead. They are wrong. There is only one bull's eye." This is
what the Expressionists, even with their new-fangled weapons, must still
discover for themselves.'[18]

Despite Schoenberg's reputation as the Expressionist composer *par excellence*, it is equally unsurprising that he would seek to impose some organisation onto the chaos that was starting to ensue. *Pierrot Lunaire* (1912), with its
Sprechgesang and darkly symbolic poetry, shows, with its use of passacaglia,
canon and other 'learned' compositional devices, signs of Schoenberg seeking
some sort of atonal order. Even at his most extreme, Schoenberg seemed to
yearn for the eighteenth-century musical Enlightenment in its search for
clarity, purity of form, and balance of construction.

The German composer James Simon also wrote on 'Expressionism in
Music' in *Musikblätter des Anbruch*. He starts by explaining how 'Impressionists
compress the world into the concept of "I", whereas Expressionists explode the
concept of "I" into the outer universe.'[19] Essentially, he agrees with many of

Auernheimer's points, though he views the movement more sympathetically. Simon points out that, with *Verklärte Nacht* (1899), Schoenberg started as an Impressionist before moving into Expressionism. The potential inference from reading Auernheimer and Simon (who was murdered in Auschwitz in 1944) is that Jewish intellectuals had good reason to be wary of Expressionism. With its relationship to Wagnerian Romanticism merely up-dated and drilled through with *angst*, it was moving away from the clear vision of rationality; Jewish intellectuals were instinctively uneasy with the irrational, a point that even comes across implicitly in the 'Expressionism Debate' of 1937–8.

Schoenberg's correspondence with Kandinsky is revealing for exactly this reason. Kandinsky had started to paint his first abstract works during 1908–9 at exactly the same time that Schoenberg felt he had broken through to achieve his own musical vision. In 1911 Kandinsky wrote an unsolicited but admiring letter to Schoenberg after hearing a performance of his music in Munich:

You have achieved in your compositions what I long for in less concrete form than music: the independence to walk towards one's own destiny. Your entire life is heard in the individual sounds of your music and reflects what I wish to show in my painting. Currently within the fine arts, there is a strong move towards construction as a means of finding a new 'harmony'. [...] My comprehension and efforts can subsequently only limp one step behind. Construction is exactly what the fine arts have so hopelessly lacked and it's marvellous that it's now being sought. Only, I think about the *way* things should be constructed.

Then, in a sentence that echoes Schoenberg's view from his *Harmonielehre* that composers needed to liberate themselves from merely providing conventional beauty or coherency, Kandinsky adds: 'I find that contemporary harmony shouldn't follow set geometrical pattern but rather strike out on an anti-geometrical, illogical path and this path is the equivalent of musical dissonance.'[20] Kandinsky made Schoenberg a member of *Der Blaue Reiter*, included some of his paintings in the group's first exhibition, and organised a performance in St Petersburg of *Pelleas und Melisande*, which the composer conducted.[21]

There followed a break in correspondence with Kandinsky returning to Russia and Schoenberg joining the Austrian army in 1914. After the war, just as Kandinsky became involved with the constructivist Bauhaus movement, Schoenberg developed his own constructivist system using the twelve-note method. Both artists had independently sought to restore order from the chaos of Expressionism. Kandinsky was keen for Schoenberg to come to Weimar, where he believed it would be possible to establish a musical branch of Bauhaus. Unfortunately, allegedly anti-Semitic remarks made by Kandinsky were reported to Schoenberg just as he was smarting from the racist indignities of Mattsee, an Alpine resort where he generally spent his summer vacation and which had begun to advertise the fact that it no longer welcomed Jewish holidaymakers. This combination of unhappy events initiated a break by Schoenberg in 1923, despite protestations of innocence by a mystified Kandinsky. There was only sporadic contact afterwards. Expressionism was thus a movement that by claiming to represent inner truth based on anarchic emotion was essentially nihilistic Romanticism. After Schoenberg, it had limited appeal to Jewish avant-garde composers.

Schreker, Expressionism and His Composition Pupils

One notable exception was Franz Schreker, whose music from the pyromaniac opera *Irrelohe* (1919–22) onwards began to develop beyond the sensually woven 'Jugendstil' textures of his earlier operas and became more abrasively dissonant. The title *Irrelohe* was taken from a railway station near Regensburg called Irrenlohe, which Schreker adapted for the name of his opera, roughly translated as 'Flames of Madness'. It was a transitional work that reflected his departure from Vienna and his arrival in Berlin. As such, it contains much that is redolent of his former musical world while exploring turbulent sounds and effects encouraged by the new. *Der Singende Teufel*,[22] composed between 1924 and 1928, is also readily classifiable as musical Expressionism, with a subject similar to Kleist's *Die Heilige Cäcilie oder die Gewalt der Musik*,[23] in which music stuns hordes of pagan Huns into submission. The more experimental *Christophorus, oder die Vision einer Oper*, composed between 1925 and 1929, brings to mind subjects as diverse *as The Sorcerer's Apprentice* and Thomas Mann's as yet unwritten *Dr Faustus*. *Christophorus* is dedicated to Schoenberg and, according to Schreker's biographer Christopher Hailey, owes much to Schoenberg's influence, with a musical language that pushes through the borders of conventional tonality.[24] It was rejected for publication by the usually supportive Universal Edition and remained unperformed during Schreker's lifetime.

Yet if Wellesz saw much in Berg's *Lulu* that reminded him of Schreker's *Der ferne Klang*, there is even more in *Christophorus* with its abrasive dissonances as orchestral colour and cinematic links between scenes that seem unthinkable without Berg's *Wozzeck* (though, intriguingly, that was not premiered until 1925). Schreker began composing *Christophorus* straight after *Irrelohe*, but only completed it much later, following a return to more familiar territory in *Der singende Teufel*.[25] By the time of his last opera, *Der Schmied von Gent*,[26] completed in 1932, Schreker had become a participant in the anti-Romantic Zeitgeist that defined much of the work of his students. Ernst Krenek's *Jonny spielt auf*, for example, had been given its premiere in Leipzig in 1927, then toured the world, launching an avalanche of similar *Zeitopern*, a genre of musical theatre that offered an ultra-contemporary setting and used an apparatus of modern acoustical artifices such as car-horns, radios, jazz bands, telephones, police sirens and so on. Many of the most successful Zeitopern were composed by Schreker's students, such as Max Brand's *Maschinist Hopkins* and Karol Rathaus's *Fremde Erde*,[27] both from 1930, and Mark Lothar's *Lord Spleen* in 1931. In February 1932, an opera by one of his brightest pupils, *Der gewaltige Hahnrei*[28] by Berthold Goldschmidt, admittedly more erotic-grotesque than Zeitoper, was first performed to great acclaim in Mannheim. Wilhelm Grosz, viewed by Julius Korngold as one of the most promising of potential Mahler successors[29] and whose *Sgarnarelle* (based on Molière) was given at the Vienna Opera in 1925, moved away from 'serious' music altogether to compose jazzy ballads, hit songs and dance numbers, including the theme-song for the film *The Santa Fe Trail*, starring Ronald Reagan.

Schreker's pupils from Vienna and Berlin are startling in their diversity. He instinctively took on individualists who would go their own way rather than follow his example. He treated pupils on individual merit, including several talented women such as Lotte Schlesinger, Zdenka von Ticharich, and Grete von Zieritz. His pupils, even more than Schoenberg's, are a roll-call of music in Weimar Germany. It is tantalising to speculate how such a group would have influenced future developments in German music had many of Schreker's most capable pupils not been forced into exile by the Nazis or, in some cases, openly collaborated with them, thus hindering their reception after 1945. As a result of the inevitable parricide that is common between gifted pupil and teacher, many of his most prominent students would distance themselves from Schreker as old-fashioned. With so much posthumous disparagement of Schreker, we can only surmise what he was like as a teacher on the basis of his remarkable class: unlike Schoenberg, he left no books or manuals behind.

Following Schoenberg's arrival as Busoni's successor at the Prussian Academy of Arts in 1925, thanks in part to Schreker's recommendation, Schreker's pupils took the conscious decision not to go down the twelve-tone route. Only Paul Pisk and Rudolf Kolisch – Schoenberg's future brother-in-law – studied with both. By choosing to study with Schreker, they showed an inclination to the trends within musical modernism represented by Stravinsky and the emerging voices of composers such as Hindemith and

Toch. Schoenberg, though seen as brilliant, was considered too doctrinaire for many independent, younger spirits of the age.

Apart from Schreker, who is finally starting to regain recognition, it appears the most memorable examples of musical Expressionism were by two non-Jewish composers: Alban Berg's operatic settings of Büchner's *Wozzeck* and Wedekind's *Lulu*, and Paul Hindemith's three short operas, *Das Nusch-Nuschi*, with a libretto by Franz Blei, *Sancta Susanna* and its libretto by August Stramm, and *Mörder, Hoffnung der Frauen*[30] written to a text by Expressionism's favourite wild-child, the artist Oskar Kokoschka. Jewish composers were showing a marked preference for an avant-garde that either adhered to well-defined laws, such as Schoenberg's twelve-note method, or, more frequently, the emerging *Neue Sachlichkeit* ('New Objectivity'), which represented developments that, though still broadly tonal, were anti-Romantic.

Ernst Krenek makes an interesting observation regarding Expressionist Jewish composers and atonality in his memoirs *Im Atem der Zeit*. In 1934, he founded a concert series called 'The Austrian Studio', the purpose of which was to show that modern music was something 'intrinsically Austrian' and not an affair relegated to (as he put it) 'subversive lefties and Jews'.[31] In a conversation regarding the programming of a liturgical concert with Dr Josef Lechthaler, the head of music within Austria's Catholic Church, Krenek is shocked by an observation which seemed at the time to enjoy wide currency: 'Alarmingly', according to Krenek, 'Lechthaler mentioned that it is no wonder the public is sceptical of new music in Austria, as it was atonal music "exclusively composed by Jews for Jews and therefore only purposeful in diverting 'an exotic minority'"'. Krenek, despite the overtly anti-Semitic founding principles of the Austrian Studio, is taken aback and answers that if this is the case, 'one should try to encourage non-Jews to listen to new music rather than disparage it. It's not right to blame the composer if only Jews attend performances of his works. In addition, it would be very simple to prove that concerts of modern music were attended by at least as many non-Jews as Jews.'[32] With regard to the other point, Krenek admits that he can only think of a single Jewish composer 'of the more dubious variety of atonal music: Arnold Schoenberg'. Lechthaler is surprised and tries to strengthen his argument by listing one atonal or twelve-tone composer after another, only to be informed by Krenek that they all come from generations of good Austrian Catholics.

Krenek was the son of a Czech army officer and a conservative Austrian Catholic monarchist. His implicit view that Jews could not be considered the same as 'Austrians' or 'Germans' confirms that even enlightened non-Jewish intellectuals sported casually anti-Semitic opinions at the time. Since 1933, he had been frequently and erroneously attacked as a Jew in the Nazi press. He subsequently expressed remorse for what he called his 'disgraceful' public protestations at these charges.[33] Indeed, his first two wives, Mahler's daughter Anna and the actress Bertha Haas, were both Jewish enough to fall foul of the Nuremberg laws.

By January 1931, there was no clear delineation of how modern music theatre was progressing. The following highlight some of the most important work chosen by the *Anbruch* editor Hans Heinsheimer for treatment:[34] Walter Braunfels speaks about his opera based on E. T. A. Hoffmann's *Prinzessin Brambilla*; Berthold Goldschmidt writes about his 'tragic-comedy' grotesque *Der gewaltige Hahnrei*; Hans Krasa (who would be murdered in Auschwitz in 1944) writes about his opera *Verlobung im Traum*, based on an amusing short-story by Dostoyevsky.[35] There are further articles by Alois Hába on his Moravian nationalist quarter-tone opera *Matka* (*The Mother*);[36] reviews of Manfred Gurlitt's reworking of the tale of girls from good families falling for soldiers and becoming prostitutes, based on Lenz's 1776 play *Soldaten*;[37] Karol Rathaus's contemporary opera *Fremde Erde* about the exploitation of financial refugees;[38] Janáček's *From the House of the Dead*, also based on Dostoyevsky;[39] Kurt Weill's opera for school-children *Der Jasager*;[40] Krenek's updating of the Orestes story in *Das Leben des Orest*;[41] Schreker writing on *Der Schmied von Gent*, which in January 1931 he was still calling *Smee und die sieben Jahre*,[42] and a revealing article by Herbert Windt – who became Leni Riefenstahl's composer of choice during the Third Reich – on the nationalist political nature of his opera *Andromache*.[43]

By 1930, the fad for Zeitoper had already peaked and was starting to give way to operas based on folktales and parables mixed with antiquity, often referred to in the press and elsewhere as the 'Bekenntnisoper' or 'operas of avowal'. As Windt unintentionally makes clear in his article on *Andromache*, this was the perfect cultural run-up to National Socialism with its Germanic chauvinism mixed with Hellenophilia. Prior to the premiere of Schreker's own 'Bekenntnisoper', *Der Schmied von Gent*, there was Wellesz's *Alkestis*, first performed at Mannheim in 1924, Pfitzner's *Das Herz* (1931), Herbert Windt's *Andromache* (1932), Weinberger's *Schwanda der Dudelsackpfeifer* (1928), Weill's *Die Bürgschaft* (1932), and Paul Graener's *Friedemann Bach* (1932). Though a number of these works were by Jewish composers, the move away from Zeitoper towards the simple rustic parable or warmed-over Hellenism was unmistakable. Schreker, in an attempt to combine what he had always done best with an appeal to contemporary tastes, seemed to critics to have cooked up a mixture of current modernism, re-packaged as a German religious morality play. Viktor Zuckerkandl's review of the new work did not make for pleasant reading:

> Schreker: the composer of distant sounds, music-box mysteries, grave diggers in the realms of pesky magic, maddening flames, and singing devils in operatic enclosures, friend of orgies and intoxication, this sworn enemy of the commonplace has decided [in his latest opera] to re-locate to Holland: the centre of portly conventional pleasures and everyday well-being. He exchanges his opium excesses for the more commonplace delights of beer and Edam cheese. The nervous haggard looks of his usual characters are now exchanged for well-rounded beer-bellies. Is this a change in his personality or has he been caught up by the spirit of the time? Probably a bit of both. Presumably continuous exaltation is even wearing for those who create it.[44]

Leaving Schreker's motivations to one side, Zuckerkandl dismisses the tonal language as mere 'paper music' and in a final flurry of journalistic mischief continues: 'nothing proves that the music so completely misses the point as the fact that with [baritone] Wilhelm Rode, we have the perfectly cast central character! What!? The great Wotan and Iago as a jolly pie-face provincial with a pot-belly!? Of course not! But since the music makes no concession to these particular characteristics, the singer doesn't need to pretend he possesses them.'[45]

The Musical Consequences of Change: Serialism

When Krenek referred to Schoenberg as the only Jewish composer of 'the more dubious variety of atonal music', he was simply stating what every musician at the time, including such reactionaries as Julius Korngold, already knew. Schoenberg was the supreme musical intellect and creative spirit of the age who towered well above his Austro-German contemporaries. His concept of twelve-tone composition ('serialism' or dodecaphonic composition) was an attempt to impose order onto the disorder that had grown out of a-tonal Expressionism. It was conceived in order to create new building blocks for Western music. Egon Wellesz, who at this time was intrigued by the sequences of modal tone-rows found in early Byzantine liturgical music, gave the following account of the development of Schoenberg's ideas:

> At this time [1917], I had an unusual encounter. A conscript wearing a filthy uniform reported to me and handed over a letter from the War Ministry. I

was asked to assess whether the bearer of this letter, a certain Josef Matthias Hauer, was insane or if he was truly a musician, a claim doubted by the military doctors. Truth be told, clothed in his dirty uniform with his eccentric manner, the soldier in question actually did make a curious impression. But the moment he started to explain his theory of composing using a system of twelve notes, I quickly noted that far from being deranged, he was extraordinarily inventive and potentially an important musician. I wrote a letter informing the authorities of my opinion and managed to secure a safe place for him as an office clerk. Several days later, Hauer appeared again with several of his compositions and began to re-explain how his theory worked.[46]

A childhood friend and important influence on Hauer was the Austrian Catholic philosopher Ferdinand Ebner, who not only wrote extensively about Hauer's music, but also published *The Word and Spiritual Realities* (*Das Wort und die geistigen Realitäten*) in 1921, resulting in him being seen as a Catholic Kirkegaard. And in fact Kirkegaard, along with the nihilist Jewish philosopher Otto Weininger, and the Bible, were Ebner's principal influences. *The Word and Spiritual Realities* would become a cornerstone of anti-clerical theology. Ethics at the start of the twentieth century were obviously not a uniquely Jewish preoccupation. But Schoenberg's declaration that the composer needed to be honest in listening to his inner voice was consistent with Ebner's more general philosophy relating to the 'I and thou' relationship between the inner ethical voice and the individual. Ebner, rather than being a 'Catholic Kirkegaard', had in truth written a Catholic extension of *Ich und Du*[47] by the Viennese Jewish philosopher Martin Buber which also explored the inner dialogue between God and the individual.

Wellesz dwells on the relationship between Ebner and Hauer, which, before coming to an end in 1920, had supplied Hauer with the terms of reference to describe melodies composed according to strict rules as 'nomos' or 'atonal Melos', which differentiated between the purity of unaccompanied melody and noise. In describing Hauer and his eventual break with Ebner, Wellesz goes on to write:

It was in fact quite difficult to have any sort of dialogue at all with Hauer. One was treated to dilettantish and arrogant monologues regarding his theories and their significance to mankind. Yet there was something valuable to be gathered when he ceased his preaching for a few moments and concentrated on how he built his system: The twelve-tone row was constructed from four groups [of notes], each consisting of three pitches. We know that this idea would be important to Schoenberg. When speaking of a-tonality, he explained that music that exists without consonance and dissonance can only be homophonic. When he showed me his twelve-tone compositions, he explained how important it was that the intervallic relationships between the different notes should only fluctuate gently. He then sang with great emotion his exceptionally simplistic melodies. Far more significant were his [later] piano works *Nomos 1*, *Nomos 2*, his choruses from the tragedies of Sophocles, and particularly his Hölderlin Songs.[48]

Wellesz told his friend and fellow Schoenberg pupil Rudof Réti about Hauer, and it was Réti who was responsible for finally bringing Schoenberg and Hauer together. Wellesz writes:

The meeting between Schoenberg and Hauer was a confrontation of two very different natures. Schoenberg's musical universe contained well-developed ideas on the melodic, harmonic and the contrapuntal components of composition in equal measure. At this point, Hauer was only interested in 'melos' constructed according to his system in which 'the same over-tones and the same sounds' were shared. [. . .] For Schoenberg, Hauer's formulas were merely the starting point that allowed him to develop his own thoughts regarding the practical construction of tone-rows. As the era's greatest master of counterpoint, it gave him the tool with which he could finally impose order on the construction of atonal music.[49]

Hauer and Schoenberg planned a jointly-written book on the subject, and Schoenberg programmed some of Hauer's piano works, performed by Réti, in one of his concerts at the Society for Private Performance. The difference in the two men's characters – and Hauer's suspicions of Schoenberg's motives – meant the book would never be written. Wellesz argued that the difference between Hauer and Schoenberg could be demonstrated by the following anecdote:

During the final years of his life, Hauer carried around flash-cards, each with a tone printed on it. He allowed friends and acquaintances to pick out cards randomly from which he constructed a melody which he then named after the person who had chosen the notes, such as, for example, the one he named after his post-man Pospischil. [. . .] In writing to his future brother-in-law, the violinist Rudolf Kolisch and leader of the Kolisch Quartet, Schoenberg explained that 'what is important in composition isn't *how* something is composed but *what* is composed! I've tried to explain this to Wiesengrund [Theodor Adorno], Berg and Webern, but they won't believe me. I can't repeat it often enough: my works are twelve tone *compositions*, not *twelve tone* compositions. In this, one confuses me again with Hauer for whom the actual composition is less important.' [50]

The Musical Chronicle of Change: *Anbruch*

With the end of the war in 1918, it was clear that society had changed. As early as 1905 the playwright and essayist Hans Müller was referring to *morbus Austriacus*.[51] By 1919, this had turned into a self-fulfilled prophecy. Universal Edition, publishers of such major figures as Mahler, Schoenberg, Zemlinsky, Schreker, Berg, Webern, Wellesz, Hauer, Bartók and Kodály, along with Casella, Janáček, Szymanowski, Weill, Eisler, Krenek, Milhaud and Malipiero, decided to launch a magazine devoted to new music symbolically entitled *Musikblätter des Anbruch (Music Leaves from a New Dawn)*. The 'Jewishness' of Universal Edition was described by Ernst Krenek:

> Fräulein Rothe (assistant to Director Emil Hertzka) was the only highly placed employee of UE who was not Jewish. Immediately under Director Hertzka was Dr. Kalmus, a relative of Hertzka's, if I'm not mistaken, and a good-natured oaf with lovely Old-Testament features. Peter Winter was the principal head of accounts, a fine, good-hearted person who was a genius in financial matters. [. . .] Among the many projects that UE supported was the monthly musical publication *Musikblätter des Anbruch*, an admittedly lame title that only made it clear that it was an artistic movement that wished to be called *Anbruch (Dawn –* a typically Expressionist term for 'beginning'), which was edited originally by Otto Schneider, a smooth roguish character who in all likelihood personified the revolutionary prototype of the coming age. I didn't much care for him.[52]

Theodor Adorno, Paul Pisk, Rudolf Réti and Paul Stefan were just some of the prominent Jewish musicians and thinkers who would join its editorial staff. The magazine's first issue in January 1919 starts with an introduction by Guido Adler, followed by articles on a variety of subjects by Béla Bartók, Frederick Delius, Oskar Fried, Hugo Kauder, Rudolf Hoffmann (one of the founding members of the Vereinigung schaffender Tonkünstler), Egon Lustgarten, Egon Wellesz, Rudolf Réti and Franz Schreker. As with the *Neue Freie Presse*, this was a publication that was dominated by assimilated, secular Jews and it quickly became one of the most influential musical chronicles of the period. It lasted for 19 years and 165 issues. Even more than its rival *Melos*, published by Schott, *Anbruch* (its title from 1929) would not so much reflect

Jewish assimilation as Jewish dominance in matters of new music. Seen in the context of a 70-year progression starting from Wagner's anti-Semitic pamphleteering of 1850, *Anbruch* appeared to represent the pinnacle of Jewish musical assimilation. The National Socialists, unsurprisingly, would see things differently and Universal Edition, along with *Anbruch*, would become Exhibit A in their propaganda campaign against the Jewish infiltration of German culture.

The Musical Consequences of Change: New Objectivity

The apocalyptic premonitions of Expressionism before the war, the horrors of the Front and the bewildering postwar reconstitution of European states resulted in a galvanising sobriety within the arts. One of the most prominent movements came to be known as *Neue Sachlichkeit*, or 'New Objectivity'. In common with *verismo*, its realist relative from the end of the nineteenth century, New Objectivity offered an unflinching presentation of reality. As it grew out of Expressionism, or more precisely as a reaction against it, the realism of the New Objectivity was intended to provoke a sense of discomfort and foreboding. In the visual arts, the influence of the Italian Futurists lent some of the best German *neusachlich* paintings a dream-like quality with stark shadows and eerie lighting.

Despite Busoni's 1907 *Sketch on a New Aesthetic of Music*, which predicted some of the ideas of Futurism, New Objectivity in music tended to eschew such mysterious and suggestive shades of light and grey, and pursued the black and white dispassionate ideals of mechanical precision. Under its broad umbrella of tonal, structured music composed as an anti-Romantic reaction against Expressionism, it included every conceivable form of technical experimentation. It was as defining musically of the Weimar Years as Bauhaus was within design and architecture. The most prominent exponents of its purest form were undoubtedly Hindemith – something of an *enfant terrible* at the time – and the more sedate Ernst Toch, though Weill and most of Schreker's composition pupils (including Krenek) were also willing participants. New Objectivity attempted to distance music from the subjectively poetic, and even in Schoenberg's circle – with its leaning towards Expressionism – there was discussion of the concept of 'musical prose'. Alban Berg and Erwin Schulhoff – who as a pianist was a valued interpreter of Berg's Piano Sonata Op. 1 – corresponded extensively on the subject, with Berg writing that 'we have long stopped regarding bar lines as a means of enchaining melody and phrasing; just look at my early clarinet works, or the later works of Schoenberg – all could be performed without any time signatures at all.'[53]

Similar developments were already under way in the Soviet Union, but in Germany and Austria, New Objectivity included diverse permutations, such as the musical wing of 'Die Novembergruppe, a loose organisation that took its name from the German Revolution of November 1918 and consisted of the composers Max Butting, Hanns Eisler, Philipp Jarnach, Heinz Tiessen, Wladimir Vogel, Kurt Weill and Stefan Wolpe; the journalist and musicologist H. H. Stuckenschmidt, several Schreker pupils, and the violinist Gustav Havemann. New Objectivity also encompassed everything from the Communist fight songs of Hanns Eisler to the Zeitoper. Eventually it accommodated the theatre songs of Weill and Paul Dessau; to these could be added the Dadaist dalliances of Stefan Wolpe and the jazz flirtations of Schulhoff and Wilhelm Grosz. What passed as Neo-Classicism in Germany and Austria could more appropriately be described as New Objectivity. Incidental music for the theatre was re-christened 'applied music' (*angewandte Musik*) and now included scores for cinema and radio. New Objectivity also provided an aesthetic home for some of the kookier experiments with sound machines, propellers, turbines, generators and strange new instruments, as well as offering space to the social ambitions of 'functional music' – *Gebrauchsmusik* and its constant companion, the *Lehrstück* (Brechtian works intended to offer political 'instruction'), in which the barriers between performers and listeners were often torn down.

Ernst Toch, the New Objectivist

In the midst of all this energetic exuberance stood a rather austere figure, almost forgotten today, who alongside Hindemith was one of the prime exponents of the age: Ernst Toch. Toch was older than Hindemith and was arguably more established as a composer by the end of the war. He thus offers a clearer image of what went into the psychology that shaped New Objectivity. With Hindemith, it is more difficult to say whether he shaped the movement through his boundless youthful creativity or if the movement shaped him. Toch, on the other hand, grew into it through a sequence of carefully considered steps. Interestingly, both Toch and Hindemith produced similar artistic responses, having approached them from very different directions.

Though Toch maintained that he was basically self-taught, he had studied – like so many other Viennese composers – with Robert Fuchs; indeed, he was only 16 when Fuchs accepted him into his harmony class. Toch's first quartet was taken up by the prestigious Rosé Quartet when he was 18. Originally he was a student of philosophy and medicine at Vienna's

University before winning a scholarship in 1909 to study composition in Frankfurt, entering its Conservatory the same year as Hindemith.

Toch's musical relationship with Vienna was unique. He recalled that his resolve to become a composer came to him when, as a boy, he heard a newspaper vendor announce the death of 'the composer Johannes Brahms' in 1897. Until then, he hadn't realised that it was even possible to be a composer. His family disapproved of his musical interests (they refused even to attend the Rosé premiere of his quartet), and he remained isolated and largely unaware of, indeed impervious to, the intoxicating sound-world of the musical developments represented by Mahler, Schoenberg, Zemlinsky and Schreker. Years later, when listening to Mahler's symphonies, Toch admitted that all he could hear were obvious compositional errors.

Following graduation in Frankfurt, Toch moved to Mannheim, where he taught the piano until – in a fit of patriotic fervour – he joined the Austrian army at the outbreak of war. His music, until his return after 1918, was pleasantly Brahmsian, its inoffensiveness sharpened slightly by the obvious influence of Reger, with whom he was in correspondence until Reger's death in 1916. If Julius Korngold could describe the early music of Schreker as 'tame', he would have referred to Toch's first works as 'timid'.

Much of Toch's music from this period is exceptionally appealing, but rarely can a musical personality have diverged so markedly as did the prewar and postwar Toch. While Julius Korngold implied that Schreker's change in style was due to opportunism, Toch's was due to witnessing the horrors of battle and the belief that, with the fall of the old order, everything needed to change. His exquisitely crafted works from before the war now seemed inappropriate. Like so many others, he saw no future in Austria, and his patriotism turned to indifference, if not outright disdain. He moved back to Mannheim, since German law compelled Austrian citizens to return to where they had lived prior to 1914. During 1919 both Toch and Hindemith took a sobering turn towards New Objectivity.

In 1921, Prince Max Egon zu Fürstenberg founded what would become the first of many new music festivals in interwar Germany in the Black Forest town of Donaueschingen. Hindemith's Third Quartet Op. 16 was given its premiere during the festival's inaugural season in 1921, and Hindemith became Artistic Director of chamber concerts until a falling out with Fürstenberg meant relocating activities to Baden-Baden. With the performance of Toch's Op. 26 quartet by the Amar Quartet (in which Hindemith played viola) in 1922, Toch also became a regular feature in Donaueschingen and Baden-Baden. By the early 1920s, both Toch and Hindemith had produced a bolder reaction to the sobering spirit of the age than was the case in art, theatre or literature, which were still largely caught up in the dying throes of Expressionism.

In 1925, an exhibition at Mannheim's Kunsthalle called 'The Art of Post-Expressionism: New Objectivity' was the first time that the style in which Hindemith and Toch had been composing was given a name, though in reference to the visual arts, and it was curated by Toch's friend Gustav Friedrich Hartlaub, director of the Kunsthalle. In 1924, Toch established a Society for New Music which would place Mannheim at the forefront of contemporary music in the 1920s – a position it maintained until 1933.

From 1922 onwards, no new-music festival seemed complete without something by Toch. In 1927, the *New York Times* printed a portrait of Toch together with Bartók in an article on new music in Germany;[54] and in 1930, another large portrait and article on Toch and Hindemith appeared in the same paper.[55] In 1932, the *New York Times* covered the performance of Toch's Piano Concerto No. 1 and a recital of his music.[56] These American reports of Toch were as nothing compared with the extensive coverage of his music in Germany during the same period. By 1929, Toch and his wife had abandoned Mannheim for a large villa in one of Berlin's greenest and plushest suburbs, where he began writing a steady stream of music for stage, radio and screen.

Why is Hindemith's music familiar to us today and Toch's largely forgotten? At the heart of this question, there are both aesthetic and practical factors. By the early 1930s, Toch had not composed nearly as much music as Hindemith, nor was he as skilled at self-promotion as his indefatigable younger colleague. Hindemith's enthusiasm for controversy and 'bad-boy' creativity would ultimately land him in trouble, first because he was too eager to find an accommodation with the Nazis in 1933, and then because the Nazis didn't want to have anything to do with him after Hitler objected to his comic Zeitoper *Neues vom Tage*,[57] in which a nude soprano sings an aria about central heating while lying in the bath. This messy chapter in Hindemith's life left him morally and ethically compromised.

Toch, on the other hand, arrived in the United States in 1933 with publication of his music in the hands of the American affiliate of his German publisher Schott, and also, thanks to the friendship of George Gershwin, membership of the American Society of Composers, Authors and Publishers (ASCAP), which allowed him to collect royalties from performances. Things looked very bright for the newly arrived refugee and his family until ASCAP's rival BMI bought up Toch's American publisher, resulting in a ruthless suppression of ASCAP composers. These were issues that Hindemith, arriving in the United States in 1940, managed to avoid by joining BMI from the outset. Unlike Hindemith, Toch had countless Jewish relatives who needed help emigrating from Austria. He had little choice but to go to Hollywood in order to earn as much as possible to secure the necessary affidavits. Hindemith became a professor of composition at Yale and was not to experience the sort of compositional hiatus that resulted from Toch's obligations to produce music by the yard for Hollywood studios.

After freeing himself from the movie industry after the Second World War, Toch embarked on a frenzy of composing in an attempt to recapture the prewar successes of works such as his Cello Concerto (first performed by Emanuel Feuermann in 1925) and First Piano Concerto of 1926. With performances of this work by the likes of Walter Gieseking with Wilhelm Furtwängler and the Berlin Philharmonic – and the premiere on 20 August 1934 at the London Promenade Concerts of his Second Piano Concerto with the composer as soloist and conducted by Sir Henry Wood – Toch seemed to have joined the European mainstream before Hindemith. Like his near contemporary Wellesz, he must have been seen by younger composers as an elder statesman of the international new-music circuit. During these years, Toch enjoyed a reputation that was nearly as exalted as Schoenberg, and his book on the construction of melody, *Melodielehre* (1923), was hailed as a companion to Schoenberg's *Harmonielehre*. (Schoenberg himself, already propagating his twelve-tone theory, neither greeted the arrival of *Melodielehre* nor acknowledged any connection.) *Melos*, Schott's answer to Universal Edition's *Anbruch*, unsurprisingly banged the drum for their house composer who, as a performer, enjoyed the additional prestige of a contract with the piano manufacturer Blüthner. The pianist and teacher Eduard Beninger in the February 1928 issue praises the First Piano Concerto in terms that tell us as much about the context of New Objectivity in which Toch was composing as it does about the work itself: 'The qualities which I wish to highlight in Toch's piano works, apart from their harmonic freedom, are the successful implementation of large cyclic structures; lack of expressive shades of light and colour; reduction of the overloaded chord and an underpinning of the piano's intrinsic neutral character by way of motorised performance technique.'[58]

As if to snatch away the last vestiges of Schoenbergian thunder, Toch even took the idea of *Sprechgesang* and developed it into something brilliantly mischievous with his three pieces for spoken chorus from 1930 entitled *Gesprochene Musik* (*Spoken Music*), which included the still famous *Fuge aus der Geographie*, or *Geographical Fugue*, translated into English by Henry Cowell and a bedazzled John Cage, who had heard its premiere in Berlin.

In public, Toch was serious and withdrawn. Berthold Goldschmidt, in conversation with the author, recalled that whenever Toch appeared at any of the new-music festivals in Germany, he seemed the very personification of the modern composer. Unbeknown to Goldschmidt, the photographer August Sander, while working on a highly regarded series of genre photos from the interwar years, chose Toch as the model for his representation of 'The Composer'.

Like Hindemith and Weill, Toch was not particularly taken with the idea of atonal or dodecaphonic music. In any case, by the mid-1920s, some of the extremes that had convulsed music had settled into the newly defined diatonic homes offered by Neue Sachlichkeit. Toch's ambition was rather to find ways of incorporating unresolved dissonances within his music without tonal derailment.

His ethical sense was as strong as Schoenberg's, as can be seen in his writings, letters and essays where we come closer to encountering the real Toch. He corresponded with nearly everyone involved in contemporary music during his lifetime and wrote countless essays, many apparently not intended for publication but meant as a means of sorting out his own thoughts. He often wrote these in German and translated them into English, perhaps as exercises to be kept alongside stacks of notebooks filled with lists of English synonyms and their German equivalents. Such essays were full of bitter sarcasm and often had intriguing titles such as *Die Germanen sind Blond* (*The Teutons Are Blond*). He also kept a 'dream journal' in which we find the confused synthesis of his present life in Los Angeles and his past. He reports dreams of being visited by rabbis and relatives from Austria, and his mortification that they have no understanding of how to behave in American society.

Toch was raised in a traditional Jewish home and it appears that his spiritual life was quite different from that of his practical wife Lili (née Zwack), the daughter of a wealthy banker. Contradictions abound between Toch's private letters and essays and his wife's 'oral history' housed at the University of Southern California in Los Angeles. If she mentions Judaism at all, it's not in relation to her own family which was apparently secular. Despite the murder of her sister in a Nazi camp, she expresses no feelings for either the religion or its domestic and social traditions. Toch is very different: even though he refused to allow himself to be pinned down as a traditional, devout Jew, he composed a number of works in exile based on Jewish subjects such as the 'Covenant' movement from the multi-composer *Genesis* Suite,[59] his *Cantata of the Bitter Herbs*, written in memory of his mother who died just before Austria's annexation by Nazi Germany, or his Fifth Symphony, subtitled *Jephtha*. His essay *Glaubensbekenntnis eines Komponisten* (*Composer's Credo*) from March and April 1945 is profoundly ethical, even spiritual:

Today there is a tendency to believe that science, in the fullness of time, will be able to explain everything. In the future, there will be no more mysteries – neither in nature nor within our inner lives. Thus would effectively be removed the need for what we generally refer to as 'religion'. But it wasn't mere ignorance of scientific triumphs that often resulted in many of the most brilliant academic and artistic minds also being believers. Indeed, it was especially these individuals who were increasingly aware of the mystery of a spiritual presence that resides within and around us. This recognition of religion has almost nothing to do with a specific church. Instead, it comes closer to the devotion found within ancient cultures that saw every event, whether happy or sad, as being enigmatically linked with human destiny. It was called yielding-up to life in the fullest sense of the word. And though science attempts to bore ever deeper while analysing the discoveries it makes, it is specifically within this border-region of the human spirit that the arts thrive. And in this region, music thrives even more than the others. [. . .] The true nature of art, which comes from religious depth and naivety, is both un-teachable and un-learnable. *This is what makes great art neither modern nor old-fashioned but timeless.* [. . .] In the past couple of decades we have seen the production of much music that both excited our interests and stimulated our wits. We discovered and gained a great deal. But at the same time, we lost something. Perhaps it will be a while before we even notice that it's missing, but in due course it will become obvious. And this 'something' is simply too important to do without. As fed up with Romanticism as we eventually became, one should not forget the basic fact *that music, in its innermost makeup, is de facto romantic.* And if sentimentality has no place in true art, we should never forget that sentimentality should not be confused with emotion. [. . .] The continued rejection of modern music comes not from our unquestioned lack of respect for it, but from our inability to love it. One usually cites atonality as the reason for this. This is of course nonsense. The development of our tonal language is natural, logical and inevitable. It cannot represent a destruction of the old but an enrichment of the new. [. . .] Atonality cannot be held responsible for what a composer wishes to express. [. . .] If the music of our century is unable to satisfy our needs as in the past, then one should not hold the technical aspects of the work's construction responsible. Rather, it is within the spiritual that one needs to look.[60]

Though this essay dates from 1945, it offers a reflection of the musical values that characterised New Objectivity and ultimately amounts to its rejection by one of its most high-profile protagonists. Reading both *Melos* and *Anbruch* in the interwar years, the impression is that the musicians and thinkers who cleaved most firmly to New Objectivity felt the need to accord music a sense of scientific legitimacy so that it could be seen as a dynamic tool in the shaping of post-1919 society – a misappropriation that would be repeated with some variation by the post-1945 avant-garde. Toch was only one of many composers in the interwar years who tried to compensate for the lack of empirical scientific evidence that music had to offer. His *Melodielehre* is highly technical and it attempts to draw conclusions and extrapolate methods where, apart from counterpoint, hardly any had previously existed.

The postwar years of both 1919 and 1946 shared common objectives characterised by the belief that through alienating human responses to music, mankind and the human condition could be lifted out of the romantic and irrational stupor that had led to the follies of war. This is symbolised in an undated postcard from Hindemith to Toch regarding the preparation of a film music event (presumably Baden-Baden's film music festival in 1928): Hindemith asks if Toch's composition will be requiring 'machines or musicians', a juxtaposition of opposing concepts. My translation uses 'musicians' to illuminate some of the alliterative irony conveyed by Hindemith's 'mechanisch oder menschlich', which sums up the ethos of *neue Sachlichkeit* by offering the alternative, more general translation of: 'will you be requiring mechanisation or humanity?'[61]

CHAPTER 7

Hey! We're Alive!

We believe that it is specifically the un-Romantic character of our era that
encourages the Art that one day could provide expression to those great events
taking place during our time.
... wir glauben, daß gerade dieser unromantische Charakter unserer Epoche die
Entstehung einer Kunst befördert, die zum Ausdruck jener großen Ereignisse
werden könnte, welche sich in unseren Tagen abspielen.

Kurt Weill, *Romantik in der Musik*, 1929

The Political Science of Music

'Wissenschaft' or 'science' as a suffix became a useful means of establishing
academic credibility in disciplines far removed from the physical and natural
sciences. With its mathematical permutations, much of the arcane fascination
with dodecaphony arose because it appeared to bring music closer to
'Wissenschaft'. A cursory glance down the index of 'scientific' articles found
in *Melos* and *Anbruch* only confirms how involved Jewish critics, writers and
musicians were in the process of making music rational and subject to empirical evaluation. Most of these writers would later be included in the notorious
Lexikon der Juden in der Musik compiled by the eminent Nazi 'Music
Scientists' Theo Stengel and Herbert Gerigk. Most of *Anbruch*'s Jewish 'music
scientists' had left their religious beliefs behind in the drive towards assimilation, and having jettisoned one set of 'irrational' beliefs, were unwilling to take
on another. Only a few of the major figures did so: Walter Braunfels and Egon
Wellesz, for instance, both became devout Catholics and many of their works
from the interwar years (and afterwards) reflect this. Viktor Ullmann became
a follower of Rudolf Steiner's Anthroposophy movement, which believed

in a quasi-pantheistic interaction between mankind and nature but also that spiritual experience could be subjected to the same objective criteria as physical and natural sciences. Much of Ullmann's work, notably his operas *Der Sturz des Antichrist* and *Der Kaiser von Atlantis*,[1] attempts to convey these complex ideas. Other composers, such as Toch and Weill, simply put the devotional life they had acquired during childhood into a drawer, taking it out now and again for personal use and occasional reflection.

The vast majority of secular Jewish composers and writers, however, were resolutely anti-religion: Korngold and Schreker are examples of composers who did not actively practise religion but wrote music that was deeply spiritual within its own terms. Those who turned to 'New Objectivity', such as Hanns Eisler, could often be militantly anti-spiritual but profound believers when it came to Communism, the secular alternative to both Judaism and Christianity, and providing a belief system as dogmatic as any formal confession. Marxist terms such as 'dialectical materialism' offered young believers the twin advantages of religious mystery and satisfyingly 'scientific' weightiness. In a deliberate attempt to draw parallels with religion, Eisler's secular cantatas and *Lehrstücke* were consciously modelled on Bach's cantatas and passions. Eisler, along with Paul Dessau and others, wrote 'secular hymns', or 'fight-songs', for Communist pageants and rallies which challenged anything conventional religion could offer. It comes as no surprise that the other great secular cult of the age, National Socialism, hijacked some of Eisler's most trenchant melodies. Young believers who had previously struck out Leftwards towards the new dawn promised by Marx now set off in the opposite direction, singing the same heart-pounding tunes with different words.

The growth of these secular religions did not happen in a vacuum. Prewar middle-class prosperity had created an entrenched and resentful underclass of urban and rural poor. To this was added the casual racism towards different nationalities that were in practice accorded second- or even third-class citizen status. The dynastic houses of Europe, supported by their established churches, saw in these disenfranchised masses cheap labour and plentiful cannon-fodder.

The World as Viewed by Max Nordau

The Austrian Zionist philosopher Max Nordau, who gave us the term 'degenerate' to describe the condition of both society and culture, wrote lengthy end-of-year summaries of the political and social state of the world, which from 1897 until 1915 appeared annually in Vienna's *Neue Freie Presse*. Dipping into these, we see how events were unfolding in a way that neither nations nor governments could be expected to control. Nordau's article from 1 January 1901 is remarkable in its casual racism as he cites the need for new markets in order to purchase the over-production of Europe. To this end he writes: 'The Chinese, like other coloured races, must finally be forced into facing the subjugation of the rest of non-whites if the superiority of the European people is not to be proved an embarrassing, anthropological mistake.'[2]

By the following year (1 January 1902) we have a run-down of the social changes occurring thanks to the emergence of a financially powerful mercantile class that demands greater democratic returns. Nordau elaborates at length on the vested interests and hypocrisy of the land-owning aristocracy and the church, exposing their twisted arguments for maintaining a feudal and greedy status quo. Nordau's Zionism was a result of the Dreyfus affair and he is merciless in his denouncement of the Catholic Church, which he calls a power as dark as that of Tsarist Russia. He accuses the church of resorting to the basest of instincts in order to maintain its grip on the European peoples: 'clericalism in France uses patriotism as a means of stirring up anti-Semitism by having those with little resent those believed to have more. French clericalism promotes patriotic bravery and courage as a means of appealing to national vanity and thus manages to associate the authority of Rome, without the slightest doctrinal basis, to France's own glorious past. This results in a state of suspicion and unease amongst the masses and encourages the seeking of continuous revenge for perceived injustices and slights.'[3]

Finally, on 1 January 1914 we reach the year in which the world would change with the eruption of the Great War. Nordau gives us his view of British imperialism and accuses Sir Edward Grey of

> disregarding the rights and aspirations of the nations. He blithely sells out the island-dwelling Greeks to the Turks, the Armenians to the Persians, the Mongolians to the Russians and congratulates himself for keeping the peace at such a low price. Mind you, he only calls it peace as long as the big nations don't start to cross swords and drag England into the fray. He doesn't lose any sleep as long as it's only small countries that break each other's necks, and the raping and pillaging doesn't interfere with rail and sea routes.

He goes on to expound on the social changes cited twelve years earlier as Lloyd George attempts to reclaim land held by aristocratic families, by decree if necessary. This has resulted in 'feudalistic lords feeling under such pressure that they are selling their land before it can be taken away, with the recent sale of Covent Garden Market by the Duke of Bedford to Mr Mallaby-Deeley for three million pounds only being the most sensational.'[4]

Nordau's ruminations on contemporary events offer a view of the social evolution taking place in the run-up to the First World War. They are the thoughts of an educated, middle-class, secular Jewish European. Born a German-speaking Hungarian, he considered himself Austrian but lived by choice in Paris. He was a medical doctor by profession and a clinical thinker with a firm conviction in both physical and social evolution. Though his ideas regarding 'Entartung' or 'degeneration' would later be appropriated in part by the Nazis, it was the institutional anti-Semitism demonstrated by the Dreyfus affair that ultimately made the militantly secularist Nordau into one of the leaders of the Zionist movement. His lengthy year-end interpretations of events add meat to the bones of empirical statistics and demonstrate that the duopoly of the church and ruling families was heading for a spectacular and utterly predictable end.

The ambitions and entitlements of the rising middle classes could no longer be ignored. The threats to this rapidly developing demographic came not only from the unravelling of the nobility. Despite the annihilation of the aristocracy during the Bolshevik Revolution, Marxists aimed their anger principally at the bourgeoisie who, with their newly acquired wealth, were seen as replacing the absolute power that was once feudal. The proletariat was left just as disenfranchised as before. Even without modern communication technology, it was clear to working people that they had been used as pawns during the Great War, thus providing grist to revolutionary mills. That many young Jews would be prominent among them should come as no surprise given the measures taken by the churches in defence of a defunct dynastic order.

The Eislers

The futility of any war in which only the old orders, along with the self-aggrandising middle classes, stood to gain, tipped the balance in favour of the social subversion that defined the family of Hanns Eisler. Charlie Chaplin, Eisler's friend in postwar Hollywood, described the ruthlessness of the Eisler siblings as coming out of one of Shakespeare's histories. Hanns Eisler's use of music as a 'political weapon' would be a defining element in Weimar Germany. Many from the political centre and right would claim that Eisler's music was a factor in this shaky German Republic becoming unstable, even ungovernable. An Eisler family time-line from the end of the nineteenth century to the middle of the twentieth helps to clarify Hanns Eisler's unique contribution, and what many saw as an unnatural union of political doctrine and music.

Rudolf Eisler, father of Hanns, was a Jewish philosopher, essayist and lexicographer who married Ida Maria Fischer, a Protestant with whom he had been living while finishing his doctorate in Leipzig. In order to maintain the appearance of working-class origins, their three children would always describe their mother from Saxony as 'proletarian', though this statement is slightly off the mark: she was an 'irregular' student at Leipzig's university (the only option available to women at the end of the nineteenth century). Her family was militantly socialist and she was published locally as an essayist, journalist and poet. Her father was in the business of distributing meat products to Leipzig's butchers, resulting in her children referring to her as a 'butcher's daughter'. Hanns later remarked that his parents met at a fair when his mother sold his father a sausage. Rudolf Eisler came from a wealthy family of Jewish merchants who disapproved of the relationship but accepted their eventual marriage, following the birth in 1895 of their first child Elfriede, who later became Ruth Fischer (discussed in the previous chapter). The family relocated to Vienna, settling in the city's comfortable Third District before circumstances forced a move to the Second, the so-called 'Matzos Quarter', where most of Vienna's working-class Jews lived. Rudolf had been denied a permanent position at Vienna's university, not, as often stated, because he was a Jew, but because of his openly declared atheism.

The children's reminiscences of home life seem surprisingly mundane for a family of future revolutionaries: music within the Eisler family was provided by Rudolf, who played the upright piano in the sitting room while singing all of the roles of entire operas and operettas. Gerhart and Hanns pretended to be figures from the Nibelungen Saga, with Elfriede as a serviceable Brünnhilde. The conductor and childhood friend of Hanns Eisler, Jascha Horenstein, recalled his class-mate as badly dressed, already bald at the age of 13, and only interested in soccer.[5] Hanns's school reports would seem to bear this out, with poor grades in all subjects except sport. That the Eisler children would become some of the most dynamic personalities in interwar Europe owes much to the Viennese secular-Jewish domestic life provided by their poor but fiercely intelligent parents.

As Ruth Fischer, Elfriede Eisler rose to the top of the German Communist Party, only to be expelled by Stalin for being too radical. She was imprisoned in Moscow for a short period before making her way to Paris, where she became an active anti-Stalinist with Trotsky, staying one step ahead of Soviet death-squads. Her lover and fellow Trotskyite, Arkadi Maslow, was not so lucky, meeting a mysterious end in Havana while awaiting his American visa. Elfriede-Ruth Fischer, fearing for her life after Trotsky's murder and the death of Maslow, suspected her American-based brothers of treachery, believing that they were the only people who knew of Maslow's whereabouts. By this point, she too was resident in the United States, firing off scholarly, anti-Stalinist publications for Harvard University. She publicly denounced her brothers Hanns and Gerhart as Soviet spies, leading to their arrest and, in the case of Hanns, ultimately to his enforced removal, which amounted to deportation in all but name.

Gerhart, who had been a genuine Communist agent, living under a false name, escaped as a stowaway on a Polish freighter before making his way back to the Soviet sector of occupied Germany. As a German returning from the West, and as the brother of Ruth Fischer, he was considered as suspect by the paranoid Stalinist regime and placed in custody. Only the death of Stalin in 1953 saved Gerhart from a show trial and possible execution. Ruth meanwhile continued her work as an expert on Stalinist affairs at Harvard until she found herself in the sights of the anti-Communist Senator, Joseph McCarthy. She avoided arrest by returning to Paris, where she lived until her death in 1961.

Gerhart went on to become a leading broadcaster in East Germany and, during his final years, even joined the Central Committee of the German Democratic Republic. He died as a highly regarded party functionary in 1968 while on holiday in Yerevan. Both of Hanns's elder siblings were audacious believers in Marxism and were both activists and propagandists.

Hanns Eisler

It is impossible to understand Hanns fully as the composer who attempted to reconcile music with political activism without knowing these essential facts about his family. His enforced removal from America in 1948 offers a well-documented account of the remigration of a returning composer from exile. His destination was the newly formed German Democratic Republic, for which he composed the National Anthem – though his first intentions had been to return to Vienna. American black-listing, however, barred him from working outside the city's Soviet sector, and as a former Schoenberg pupil he was unable to find an academic position in Austria, which had stuck to a remorseless musical conservatism following the mass exodus of Viennese progressives to Berlin after the First World War.

Though he kept an address in Vienna until 1953, his eventual move to East Berlin could be understood as one made reluctantly. His Marxist wife Louise, with aristocratic Jewish, Austro-Hungarian lineage, disliked the Stalinist incarnation of Communism and after 1953 refused to join him, eventually marrying one of their closest friends, the prominent Austrian Communist Ernst Fischer. Eisler's musical output broadly falls into four distinct periods, with consistent stylistic elements common to all. The first period goes up to his break with his teacher Schoenberg in 1922–3 and the complete rupture between the two men that ensued in 1926. At this time he moved into 'agitprop', a genre which he more or less established single-handedly in Germany; there then follows the music of exile, and finally the music of remigration which not only quietly echoed his agitprop and exile years with copious scores for stage and screen, but required him to conform to the conditions imposed by the new state with which, for better or worse, he had now become so closely identified.

Eisler's poor school reports gave no indication of the brilliance of his mind, or the penetrating insight of his writing. After Wagner, few musicians had written so extensively and incisively on such a wide variety of social and political issues. As with Wagner, the socio-political component of Eisler's writings nearly outweighs his thoughts on music. He was contrary both as composer and as a person, seemed to enjoy his many contradictions, and frequently referred to them. For example, he saw the contradiction of being a twelve-tone composer, despite the fact that few prominent composers viewed as 'Jewish' apart from Schoenberg chose to take up what most found an isolating musical language with limited popular resonance.[6] Most of Eisler's serial works, however, provide an immediate point of contact with the listener while avoiding any sense of tonal dislocation commonly found in Schoenberg and most of his adherents. Other works are in a richer, post-Romantic style, though Eisler vehemently rejected any suggestion that music could go beyond the immediately rational. He simply did not believe that Wagner's 'German spirit' could be the source of great art.

Through all these contradictions and disparate styles, one element remains constant: his desire to communicate without musical impediments. His break with Schoenberg came about because he felt his teacher's output had isolated itself from the common man. He satirised the idea of *l'art pour l'art* in his *Pierrot Lunaire* epigone *Palmström* (1924), and again in his 1925 *Zeitungsausschnitte* (*Newspaper Clippings*), in which he takes personal announcements from a daily paper along with an assortment of provocative short poems, setting them as atonal art-songs.

Eisler's arrival in Berlin and his participation in agitprop theatre – his collaborations with the charismatic agitprop performer Ernst Busch and the writers around Bertolt Brecht, to say nothing of his frequent collaborations with Brecht himself – took his music in a new direction. An Eisler 'fight-song', with its four-square march-rhythms, was meant to be sung at rallies and be instantly memorable. Incidental songs from stage works were allowed more harmonic and melodic sophistication, but did not sacrifice immediacy. His magnum opus, the *Deutsche Sinfonie* (1930–59), along with many of his secular cantatas, are twelve-tone works, yet their musical language is neither alienating nor any more demanding than tonal works from the same period by Shostakovich or Prokofiev. In keeping with his contradictory tendencies, one of Eisler's most notable serial works, the quintet *Vierzehn Arten den Regen zu Beschreiben* (*Fourteen Ways of Describing the Rain*) composed in 1941, and dedicated to Schoenberg on his 70th birthday in 1944, was far removed from his customary aim of approachability. It is exquisitely refined and febrile in character. As an act of reconciliation with his former teacher, it was warmly appreciated and Eisler was proud of Schoenberg's grateful and complimentary remarks, though he admitted that it might be generations before the general public would be able to appreciate its beauty.

Eisler's album of songs composed in exile, later entitled the *Hollywood Songbook*, contains settings that cover all his compositional styles. Today it has become common practice for a selection of some 40 of these to be presented as a 'cycle'. The only cyclical thing about them is their multi-layered narrative of exile. The majority of the texts are by Brecht, but Eisler includes other writers such as Rimbaud and Hölderlin. We shall return to Eisler later, but his contribution to interwar musical life and his creation of 'agitprop' as a musical genre place him in a central position among composers of the post-assimilation generation.

Chuck out the Men! Jewish and Objective – Berlin Cabaret

Eisler was not the only young composer of the interwar years attracted to the idea of crossing musical boundaries. Much of what has loosely been called 'Berlin Cabaret' is in fact a hotchpotch derived from different sources and different styles. Today, *variété*, *revue*, *cabaret* have all been jumbled together with stage and screen *Schlager* ('hit songs') along with political fight-songs and agitprop to form an encapsulation of interwar Berlin. Some of the most familiar numbers are theatre songs taken from Weill's *Dreigroschenoper*, *Happy End* and *Aufstieg und Fall der Stadt Mahagonny*.[7] Others were genuine cabaret songs performed as part of programmes satirising local issues or the politics of the still new Republic. Some of the most memorable were composed by Friedrich Holländer, including the feminist *Raus mit den Männern!* (*Chuck out the Men!*), made famous by one of Berlin's most popular performers, the lesbian Claire Waldorf. Another important Holländer song illustrating conditions under the new system was his scathing *Münchhausen*, a hypnotic strophic number with a never-ending list of the lies used to keep social injustices in place.

Much of the appeal of this music to modern listeners is to be found in the sexual references stemming from the politics of the day. There is no doubt that German and Austrian societies were more unbuttoned about such things than their Anglo-Saxon cousins. As early as 1908, the *Neue Freie Presse* ran a front-page debate regarding the pros and cons of sex education in schools,[8] and in 1919 it became obligatory for all 14-year-olds. Felix Salten was the author of the children's classic *Bambi – a Life in the Woods* and of the anonymously published volume of erotica *Josephine Munzenbacher – die Lebensgeschichte einer Wienerischen Dirne von ihr selbst erzäht (Josephine Munzenbacher – the Story of a Viennese Whore as Told by Herself)*. Salten seems to have caught the mood of the day and he wrote persuasively in defence of the new educational ordinance.[9] As early as 1897, the Jewish Berlin-based sexologist Magnus Hirschfeld was presenting frank arguments in defence of homosexuality, and Mischa Spoliansky's gay-liberation number *The Lavender Song* along with his *Masculinum-Femininum* provided the soundtrack for the Berlin of Thomas Mann's openly homosexual son Klaus and the British writer Christopher Isherwood. Figures such as Magnus Hirschfeld, Sigmund Freud and Arthur Schnitzler (the playwright whom Freud considered his alter-ego), along with Felix Salten and his genius for both children's stories and pornography; the political writer, satirist and poet Kurt Tucholsky were all Jewish and, even by today's standards, not remotely squeamish about sex.

Stefan Zweig in relating the social changes that came about after the war believed that young people held their elders responsible for the catastrophes of the day and that 'eleven- and twelve-year-old children, all sexually enlightened, went on camping expeditions in groups with names such as *Wandervögel* (*Birds of Passage*)'. '[. . .] one even rebelled against the laws of nature'. Zweig goes on to relate how 'girls cut their hair to look like boys, and boys shaved in order to look more feminine'. Conspicuous male and female homosexuality was not the result of what Zweig called 'a natural sexual preference', but an act of 'open rebellion'. Fashion became shockingly revealing, literature became 'activist and politicised', and music 'lost the coherency of melody and harmony'. But Zweig becomes most incensed at the German language losing its grammatical rules and is horrified at the truncated spelling of telegrams being used in general communication.[10]

Raunchy and racy cabaret texts were set by any number of popular composers, but the Jewish composers Holländer, Spoliansky and Rudolf Nelson penned the most famous and certainly some of the most amusing. Whether or not enlightened non-religious Jews felt more at ease about sexual matters than non-Jews, there can be no doubt that Berlin Cabaret would be unthinkable without their openness. Needless to say, this was used as anti-Semitic ammunition in the run-up to the Nazi dictatorship, though even the

Nazis were happy to promote a non-puritanical line as long as it was in the interest of propagating the Aryan race.

During the 1950s, German historians decided that a distinction was needed between cabaret songs that were seen as sleazy and those which were socially critical, though no such distinction had been made during the years of the Weimar Republic. 'Kabarett' was taken to represent the political and socially critical, while 'Cabaret' referred to the rest.[11] Peter Jelavich's book entitled *Berlin Cabaret* defines both variants as the following:

> Cabaret/Kabarett consisted 'of a small stage in a relatively small hall, where the audience sat around tables. The intimacy of the setting allowed direct, eye-to-eye contact between performers and spectators. The show consisted of short (five- or ten-minute) numbers from several different genres, usually songs, comic monologues, dialogues and skits; less frequently dances, pantomimes, puppet shows, or even short films. They dealt in a satirical or parodistic manner with topical issues: sex (most of all), commercial fashions, cultural fads, politics (least of all). These numbers were usually presented by professional singers and actors, but often writers, composers, or dancers would perform their own works. The presentations were linked together by a conférencier, a type of emcee who interacted with the audience, made witty remarks about events of the day, and introduced the performers.[12]

In German, cabaret was already being spelt with a 'c' and a single 't' by 1900 to emphasise the connection with such outré Parisian venues as Le Chat noir, founded in 1881 by the poet, rogue artist, and erstwhile Montmartre hydropath Rodolphe Salis, Baron de la Tour de Naintré. It was an organic offshoot of the Naturalist and Realist movements represented by writers like Zola and it created the impression of a counter-cultural 'salon' of prostitutes, pimps and pickpockets, along with the many artists and Bohemian intellectuals who sought their company. A hint of Salis's ability to amuse can be gleaned from the Berlin journalist Paul Goldman, who wrote in Salis's obituary in 1897 that it was difficult to imagine how such a 'good-time-lad would ever have tried to tangle with anything as po-faced as dying'.[13] From Paris, cabaret moved to Barcelona's Four Cats and to Simplicissimus (known as 'Simpl') in Munich in 1903, providing naughty respite from straitlaced, Protestant Berlin. It took its name from the satirical publication *Simplicissimus*. 'Destined to keep all of Germany high and low on its toes for several decades, *Simplicissimus* attacked the makers, purveyors and accepters of authority, literary kitsch and hypocritical morality. Its spirit made it the kin of cabaret.'[14]

Simpl was frequented by such figures as Frank Wedekind, and eventually such literary luminaries as Joachim Ringelnatz and Karl Valentin were recognised as house poets. It was also allegedly the source of literary 'Dadaism', with the term 'Dada' used for the first time by Marietta di Monaco in a recitation by the poets Klabund and Hugo Ball.

The subversive ideas that formed the basis of what we now think of as Berlin Cabaret started in the Café des Westens,[15] colloquially known as Café Größenwahn ('Café Megalomania'). Opening as the first coffee house in Berlin's boulevard Kurfürstendam in 1893, it was initially called Das kleine Café before being renamed Café des Westens in 1898, where it became a meeting point for the city's Bohemian community. The first two official Cabarets in Berlin, Ernst von Wolzogen's Überbrettl and Max Reinhardt's Schall und Rauch ('Wind and Froth'), were both conceived at tables in the Café des Westens. It provided a salon atmosphere for average Berliners who were not necessarily part of the 'salonnière' circles of Berlin's upper bourgeoisie, offering an informal meeting place where they could mingle with artists and intellectuals. Much later, it was where the idea for Brecht and Weill's *Threepenny Opera* was born as well as Friedrich Holländer's seminal chanson *Ich bin von Kopf bis Fuß (Falling in Love Again)*, immortalised by Marlene Dietrich in the 1930 film *The Blue Angel*.

In the years leading up to the First World War, Café Größenwahn, as Café des Westens more commonly came to be known, was the meeting point for Berlin's Expressionist writers and painters, and only began to fall apart when the right-wing press started to make claims that the 'vermin of Berlin's arts crowd' were turning the Western districts into 'a swamp'. In 1913 the café's owners moved further down the Kurfürstendam, while the artists and intellectuals largely stayed put until 1915. In 1920 a cabaret Größenwahn was opened where the original café had stood until 1913. The cabaret continued until 1922 and its accompanying café was described by the journalist Stephan Grossmann in 1921 along the following lines:

There has never been a meeting place for artists that takes itself quite as seriously as Café Größenwahn, also known as Café des Westens. One hardly ever hears any laughter as it's expected that you sit and stare straight ahead or abruptly toss your head with a frozen look in the opposite direction. Ordinary people arrive in the evening to have a look at the many 'Megalomaniacs', but soon realise that outer and inner differences between themselves and such geniuses are surprisingly small. Arguments ignite easily. The Berlin native is a child of reason and his idea of an orgy is 'the conversation'. In other places, people may have more music in their souls or a sense of exuberance or, at the very least, a philosophy arising out of personal experience. [. . .] In Berlin, however, everything is argued about – naturally they argue over 'questions', and the worst aspect of this dreadful place was their arguing over the question of *sex*. My God! Elsewhere people simply get on with it, especially the young; here, they debate sexual relations. Women in high-boots and masculine waist-coats stride alongside long-haired youths who wish to project their femininity: Strindberg's Miss Julie or Wedekind's Alwa Schön.

There would, however, have been a fail-safe means of achieving total silence in this din of continuous yakety-yak. All it would take is to have someone standing at the entrance threatening to throw out anyone if they so much as breathed the following references: 'Tilla Durieux', 'Strindberg', 'Professor Freud', 'Herwarth Walden', 'Rosa Luxemburg', 'Magnus Hirschfeld' or 'Arnold Schoenberg'. Before you knew it, all of the gasbags would be chucked out the door! These people only live for today and would be condemned to a Trappist existence if their weekly theatre guide suddenly went up in smoke. It was dear old Johann Nestroy who said of such creatures: 'Zeitgeist – nothing but Zeitgeist.'[16]

Berlin may have been more straight-laced and aggressively censored than Munich, but it did have two important Cabarets. The first to appear was Ernst von Wolzogen's Überbrettl in 1901. In English, 'Rickety Boards' is perhaps the closest translation to the German diminutive 'Brettl' and the name designated a makeshift stage where someone would stand up and sing a bawdy song. Thus Überbrettl implies a more exalted version of a temporary stage. It was while the ensemble of Überbrettl was performing in Vienna in 1901 that its house composer, Oscar Straus, introduced Wolzogen to Schoenberg, who had already composed eight *Brettl-Lieder*. These songs had been taken from a collection of poems called *Deutsche Chansons* compiled by Otto Julius Bierbaum and included not only verses by himself but also by writers such as Frank Wedekind, Richard Dehmel and Gustav Falke. Bierbaum, in his introduction to the published collection, called for Germans to use poetry in the same way that applied artists were producing furniture. Through such functional means, Bierbaum wanted to elevate German proletarian tastes beyond the seedy dives that were referred to as 'Tingeltangels'. But it was in appealing to a sense of Teutonic self-improvement that he lost a good deal of the Latin abandonment found in the cabaret texts and songs of Paris and Barcelona. Wolzogen's Überbrettl would provide Schoenberg with early conducting experience and it is also likely that at least one of his *Brettl-Lieder*, Falke's

'Nachtwandler' ('The Somnambulist'), was performed before Schoenberg's departure in 1902. Paul Goldman explained the origin of Überbrettl and offers an account of its opening:

> The Überbrettl has finally opened at the Secessionist Theatre and was the most successful event that this Alexander-Platz venue, uniquely dedicated to Secessionist celebrations, has thus far witnessed. In fact, the box-office confounded us with that most astonishing of Secessionist contradictions: a sign reading 'Sold Out'. An extremely glittery public including the entire artist community of Berlin arrived in droves. [...] At this point, it's worth explaining what exactly is meant by the term 'Überbrettl'. In all likelihood, it probably doesn't mean much of anything. It's just a name. One planned a show to put on and then hunted around until a silly name could be found: 'Überbrettl'. Wolzogen, the founder himself, explained: 'There is the Über-Mensch ... why can't there be an Über-Brettl?' ... It's best simply to note that its self-proclaimed main purpose is to elevate the general taste of society. [...] Some have referred to the Überbrettl as 'literary Variété', as if only the 'literary' had any innate value. [...] The short introductions spoken at the start of each act were exactly right inasmuch as they were scrupulously absolved of any literary pretentions. [Wolzogen] took the good where he could find it and succeeded in using silly patches and scraps to make a jester's tuxedo. This was gaudy theatre made from an arrangement of short pieces. In fact, this is exactly the right expression and it need only have been printed on the programme: 'Überbrettl is gaudy theatre, in which a lot happens and much more besides.' It's mimed and sung, declaimed and danced. Gaudy, gaudy, gaudy is the solution. Lovely women; lovely German lyrics; a lot of lovely light, a lot of lovely colour; a bit of circular poetry; a drop of genius and pinch of nastiness; politics; literature; a shadow-dance; a waltz and, at long last, our long-awaited friend Pierrot, who, once again, out of unrequited love commits suicide. Gaudy Theatre! The thinking seems to be, that whatever you may have seen on a stage before, you can see here! Gaudy theatre is called in French variété. Actually, there can be no more literal translation. So as far as I'm concerned, the Überbrettl is variété. Or it's just the Brettl, since for the most part the programme consisted of songs, just as they should be sung while strutting over the boards. Only this selection of songs is a bit more tasteful than the ones heard on most 'boards'. [...] The Gaudy Theatre is actually a better set of boards, a Tréteau supérieur – an Above-board! So the word 'Überbrettl' has a meaning as well, which means we can finally sit back and relax.[17]

The second venue, Schall und Rauch, was opened at almost the same time by the theatrical genius of the day, Max Reinhardt, offering a parody of Schiller's *Don Carlos* (much admired by Thomas Mann) in its first season in 1901. In fact, in its initial formation it only lasted a single season before moving to a small theatre in Berlin's Unter den Linden, where it began a steady migration away from parody and satire towards conventional theatre. After the war, Friedrich Holländer, along with his wife, the singer Blandine Ebinger, established their own cabaret ensemble which they named after Schall und Rauch in the cellar of Reinhardt's Großes Schaupsielhaus, where they were joined by notables such as the composers Werner Richard Heymann and Mischa Spoliansky, and the writers Walter Mehring, Kurt Tucholsky and Joachim Ringelnatz.

German society experienced a number of changes during the interwar years that provided fertile ground for the unique genre of Berlin Cabaret. These included the official lifting of censorship, extreme poverty, and the general seediness that permeated the bourgeoisie. By this time, it wasn't just Bohemian artists who were choosing to spend time with pimps, prostitutes and pickpockets. Girls and boys from the best families were working the streets and clubs to pay for their next meal. Social Realism was no longer an artistic movement but day-to-day reality. The American composer George Antheil, arriving in Berlin in 1922, offers the following account:

> Almost the very first night I came to Berlin I met a young prominent German newspaperman and his pretty and intelligent young wife. It was obvious that they were very much in love with each other. It was also rather obvious that they were both starving. It did something very queer to me when, three nights later, I saw this girl in another quarter in Berlin, soliciting. When she saw me she was horrified, turned and ran.[18]

A theatrical venue where performer and spectator were virtually interchangeable chimed well with the Neue Sachlichkeit ethos of 'Lehrstück' and Gebrauchsmusik, but satire was also a way of coping with the conflicts that arose between grim reality and face-saving respectability. Hanns Eisler's critique of Friedrich Holländer's 1927 revue *Rund um die Gedächniskirche* (*Ring-Round the Memorial Church*[19]) in the Communist publication *Die Rote Fahne* (*The Red Flag*) takes these issues to heart in what he sees as frivolous treatment of a serious subject. 'Today, every sensible banker and factory owner counts himself a democratic republican with capitalism along with modern finance making up the superstructure perched on top of our democratic republic.'[20] Eisler is furious that the enforced prostitution of young girls is sanitised in Holländer's revue:

> Cleverness, spirit and satire need a true enemy in order to grow and be effective. Where there is cleverness and spirit, there must also be both conviction and an enemy against whom one unleashes cleverness and spirit, since all other weapons are pointless. Cleverness and spirit are the characteristics of the oppressed, of the fighters, not however of those who flirt with our rulers. [. . .] These were the thoughts that sprang to my mind while watching the revue *Ring-Round the Memorial Church* for which Friedrich Holländer has written some fairly lame music. It is of course possible to pull off such petit-bourgeois satire with acts that brim with more, or perhaps less, talent. Holländer and his author, Moritz Seeler, have chosen to get by with less. The Haller revue *A Thousand Sweet Legs* or James Klein's *Everybody Naked!* appears profound in comparison with this boring rubbish, as at least they're more honest and don't pretend to possess any sort of conviction and actually only want to earn lots of money with lots of naked girls.[21]

This judgement was harsh on Holländer, who had studied composition with Engelbert Humperdinck long before establishing himself at Schall und Rauch. Even before becoming widely known as the composer of the film music for *The Blue Angel*, he had spent the years 1921 to 1923 composing for the singing actress Trude Hesterberg and her cabaret *Wilde Bühne* (Savage Stage) in the cellar of Theater des Westens, before opening his own highly successful theatre in 1931 in the same location which he called, *pace* Bierbaum, Tingel-Tangel. Holländer went on to set texts by Macellus Schiffer that were made famous by Schiffer's wife Margo Lion on whose vampish appearance the young Marlene Dietrich modelled herself.

Whether it was Oskar Straus, Arnold Schoenberg or Max Reinhardt, there was a strong Jewish presence from the outset in German cabaret. If, at the beginning of the century, the non-Jewish Bierbaum had a feeling that the common man should be lured away from the sleaze of the 'Tingeltangel' with edifying poetry, by the interwar years Jews had recognised that cabaret, revue and variété were entertaining ways of earning a living. Holländer, Franz Wachsmann (pianist with the fashionable jazz ensemble the Weintraub Syncopators, and Holländer's orchestrator for *The Blue Angel*), Mischa Spoliansky, Werner Richard Heymann and Rudolf Nelson were making enormous contributions to a genre that was socially critical as well as amusing. But penning hit-songs with funny lyrics, cabaret, light music and operetta also offered a good number of talented young Jews a pleasurable and lucrative means of moving seamlessly out of the distinctively Jewish cabarets and theatrical troupes of Eastern Europe. With German as a second household language, these performers often grew up with an irreverent means of turning the language's complex syntax upside down, or spinning puns from unlikely linguistic combinations.

When Eisler wrote of 'cleverness and spirit' as characteristics of the oppressed, he did not need to use the word 'Jew'. Indeed, he probably wouldn't have, since, to his generation, there was an uncomfortably close relationship between Communists and anti-Semitic propaganda which often ignited Jew hatred even among young Jewish Communists. At one point, Eisler's sister Elfriede had to be warned against making anti-Semitic pronouncements in political speeches.

Emblematic for both time and place was the extravagant 1927 revue *Hoppla, Wir Leben!* (*Hey! We're Alive!*) by the Jewish political writer and revolutionary Ernst Toller. During the short-lived days of Bavaria's Soviet Republic in 1918–19, Toller had been placed in charge of assembling a 'Red Army'. Its fall left Toller serving a five-year prison sentence, grateful that a series of legal coincidences had saved him from execution. His trial was a sensation and he became not only a public darling, but also an avowed pacifist and an influential social critic. *Hoppla, Wir Leben!* opened in Hamburg before transferring to the theatre on Berlin's Nollendorfplatz run by the avant-garde director Erwin Piscator. It would become the essence of the Weimar Republic's zeitgeist. *Hoppla, Wir Leben!* tells a largely autobiographical story of a revolutionary, spared from execution and subsequently released from a lengthy prison sentence into the present. It offered a satire of the new world of financial stability brought about by Germany's central statesman of the day, Gustav Stresemann, and by showing a panorama of the Republic's betrayed principles, hypocrisy and corruption. At the end of the revue, the main character is returned to prison, having been falsely accused of murdering one of his former revolutionary comrades, who had himself become a corrupt government minister. The sequence of scenes offered a journey through all of Weimar Germany's social and political permutations.

Felix Salten reviewed its Viennese premiere at the Raimund Theatre in November 1927 and, perhaps compelled by local loyalties, mentions that in many respects, this production was superior to its Berlin run. He then proceeds to explain various key moments:

'Hey! We're Alive!' The phrase which lends this revue its name is heard five times emanating from various quarters of the stage: from the broadcasting console of the radio studio, from the private dining room where a government minister is taking a bribe, from the office of a journalist, from a brothel where a young girl is being taken by an elderly count, and from the dingy dive of a group of workers having a meal. The stage is assembled in such a way that all of these venues are instantly visible and the actions are all concurrent. Various other dramatic devices are employed throughout, such as actors mixing with the audience, newspaper-sellers shouting from the top balcony 'Extra! Extra!' before tossing sheets of newsprint on top of the audience seated below.[22]

'It's a revue, but without the girls', explains Salten, who adds that Piscator and Toller haven't created a piece of theatre so much as wedged their weltanschauung onto the stage. Revolutionary use is made of montage, film, music, transparencies and agitprop. 'Toller's work is as current as the editorial commentary that's read in the daily paper: full of harangue in the manner of someone addressing a mass-meeting, there is the aggression and gesticulation of the cockiest of political posters.'[23]

Composing for films

The music for *Hoppla, Wir leben!* was written by the Viennese-born composer Edmund Meisel, and in his review Salten mentions that one of the cinematic sequences used in the work reminded him of *Battleship Potemkin*. This should not have come as a surprise since Meisel had composed its music. The director of the film, Sergei Eisenstein, had more or less come to the conclusion that he did not want a single score as musical underlay, but preferred each country, region, territory, indeed even each generation, in which the film was shown, to have its own musical soundtrack. Meisel therefore arrived in Moscow to view a screening in preparation for the film's German distribution. Eisenstein mentions in his autobiography that the screening was shown with an accompanying cacophony as work was being carried out on the central heating system in the cinema. Eisenstein suspected that Meisel had later incorporated these sounds into his score.[24] He was very taken with Meisel's music and later mentioned that the perfect combination of sound and vision that he achieved in *Alexander Nevsky* in 1938 (with music by Prokofiev) would never have been possible without Meisel's pioneering work on *Potemkin*.[25] Unfortunately, a year before Meisel's untimely death in 1930 at the age of 36, Eisenstein and Meisel fell out: Meisel had instructed the projectionist at the London premiere of the film to show it at a slightly slower speed in order to accommodate certain rhythmic elements of the music, a request that did not go down well with the director.

Film composition was a fairly new art form in 1927. The large number of Viennese Jewish composers drawn to the medium is well documented, but it is an extraordinary coincidence that Edmund Meisel should be yet another, given that he was born in Vienna but raised in Berlin, and writing the music for one of that city's most iconic cinematic representations, Walter Ruttmann's 1927 film, *Berlin: die Sinfonie der Großstadt* (*Berlin, the Symphony of a Metropolis*).

Eisenstein's thoughts on the marriage of film and music were developed later by Hanns Eisler, who started working in Soviet cinema in 1932 with the Dutch director Joris Ivens. The techniques Eisler acquired during this period informed his 1947 book *Composing for Films*, co-authored with Adorno.

Meisel and Eisler had similar backgrounds. Meisel was born in Vienna, but moved as a small child to Germany; Eisler was born in Germany and moved to Vienna. Both came from secular Jewish backgrounds and were political activists. Meisel composed songs for Ernst Toller's *Hoppla, Wir leben!* and Eisler joined him at Piscator's Theatre in 1927 with a production of the play *Heimweh* (*Homesickness*), by Franz Jung. Meisel scored Ruttmann's *Berlin: die Sinfonie der Großstadt* in 1927, predating Eisler as a film composer, but Eisler soon caught up, providing music in 1932 for *Kuhle Wampe, oder wem gehört die Welt?* (*Kuhle Wampe, or To whom does this World Belong?*), starring Ernst Busch with a screenplay by Brecht and directed by Slatan Dudow. Although both young composers were curious about the juxtaposition of image and sound, Meisel's score for *Berlin: die Sinfonie der Großstadt* employs acoustical effects and often rushes forward with a musical sweep that anticipates Hollywood. Kurt Weill found these characteristics in conflict with the aesthetics of the age and clearly did not approve:

The purely illustrative music of [Meisel's] *Berlin* film score lies well outside the development of film music, such as I would imagine it and which I believe to be the only possibility. Without wishing to make qualitative judgements on the score, I believe that resorting to expressive devices from the past to solve the issues of film music is wrong. Objectively speaking, this music is offering purely melodramatic means in a Veristic style which completely contradicts the epic character of modern cinema [. . .] for example, at the beginning of the film, we see a train approaching Berlin and hear the rattling of wheels on the tracks. Meisel illustrates this literally to the point that after a few seconds we start to wonder, what's going to happen now? At any point something has to happen: an accident, a robbery, a crash with another train; but in fact and against all expectations, nothing of the sort occurs. And such moments are repeated throughout, with one frustrated build-up closely followed by another. What is utterly overlooked, however, is that though the outward expressive devices are continuously built up, the work itself does not offer the same intensity. We need an objective, *concertante* score, a creation that runs under the images of the film and not a literal illustration of these images.[26]

Eisler's film music takes these ideas even further by presenting a counter-illustrative score that often draws stark contrasts between the visual and the aural. During his work with Ivens, Eisler's scores moved beyond the purely illustrative to create a parallel emotional dialectic that draws out greater depth from the film by contrasting images against unexpected musical effects. By 1941, when he set his *Fourteen Ways of Describing the Rain* to Ivens's short experimental silent film *Rain* from 1929, we are confronted with any number of dislocating moments between viewer and listener. With the 1955 Auschwitz documentary *Nuit et brouillard*, directed by Alain Resnais, Eisler employs the starkest of music-to-visual counterpoint, anticipating Hannah Arendt's concept of 'the banality of evil': he underscores the gas-chambers with music of unapologetic banality, leaving the viewer with a deeply unsettled impression.

Music for the Masses or Mass Appeal

The age of Aestheticism, vigorously defended by Hanslick during the mid-nineteenth century and which had continued to enjoy wide currency, was now seen as elitist. Even the age of post-Wagnerian Romanticism that super-seded it (as represented by Zemlinsky, Schreker and latterly, Korngold) was resoundingly discredited by Weill in his 1926 essay on 'The New Opera'. What was required, he argued, was a shedding of pretentiousness and the need to find the most immediate contact with a broad public. Radio thus facilitated Weill's 'immediate contact' aspirations, though the technical limitations of its early days made satisfactory broadcasts of complex and finely differentiated music nearly impossibly and seemed thereby to confirm the fundamental redundancies of post-Romanticism. Music now had to be brief, instantaneous and memorable. It had to escape from the bourgeois prisons of the concert hall and opera house, and feed the culture-hungry masses. Jazz, dance music and light entertainment were not only genuinely appreciated by a wider population, but also provided Jewish composers and writers with an entrée that earlier generations could not have dreamed of. Why battle to be counted among the elite, when so much more could be achieved by sticking with the masses? Ralph Benatzky, the popular (non-Jewish) composer of *Im Weißen*

Rößl (*The White Horse Inn*),[27] may have been over-generous in his diary entry for 1 January 1928, but it contains more than an element of truth:

> There is only one truly good and ideal public: the Jewish one! If there are a number of Jews in a room, there'll be both laughter and tears; there is warmth and gratitude as well as comprehension and recognition; and if there are a lot of Jews in a city, one can always count on a ready public. The intellectual agility of this race, the ability to comprehend everything in a moment, their cultivation, their talent for punning and wordplay are ideal for the creative artist, and it is no coincidence that a huge number of this nation are recruited to make up the largest contingent of performers, writers and composers. Of the Viennese composers, meaning for example Lehar, Strauß [*sic!*], Kálman, Fall, Granichstädten, Eysler, Stolz, Engel-Berger, Erwin, Krauss, Werau, R. Fall, Katscher, Ch. Weinberger, etc., only Lehar and myself are Christians. Of Vienna's publishing houses: Weinberger, Herzmansky, Hein, Callé, Marischka, only Herzmansky is Christian, and of the librettists, I simply can't think of a single one who isn't Jewish. And the same is true of actors and actresses, singers, dancers etc., non-Jewish performers are rather few and far between, and one shouldn't even mention the situation regarding theatre managements. Perhaps it's a bit different in the world of so-called 'serious' music, and perhaps this hypothesis should be tested, but I'm quite sure the results wouldn't be that different.[28]

Benatzky's enthusiasm leads him to make numerous factual errors, but he throws a positive light on what would be turned just a few years later into Nazi anti-Semitic propaganda and confirms the popular perception of Jewish prominence in light music.

Operetta by Jewish composers and librettists suffered a particularly iniquitous post-Hitler legacy. The Third Reich's guardians of public morality removed popular works and replaced them with alternatives from which all social satire and sauciness had been removed. With post-1945 revivals of previously banned works, the puritanical policies of the Nazis continued with the fastidious removal of sexual innuendo and the employment of actors and actresses who represented a harmless winsomeness far removed from their predecessors, leaving operetta with a saccharine reputation that it absolutely did not deserve.[29]

New Objectivity was the determining aesthetic of the serious artistic movements in the Berlin of the Weimar Republic, representing not just a rejection of Romanticism, but a resolute Counter-Romanticism. Accelerated by the hot-house atmosphere of various new music festivals such as those in

Donaueschingen and Baden-Baden, along with further events organised by the Allgemeiner Deutscher Musikverein (ADMV) and the International Society of Contemporary Music (ISCM), bright young composers began a process that turned music into a commodity, or at the very least, put it to 'practical' use. With music's application for stage and screen, it became a function or indeed, a utility. Brecht said to Eisler that music captured his verse like 'a fly in amber', implying that music was the means rather than the end.[30] Rejecting music's implied ability to communicate on an abstract 'spiritual' level meant that it was neither more nor less intrinsically valuable than graphics or carpentry. Indeed, Eisler's agitprop songs were considered by Piscator's avant-garde circle as the musical equivalent of John Heartfield's striking political posters. New Objectivity was aimed at the masses for them to use as they felt best. The spirit of the Weimar Republic meant that music had lost its position as an aristocratic accompaniment to balls and banquets or even as a bourgeois pretension to cultivation.

Eisler, however, did not feel that this should compel composers to pitch their work down market. As early as 1935, he was stating clearly that the avant-garde had a responsibility not to isolate itself from the masses.[31] But in 1950, he elaborated these earlier thoughts in another essay that strikes us, in retrospect, as a clear-sighted prophecy of where the emerging avant-garde in postwar Europe was heading: 'If modern – that is serious – art distances itself continuously from the broader masses, then it becomes continuously more cynical, decadent, nihilistic and formalistically isolated; monopoly-capitalism's cultural industry has always understood the masses: for them, "true" art is merely merchandised art.'[32] Just as Ernst Toch would ultimately distance himself from the steely-eyed gaze of New Objectivity in American exile, Eisler, living in the Communist East, would clarify his earlier stance: appealing to the masses did not mean composing music with mass appeal.

CHAPTER 8

A Question of Musical Potency
The Anti-Romantics

What is it that we call modern? We aren't so foolish as to fall for the belief that all advancement is progress. We know that a new way of painting, a new palette of colours, a new sense of harmony, a new instrument doesn't represent progressive attainment in an absolute sense. These are only the outer symptoms of inner permutations brought about by the tide that continuously sweeps everything away. And we believe in this tide and the change it brings and call it life. And this is what we call modern: what ebbs and flows within us, changes, yields fruit and carries us along.

Was ist es denn, was wir 'modern' nennen? Wir sind nicht töricht genug, an eine "Entwicklung" der Kunst im Sinne des Fortschritt-Philisters zu glauben. [. . .] Wir wissen, daß eine neue Mal Technik, eine neue Farbenskala, eine neue Harmonieverbindung, ein neues Instrument, keinen Fortschritt, keine Errungenschaft im absoluten Sinne bedeutet, daß dies alles nur äußere Symptome innerer Umstellungen sind, bedingt durch den ewigen Fluß und Wechsel der Dinge. An diesen Fluß und Wechsel aber glauben wir, denn er ist das, was wir Leben nennen. Und dieses nennen wir modern: was innerlich fließt, wechselt, zeugt und trägt.

Paul Bekker, *Musikblätter des Anbruch*, 1920

To musical conservatives, Hans Pfitzner's pamphlet *Die neue Aesthetik der musikalischen Impotenz. Ein Verwesungssymtom?* (*The New Aesthetic of Musical Impotence: A Sign of Decay?*), written in 1919 and published the following year, must have seemed like a godsend. It was a response to the critic Paul Bekker, the author of a popular and well-received biography of

Beethoven in which he suggested that the music of the early twentieth century was the fruit of Beethoven's legacy. As reactionaries and progressives both claimed Beethoven as their own, Pfitzner's attack on Bekker was intended to dispute the legitimacy of the modernists' claim. However, Beethoven was only the *casus belli* of Pfitzner's tract on 'musical impotence'. It irked him that a year earlier Bekker had suggested in a pamphlet that the only contemporary composer who could be considered a legitimate successor to Richard Wagner was Franz Schreker.[1] Bekker had arrived at this conclusion after careful consideration of the potential claims by a number of other composers, including Pfitzner.[2]

It is worth focusing on one central point in Pfitzner's essay as this would ultimately harness many intellectuals into the anti-Semitic thinking of National Socialism. Clearly, there was more at stake than the question of which strand of musical development had a legitimate claim to Beethoven's inheritance, and accordingly Pfitzner moved the debate to something even more profound by making a claim on behalf of musical conservatives of the German soul itself. Composers of all musical tendencies believed that music was somehow a privilege uniquely bequeathed either by fate or by God to the German people. Pfitzner, in common with Wagner (whose *Das Judenthum in der Musik* he described in his own tract as 'serious, brave and loving'[3]) saw Jews as non-German foreigners. He goes on to accuse the Jewish Bekker of leading an international assault, and uses the words 'international' and 'Jewish' in tandem so often that they soon become interchangeable. 'International' thus becomes the opposite of 'German'. The Communist Party was at this time called the 'International', which was described as 'Bolshevik': thus, 'international' = 'Jew' = 'Bolshevik' = 'non-German'. In due course, other euphemisms for Jews would stand in for 'international', 'cosmopolitan' emerging as a favourite used by both National Socialist and Communist anti-Semites alike. Ultimately, all these euphemisms meant outsiders, usurpers, parvenus, *Möchtegerns* and confidence tricksters. To Pfitzner and others, such as his journalist ally Alfred Heuß, editor of the nationalist, conservative *Zeitschrift für Musik*, these were merely synonyms for 'non-German'.

Paul Bekker was born in Berlin and was briefly a violinist in the Berlin Philharmonic before leaving to work as a conductor in Aschaffenburg and Görlitz. He started writing music criticism in 1906 and from 1911 to 1923 he was chief music critic of the *Frankfurter Zeitung*, Germany's liberal answer to Austria's *Neue Freie Presse*. This placed him in a similar position to Julius Korngold, and their rivalry was legendary. In an open letter to Korngold from 1924, Bekker wrote the following attack on him:

My dear Dr Korngold!

One taunts those whom one loves – this truism occurred to me as I recently read in the *Neue Freie Presse* your anguished cry regarding atonal insanity and the demise of human feeling and passion. I continued to be reminded of this truism as I noticed that despite these human catastrophes, you still managed, somehow, to intone your predictable grandiose song in praise of the natural order. It was at this point that I suddenly realised that it was my own good self you meant when naming the un-credited spokesman for the 'journalistic pulp' that calls itself the 'Vienna Newspaper for Atonal Music' [*Anbruch*]. So, I thought to myself, you really love me, don't you Julius? Why deny it? Only a deep love can bring forth such great pain, such grievance and such anger. [. . .] For this reason, I shall attempt to explain why I, Julius, cannot love you, at least as far as such things can be accounted. [. . .] You see, Julius, I happen to view Beethoven as being different from Wagner, just as Krenek is different from Schoenberg. I see two operas by Schreker from different perspectives and am proud of the inconsequence that it does not result in me being against Schreker, though he doesn't happen belong to the [atonal] 'movement'. [. . .] When I walk through the garden, I cherish the apple tree, the pear tree, the peach tree, the roses and the thistles. I do not value a single one of these to the exclusion of others. Rather, I am conscious of the fact that apples, pears and peaches are fundamentally different in both taste and appearance. I still enjoy eating all of them, according to the individual tree's fruit and whims of the season. I'm delighted by the rose. As far as the thistle goes – please don't blush, Julius – I must admit it pleases me the least of all. But I think to myself, God also created the thistle and he surely must know why. For that reason, it should continue to stay where it is, growing and bringing whatever fruits it may bear – even if only asses enjoy eating it.[4]

On the recommendation of Leo Kestenberg, Musical Advisor to the Prussian Ministry of Culture, in 1923 Bekker was made director of the opera house in Kassel, where he worked closely with Krenek. As Krenek relates in his memoirs, one of Bekker's first productions was, ironically, Pfitzner's *Der arme Heinrich*, mounted prior to Schreker's *Die Gezeichneten*, which was scheduled 'towards the end of his directorship'.[5] Bekker had written, in addition to his Beethoven monograph, biographies of Offenbach and Oskar Fried, along with numerous articles and essays on Schreker, Mahler, 'Art and

Revolution', and other aspects of German music of the day. The Nazi *Lexikon der Juden in der Musik* accords him a particularly blistering entry:

> Bekker, Paul (H [= Half Jew]), * Berlin 4.12.1882, + New York 1937: music critic; from 1925 director of the State Theatre in Kassel; 1927–32 director in Wiesbaden. Famous writer during the time of general decline; well-known by his work at the *Frankfurter Zeitung* (1911–1925); promoter of such degenerating tendencies as Mahler, Schoenberg, Schreker etc. Hans Pfitzner directed his polemic *The Aesthetic of Musical Impotence* against him, in which he states clearly that 'Whoever took the nihilistic views seriously of this "Frankfurt darling", in proclaiming who the legitimate successors to Beethoven and Wagner were, wasn't in a position to tell the difference between the production of art and shit.'[6]

The lexicon goes on to detail the withdrawal of Bekker's German citizenship and accuses him of hiring only Jewish minions to carry out his work while at Kassel (though Krenek, as we have seen, was certainly not Jewish). It goes on to recycle Pfitzner's accusations of Bekker's Bolshevism, which were so ludicrous that when Pfitzner brought them up in his *Impotence* polemic, Bekker never even bothered to address them.

In an article entitled *Beethoven und die Moderne*,[7] printed as part of the Berlin Staatsoper's Almanac in 1926, Pfitzner had his own chance to reclaim Beethoven from the modernists. Julius Korngold, in his review of this morose essay, wrote:

> It would occasionally appear that the pessimism which befalls the composer of *Palestrina* may compel him to give up composing altogether. 'All music has something of the wilting bloom about it', he opines, before suddenly reaching for yet another of his many contradictions and dismissing this thought by expressing the belief that the creative artist's sense of self-preservation is such that he cannot find the wherewithal to stop believing in himself. Good. Inevitably, the sun must set, 'but should and must one', he wails, 'speed up this inevitability by throwing muck at the horizon?' This is a singularly powerful thought that appeals to us more than Pfitzner's latest bloodless musings. However, it could be argued that most of the muck thrown at the horizon comes from those who write about it rather than from those who compose.[8]

It would be wrong to suggest that Pfitzner was placing himself in the same aesthetic position as Wagner with *Das Judenthum in der Musik*. In fact, he was aesthetically closer to Hanslick in matters of musical purity and its inappropriateness in disseminating extra-musical ideas. It was, in Pfitzner's opinion, Bekker's cheek at placing non-musical concepts at the heart of understanding Beethoven that became one of the most contentious points of his biography. For Pfitzner, the inspiration of the musical idea must come uniquely from within the music itself. On the other hand, his German Nationalism was obsessive and it would appear that this very non-musical impulse was the agenda behind his cantata *Von deutscher Seele*[9] to texts by Eichendorff, first performed in 1922. Thomas Mann explains the origins of Pfitzner's German nationalism as follows:

> Until the height of summer in 1914, the composer believed that as far as he was concerned, the devil could take politics. He saw himself as a Romantic composer, that is to say a *national*, but not a political composer. It was with the outbreak of war that he realised that national feelings would inevitably be transmuted into the political: this introspective, gentle and cerebral artist thus transformed himself into a power-seeker. He longed for the warrior triumph of Germany: at the height of the morality-debate on the waging of U-boat attacks, he dedicated a chamber work to Admiral Tirpitz. In a word, Germany's national composer had politicised himself into the anti-democratic nationalist. And who should be surprised? He was steeped in the spirit of German music as no one else. His fundamental instinct [. . .] was antagonistic to such foreign things as European intellectualism or the artifices of democracy.[10]

Pfitzner had already thrown down the gauntlet in 1917 in an anti-Futurist polemic directed against Busoni, whose *Sketch of a New Aesthetic of Music* had appeared ten years earlier. The tract *Musical Impotence* caused far greater controversy. According to Pfitzner, 'international' influences included Impressionism, and the fact that both Schoenberg and Schreker had used Impressionistic effects in their earlier works only confirmed, in his view, how un-German they were. His use of the concept of 'impotency' as an aesthetic idea, with its alternative notion of 'potency' (implying, of course, Pfitzner himself), carries forward the subliminal idea of the artist as hero and the female as non-creative and passive, thus preparing the way for Nazi propaganda that would dismiss music by Jewish composers as 'weak and effeminate'.

The responses to Pfitzner's polemic were many and varied. The German music historian Eckard John, in his book *Musik-Bolschewismus* of 1994, sees it as a pivotal moment in the politicisation of music. The German musicologist Alfred Einstein, writing for British readers, makes the point that Pfitzner was only stating what the historian and philosopher Oswald Spengler had cited in his ultra-conservative *Downfall of Western Civilisation* (1918).[11] Einstein goes on to cite Pfitzner's point of view, more in sorrow than anger, as a symptom of Germany's lingering plight over Romanticism:

> We must go a different way if we want to overcome the pathos, the overbearing sentimentality, and the natural aversion to romanticism. Germany was deeper under the spell of Romanticism than any other country. Romanticism was indeed a specifically German creation. We must overcome this disease, and therefore cannot afford to treat the attempts at deliverance as a question of fashion, no matter how ridiculous the gestures these attempts may produce. [. . .] We believe that we write new music: yet we only avoid writing old music. The old music no longer exists, and the new music does not yet exist as a positive expression of our times. We, too, try to parody and to ridicule the bourgeoisie and the sentimentality of romantic music [. . .] to come near a so-called musical 'Gothic' by linear development of melody or to do away with the old methods of composing by inventing new matters, and by depriving all motives, themes, and concords of the original soul, to create the *tabula rasa*, the chaos which is to bring forth a star. The star is not born yet, neither do we know whether it will be born, but we know that we cannot go back and that our present evolution is necessary even if there are few spectators. The evolution will be all the quicker the more passionately the issue is fought.[12]

If Einstein's view was that Germany was stuck in some sort of late-Romantic time-warp, Alban Berg highlights the associations between Pfitzner's German nationalism and his use of unfettered emotion as a blunt object against reason. He starts by quoting from Pfitzner's own essay: 'With such a melody [Schumann's *Träumerei*] we simply float on air. Its quality can only be recognised, not demonstrated; there is no intellectual path to its understanding. Either one comprehends its beauty innately through the delight one feels or not. He who cannot empathise has no arguments to bring, nor can he be met with counter-arguments. One can only play the melody and say, "how beautiful". What it says is as deep and clear and mystical as truth itself.'[13] Berg then offers the following observation:

> To read these words from a composer of such standing as Pfitzner must have been to many musicians, certainly it was to me, a grave disappointment. In addition to everything else, they come from a book that is so full of erudition that it hardly omits a single field of human intellectual

endeavour in its contents. In equal quantities it offers philosophy, politics, music history and racial-theories; aesthetics, ethics, journalism, literature and frankly, God knows what all else! The one place it leaves us wanting most is precisely the area it was meant to cover, namely music. It takes a position right from the outset that suppresses every possibility of judging good from bad.[14]

Pfitzner would appear to speak to a small group which had preserved the instinct to recognise melodic quality – a group of which Berg happily counted himself a member. Pfitzner is quoted as making the 'German demand' which he sets forth as: 'Those of us who still have this sense of quality must be brave enough to romanticise!'[15] Berg responds:

For my own part, I'll choose to leave the romanticising to that much larger group from whom the sense of melody has not yet been driven. Instead, I'll preserve my own, if not nobler, at least more objective relationship with music. In any case, I suddenly realised that the tiny group he believed he was addressing may not be that tiny after all. He addresses this question of innate musical quality by picking up that most difficult of nuts to crack, Schumann's 'Träumerei' from his *Scenes from Childhood* ... a work that to my knowledge, even during Schumann's lifetime, was in no particular [aesthetic] danger.

Berg then turns his attention to some of the most fatuous of Pfitzner's generalisations regarding the intrinsic perfection of *Träumerei* and deconstructs them bar by bar. Berg is annoyed that Pfitzner's attack on modern music is vague and offers no concrete examples. He provides counterevidence of innate melodic quality in contemporary music by proffering 'Ach Knabe, du mußt nicht traurig sein', taken from Mahler's Wunderhorn song, *Der Schildwache Nachtlied*. For good measure, he throws in the second subject of Schoenberg's First Chamber Symphony as an alternative example.[16]

Julius Korngold finds much to agree with in Pfitzner's essay and would certainly have welcomed any attack on Bekker (the only major critic who would disparage Erich Korngold's opera *Die tote Stadt* later in 1920). But his brief summary is revealing:

Readers who know our point of view in such questions will find immediate conviction in a polemic that Hans Pfitzner has recently published entitled *The New Aesthetic of Musical Impotence: A Sign of Decay?* Pfitzner, in response to what he sees as a dubious understanding of Beethoven, peevishly defends the uniquely and specifically musical. Nothing that Hanslick would have said could have been more clearly stated. The determining factor for Pfitzner is musical 'potency', which is the result of the imagination and expressed in individual thematic and melodic creativity. Like a high-strung fighting-rooster with his cocks-comb inflated to full fury, he attacks any and all who dispute this perspective. He's savage with any belief that music may be able to express extra-musical content, and he's against all attempts to impose new-fangled sound-experiments or decadent tonal systems that potentially discredit the supremacy of melody. He is equally savage with anyone and anything that may try to reverse the fundamentals of thematic and melodic structures, thereby undermining the foundations of musical architecture. Behind any attempt to do things differently, Pfitzner finds mere incompetence while hammering away at perceived 'impotence'. Alarmingly, he had the misfortune while wielding his mighty sword of German music to raise it against a composer who, if fact be known, is in possession of considerable musical potency: Gustav Mahler, who cannot reasonably be held responsible for all of the crazy ideas that have lined up in his name after his death. Mahler, to whom the plasticity of harmony and melody were fundamental to everything he composed, would have been bemused at such accusations. All of the pan-German excesses and excursions within this book dull the ringing purity of Pfitzner's battle cry. The Wagner who composed *Meistersinger* is a happier example to cite than the Wagner who addressed matters regarding [the Jewish] race. If we simply ignore the nonsense and follow his basic reasoning, we can find much to recommend.[17]

Reading Korngold's appraisal, along with Berg's counter-attack, we sense a shift within the musical landscape of Jewish assimilation and its many detractors. The positions of Wagner, the German superiorist who heaped function upon function onto opera until he had created a *Gesamtkunstwerk*, and his opposite pole, the aesthete Hanslick (who was of Jewish descent, and therefore, according to Wagner, not German), had now been reversed. Pfitzner, in his attempt to rescue Wagner from 'non-German' Jewish Wagnerians such as Mahler, Schoenberg and their followers, had unwittingly resorted to representing the composer Wagner in the purist aesthetic image of his arch-enemy Eduard Hanslick.

Korngold goes on to say that in Vienna, the issues that Pfitzner addresses are in any case irrelevant, as younger Viennese composers have abandoned the experimental 'impotency' that Pfitzner derides. He cites as examples the Schreker pupils Felix Petyrek, Egon Kornauth and above all, Wilhelm Grosz, who have exemplary skills in all disciplines and show great creativity. Korngold is particularly fulsome in his praise of another young Viennese composer, Hans Gál, and congratulates him on the success of his recent opera *Der Arzt der Sobeide* (*Sobeide's Doctor*) in Breslau.[18] The point that Korngold makes is that there were a number of composers for whom the de-sensitised New Objectivity was irrelevant. However, it was equally valid that these young composers did not see themselves as slavish adherents to the Wagnerian Romanticism of the previous century. They saw their own music as a reflection of their individual personalities and their singular melodic and harmonic ideas which were all that was needed to view themselves as 'new' and 'modern'.

As we have seen in Krenek's conversation with Josef Lechthaler in the previous chapter, this was particularly the case among Jewish composers. With the exception of Schoenberg, Austro-German Jewish composers still saw themselves as vulnerable to accusations of not being sufficiently 'German'. They did not want to risk new-found, albeit cautious, successes for the uncertain glories bestowed by future generations potentially more able to comprehend what contemporary audiences found alienating. This was simply not the case with the more self-assured children of the non-Jewish bourgeoisie, many of whom congregated at the more extreme margins of the avant-garde such as Webern, Krenek and Berg. If Jewish composers were to count for anything, they needed to write music, even 'modern' music, which appealed to the public of the day in all of its many permutations. On the other hand, many of the brightest and most talented of them recognised that continuing with Austro-German Romanticism in the manner of Wagner and Liszt was not a viable long-term solution either, despite its undoubted appeal amongst the largest section of the concert- and opera-attending public. A group of young composers, predominantly Viennese and predominantly pupils of Guido Adler, decided that the solution was to write new music by reaching back to models provided by a previous era. As such, they intellectually, if not always aesthetically embraced the values of Mendelssohn's 'old German School'.

Anti-Romanticism

Hans Gál was one of the most successful of these musicians who had studied with Brahms's friend and musical executor, Eusebius Mandyczewski. Together, Gál and Mandyczewski edited the complete works of Brahms, a feat that was highly regarded by all musical factions. With Mandyczewski editing only Brahms's vocal works, it was left to Gál to provide critical editions of everything else, drawing him more deeply into Brahms's world than any other composer of the time. When Hanns Eisler was asked what the hardest part of exile was, his reply was abandoning his treasured set of the complete Brahms edition in Berlin.[19] Gál was very conscious that he needed to be vigilant against Brahms influencing his own work as a composer, especially as work on the edition took place at a time when Robert Fuchs as Vienna's principal composition professor was also promoting a strict Brahmsian line at the music academy. With the North German's musical spirit guiding so many of the city's young composers, in later life Gál withdrew pieces he felt were unoriginal or, worse, derivative.

As Julius Korngold relates, Gál was a master of his craft. There are no flaws to be found in his harmony or counterpoint unless they are intentional. He was an accomplished pianist and a fine cellist and, as with many other Adler students, he was also a musical polymath: his doctoral dissertation had been on the stylistic characteristics of the young Beethoven, a subject that would have been close to Pfitzner's heart. In 1925 and 1928, he edited volumes of Strauss waltzes, marches and polkas for Adler's *Denkmäler der Tonkunst in Österreich*. Gál was, in many ways, the archetypal composer of his day and he could potentially stand as a representative of musical creativity during the years of the Weimar Republic. Certainly, he was more regularly performed in mainstream venues than the likes of Eisler, Weill, Toch and even Hindemith, though with the press feasting on their controversies, they attracted more discussion, generating often scurrilous publicity.

Gál, in comparison with these *enfants terribles*, was conventional without being derivative, and he could never be accused of banality or empty sentimentality – he was no nostalgic Romantic. Nevertheless, he may have had some sympathy for Pfitzner's music and even his ideas, while avoiding any allegiance to his wilder polemics. Gál took the more considered view that modern music should grow organically out of the nineteenth century while retaining its classical integrity, with roots in Mendelssohn, Schumann and Brahms. In this respect, it could be inferred that he shared some of the neo-classical tendencies of Stravinsky. Gál, however, was both too individual and too conventional, too firmly rooted in the German school to travel down the paths of Constructivist neo-classicism favoured by Russian, Italian, French and Spanish composers, along with the likes of Hindemith, Weill and Krenek. For Gál, unresolved dissonance remained a means, never an end.

The critical praise heaped upon the premiere of Gál's second comic opera, *Die heilige Ente*,[20] first conducted by Georg Szell (a colleague of Gál's from his student days) at Düsseldorf in 1923, is revealing. According to the critic Paul Nettl, with Gál one had found a worthy successor to Lortzing, Nicolai, Cornelius and Goetz.[21] Such praise needs to be understood in the context of the growing reaction against Wagnerian Romanticism at the time, and, with a few notable exceptions, the lack of comic opera since the end of the war. By 1925, Julius Korngold was irritated that *Die heilige Ente* had yet to be heard in Vienna.[22] He would have to wait until a radio broadcast in 1929, which Josef Reitler reviewed as follows:

> Hans Gál's opera *The Sacred Duck* has been a long-established success in Germany, and finally, thanks to RAVAG's broadcast, we too have been able to hear it in Austria. [. . .] Chinese gods swap the brain of a Mandarin official and a coolie, a bigwig and a ne'er-do-well, which leads to much exotic confusion. The music is also exotic, though never forcibly so. The composer has successfully created a lyricism of lovely, melodic warmth with a consistently appealing orchestration. Opportunities for many amusing turns are plentiful and are readily taken advantage of.[23]

Most intriguing about this peculiar opera – with its Chinese opium dens, bored gods, and a farcical duck – is that from its premiere until the arrival of the Third Reich in 1933 it remained in the repertoire of a number of opera houses, including Berlin's Städtische Oper, where the soprano role of Li was sung by Franz Schreker's wife Maria in one of her rare ventures away from the music of her husband. From 1923 to 1933, *Die heilige Ente* made the rounds of most of Germany's important provincial houses, including Breslau, Weimar, Aachen, Kassel (under the Bekker–Krenek regime), Königsberg, Karlsruhe and Cherznowitz. It also enjoyed a successful run in Prague in 1926. The 1929 Viennese broadcast was the first twentieth-century opera to be recorded by the recently-established RAVAG. The critic Karl Heinzen, reviewing the premiere in Düsseldorf, was fascinated by Gál's use of 'oriental colours', though stylised *chinoiserie* was much in vogue at the time: Toch had enjoyed a considerable success with his *Chinese Flute* songs of 1922, and other composers such as Egon Wellesz and Julius Bittner had also composed songs on texts lovingly orientalised by the German poet Hans Bethge, who had provided the texts on which Mahler's *Das Lied von der Erde* was based. Heinzen's review confirms that the Düsseldorf audience was enthusiastic and demanded that Gál should acknowledge an ocean of applause.[24]

Following its premiere, further productions of *The Sacred Duck* were mounted in Breslau and Berlin by the director Heinz Tietjen, who later under Hitler would be Artistic Director in Bayreuth. Hanns Gutman, reviewing the Berlin performances for *Anbruch*, wrote 'the score of this opera demonstrates how the orchestra has developed throughout the nineteenth century and is handled with the same virtuosity as Mahler and Strauss'.[25] Gutman goes on to admire the exotic nature of Gál's music with its use of fourths, fifths and whole tones.[26] He singles out Maria Schreker, to whom he pays a back-handed compliment by saying that though she is far and away the most enchanting creature on 'any opera stage today', she is vocally unable to surmount the acoustical difficulties of [the newly renovated auditorium of] Berlin's Charlottenburg Opera.[27] This small niggle aside, a resounding success is reported by all.

In his memoirs, Krenek recounts the flood of new operas from this period that were not revived after their premieres, a statement confirmed by a glance at the schedules of any German opera house. Even those works from the interwar years now seen as seminal, such as Krenek's own *Jonny spielt auf*, Max Brand's *Maschinist Hopkins*, Paul Hindemith's *Neues vom Tage* and Kurt Weill's *Aufstieg und Fall der Stadt Mahagonny*, only had runs of a few seasons, though some took place outside of Germany. *Jonny spielt auf*, for instance, even made it to the Metropolitan Opera in 1929, where it was received by a perplexed local audience who had no idea that Krenek's gently syncopated beer-tent music was actually supposed to represent American jazz. Some works such as Berg's *Wozzeck* and Korngold's *Die tote Stadt*, along with Schreker's three most successful operas and Strauss's *Der Rosenkavalier*, continued successful, though not unbroken runs in Germany's many opera houses. However, with the exception of *Wozzeck*, all of these operas had been composed before 1920. The list of one-season wonders composed after 1920 makes the tenacious hold of Gál's Chinese fairy-tale opera all the more remarkable.

In 1927, Gál's publisher, Universal Edition, produced a special edition of *Musikblätter des Anbruch* on the subject of 'Opera' and commissioned Gál to write a contribution on the problems of 'comic opera'. The article is illuminating: Gál highlights operetta as encroaching on the territory of the traditional German comic opera, and acknowledges that the genre, deriving from its French ancestor of a century earlier, uses far more drastic means to give the public what it wants – namely, unencumbered light-weight musical theatre. For this reason, it has proved a strong adversary against which the traditional German *Spieloper*, or comic opera, stands little chance. He cites Strauss's *Rosenkavalier* as the only recent comic opera to establish itself in the repertoire. Gál goes on to analyse several works that should have been popular but failed, such as Busoni's *Arlecchino*, which he sees as miscalculating its use of parody. He argues strongly for a return to the traditional model of the *Spieloper*, as composed by Nicolai, Lortzing and Flowtow, citing the very lineage in which Paul Nettl saw Gál's own *Sacred Duck*.[28]

Surprisingly, Gál does not mention *Die Vögel*,[29] a comic opera by Walter Braunfels based on Aristophanes, also published by Universal Edition, which enjoyed considerable success in 1920 when it was first performed in Munich under Bruno Walter. Braunfels followed this with another comic opera that, according to Alfred Einstein in *Anbruch*, seemed to fit Gál's directives for the genre to a tee.[30] Entitled *Don Gil von den grünen Hosen*,[31] it had a prestigious and successful premiere in Munich under Hans Knappertsbusch in 1924. Despite an original text by Tirso de Molina (1571–1648), *Don Gil* did not offer the clever amusement of Gál's librettist for *The Sacred Duck*, Karl Levetzow. Thanks to the success of *Die Vögel*, Braunfels was a far more commercial proposition than Gál, and following *Don Gil's* premiere, it was instantly taken up in Stuttgart, Königsberg, Leipzig and Cologne, before slipping permanently from view in 1927. Its disappearance puts the more enduring success of Gál's *Sacred Duck* into sharper relief.

Unlike Schoenberg, Schreker and many other Austrians, Gál did not migrate to Berlin after World War I. He assumed Bruckner's position as harmony teacher at Vienna's University until 1929 when, on the recommendations of Strauss and Furtwängler, he was offered the Directorship of the Music Academy in Mainz. Gál thus landed in the centre of the musical establishment.

The conductor Erich Kleiber was referred to as Gál's 'twin': not only did they share a birthday but they were placed next to each other throughout their school years, and it was believed that they even shared a certain physical resemblance. Gál's fellow piano pupils under his teacher Richard Robert included Georg Szell, Clara Haskil and Rudolf Serkin; his champions included Fritz Busch in Dresden, Wilhelm Furtwängler in Berlin, and the Rosé and Kolisch Quartets in Vienna. Gál was a committee member with Alban Berg and Ernst Toch of the Allgemeiner Deutscher Musikverein, an organisation that was a major platform for contemporary and experimental music. He was an occasional contributor to both *Anbruch* and *Melos*, and during the interwar years he was published by Universal Edition, Simrock and Schott. He won the first Austrian State Prize for music in 1913, a prize he won again in 1958. Gál's other operas were well received, but never enjoyed the success of *The Sacred Duck*. His last opera, a grotesque in the manner of Berthold Goldschmidt's *Der Gewaltige Hahnrei*, successfully premiered in Mannheim in 1932, was *Die beiden Klaas*,[32] scheduled for a double premiere in Hamburg and in Dresden in 1933 under Fritz Busch. Like Goldschmidt's *Hahnrei*, scheduled for performances in Berlin, it too was abruptly cancelled by the Nazi regime.

The *Realpolitik* of Schott & Sons: 1933

After the cancellation of *Die beiden Klaas*, Gál returned to Vienna and attempted to have the opera performed at the Volksoper. At this point, he received a revealing letter from his publisher Schott in Mainz. The proprietor himself, Dr Ludwig Strecker, wrote to Gál explaining that the cancellation was due to misgivings about the libretto. Strecker goes on to explain: 'only because of the text, quite apart from the opera's other "compromising moments". At present, you're simply too far from the firing line to recognise the drastic change in the course our company is presently being forced to take, a point I mention only in passing.'[33] If we are to believe Strecker's letter, the objections to mounting the work in Hamburg were not due to Gál's Jewishness. He had already been removed from his position as Director of the Music Academy in Mainz for this reason, following the Nazi take-over of the town council in 1933 and a high-profile anti-Semitic campaign in the local press. There was no need for his publisher to be squeamish on this point. The 'compromising moments' referred to by Strecker most likely included a scene, shown in a split set, with two couples in bed with each other's spouses. The objections within the 'new situation in Germany' were presented as moral rather than racial. Sexual incontinence, however, was a frequent anti-Semitic charge that was probably understood without having to be spelt out. Presumably unknown to Gál, Ludwig Strecker, under the pseudonym of Ludwig Andersen, would soon make a name for himself in Hitler's New Germany as librettist for a remarkable number of stage works and oratorios with obvious nationalist sympathies.[34] Gál's attempts to move the premiere to Vienna's Volksoper were thwarted by financial difficulties, and the work was not performed until after the composer's death when York Opera, a provincial ensemble in the North of England, took it up in 1990.

As confirmation that Schott was not reticent in discussing racial issues, a letter sent to Erich Korngold from Willi Strecker, Ludwig's brother, dated 11 October 1933 (nearly a year before the letter to Gál regarding *Die beiden Klaas*) confirms that the proposed operatic treatment of something called *The Marriage of Ariane* was unacceptable because of its explicit 'racial content'. He mentions that he's relieved that Korngold has removed some provocative material and tells him that had he not done so, he would have landed without question on the blacklist. Interestingly, Strecker confirms that, 'thank heavens', Korngold's name has not yet come up in discussions of composers to be banned from performance. Strecker goes on to explain that non-Aryan authors are treated more severely, and the merest hint of questionable material could lead to difficulties: 'Even if the tone coming out of Berlin on the Jewish question appears more conciliatory with matters of artistic merit being placed above all other factors, the mood in the provincial Leagues for German Culture is at present so aggressive that no theatre director or even orchestra conductor dares to perform a work of Jewish authorship without danger of public demonstrations. You can't imagine the difficulties our publishing house faces with constant charges of "cultural Bolshevism" and "international

Jewish tendencies". It would be fuel to the fire to all of those who have had their rejected manuscripts returned from us.'[35]

In February 1933, only weeks after Hitler's appointment as Federal Chancellor, Gál enjoyed his last interwar premiere in Germany with his Violin Concerto played by Georg Kulenkampff with Fritz Busch conducting the Dresden Staatskapelle. Gál was a popular teacher, performer and administrator. If his music was thought emotionally contained, it was nearly always melodically engaging and harmonically intriguing. He had become so established in German musical life that he simply couldn't comprehend the reality of the anti-Semitic press campaign waged against him, and his dismissal as director of the Mainz Academy in 1933. Efforts by the local mayor, along with pleas from Furtwängler, were to no avail. Local Nazis eventually succeeded in removing the mayor as well. Uncomprehending, and convinced that such madness would only be temporary, Gál took his family to the Black Forest, where he composed a beautiful and poignant violin sonata. Unusually for a work from this period, he did not give it an opus number, perhaps because, in spite of even the loss of home and livelihood, its unapologetic expressiveness was something he viewed as atypical.

As such, Gál stands emblematically as the 'typical' Jewish composer of the Weimar Constitution years, though he was only one of many composers such as Walter Braunfels, Max Ettinger, Wilhelm Rettich, Ignaz Waghalter and Egon Wellesz, who in their different ways maintained a cautious distance from the various trends of New Objectivity. Gál certainly enjoyed more commercial success than the followers of Schoenberg, or modernists such as Ernst Toch or Wladimir Vogel, and stood squarely in the middle of where social and cultural assimilation had landed him. By the time he was awarded the 1958 Austrian State prize, headed by a committee consisting of Egon Kornauth and Joseph Marx, it was tacitly acknowledged that Jewish cultural assimilation had produced in Gál a composer who represented the most deeply-held values of the Austro-German traditions.

Egon Wellesz

Egon Wellesz, another Guido Adler pupil, also felt that music could find new means of expressing itself by emulating older models while avoiding the excesses of nineteenth-century Romanticism. If Gál saw the traditional forms of quartets, sonatas and suites as perfect vehicles for new musical ideas, Wellesz believed that musical theatre could reinvent itself by returning to the formal pageantry of the French Baroque. However, Wellesz was harmonically and tonally far more adventurous than Gál and the largest difference between them was that Wellesz was inclined to greater expressive extremes than his more restrained colleague. As both had completed doctorates in music history under Adler, they appeared to lend weight to Wagner's accusation that Jews returned to the past because they ostensively lacked the soul of the native German that would give them the confidence to shape the present. What Wagner – wilfully blind to the intentions of his own setting of Teutonic mythology – did not take into account was that composers such as Gál and Wellesz saw the past as offering the means of shaping the present. It was a view that was shared by that most revolutionary of Jewish composers, Arnold Schoenberg, who like many of his contemporaries saw Wagner himself as the key-stone within German music's recent past.

Wellesz was a far more complex individual than his younger colleague Gál. In many ways assimilation could explain his artistic development, and his conversion (with his wife Emmy) to Catholicism in 1917. Nevertheless, the evidence suggests that their conversion was made not for reasons of social convenience, but from religious conviction. This did not stop fellow modernist (and devout Catholic) Ernst Krenek from voicing doubts: '[Within the ISCM] Egon Wellesz was ideologically a bit of the odd man out, though I was told that he had studied for a period with Schoenberg. [. . .] He composed along the lines of what I would call "measured Modernism", hustling and bustling about while musically pursuing a cautious middle path. He had converted to Catholicism, something he continually fussed about, but managed to gain access to high social and political circles.'[36] What Krenek referred to as 'gemäßigt Moderner' ('measured modernist') was, in Wellesz's case, an attempt to create a contemporary idiom that, like Gál's, was the result of new works emerging through a prism of the past.

Viewed superficially, Gál and Wellesz had much in common: both had completed their doctorates under Adler and contributed to *Denkmäler der Tonkunst in Österreich*; both were Jewish Austrians of Hungarian extraction. But whereas Gál was grounded in the very bedrock of the Austro-Germanic tradition as represented by Bach, Mendelssohn, Schumann and especially Brahms, Wellesz was one of the first to explore the early Austro-Italian Baroque, which he referred to as 'the bridge to Haydn'. His dissertation was on Giuseppe Bonno (1711–88), the Viennese-born Italian who was predecessor to Antonio Salieri (1750–1825) at the Court in Vienna. From 1905, along with Berg and Webern, Wellesz was one of Schoenberg's first pupils at Vienna's Schwarzwald School. He was also one of the founding members of the ISCM, many of whom were musicians from Schoenberg's circle.

Yet despite being Schoenberg's first biographer in 1920, he was by no means a blind disciple. Wellesz was also a Francophile and one of the first to promote

Debussy's music in Vienna. His orchestral *Stimmungsbild*, from 1912, entitled *Vorfrühling*,[37] has impressionistic colours and an opening flute solo that could be considered a dark central-European view of Debussy's *Prélude à l'après-midi d'un faune*. Bartók was an early admirer of Wellesz and managed to procure him his first contract with the Budapest publisher Rózsavölgyi. In due course, both composers would move to Universal Edition in Vienna. Béla Balázs, Bartók's librettist for *Duke Bluebeard's Castle* (1911) and author of his ballet *The Wooden Prince* (1914–16), also wrote the scenario for Wellesz's first stage work, the ballet *Das Wunder der Diana*[38] from 1914–17. The two composers remained in close contact, both took part in the Congrès de musique arabe at Cairo in 1932, and they were frequent colleagues at various ISCM events.

Such an unusual and knowledgeable voice among Vienna's progressive musicians was a puzzle to the conservative Julius Korngold. He was impressed by the young man's intelligence and talent, but this admiration was not reciprocated: Wellesz mentions Korngold in the earliest pages of his memoirs as a critic of 'despotic power with the ability to poison relationships between composers who otherwise would have admired one another'.[39] Korngold's impressions of Wellesz are prescient. They date from 1919 and, as can be seen in his review of Wellesz's piano *Idyllen*, Korngold had high hopes for the 34-year-old composer:

> In Egon Wellesz's fine and delicate work *Idyllen* [Op. 21] we can clearly hear the composer's admiration for French Impressionism. Is this perhaps a conversion away from his grim radicalism of earlier days? We ask this question eagerly of the erudite young composer whom we also greet as a fellow critic within our midst. One may hopefully be able to deduce as much from his essay in the latest edition of the *Berlin Rundschau* in which he tells us that he is now studying the melodic structures of the music of antiquity and even that of folk music. If, as he writes, this leads him to greater simplicity and a more sincerely felt expression, then we may be witnessing some interesting changes taking place amongst the circles of Vienna's modernists.[40]

He even keeps faith with Wellesz after a performance of the Second String Quartet a few months later:

> Newness in music is never the result of mixing and matching. [. . .] Experimentation as an attempt at being different and writing music that addresses the 'problematic' is merely incompetent and not 'new' at all. And as for crowbarring old music into new: well, here in Vienna during the past fifteen years, we've heard quite enough of this gimmick, though I believe at

long last we may have finally seen it off. The latest apostate of this movement is our young colleague Dr Egon Wellesz, who appealed recently for a return to the melodic element in the manner of earlier days – even suggesting a return to the folk song. His string quartet [. . .] should not deceive us. It's a work that originates from over a year ago and cannot be attributed to this latest conversion. It's fundamentally a sin of the past and is best viewed as a clinical demonstration of all the problematic nonsense that this would represent.

We find ourselves confronted in this work with something I refer to as 'negative composing'. [. . .] Yet the movements (naturally, they're not laid out in any kind of traditional sequence) never actually lose sight of a fundamental idea, while at the same time giving no hint of what one might conceivably identify as (this reddest of red-rags to the extremists) a structural tonic. [. . .] There is simply one essential fact that is impossible to get around: that which is artificially concocted and remains far from traditional tonality neither sings nor speaks to us. Otherwise, Wellesz offers us many interesting tonal combinations and instrumental effects.

Dr Wellesz [. . .] has a very real talent for composing music. His technical facilities are convincingly well beyond most of his colleagues, regardless of whether they strike out towards the musical left or the musical right. He should perhaps consider forgetting his dead-end developments concerning music from antiquity and listen to the purity of his fundamentally unprejudiced and naive musical heart.[41]

Within a few years, Korngold's hopes for Wellesz had been dashed. Wellesz was a co-founder of the International Society for Contemporary Music in 1922, an organisation that Korngold dismissed as 'German infiltration' of Austria's musical heritage.[42] Given that the other founding members – Rudolf Réti, Hugo Heller, Rudolf Bing and Emil Hertzka – were Austrians, this was obviously an absurd assertion.[43]

Wellesz offers a far more accurate account of the founding of the ISCM in his memoirs, explaining that it had started off as a suggestion made by Réti. Its immediate objective, however, was to be the first international music festival that drew the many national contemporary music festivals together.[44] Heller was to sort out the finances and he brought along Rudolf Bing, who would take on the administration. Hertzka, as owner and director of Universal Edition, stood by as consultant. Wellesz travelled to England to discuss contracts with Robert Mayer and his wife Dorothy, and in Paris en route he met Milhaud and Honegger, who were also enthusiastic about the concept of an international contemporary music festival. Wellesz writes – and this is perhaps the 'German' reference that irritated Korngold – 'thanks to the coop-eration of all participants, particularly those from Germany, we scheduled the Salzburg contemporary music festival for August 1922 and it was a big success. It was the first time since the end of the war that musicians from Europe and America had participated in such an event together. Old relation-ships were renewed and new friendships were made. [. . .] It was decided that the event should not be a one-off.'[45]

A meeting was held in January 1923 in London, where it was decided that the organisation should be given a name. It was at this point that it was chris-tened the International Society for Contemporary Music or ISCM. It would be based in London, and Edward Dent, who was British, would act as its President. There was to be an international jury of five selected members who would decide what was performed. The first jury members were Wellesz, André Caplet, Ernest Ansermet, Hermann Scherchen and Alexander Zemlinsky. The first official chamber music festival under ISCM auspices was held the following summer in Salzburg, with the orchestral concerts held later in the year in Prague. The third ISCM Festival, held in Venice, became one of the milestones in the relationship between Stravinsky and Schoenberg, both of whom were accompanied by their circles of respective acolytes: Stravinsky ignored Schoenberg, and Schoenberg was visibly rude to Stravinsky, estab-lishing a pattern that would be maintained throughout the rest of their lives, including the years they jointly spent in exile in Los Angeles.

Edward Dent offers his own version of events as reported in *The Times* in 1934:

One day Wellesz and I were invited to a local committee to consider the future of Salzburg as a 'festival Town'. I suggested that they should run a six-week festival from the beginning of August to the middle of September inviting all sorts of musical and dramatic bodies from different countries to take part in turn, and publishing early each year a day-to-day diary of all the events including plays, concerts, operas, folksong and dance meetings, church music and the Marionette Theatre.

This was received with blank amazement, and it was evident that they all thought me only fit for a lunatic asylum. The local committee was interested mainly in Max Reinhardt and a project – for which it was assumed the Americans would pay, of course – to disfigure the beautiful park of Hellbrunn by building a theatre there for him in the shape of a monstrous wedding-cake. Prague solved our problem for us by inviting us to that most musical of all European cities in 1924, and in 1925 we divided the festival between Prague and Venice. Our French friends had always told us that the

Italians would never form a national section, as they were all too busy quar-
relling among themselves; but for once the French were wrong, and we have
had three festivals in Italy (Venice 1925, Siena 1928, and Florence 1934)
which have been among the most brilliant in our history.[46]

Other than Scherchen and the British (but German-born) Robert Mayer,
Germans did not predominate in the ISCM in these early days – certainly not
to the extent that Korngold could speak of an 'infiltration of Austrian music'.[47]
Indeed, the ISCM appeared to be overwhelmingly Austrian in its initial
membership even if its President was British. This did not deter Julius
Korngold from founding, with the help of colleagues at the *Neue Freie Presse*,
something called *Der Österreichische Kulturbund*,[48] which from 1923 was
holding alternative new-music festivals led by himself and Julius Bittner. The
'Kulturbund' festival for 1923 in Vienna (8–11 August) included works by
Richard Strauss, Joseph Marx, Franz Schreker, Wilhelm Kienzl, Erich
Korngold, Wilhelm Grosz, Julius Bittner, Max Springer, Egon Kornauth, Hans
Gál and Bernhard Paumgartner, along with some early Schoenberg songs and
Zemlinsky's First String Quartet, which, according to Alban Berg, were
included as 'fig-leaves' to disguise the blatantly conservative strain of Austrian
music being presented.[49] Though the occasional mention of the Kulturbund
is made right up through 1929, it never approached the prestige of the ISCM.

It was through his wife, the art historian Dr Emmy Wellesz née Stross, that
Wellesz developed a deep interest in Byzantine music and, together with the
English Byzantine scholar H. J. W Tillyard, deciphered middle-Byzantine
Neumic notation in 1916. Wellesz would eventually become as highly regarded
for his expertise on Byzantine music as for his work as a composer. Though
this interest did not colour much of his own music – only his *Festliches
Präludium* Op. 100 and *Mirabile Mysterium* Op. 101[50] set out explicitly to
make the connection – his fascination with Byzantine chant gives an indication of Wellesz's eclectic musical tendencies. If we look at his first fifteen opus
numbers, we are confronted with a dizzying array of musical identities,
seeming to represent entirely different musical personas. His earliest piano
works and songs, the pieces that impressed Bartók, are nothing short of proto-
minimalism akin to Satie. During the early days of the twentieth century, they
must have sounded quite radical in their unremitting simplicity. Other works
are sharp and aggressively atonal, while a number are closer to French
Impressionism than to the Austro-German Impressionism that was so
characteristic of Schreker, early Schoenberg and Zemlinsky.

In addition to his relationship with Balázs, Wellesz collaborated with
other literary giants of the day such as Hugo von Hofmannsthal and Jakob

Wassermann. Though he was a much more eclectic composer than Gál, another factor that united them was the distance they kept from New Objectivity. Wellesz, however, believed that atonality and twelve-note techniques were expressive devices that could be applied when conventional tonality no longer sufficed to communicate what the creative voice demanded. This was not a view shared by Gál, who explained in a concert interval broadcast in the context of a discussion on aleatoric music, 'Music is a succession of clearly conceived, closely linked events in which every note has its organic function and its proper place, just as every word has in a well-built sentence and every sentence in a well-reasoned paragraph. This is what music as an ideal has been for the last 500 years and nothing has happened in my lifetime to shake my confidence in the fitness of this definition.'[51] He expressed himself even more clearly in an interview in 1971: 'Well, I do believe in tonality as much as I believe, say, in gravity; I have it in my musical constitution, and I cannot imagine music without tonality. In my consciousness, tonality is as firm as a rock. But I have never theorized about it. We are subject to gravity, but we have learnt that weightlessness exists. So atonality may exist, but I cannot imagine it any more than I can imagine weightlessness. I am speaking of myself; I have accepted the fact that people can live without weight and without tonality. I am afraid I can't.'[52] Such statements obviously left no quarter for the musical abstraction afforded by atonality; nor would Gál be convinced by claims of coherency in Schoenberg's twelve-note system.

Wellesz maintained a unique position among opera composers of the day. His desire to recreate the splendour of the high Baroque is explained in an article he wrote entitled 'Das Problem der Form' ('The Problem of Form') for the magazine Von neuer Musik in 1920 and it is quoted by his wife Emmy in her completion of his memoirs:

During the years of the First World War it became more and more evident that outward events should not impose demands on the contemporary musician. Rather, the artist should lift his gaze to his surroundings and search for a firm footing on something solid and sacred that is totally enclosed by a wondrous tradition. The dramatic artist need not speak of himself or of his own destiny, or even of individual destinies. Instead, he should speak of the things that are interconnected within this world and the outer-world. I have a vision of a dramatic work in which song is combined with dance in a near cultic fashion so that aspirations of our time which have been absent from the operatic stage can be revealed in the context of something with which we are already familiar. This form is best revealed using material that is timeless and detached from period. It is placed in a distant world that speaks to our world today and from where we are offered a view into a higher plane. The secret of great art is thus found in the recognisable from our own world combined with the incommensurable. [53]

According to Emmy, this was an idea that came to Wellesz following lengthy conversations with Hugo von Hofmannsthal, who was enthusiastic about returning to antiquity as a source of reinterpreting material for contemporary audiences. The hybrid dance-opera, a continuation of Baroque practice, became very much a Wellesz speciality and – apart from the familiar collaborations with Richard Strauss – their libretti remain the only other texts supplied by Hofmannsthal to a composer.

Wellesz further exploited the chorus as a dramatic device that comments on the action, while at the same time moving rhythmically in such a way as to provide additional narrative illustration. This idea of movement generated Wellesz's further interest in dance, and probably no other composer of note from this time apart from Stravinsky wrote so much music specifically for ballet. Wellesz's *Persisches Ballet* (*Persian Ballet*) of 1920, his one-act *Achilles auf Skyros* (*Achilles on Skyros*) from 1921, based on a scenario by Hofmannsthal, and his exclusive use of percussion in *Die Nächtlichen* (*Those of the Night*, 1923), were considered pioneering in German contemporary dance. In discussions with the choreographer Kurt Jooss, Wellesz developed the opera-ballet *Opferung des Gefangenen* (*Sacrifice of the Prisoner*) in 1924–5, based on a scenario by Eduard Stucken. It was to be the third part of Wellesz's 'Heroic Trilogy' which already consisted of two works to texts by Hofmannsthal: the short opera *Alkestis* and the ballet *Achilles auf Skyros*. *Opferung des Gefangenen* was a further hybrid of theatrical genres in that each character was accorded both a dancing and a singing persona, a device employed nearly a decade later by Kurt Weill and Bertolt Brecht in *The Seven Deadly Sins*.

Apart from his short comic opera from 1927, *Scherz, List und Rache*[54] based on Goethe's libretto for the composer Phillip Christoph Kayser (1755–1826), Wellesz remained during his interwar years wedded to the world of antiquity. *Die Bakchantinnen*,[55] 1929–30, would be the culmination of this experimentation with dance, movement, chant and pageantry.

Wellesz's previous operas had enjoyed success in German opera houses. Ernst Toch was taken with *Alkestis* following its premiere in Mannheim, and the two composers became friendly despite their very different aesthetic ideas: Wellesz's highly individual style was, if anything, extraordinarily *subjective*, propelling him beyond the conventional boundaries of new-objective Modernism, while steering clear of Expressionistic excesses.

The premiere of *Die Bakchantinnen* under Clemens Krauss at the Vienna State Opera in 1931 was an unqualified success, not just with new-music enthusiasts, but with the general public. Its position as one of the most successful experiments in musical theatre from the interwar years was thwarted by the Nazis when they forced the cancellation of a planned 1933 Munich production. Its high energy, a result of an often relentless syncopated rhythmic drive combined with a declamatory and sometimes Monteverdian treatment of text, is perhaps only matched in originality by the two operas of Wladimir Vogel, *Wagadus Untergang durch die Eitelkeit*[56] of 1930 and *Thyl Claes* from the 1940s, both of which combine rhythmic spoken chant with a mixture of often seductive harmonic lyricism. Neither of these extraordinary works, however, enjoyed the critical recognition of *Die Bakchantinnen*.

Wellesz wrote over 40 articles for *Anbruch* and he features as the subject in nearly as many again. It is surprising that *Die Bakchantinnen*, which uniquely among Wellesz's stage works was not published by Universal Edition, is not singled out for a dedicated essay, as previously with his major works. The most substantial review came from Julius Korngold in the *Neue Freie Presse*, spread over the first four pages of the newspaper. The critic astonishes first of all with his understanding of Euripides as a historian, author and poet. The breadth and depth of his classical education informs his review of Wellesz's treatment. He mentions the history of classical subjects and opera, and he correctly identifies Gluck as Wellesz's model. He also sees *Die Bakchantinnen* as part of a larger trend that includes Stravinsky's *Oedipus Rex* and admits to a certain bemusement that contemporary operatic fashions appear to offer up various versions of the *Zeitoper* and its diametrical opposite: works that hearken back to antiquity. He praises the way Wellesz solves dramatic problems, and mentions that the best bits of the opera are those involving the chorus, and that 'fortunately, there are a lot of scenes with chorus'.[57] He goes on to write that Wellesz's connection with Schoenberg's circle and his association with the ISCM will guarantee no shortage of admirers and positive publicity. From here, however, the review goes downhill, but not in the way one might expect. And as is often the case with Korngold, it is the very points he criticises that make the work so remarkable.

The tragedy of an opera such as *Bakchantinnen* is its lack of emotional expression.

[...] After letting this first hint of the work's most fundamental flaw slip out, something not remotely compensated for by the cacophony of semi-atonality and heterophony, let us at least hasten forward to praise the restless industry of the composer and his courage in risking what amongst his colleagues would be seen as a bathetic retrospective into antiquity. In point of fact, he goes all the way back to – dare we mention the name? – Monteverdi. And along with fellow Viennese composer Alban Berg, we must also emphasise the seriousness, character and the artistic idealism of Wellesz as well.

Since we have mentioned Alban Berg, perhaps a comparison with *Wozzeck* will inform the reader as to the style and manner of *Bakchantinnen*. Wellesz is not as intransigent in his atonality as Berg and when he does resort to it, it is on a totally different level. There are triads in *Bakchantinnen*, even C-major triads: allegiances to a key-signature! This is indeed a man with whom we can do business! Atonality and polytonality crash against one another in vertical directions, in other words, in the notes heaped together as chords and the layering of voices. Horizontally, the lines are generally tonal and the ability to comprehend and follow a melody is not as limited as with *Wozzeck*, in which much of the singing is not singing at all but is in fact, non-melodic speech. [. . .] As this work, however, misses its fundamental harmonic power, one cannot get away from the thought that much of it is merely worthy, or over-eagerness to score points with party dogmatists. Alban Berg's methods are more organic and thus – a surprising conclusion – more tolerable, as they are rooted in colour and polyphony in a more orthodox 'Schoenbergian' style. [. . .] The predictable atonal avant-garde devices are employed also by Wellesz: a lot of secessionist movement-choruses, escaping into an ostinato bass that hammers away like the Russians, Stravinsky or Prokofiev. This constant reminder of how he can compose wrong-sounding music, the scrupulous avoidance of anything that might possibly sound like a natural cadence; in a word: this *negative composing*.[58]

There follows a further comparison with *Wozzeck*, concluding with the observation: '*Wozzeck* in its everyday use of language is more original – as indeed Alban Berg is the more spontaneous and differentiated – and in fact technically superior composer.'[59] To be damned by Julius Korngold in an unfavourable comparison with Alban Berg was no doubt insulting, especially as Wellesz had campaigned assiduously to have *Wozzeck* first performed in Berlin, and even more because Korngold had rarely condemned a work as thoroughly as he had *Wozzeck*, suggesting that people attending performances might prefer to leave their ears at home (though in fairness, Korngold is generous in his praise of Berg's undeniable brilliance).[60] Clemens Krauss left the Vienna Opera in 1934, and *Die Bakchantinnen* was not revived in Austria. Wellesz had in any case turned a corner: *Die*

Bakchantinnen would be his last stage work until *Incognito*, an opera based on William Congreve written for the Oxford Opera Club in 1950 and submitted to a competition run by the Arts Council of Great Britain. After *Die Bakchantinnen*, Wellesz next turned to a sequence of tone-poems based on Shakespeare's *The Tempest*, which he entitled *Prosperos Beschwörungen* (*The Spells of Prospero*), a project that subsequently provided Wellesz – living in British exile after the war – with a template for an exploration of that most Austro-German of musical forms, the symphony. All nine of Wellesz's symphonies were written in the last 25 years of his life, the first of them completed in 1945.

The most potent of Prospero's spells, however, saved Wellesz, Bruno Walter and Ernst Krenek from Nazi arrest and certain annihilation. Walter had programmed a series of concerts in Amsterdam in which the works of two living Austrian composers would feature: Wellesz's *Prospero* and Krenek's Second Piano Concerto. Krenek had composed this to be simple enough to perform himself, since he needed income following the banning of his music in Germany.[61] The Jewish Austrian pianist and noted Schoenbergian, Peter Stadlen also attended the performances, which took place over the weekend of Hitler's annexation of Austria and triumphant march into Vienna. Wellesz, Walter, Krenek and Stadlen all fled to England. Gál would follow soon thereafter and together, he with Wellesz and Stadlen would remain in Britain, becoming respected writers and academics, while their reputations as composers were of only marginal interest to the British musical establishment. After the war, Gál, with the help of Rudolf Bing, became one of the founders of the Edinburgh Festival.

What both Gál and Wellesz represented was the view that there were different ways of reacting to the post-Wagnerian Romanticism identified by Alfred Einstein as the 'debilitating condition' that undermined German music's capacity of reinventing itself, and thus maintaining its supremacy. There were, however, several young, Austro-German Jewish composers who believed that the musical ideals of Wagner represented the better way forward, lining themselves up behind such established figures as Richard Strauss, Hans Pfitzner, Siegfried Wagner and Franz Schmidt. To them, post-Wagnerian Romanticism was not at all a spent force but a legitimate direction that offered plenty of scope to a younger generation of composers.

CHAPTER 9

The Resolute Romantics

A fight between the constructive power of rhythm and the gentle soothing of harmony: this is the fate of music that produces undreamt of stimuli through both strength and weakness while ardently reaching for a new sense of unity. A magical place is discovered and with it, the craving for new sensations. As these sensations become exhausted, chaos threatens while the creative urge drives us further and further towards new shapes and forms. By the time we have circuitously reached this point, we shall discover sensuality and intellect in fierce conflict.

Kampf zwischen der aufbauenden Kraft des Rhythmus und der verfeinerden, verweichlichenden Harmonik: das ist das Schicksal einer Musik, die zwischen Kraft und Schwäche ungeahnte Reize gewinnt, aber sehnsuchtsvoll nach einer neuen Geschlossenheit ausschaut. Ein Wunderland wird entdeckt. Der Schritt zur Reizsamkeit wird getan. Das Reizsame nutzt sich ab. Das Chaos droht. Aber der schöpferische Geist drängt zu neuer Gestaltung, zu neuer Form. Die Zeit, da auf weitem Umweg solches geschieht, ist eben jene, in der Sinnlichkeit und Intellektualismus sich stark befehden.

Adolf Weißmann, *Die Musik in der Weltkrise*, 1922

The Romantic Renewal and Houston Stewart Chamberlain

At this point, it's worth recalling the cultural upheaval resulting from the First World War. Though Germany and Austria had sued for peace in 1918, they assumed that the war, which had ground on for four years, had ended in a stalemate. Neither side had gained any significant advantage and both had suffered unimaginable casualties. Germany, Austria and their allies sustained losses of approximately 8.5 million, compared with the 5 million casualties of the Entente and its various partners. But the sabre rattling and armaments race before 1914 had been as intense among the Triple Alliance of France, Russia and Britain as it was among the Germans. The gunshot in Sarajevo was, from the Austrian perspective, an act of aggression. For the rest of the world, it was merely the starting pistol that unleashed pent-up tensions throughout Europe. By 1914, Germany as a unified state was only 43 years old; unification had come at a cost to the French, and with the accession of Wilhelm II the new state gained imperial aspirations with only limited room for geographical expansion.

These ambitions need to be put into context. Wilhelm I, who became the first German Emperor in 1871, was born in 1797, only 11 years after the death of Frederick the Great. Wilhelm went on to live to the age of 91. When he died in 1888, his son, Frederick III, only survived him by 99 days before the crown passed to Wilhelm II, who remained Emperor until the fall of the House of Hohenzollern in 1918. Wilhelm I was a Prussian with little comprehension of Bismarck's united Germany. He believed that being Emperor of Germany was a distraction from being King of Prussia, and legend has it that on the eve of his imperial coronation in Versailles, he wept with despair. Wilhelm II, however, was a child of the Empire and thus the first (and only) German Emperor whose allegiance to Prussia was secondary to his allegiance to Germany. His Germany had, since 1871, undoubtedly become more Prussian, but Prussia had also become more German. Wilhelm II was a man who looked forward to the twentieth century, while his grandfather had looked back to the eighteenth. While Wilhelm I found Bismarck a necessity who aided the mechanics of running the complex network of German states beyond Prussia while managing a compliant but irritating parliament, Wilhelm II dismissed him, sending him into long overdue retirement.

Several factors might be held responsible for starting the war: most obviously, it was the Austrian need to avenge the assassination of their future Emperor and his wife. Nevertheless, Germany found it convenient as an excuse to flex its muscles on a global scale in competition with France and Britain. It presented Austria with an opportunity of establishing its hold amongst the remnants of the Ottoman Empire in the Balkans and thus bettering Russia. One could even blame the British – fearful of Germany as a rival colonial power – and the French, over-eager to regain Alsace-Lorraine and to redress their defeat in the Franco-Prussian War. Even the Americans were not entirely blameless; though at first reluctant to participate, they too eventually joined in the European brawl if only to keep German expansion in check. In short, the world was ripe for conflict. The fears that had been projected into art and literature for decades had finally been fulfilled. Nobody knew how it would end, but everyone thought that they would be better off, almost regardless of the outcome.

Yet even before the war, it was clear that a new age was imminent. Mechanisation held the same hidden promises that technology holds today. If the war could produce an undisputed victor it was science's transmutation into industry, which had provided the advanced weaponry of modern battle. By 1918, it had supplied the tools for conquering both the monarchy and the church. Even if the old order had passed, the strong emotions that once pounded in every patriot's heart, and continued to find expression in art, literature and music, had not been totally destroyed and demanded new validation.

Empirical scientific investigations did not pretend to provide all of the answers to nature's great mysteries, but the better scientists already knew what they didn't know and were confident that they could carry on finding things out without recourse to religion or philosophy, and increasingly without recourse to ethics, as witnessed by the use of U-boats on civilian passenger liners and poison gas on the battle-field. By 1923, Felix Salten, with his story of Bambi, and Leoš Janáček, with his opera *The Cunning Little Vixen*, presented children with very secular views of reproduction, life and death as part of the natural order. Animals are anthropomorphised into sentient, thinking humans, while their nature and the world in which they live remain both ruthless and savage. At the same time, Adolf Hitler would begin writing *Mein Kampf*, in which he interpreted the 'natural order' as the subjugation of the weak by the strong. This extrapolation of pseudo-Darwinian concepts meant that arguments that had previously denied Jews German identity because they were not in possession of the German spirit were now replaced with the view that Jews, Slavs and others were inferior biological 'races', subject to annihilation by the more powerful Aryans who were, by some as yet unexplained 'scientific' logic, the natural conquerors of all others. Thus post-Wagnerian Romantics could continue their anti-Semitism unimpeded, firm in the belief that science provided their validation of racism as effectively being the law of the jungle. Where this would lead is related by Victor Klemperer 10 years later in his diary on 10 April, 1933: 'It's like Spain in the 15th Century, but in those days, it was only a question of religious beliefs. Today it's all about zoology.'[1]

Houston Stewart Chamberlain

One of the most notorious manifestations of this wilful and opportunistic misunderstanding of Darwinism was to be found in the writings of Houston

Stewart Chamberlain, the English-born son-in-law of Richard Wagner. The theories set out in his seminal work *The Foundations of the Nineteenth Century* (1899) are examined in a series of four lengthy articles in the *Neue Freie Presse* from 1905 by the Jewish philosopher and theologian Ludwig Stein, who declares Chamberlain's racial theories to be a manifestation of the Romantic movement and refers to him as 'the troubadour of racial imperialism'.[2] He compares two English Chamberlains, Houston Stewart and the unrelated Joseph, by noting that Joseph Chamberlain's enemies were specifically the Boers and anyone else who got in the way of British imperial ambitions, whereas Houston Stewart's enemies were anyone and anything resembling a mixed race: the Semitic races in general and, specifically, the Jews. Joseph Chamberlain, according to Stein, was the 'national imperialist', Houston Stewart Chamberlain, the 'racial imperialist'.[3]

The latter's views on Teutonic racial imperialism led to a close relationship between him and Kaiser Wilhelm II, who was captivated by Chamberlain's ideas. The Kaiser's approval confirmed Chamberlain as a major figure in Germany (he was actually living in Austria at the time of writing *The Foundations of the Nineteenth Century*) despite devastating reviews in many scientific journals. One that is quoted by Stein offers a summary of how pseudo-scientists of the day, such as Chamberlain, were presenting themselves: 'In short, this is an extremely bad book, unclear and illogical in its development of ideas and written in an un-gratifying style, full of false modesty and genuine arrogance; full of genuine ignorance and false scholarship.'[4]

On the other hand, Stein goes on to quote Karl Joël, the Basel University rector who was 'among the leading experts of the Philosophy of Romanticism', and wrote of Chamberlain's *Foundations of the Nineteenth Century*: 'The book lives and inflames with passion, it incites feelings of the most objectionable hatred while eliciting enthusiasm through its own conviction. It is at once so gloriously bold, so presumptuous in offering up uncensored ideas, so refreshingly irreverent, gleeful, free and so contradictory that it has more of the characteristics of a person than a book.'[5]

Stein then brings up a compilation of essays and articles by the sociologist Friedrich Otto Hertz, *Modern Racial Theory* (later published as *Race and Culture*), as a total rejection of Chamberlain's work. Hertz takes apart the contradictions and inaccuracies in Chamberlain's book. Yet, according to Stein, 'Chamberlain's response would only be a smiled, "But dear sir, I'm merely a dilettante – as I expressly explain in the foreword of the fourth edition of my book."' Stein goes on: 'In order to disprove Chamberlain, it is necessary to offer psychological explanations of the man himself. Chamberlain speaks to the tendencies of our time. Let us say this very clearly, he speaks to the deepest responses that reside in people's soul. Everyone knows that "feelings" are not things that can be disproved – at best, they can only be analysed and thus laid bare so that at least the more irrational of the components may be disproved.'[6]

In fact, Chamberlain admitted in a letter to Stein that what he felt distinguished *The Foundation of the Nineteenth Century* 'is its total lack of caution.'[7] He goes on to state that he has not written a new theory of race, nor has he updated the widely admired theories of Joseph Arthur Comte de Gobineau, the aristocratic father of the theory of 'race as a determinant of culture' and a great influence on Richard Wagner's thinking. Chamberlain continues his explanation to Stein:

> Race is to the collective what personality is to the individual. [. . .] One can in any case only define ideas, not things – race as well – it's equally impossible to define the colour blue or green. [. . .] One need only note the establishment in 1904 of the 'Racial Archive' by professors Plate, Ploetz and Nordenholtz – men who are not by any stretch of the imagination fantasists. Indeed, it is an archive that has had numerous contributions made by such distinguished scientists as the zoologists Ziegler, Ratzler, Hueppe, etc. It only proves where science is trying to lead us and gives us an indication as to which path is the correct one to follow – as such, one is able to dismiss the journalist and feuilletonist who attack research on race as a legitimate concern. Such is scientific research: a search for truth, against ignorance. [. . .] Yet one must be prepared to carry on and not be frightened of discovering the truth. As I myself am a man with the deepest respect for science, I totally reject the pure speculative hypotheses of Gobineau [. . .] rather, my views are based on those that can be inferred by Darwin's own writings on race and its origins.[8]

Stein then lays out the arguments surrounding Chamberlain's 'subjective conviction' and, in sentences that recall Schoenberg, he writes that he is merely 'listening to his inner voice, regardless of the consequences'. Chamberlain's arguments regarding race are 'race is a fact. Everyone is aware of it.' But as Stein points out, he is oblivious to the possible findings of future evaluations of a not-yet-understood science: 'Yet his belief that believing is all that matters flies in the face of the many things we have believed in the past and have had to reject as evidence came to light that disproved that which we had known "deep in our hearts" to be true.'[9]

In placing the Romantics in opposition to the Enlightenment, Stein writes that 'irrationality is not to be countered by rationality' and quotes another review of Chamberlain's book by the Viennese psychiatrist Otto Pötzl, who wrote: 'Chamberlain's "Teutonic races" are a purely intuitive, artificial and personal concept. His thoughts regarding "race" are equally part of his intuition and must thus be ascribed to his personal domain. The idea behind race breeds further ideas regarding race which inevitably lead directly back to [Chamberlain's] original idea. As a result, it turns itself into a circle of definitions which removes intuition itself from being subject to definition.'[10] *Ratio intuitiva* (intuitive reasoning), Stein argues, is the most defining element of artistic natures and this is what he ascribes to Chamberlain – as with the philosophers René Descartes, Baruch Spinoza and Friedrich Nietzsche. 'Such mystics see no higher judge of truth than the certainty that comes from their inner voice and their inner self.' Stein continues: '[A] scholar such as Chamberlain who as a philosophical historian sees race as the key to all life on earth [...] should not be implementing such fundamentally mystical concepts as "racial purity", something he describes as "an amusing mind-game" ["lustiges Gedankending"]: racial purity inhibits rather than expands such explanations. His references to 'the sacredness of racial purity' are not ideas that can be brought to empirical tests if they are to be thought of merely as "amusing mind-games".'[11]

Stein goes on to write that, with Chamberlain, it is the duality of scholar and artist that accounts for the many contradictions in his concepts and ideas. For Stein, it is often the scholar who is victorious over the artist, but usually it's the other way around. He writes:

> 'With my mind I am a follower of Spinoza, with my heart I am a devoted Christian' is the fundamental destiny of all Romantics. Chamberlain is the strict nominalist and actually sees this as a characteristic of the Anglo-Saxon races. According to Chamberlain, 'the social manifestation of nominalism is individualism'. Yet these sober observations collide abruptly against Chamberlain's ideas regarding race. Ultimately, the Romantic irrationalist, instinctive philosopher, mystic and artist in Chamberlain are stronger than the logistician and scholar. His heart has conquered his head.
>
> Chamberlain distances himself substantially from Gobineau and makes it clear he does not wish to be thought of as a Gobineau disciple. Yet we must challenge this 'racial imperialism' and 'racial Romanticism' that Chamberlain claims to be a characteristic of the Teutonic people. Undoubtedly the most Romantic concept put forward by the philosophical historian is indeed the concept of the 'Teutonic race'. Chamberlain himself dismisses the misty-eyed views of German Romanticism of heraldry and minstrels, folk songs and minnesingers. He despises the notion of this sort of Romanticism that

'throws shadows in all directions and thus becomes the basis of explaining all mystical experiences'. [. . .] The masters of modern culture, according to Chamberlain, are the Nordic races. He gives them the collective name 'the Teutons' [Die Germanen] which he has taken from Tacitus, despite using the term in ways that Tacitus would not have recognised. He admits as much [. . .] but with this new concept, he accords a practical identification to an ethnic grouping within current human history. We wish to address a final word on [. . .] 'racial Romanticism' as laid out by [Chamberlain] regarding this new ethnic entity that he implacably places against the Jew. [. . .] Chamberlain's protestations that he is not a Romantic must be seen in the context of Nietzsche and Schopenhauer, who would also not have welcomed this particular moniker. [. . .] The mind offers us logic, while feelings offer us the mystical. The two are in constant conflict and from the one we have science and technology measured in units, while from the other we have religion and [artistic] creativity. [. . .] The duality of mankind consists of reason and emotion which remain in continuous alternation with each other and are variously described as Classicism or Romanticism.[12]

Stein expands this duality by stating that the predominance of Classicism leads in the long term to a stifling of the personality, the individual and to eventual authoritarianism. Against this, the Romantic is the born revolutionary. According to Stein, it was implicit from Chamberlain's writings that the world was now about to enter a new age of Romanticism:

For the Romantic, nothing is more characteristic than worshipping at the cult of genius. Emotions are the progenitors of all values [. . .] yet the highest of all values is that of 'the genius'. Only the artist reaches such exalted states of humanity according to the Romantics. The Romantic cries that the artist stands atop humanity as Nature stands atop a pedestal. It is the new aristocracy, the aristocracy of the mind, the spirit, the creative individual: it is 'the artist as aristocrat', an idea in which both Wagner and Schopenhauer luxuriate. [. . .] For Nietzsche, the idea of the complete person is the 'superman', for Chamberlain, it is the 'Teuton'. Yet in truth, the 'Teuton' is merely the collective of Nietzsche's formula, and Chamberlain's Teuton becomes the Super-race.[13]

Race, often referred to as 'blood', thus became the new, all-defining answer to most of nature's riddles. This new world which was being shaped by ideas wilfully extrapolated from science by arrogant 'dilettantes' such as Chamberlain was a reaction against the sentimental romanticism of the German people as historic Teutons by elevating them into the more dangerous notion of the German people as *racial* Teutons.

The Jewish Response to Neo-Romanticism

Though written as early as 1899, Chamberlain's book was incorporated as a philosophical foundation for National Socialist racial dogma. It was against this background that various anti-Romantic movements were assembling themselves, including those composers who exemplified 'New Objectivity', or others who wished to return to classical models such as Hans Gál, reaching for Mendelssohnian templates, and Egon Wellesz, returning to a form of musical theatre based on Baroque opera. In his *Judentum und Modernität*, Leon Botstein also sees this return to older models as a Schoenbergian aspiration. Certainly, the earliest compositions of Schoenberg, as well as those of Schreker, Toch and particularly Zemlinsky, were based on a more classical, Brahmsian ideal before they turned, with the exception of Toch, en masse towards the harmonic Wagnerian opulence of fin de siècle Vienna.

With the exception of Hindemith, the most popular and successful of these composers, reacting against Romanticism, whether writing music for education or for the workers of a new society, or re-interpreting the musical past, were Jewish Germans and Austrians. As Stein wrote of Chamberlain, the Romantic notion of being racially and culturally German was 'implacably placed against the Jew'. And as the dust began to settle after the First World War, Jews even found themselves blamed for Germany's 'defeat' and subsequent humiliation, despite the disproportionate number of Jewish soldiers who fought for the Kaiser and the most potent of all wartime poems *A Paean on Hate For England*, with its battle cry of 'God condemn England – God condemns her!', having been penned by the fanatically patriotic Prussian Jew, Ernst Lissauer.

The suspicion ran that a new order, represented by the republic based on the Weimar Constitution existing without monarchs and a humbled church, suited these non-German Jews. As 'non-Germans', it was suspected that they had even 'profiteered' by the war and its aftermath. It was thus easy to argue that the music they were composing was also 'foreign' and 'un-German'. Even if Jews had made the greatest declarations of loyalty to the various Emperors under whom they fought, it was clear to 'racial Romantics' that the German soul, as defined by Wagner and bizarrely seconded by his German-speaking, Francophile, Magyar son-in-law, Liszt, remained an impossibility for the Jew; 'German Jew' and 'Austrian Jew' could therefore only designate citizenship rather than nationality. In a Kafkaesque twist, even Lissauer's *Paean of Hate*, which during the war was issued to every German soldier, was later declared by anti-Semites as fundamentally 'un-German' and a symptom of a uniquely Jewish hatefulness.

Throughout the interwar years, German Romanticism continued to exert a tenacious hold, as much due to the political fallout of the war as to any of the developments discussed in the previous chapters. Many non-Jewish composers continued to compose music that was ripe with associations of German Romanticism – 'folklore, heraldry and minnesingers' as described by Chamberlain – the idea being that, despite Chamberlain's protestations, this was an expression of being 'German'. The most prominent among them were Wilhelm Kienzl, Joseph Marx, Hans Pfitzner, Emil von Reznicek, Max von Schillings, Franz Schmidt, Max Trapp, and above all, with his eighteen folk-tale influenced operas, Richard Wagner's son Siegfried.

Adolf Weißmann, who was himself Jewish, uses the concept of 'race' as the great clarifying agent in his book *Musik in der Weltkrise*,[14] from which there is a quotation at the head of this chapter. Weißmann offers a *Who's Who* of younger composers who don't follow the more immediately identifiable modernist trends. He refers to these composers as trying 'by different means, many on the other side of art's now broken line, to seek new solutions'.[15]

The list is fascinating as there are names that are unknown today and many that are familiar, but in different contexts. Weißmann writes:

There is one composer who has become the mouthpiece of all modern directions without taking on more than their outer characteristics: the influences on Sigfried Karg-Elert were too broad [. . .]. Receptive and adaptable to so many influences, he became far too prolific. This sort of Modernism remains without significant effect.

Another hope was Rudi Stephan who fell in the war – an anti-Romantic of amassed strength [demonstrated by] such semi-mature works as *Music for Orchestra* or the erotic mystery play based on Otto Borngräber, *Die ersten Menschen* (*The First People*).

Julius Weismann [later a prominent supporter of the Nazi regime] is a composer who is enthusiastically hard at work and writes in a style somewhere between Brahms and Modernism that not only seeks but finds a sense of unity. He is no revolutionary yet remains unconventional and keeps himself largely within the more reticent realms of chamber music.

A set of Orchestral Variations similar in style to Richard Strauss confirmed the exceptional musical talent of the promising young [Jewish composer] Georg Szell. He is a [sensitive] artist who commands a poetic talent for colour while renewing traditional orchestral architecture.

Paul Graener [a prominent composer under the Nazis post-1933] writes for both stage and the concert hall, allowing the new to resonate gently in everything he writes while distilling it into a quiet, symphonically based language. He has had a much-regarded success with his setting of Christian Morgenstern's *Gallows-songs*.

Wilhelm Kempff [active as a pianist during the Nazi years] improvises polyphonically; Walter Braunfels [a Catholic composer of Jewish provenance] brings 'New-German' to ever greater heights as noted in his [symphonic work] *Fantastic Visions* – which, by the way, were not overly 'fantastic'.

Quite remarkable, however, is [the Jewish composer] Erwin Lendvai. The Hungarian native started off in the style of the day. Puccini was an influence in Milan. One clearly recognises in his music a sense of orchestral colour and harmonic individuality. Soon however, he turned his back onto the contemporary. The more he studied German choral music, the greater his antagonism directed against every type of emotional stimulus. Whatever the psychological reasons of his sudden 'about-face', one must still recognise a serious musician of unusual ability and knowledge who has cultivated a sober artistic language and thus offered an important contribution to our musical life. Lendvai wishes to resurrect the stylistic purity of earlier music. He objects to all chromaticism, against augmented intervals; he desires a less fulsome type of voice leading. In chamber music, he promotes an appealing yet near chaste stylistic purity. But his most important achievement must remain his choral works. . . .

There are, however, true Romantics still to be found amongst the younger generation of composers such as [the future ardent Nazi] Max Trapp, who in his chamber works and symphonies looks backwards, usually with a nod towards Richard Strauss while giving voice to the simplest of emotions – an artist who clearly prefers living in the realms of Mörike and offers up a gentle lyricism with his puppet show *The Last King of Orplid*. Another supporter of the Romantics is Walter Niemann, a passionate yet extremely clever Brahms-worshipper who sanctifies his love for the piano by composing works which are both musically and structurally beautiful; another one in this mould is Leo Schrattenholz, who remains pleasant enough kept within his small sphere. Aspiring to much more is [the Jewish composer who would later be murdered in Auschwitz] James Simon, and [the Jewish composer] Hugo Leichtentritt, both of whom appear to have their creativity inhibited by their exceptional erudition. They are rooted to a modern style of their own that they wish to evolve, and Leichtentritt has progressed from chamber music to art-song and even opera.[16]

Weißmann also takes a look at the composers who are influenced by d'Albert and Italian *verismo*. This is an area where he finds much to praise for literary choice and some fine music. Yet, ultimately, he concludes that some element is missing that condemns them to what he calls 'a mere paper existence'. 'Apart from d'Albert and the Italian masters, we find composers marching down similar paths such as [Hermann Wolfgang] von Waltershausen, who wrote his own libretto for his opera *Colonel Chabert* in a free adaptation from Balzac. This highly theatrical text lost something in its musical adaptation, though its strongest points were those that focused on the stage. This is quite different from [the Jewish composer] Ignaz Waghalter whose setting of Paul Eger's libretto of Machiavelli's *Mandragola* grips while filling what is essentially a not very musical subject with such quantities of musical ideas that both the saucy tale and the delightful music charge forward together.'[17] Weißmann then goes on to deal with the Dutch composer Jan Brandts-Buys, whose opera *The Tailors of Schönau* had enjoyed considerable success, the Viennese composer Julius Bittner whose opera *Das höllisch Gold* was more successful still, and even comments that Leoš Janáček has, with his opera *Jenůfa*, composed a work that follows in the 'general racial style' of his Bohemian predecessors, Smetana and Dvořák. He singles out the German Italian composer Ermanno Wolf-Ferrari as a 'post-Wagnerian classicist' who changes from one work to the next. Another German composer to engage with Italian *verismo* is Paul Graener, whose opera *Don Juan's Last Adventure* and *Theophano* are praised in passing, while Walter Braunfels's *The Birds* 'hovers somewhere between Wagner's *Meistersinger* and Richard Strauss' *Ariadne auf Naxos*'.[18] Weißmann continues:

> And again we bump into both [Franz] Schreker and [Erich Wolfgang] Korngold. It's no coincidence that these two Viennese are more successful with their operas than any of their contemporaries. Neither is problematic. Schreker attempts to make the erotic profound, he writes his own texts that take us from the flighty historic romanticism of [the Viennese artist] Hans Makart to the most profound. But his *Spielwerk und die Prinzessin*, *Die Gezeichneten* and *Der Schatzgräber* are not the fulfilment of the promise shown by his opera *Der ferne Klang*. They are the result of compromised efforts, highly polished naivety and full of effects while lacking individuality. Yet as a type of hybrid musical theatre, they have their unique place.
>
> Erich Wolfgang Korngold, on the other hand – composer of *Violanta*, *Der Ring des Polykrates* and *Die tote Stadt* – is the only true contemporary opera composer who has been able to balance the many different factors demanded by musical theatre. He is the only one who allows the voice to soar above the

superb instrumentation of his orchestral writing, and he's the only one after Puccini who has the courage and the ability to overcome all of opera's many inherent problems. Of course, it must be understood that this is only possible by sacrificing his individuality.[19]

Weißmann's views on Mahler remind us how idiosyncratic the age was in which he was writing. Mahler's significance for such Jewish 'Romantic' composers as Schreker and Korngold was very different from what it was for Schoenberg, Berg and Webern. For modernists, Mahler had crashed through boundaries that allowed the next generation to explore regions beyond the confines of Romanticism. For the 'resolute' Romantics, however, Mahler was a composer who opened a vast landscape of extremes in which they could continue to roam. Weißmann writes:

There is a Mahler problem. [. . .] It lies firmly in the personality of the man himself. [. . .] Mahler is a Jew. He is [also] a Jew of this new age while being at the same time a great symphonist. Is it believable that the so-called death of the symphony – the musical idiom so hallowed by Beethoven – should be revived by a Jew? The connections between race and music are finally being examined despite frequent criticism. [Mahler's] ideals may be questionable, but his Jewishness cannot be denied as an important component in his creativity, even by those who think that ignoring it does him a favour. This Jewish blood is important. Always heated, it attempts a great deal while rarely scaling great heights. It pushes towards dispersion as easily as it pushes towards cohesion. But it has the ability to flow in such a fashion that the Jewishness to which he was born is joined in an inseparable and noble union with the German nature that has always accompanied him. Thus metaphysical thought and intensified emotion become the inheritance of a neurotic creativity. Indeed much more: they march forth into the Beyond where there are no borders – they take on the traits of the transnational. Even in Mahler's [own] spirit, Jewishness has gouged deep furrows. [. . .] In such a hyper-sensitive, creative spirit, nerves are always ready to blast the body asunder. He may feel himself German to the last fibre of his being, but his strength comes only from his state of continuous nervous agitation. Journeys into the metaphysical with emotions pumped to their most extreme are joined in a passionate yet necessary fanaticism. His relationship with nature runs deep; one could almost call it naïve. He wishes to be part of his people and to be a real Austrian. But he remains tortured and tormented [. . .] as a modernist, as a passionate interpreter of the works of others, as a Jew. This is the spirit that invades his music and drives him to the demonic. This accounts for the countless contradictions in his work and also accounts for its 'profound' shallowness, a half-ironic creativity that makes counterfeit appear to be real gold. This accounts for his ingenious re-creation of the sound-worlds of forests and glades. But the most tellingly racial characteristic of all is his Christian fight for sanctity. [. . .] His ability to recreate music is no less passionate than that to create it. Mahler is the consummation of the German into the Jew. Wagner's words, 'To be German means to do something because it *must* be done', were for Mahler: 'To be German is to do what must be done to the point of self-annihilation.' Thus was the life of a man living in a state of perpetual tension: a self-flagellator continuously whipping himself into a state of ecstasy.[20]

Julius Korngold summarises much of this important book's content in an extended review offering, again, a view from a bygone age:

The crisis actually starts with the Romantics, the French and the Germans; it's based on a high-strung state of nervous tension that requires constant stimuli. One of the 'crises' has to do with rhythm and the fact that its enno-bling strength is threatened; then [along] comes the 'crisis' of harmony, which works against rhythm and has now moved to the foreground estab-lishing itself as the basis of musical sound. Our nervous state demands new colours; ergo, another 'crisis'. Melody is being atomised by motifs and by the distraction of colour; [obviously] another 'crisis'. Regarding form and above all *sonata form*, well, it's of course yet another 'crisis'. The French, Berlioz more than anyone, started this process. From there followed the Francophile Liszt with his programmatic works that increased spiritual asso-ciations and expanded music's harmonic palette. This had already been started by Wagner, who heightened theatrical and emotional experience. Naturally this dissolves traditional structure but employs its motifs in sequential manners in the service of providing yet further nerve-tingling experiences. Even with the great Romantic musical poet Schumann, one notes a lack of rhythmic pulse and, as for form, Mendelssohn only looked backwards. [. . .]

People have become inartistic – their folk music is no longer creative. The artist turns away from his own community and is engrossed only with himself, while honing only the technical perfection of his handicraft. He is distracted by the orchestra that offers colours that not only enchant but also deceive, thus forcing him to expand the melodic and undermine the purity of tonality. It has driven him towards the programmatic which may encourage the intellect but weakens the instincts. Artistry and music part company.

It was with the Impressionists that inventive musicians started to hunt down connections between music and painting. Growing out of Debussy's French Impressionism is a German formless play with colour without spiritual basis, in fact without even a foundation of technique. There is no world-view or strong inner-need to express oneself that can survive the crash brought about by lack of technique and imagination. The fear of being thought conventional inhibits the urge to write melody, thus destroying music's architecture and trampling on its innate narrative. Arriving from Italy we are confronted with Futurism. At the moment, any noun with the suffix 'ism' offers an excuse for endless, pointless experimentation. First we had 'Expressionism' which, searching for a new primitiveness, camouflaged inability and chicanery. Weißmann does not overlook the many accompanying sub-groupings or the 'dictatorship of the minorities' as he calls them.[. . .] But the confusion resulting from intellectual experimentation [. . .] leads us to the final step: atonality. Chaos now reigns supreme.

But having dazzled us with his diagnosis, Weißmann then appears to be suffering from the symptoms of the very same musical affliction. Just as he points out the misguided, powerless inability that has resulted in the 'crisis', he suddenly backs away and proclaims that the ensuing chaos itself is fruitful![21]

Korngold has interesting things to write about Weißmann's views on Mahler:

A particular trouble-maker for Weißmann's scalpel-sharp observations [is Mahler], who as a hypersensitive individual, exists in a continuous state of near hysteria. He is the culmination of the Jew whose German nature has resulted in total self-annihilation to his art. In fleeing from reality, Mahler, the man of the theatre, finds a metaphysical refuge in his own variety of the Symphony. In his ecstasy, he senses relationships [. . .] with Goethe's *Faust*, and within the ethical and metaphysical he is related to both Beethoven and Wagner. Yet ultimately he remains a minstrel yearning for the 'original sound' and longing for the community and culture of his native country.[22]

As can be understood from reading Weißmann and the controversy his book ignited, Romanticism was far from being a spent force by the early 1920s. A number of composers felt that the late-Romantic ideal of overloading the senses was still the best way forward for music. Clearly, this style was popular with audiences, as evidenced by the success of Schreker's operas, along with those of Richard Strauss, Puccini and Eugen d'Albert. These remained the preferred repertoire for any opera house seeking to appeal to popular tastes.

Unexpected Developments

Then a quite unexpected change occurred, the significance of which can be sensed from an examination of the list of operas performed in German-speaking Europe during the 1927–8 season, compiled by the music historian Wilhelm Altmann. It was in 1928 that the 27-year-old Ernst Krenek's *Jonny spielt auf*, a risqué opera featuring a black jazz violinist as its central character, was performed at the Vienna State Opera. Following its premiere in Leipzig on 10 February 1927, it went on to have 421 performances in some 45 different houses during a single season. It's interesting to compare this with the second most performed opera, d'Albert's *Tiefland*, which clocked up 296 performances on 51 different stages. Pfitzner's *Der arme Heinrich* and *Das Christelflein*, with a combined total of 80 performances in 39 houses, were more popular than his highly demanding *Palestrina*, which achieved only 28 performances in six houses. Puccini remained one of the most popular composers with 876 performances and 167 different stagings of his five most popular operas, while Strauss's operas clocked 416 performances, with *Rosenkavalier* alone making up more than half of these. Even Janáček's *Jenůfa* had a remarkable 77 performances, though this was down from the 96 performances of the previous season.[23]

When we start to look at Jewish composers, however, we get a different picture. Schreker's operas, once so dominant, are in steep decline: *Der ferne Klang* appears in only two opera houses for eight performances; *Die Gezeichneten* has only three performances; and *Der Schatzgräber*, which had been the most popular of all, has only five performances. Zemlinsky has only ten performances divided between two operas, *Eine florentinische Tragödie* and *Kleider machen Leute*. Weill's *Der Protagonist* receives 11 performances on three stages; Wellesz's *Alkestis* has just four performances, while Gál has to make do with five performances of two operas. Even Korngold's *Die tote Stadt* has gone down from 20 performances in the previous season to just 14 in four opera houses; his *Violanta* also runs in only four theatres for a total of nine performances. Braunfels's *Don Gil von den grünen Hosen* has also gone down to 11 performances from 17 the previous season. The older generation of Jewish composers, meaning those born before 1895, were giving way to a younger generation of composers who were turning towards the trend of the *Zeitoper*, with radios, motorcars, flappers and other accoutrements of the roaring twenties. Even such stalwarts of the opulent sound-world of fin de siècle Vienna such as Schreker and Zemlinsky would start a process of paring down their music in an attempt to adjust to the demands of the time.

In any case, it was beginning to become apparent that music claiming a German 'Romantic' heritage was starting to take on subtle political and nationalistic overtones. Within only a year, it was a lot less subtle. In January 1931, Hans Heinsheimer wrote a leading article in *Anbruch* called 'The Secret Terror' that examined the political situation in 1930. Heinsheimer advises that a careful eye must be kept in light of a recent development: the film *All Quiet on the Western Front* had to be taken out of cinemas in Berlin and Vienna as it was seen to offend the nationalist mood. The same trend afflicted music as well: Kurt Weill's *Aufstieg und Fall der Stadt Mahagonny* was removed from the schedules of Max Reinhardt's theatres. Heinsheimer quotes correspondence from opera house directors, as well as from members of the public, with their references to 'what one should expect as a Christian and a German' from publicly subsidised theatres. The article is followed by another called 'A Look into the Third Reich' in which a comprehensive list of works is shown from Thuringia's theatres where a local Nazi government had been in place since 1929. The scheduling of theatres in Jena and Gera was merely anticipating what would happen throughout Germany after 1933.[24]

Returning to the 1927–8 season, Altmann goes on to analyse his statistics further: *Tiefland* has the most productions overall, followed by *Madame Butterfly*, *Tosca* and *Jonny spielt auf*, *Der Rosenkavalier* and *La Bohème*. Altmann also cites the number of performances too, concluding that the total of 421 for *Jonny spielt auf* breaks every record he has ever kept for a single work in a single season. Berg's *Wozzeck*, first performed to such acclaim in 1925, is missing from the 1927–8 season altogether, as are previously successful operas such as *Die Vögel* by Braunfels, and Zemlinsky's *Es war einmal* and *Der Zwerg*. Hindemith's *Cardillac* (1926) received 45 performances, as did Max von Schillings's more established *Mona Lisa*, which had enjoyed unbroken popularity since its premiere in Stuttgart in 1915. Altmann's list indicates that musical tastes were shifting not only towards the contemporary thrill offered by *Zeitoper* but, more revealingly, by the angular musical language that was moving away from the Romanticism of earlier works by Schreker, Zemlinsky, Korngold, Braunfels and even Strauss and Pfitzner. Puccini seemed to remain immune to these changes in taste, as did the unshakeable popularity of d'Albert's *Tiefland* and Strauss's *Rosenkavalier*.[25]

The huge success of *Jonny spielt auf* would dramatically alter the shape of opera scheduling over subsequent seasons. If the popularity of late-Romantic operas by Jewish composers had started to wane, a younger generation of Jewish composers was busily compensating with *Zeitopern*. Many of the most successful, such as *Maschinist Hopkins* by Max Brand (120 performances in the 1929–30 season), Wilhelm Grosz's *Baby an der Bar* and Karol Rathaus's *Fremde Erde*, emanated from the same stable that had produced Krenek: the composition class of Franz Schreker. But even Krenek's record of 421 performances was broken in the 1929–30 season by the 490 performances clocked up by *Schwanda der Dudelsackpfeifer*,[26] by the Jewish Czech composer Jaromír Weinberger.[27] *Schwanda* was neither modernist, nor a jazzy *Zeitoper*. It was an entertaining Bohemian folk-tale about devils, ice queens and the human foibles of its central folk hero. Weinberger may have studied with Reger – regarded as the spiritual father of many New Objectivity composers – but he was no 'New Objectivist'. The music of *Schwanda* is far closer to Dvořák than to Hindemith.

There are several superficial parallels in the biographies of Weinberger and Erich Korngold: they were more or less the same age, with Weinberger born a year earlier than Korngold in 1896; both were born in what is today the Czech Republic, with Korngold maintaining the Austrian citizenship that all Czechs born before 1919 received automatically, and Weinberger taking the steps to become a citizen of the newly founded state of Czechoslovakia; both were child prodigies and non-practising Jews, and both had a solid classical training while finding that perhaps their true metier lay with lighter opera. Here, though, we encounter a certain creative contrary motion between the two, with Korngold moving towards light music in the second half of his life with *Die stumme Serenade*,[28] following his last opera *Die Kathrin*, which was essentially a large-scale operetta. Weinberger, on the other hand, started off composing lighter operas, but his last work, *Valdštejn* from 1937, was a serious work based on Schiller's *Wallenstein* trilogy. Neither composer made major changes to their musical idiom whether in lighter or more serious operas. Both saw traditional tonality as adequate for their needs, and neither forgot the importance of guaranteeing an audience aural delight. Weinberger would ultimately remain a 'one-hit-wonder' with *Schwanda*. Korngold, on the other hand, was a more subtle composer whose influence on twentieth-century popular culture would extend well beyond the world of Vienna's *haute bourgeoisie*. With his consolidation of what later became the 'Hollywood Sound', Korngold established not only a new genre within applied music, but, through cinema, unleashed a more powerful fusion of image and sound than even Wagner could have anticipated. The 'crisis' that Weißmann had written about concerned the futility of the continuous 'over-loading' of emotional, or as he expressed it, 'nervous' stimulation. This was the crux of the dilemma in musical Romanticism. Weißmann would never have foreseen Korngold's Hollywood scores as the answer to the critical question of where it could possibly lead.

Korngold: The Resolute Romantic

There was a much-circulated quip about Korngold attributed to Ernst Toch, one of the principal exponents of Germany's New Objectivity who had also ended up composing film music in Hollywood: 'Korngold has been composing music for Warner Brothers his whole life. It's just that when he was a kid, he didn't know it at the time.' No statement could make the point more clearly that Korngold's brand of early twentieth-century Viennese Romanticism determined what would become known as the 'Hollywood Sound'. With this in mind, it is hardly surprising that Hollywood quickly became a happy repository for many more of Europe's Jewish 'resolute Romantics'.

Korngold considered his most important work to be the opera *Das Wunder der Heliane*. This huge work is almost a third longer again than his previous opera, *Die tote Stadt*, and it demands large forces similar to Strauss's *Die Frau ohne Schatten*, an obvious model for *Heliane* with its generically named roles (The Ruler, The Stranger, The Warden, The Messenger, and so on). It was the culmination of Korngold's harmonic and melodic development and represented the 30-year-old at his creative peak. According to his father Julius, its premiere in 1927 should have guaranteed Erich's position as the leading composer of his generation. Yet grievances that had grown out of Julius's determination to undermine anyone at the opera who followed Mahler, his erratic treatment of artists who supported (or ignored) his son Erich, and the general spirit of the age resulted in the young Korngold's biggest professional disappointment. A Korngold 'failure' was still more successful than many other composers' 'successes', but the clash of Viennese premieres between Krenek's *Jonny spielt auf* and Korngold's *Heliane* resulted in more than just a public slanging match, it was a true *Kulturkampf*. On the one side was Erich with his string of commercial successes and his powerful father. On the other was Krenek, a young man who had managed to tap into the spirit of the age with the most popular opera on any German stage at any time. Erich Korngold, who had been regarded as sufficiently modernist to be represented at the ISCM festival in 1925, decided at this point to become the champion of late-romanticism.

Even when still seen as a modernist, Korngold was never interested in following in Schoenberg's footsteps. But a letter from Rudolf Réti inviting him to propose works for the 1925 ISCM festival in Venice indicates that atonal and serial music were by no means the sole criteria of the musically progressive.[29]

The Kolisch Quartet performed Korngold's First String Quartet at the 1925 Venice Festival in a series of concerts that also featured music by the Schoenberg pupil Hanns Eisler. By then, Eisler was in the process of breaking with his teacher and was writing music reviews for the Communist paper *Die Rote Fahne*. He reviewed both *Heliane* and *Jonny spielt auf* for the paper and starts his review of *Heliane* with a quip about prodigies already being as untalented at the age of six as other people are at the age of sixty. He then cuts straight to his conclusion: '*Das Wunder der Heliane* is an unbelievably bad and ill-conceived work.' He offers a potted version of the plot while damning the librettist Hans Müller as 'a typical lower-middle-class writer': 'This kind of opera-*Schlock* simply should not be put in front of any public unless it's intended as a joke. [. . .] The music is intoxicating, unoriginal and lives less from its creativity than it does from its appealing effectiveness, which of course only comes across today as boring.'[30] Eisler's review of *Jonny* is possibly even more scathing, though his points are far more political than musical. He hates the easy sense of entitlement expressed by all of the principal characters as they travel in luxury and stay in expensive hotels. 'This is a seriously botched opera plot! [. . .] Like most modern operas these days, it's resolutely petit-bourgeois and despite the presence of locomotives and cars, it doesn't reflect our time at all. As for the music, one can only say that the otherwise talented Krenek has totally messed this one up. It's astonishing how poorly orchestrated it is and the dance numbers aren't as good as those heard in the cheapest beer-halls. Only at the end are we offered anything decent – but that's after sitting through two-and-a-half hours of tedium. Stylistically, it's a mixture of Puccini, d'Albert and Stravinsky. It's pity to think of all the money they invested in this worthless dud.'[31]

Heliane vs Jonny

With the music of Korngold's *Heliane* anticipating so much that would become familiar to generations of film lovers, and in the light of Eisler's reviews and its general reception at the time, it is worth recounting how the work came to be written in such a hostile musical environment. The Viennese poet Hans Kaltneker, fascinated by *Violanta*, managed to pen an opera text that he presented to Korngold called *Die Heilige*. He died soon afterwards at the tragically young age of 22. Julius dryly describes *Die Heilige* as recounting 'sexual difficulties' beyond those that featured in the poet's other works.[32] It was apparently not possible to set in its original form, and the Jewish playwright Hans Müller, who had been the librettist for *Violanta*, was approached to rework it for the stage. In doing so, he reduced the sexual aspect and concentrated on the themes of love and redemption set in a joyless totalitarian country.

As with most important Korngold premieres, the Hamburg Opera and Egon Pollak won the rights to the first performance, with local soprano Maria Hussa (who would also sing the role of Anita in Krenek's *Jonny spielt auf*) in the title role. It opened on 7 October 1927 and the Viennese premiere followed three weeks later, running for a further 26 performances. Korngold composed the title role with Maria Jeritza in mind but, as she was singing *Violanta* at New York's Metropolitan Opera; Lotte Lehmann stepped in as a replacement. The tenor role of Der Fremder ('The Stranger') was sung by Jan Kiepura. The Hamburg premiere was a public and critical success, and continued with a run of a further 18 performances. In Berlin, however, Hanns Eisler was not alone in his savage dismissal of the work as outdated and irrelevant. Both the cast and even the conductor, Korngold's friend Bruno Walter, distanced themselves from it in the light of the unrelentingly harsh and dismissive press.

The symbolism of *Jonny*, a black New World jazz musician stealing a violin from an Old World classical virtuoso who is killed in a final race to regain possession of the instrument, was not lost on Julius Korngold. Krenek's throwing down the gauntlet against the sanctity of European culture was triumphantly picked up by Julius Korngold. Indeed, European culture had a particularly powerful hold on Jews of Julius's generation just as it was being viewed as an irrelevant inheritance by non-Jews of Krenek's generation. The spirit of the age, however, condemned Julius to defeat before the first battle had even been fought. It was a further twist of fate that this crucial battle would involve a work written by his son Erich. After its premiere in Leipzig on 10 February 1927, *Jonny* went on to conquer the mightiest bastions of opera, including New York's Metropolitan Opera. It was translated into 18 languages and, worst of all for the Korngolds, it was scheduled to come to Vienna in time to clash with *Das Wunder der Heliane*.

The *Kulturkampf* between *Jonny* and *Heliane* manifested itself in often quite bizarre ways. Austrian Tobacco created two new brands of cigarettes called *Jonny* and *Heliane*; even more surreal was that behind closed doors, anti-Semitic National Socialists were making common cause with Julius Korngold. In an Orwellian twist, and in order to rid the State Opera of a work written by the non-Jewish Krenek, he and the character *Jonny* were made out to be 'Jewish polluters'.

To Julius, *Jonny* was narcissistic nonsense.[33] Journalistic scorn for *Jonny* in the otherwise liberal *Neue Freie Presse* is notable by the paper's utter silence during the run-up to its much anticipated premiere. It was thoroughly trashed by Julius in subsequent reviews, both in his feuilleton and in an unsigned leading article on the front page. Perhaps nothing better expresses the paper's contempt for the work than a short paragraph to be found in its 'Kleine Chronik' on 10 November 1928 announcing the appearance at Vienna's Konzerthaus of an American jazz singer named Jack Smith: 'We assumed that it would be inevitable that with the State Opera presenting Variété, it was only a matter of time before we encountered a bar-room singer from America without a voice at the Konzerthaus.'[34] This was tame compared with the German nationalist newspaper *Deutsch-österreichisch Tageszeitung*, which attacked *Jonny* with the sort of anti-Semitic vehemence that had become the weapon of choice against anything with which the Pan-German Austrian press disagreed.[35]

Heliane was understood by many as mere cannon fodder in Julius's war against progressive musical developments perpetrated by composers who were of similar age to Erich. Like many Austrian nationalists, Krenek had little time for Prussian Berlin and he retreated to Vienna following the unexpected success of *Jonny*. Krenek described visiting a performance of *Heliane* as 'either the high-point, or the low-point of this particular period, depending on your point of view'.[36] In writing more extensively about Korngold in his memoirs, he mentions the tragic elements in the relationship between father and son which made it easier to sympathise with Erich, and how his best music was written while he was still a teenager (and at the front line of the avant-garde). From Krenek's perspective, Julius had kept Erich from following his natural instincts and hindered the boy's talent. He recalled meeting Erich many years later in Los Angeles after the death of Julius and described him as being 'a broken and disillusioned man who had nothing to show but a handful of long-forgotten film scores'.[37]

Heliane failed to achieve the success of either *Die tote Stadt* or *Jonny spielt auf*. Krenek's opera had shown how far into the past Korngold had retreated. Yet on the other side of the world, an event took place on the day before the Hamburg premiere of *Heliane* that would have a far-reaching effect on Korngold's future and ultimately render the attacks on him irrelevant. Hollywood released *The Jazz Singer*, the first commercially successful motion picture with synchronized sound. Even before the arrival of Hitler, more and more Austrian and German talent had relocated to America, where Hollywood's appetite for all things European seemed to equal Europe's appetite for all things American.

Korngold the Arranger

The truth was that the cultural fights picked by Julius had put his son Erich in an impossible position. Moreover, until he was conscripted into the army at the age of nineteen, he had – according to Julius – not been allowed to leave the parental home unaccompanied.[38] It was clear that Julius had also pushed him into situations where he was unable to have his works judged without prejudice. Taking a side step as an arranger of other people's music was the perfect antidote to Julius's attempts to influence every aspect of Erich's life and helped to neutralise Julius's use of Erich as a weapon in his public battles. While it is true that Erich's most progressive music was composed while still a teenager, he equally loved the nostalgia of Viennese operetta. In arranging the works of others, he saw a chance to get closer to music he adored and to earn enough money to achieve financial independence. This prepared Erich for his future as a film music composer by forcing him to supply music on demand and to work together with a team to a strict deadline. Viennese composers were never shy about arranging operetta: Schoenberg and Zemlinsky did so frequently and often gave similar assignments to their pupils.

Erich Korngold first met his future wife Luise von Sonnenthal in 1917. She was the granddaughter of Adolf Ritter von Sonnenthal, one of the great actors of the Burgtheater and one of the first prominent Jews to be knighted following the 'emancipation' of 1867. Luzi, as Erich called her, was an actress who had starred in several films. In addition, she was an extremely accomplished pianist. Yet despite coming from one of Vienna's most prestigious families, Julius was against the relationship. He was hostile to any relationship that questioned his position as absolute mentor over every aspect of Erich's life. In his memoirs, he grudgingly acknowledges Luzi's abundant gifts, but hints darkly that she was responsible for bringing Erich into the world of cinema.[39]

Johann Strauss's operetta *Eine Nacht in Venedig* from 1885 had been one of the composer's greatest disappointments. His widow, Adele, thought that if it were to be carefully reworked for more modern tastes, it could enjoy the success previously denied. The Korngolds knew Adele, and Erich loved Strauss's music. Korngold eagerly took the opportunity offered by the multi-talented writer, performer and entrepreneur Hubert Marischka to arrange and conduct performances of the work which would feature the popular tenor Richard Tauber. A long run at the Theater an der Wien followed a successful opening on 25 October 1923. It then travelled through Austria and Germany, returning to the State Opera with a cast including Maria Jeritza, Adele Kern, Alfred Jerger, Koloman von Pataky, and Hubert Marischka himself.

Cagliostro in Wien was the next Strauss operetta that Korngold adapted and updated. This too was a success, opening at the Bürgertheater[40] on 13 April 1927. Korngold went on to concoct a Johann Strauss pastiche entitled *Das Lied der Liebe* as a vehicle for Richard Tauber, as well as arranging two operettas by Leo Fall: *Rosen aus Florida* and *Die geschiedene Frau* – which opened at Berlin's Theater am Nollendorfplatz on 1 February 1933, two days after Hitler's appointment as Reich Chancellor.

Korngold's association with the theatrical wizard Max Reinhardt was the single most important collaboration of his professional life. Ultimately, it would save him from the Nazis and, over time, Reinhardt became Erich's principal artistic advisor and an effective antidote to his father. In the short term, they were responsible for two of the biggest theatrical successes of the decade. Early in 1929, Reinhardt proposed that Korngold adapt Offenbach's *La vie parisienne*. However, Korngold thought the work weak and they settled on *Die Fledermaus* in a new arrangement that required three singers in the principal roles, with actors in the other parts. The opening at the Deutsches Theater in Berlin on 8 June1929 exceeded all previous public and critical successes. *Die Fledermaus* ran throughout Europe, including in Paris, where it was given under the French title of *Chauve-souris* at the Théâtre Pigalle conducted by Bruno Walter. It even made it to Broadway in 1942, where it enjoyed a run of 520 performances.

The Great Waltz, or *Walzer aus Wien* as it was called in German, was to become Korngold's biggest operetta success. The book was written by Hubert's brother Ernst Marischka and Heinz Reichert, and the score was a compilation of numbers composed by Johann Strauss Father and Son. Korngold drafted in Julius Bittner to help. He was not only a family friend and the composer of the popular opera *Das höllisch Gold*, but he was also elderly, suffering from acute diabetes and near penury. In truth, Bittner was too ill to contribute much, but with the work's success and the ban on Jewish composers after 1933 (which of course included Korngold), Bittner became the only arranger to receive a credit. The Korngold Collection at the Library of Congress includes a deeply moving letter from Bittner's son, a returning prisoner of war, in which he expresses his most humble gratitude to Korngold for giving his parents the financial stability to survive the Nazi years. Bittner died in 1939, and the royalties kept him and his wife solvent.

Walzer aus Wien was a hit from the moment it opened at Vienna's Stadttheater on 30 October 1930. It opened in London the following year as *Waltzes from Vienna* and ran for 600 performances, with a similar success in Paris as *Valse de Vienne*. In 1934, it reopened in London under the new title *The Great Waltz*, by which it became known to English-language audiences from various film versions. It opened as *The Great Waltz* on Broadway at the Center Theater directed by Hassard Short on 22 September 1934 and ran for a further 289 performances. All of the film versions, including the one directed by Alfred Hitchcock in 1934, would mischievously keep to the original Korngold treatment while using arrangements by house composers, thus evading the considerable royalty payments due to Korngold and Bittner.

Reinhardt had not given up on his wish to mount an Offenbach operetta, and at Christmas in 1930 he finally persuaded Korngold. *Die schöne Helene* (*La belle Hélène*), with a new libretto by Egon Friedell and Hanns Sassmann, became their second international success. It opened at Berlin's Theater am Kurfürstendamm on 14 June 1931. After a run of 144 performances, it moved to London's Adelphi Theatre, where it was entitled simply *Helen*. Léonide Massine was the choreographer and Korngold conducted the opening performance, attended by the likes of Noel Coward, J. B. Priestley, Ivor Novello, Vivien Leigh, Tallulah Bankhead, Laurence Olivier, Sybil Thorndyke and Gertrude Lawrence.[41]

From 1933, Korngold's opportunities for work in Nazi Germany – including the many operetta arrangements – disappeared. The family retreated to its comfortable estate at Schloss Höselberg in Austria's Salzkammergut, where Erich began composing a new opera, *Die Kathrin*, even though there was no hope of it ever reaching a German stage under the new regime. Reinhardt, however, had managed to land a contract in Hollywood where he had accepted an offer from Warner Brothers to direct a film version of Shakespeare's *A Midsummer Night's Dream*, for which he asked Korngold to provide the score. Korngold arranged Mendelssohn's incidental music along with extracts from the composer's other works, ingeniously joining them together by scrupulously composed Mendelssohnian links. The move from arranging operetta to film could not have been more natural; that it should be Mendelssohn who would provide the musical opportunity carries its own intriguing symbolism.

Hollywood

Hollywood's moguls were mostly Eastern European and Russian Jews themselves, and they must have felt a touch of *Schadenfreude* as they scooped up the cream of Western European talent following Hitler's rise to power. Most of the newcomers were assimilated, urban Jews who were intimidatingly glamorous and sophisticated. Certainly Jack Warner, head of Warner Brothers, felt their arrival provided the opportunity to move away from low-budget gangster films and to smarten up the studio's image. At the same time, cultural insecurity meant he made agreements with this abundant talent that did not tally with his normally canny business instincts. One of these untypical deals was Max Reinhardt's film of *A Midsummer Night's Dream* – which gave Warner Bros the prestige of filming Shakespeare before its rivals at MGM or Paramount. Reinhardt's theatrical reputation was legendary, and his staging of the play at the Hollywood Bowl the previous year had left everyone open-mouthed. It was assumed he would be a cinematic natural.

What Warner had not taken into account was a European sophistication that took little notice of the company's central business precept – to produce mass-market movies with as little financial outlay as possible. Warner Brothers was famous for never going over budget. With Reinhardt's *Midsummer Night's Dream*, all the rules changed. Its expensive stars spoke lines in a weighty Shakespearian language that many movie-going Americans had difficulty following. The film may have been a *succès d'estime*, but it was a financial disaster. A combination of panic and cultural insecurity even saw Warner agreeing to another Reinhardt contract to make a film version of Georg Büchner's play *Dantons Tod*, while simultaneously taking measures to make sure such financial folly would never get beyond the planning stages. If it had, Korngold would have finally been able to supply Reinhardt with an original score, an ambition that was never to be realised.

Korngold's arrival had a galvanising effect on the Warner Brothers music department. Though many studio composers from this time are now well known, such as Alfred Newman and Max Steiner, none arrived in Hollywood with a career as firmly established as Korngold's. They supplied music by the minute and used stopwatches to measure to the second what was required. A team of orchestrators and arrangers would then flesh out sketched ideas. Korngold's practical mastery was unheard of. He conducted with authority, played the piano like a virtuoso and orchestrated as he composed, leaving details to assistants like Hugo Friedhofer. Most astonishingly, he knew instinctively how much music was needed for, say, twelve inches of film, and never used a stopwatch. The film version of *A Midsummer Night's Dream* launched not only Korngold's Hollywood career, but also those of many in its cast: Olivia de Havilland and Mickey Rooney made their film debuts and the role of Bottom was improbably played by James Cagney.

On completion of the film, Korngold returned to Austria in May 1935 to continue work on *Die Kathrin*. New contracts from Warner Brothers had already been offered to him for further projects with Reinhardt and Ernst Lubitsch. Paramount wanted him to compose the music for their newest signing: Jan Kiepura, the heart-throb star of Korngold's opera *Das Wunder der Heliane*, recently exiled from Hitler's Germany. The resolute Romantics of Vienna and Berlin had found their refuge from Europe's cultural and political dictatorships, and it was called Hollywood.

CHAPTER 10

Between Hell and Purgatory

I, as a Jew, expect the redemption of the world to come to us through a renewal
of a pure and genuine Christianity.
Ich als Jude erwarte die Erlösung der Welt von der Wiedergeburt eines reinen
und echten Christentums.

Speech by Franz Werfel in Vienna, 4 March 1932

We have eradicated International Jewry from cultural life; we have purged the
theatres and cinemas and we have returned a respectable press to the German
people. We have placed our entire intellectual and cultural life onto a new
foundation.
Wir haben das internationale Judentum aus dem Kulturleben ausgemerzt, wir
haben die Theater und Kinopaläste gesäubert, wir haben dem deutschen Volk
wieder eine anständige Presse gegeben und wir haben das ganze Geistes- und
Kulturleben auf eine neue Basis gestellt.

Speech by Josef Goebbels in Hamburg, 3 March 1933

At the end of 1932, there was much to occupy the largely Jewish contingent of
journalists at Vienna's *Neue Freie Presse*. The 300th birthday of the philosopher Baruch Spinoza was celebrated on 24 November,[1] though despite the
detail of the accompanying articles, it was far more subdued than the retrospective the paper had produced on the 250th anniversary of his death in
1927.[2] It was a last gasp of rationalism: the Dutch Jewish philosopher had laid
the intellectual basis for the Enlightenment that became the foundation for
two pillars of German Humanism: Lessing and Goethe. In 1933 the readers of
the *Neue Freie Presse* were offered a reminder of the conflicts between Wagner

and Brahms, with a variety of articles and feuilletons: it was 50 years since Wagner's death and 100 years since Brahms's birth. The anti-Semitism of Wagner goes unmentioned,[3] though the Austrian journalist deplores the brutalised co-opting of Wagner by 'the new politics of today' and paints his German nationalism in wilfully Kantian colours. Similarly, the philo-Semitism of Brahms passes without direct comment.[4] Brahms's support for the Liberal Party, the basis of the paper's editorial philosophy, is considered more relevant – and tacitly it amounted to much the same thing. Mahler's beloved soprano Selma Kurz also died in 1933, making it a poignant year for Julius Korngold, who had been one of her most ardent supporters. More irksome for Julius was the continued success of his son's work as an arranger of operettas, most recently Offenbach's *Helen*, which opened to sensational reviews in London.

And then there were the political changes taking place in Germany: Hitler's appointment as Reich Chancellor on 30 January 1933, the burning of the Parliament the following month and the imposition of the Reichstag Fire Decree on 27 February, suspending civil liberties and allowing the Nazis to embark on the systematic suppression of all opposition. This was followed on 23 March 1933 by the Enabling Act, sanctioned by the German Parliament, which gave Hitler absolute dictatorial powers, and given the totally inappropriate title 'Law to Remedy the Distress of the [German] People and Reich'.[5]

On New Year's Eve 1933, an anonymous editorial was printed in the *Neue Freie Presse* entitled 'Between Hell and Purgatory'. It is an intriguing article, presenting the reader today with a combination of clairvoyance mixed with blindness, and wisdom tempered by fear and doubt. As with most leading articles in the paper, it is full of historic and literary allusions, starting with a quote from the fourth-century Greek sophist Alcidamas: 'The Gods set all humanity free – nature has yet to make them into slaves.'[6] The article goes on to deal with contemporary macro-economic issues and the insanity of further defence spending. The writer is justifiably fretful regarding the delicate nature of relations between France and Germany, and is sceptical about Roosevelt's financial plans, which he views as reckless and unproven. But developments in Germany are the cause of greatest concern:

> It becomes more and more difficult to greet the developments of the age using words that offer mere credulity. It's as [*Götterdämmerung*] when during night's darkest moment, the rope of fate being woven by the Norns suddenly snaps, cut by a curse as forbidding as a peak within the distant mountain range. By this we mean that a normal evaluation [and interpretation of the end of the year and its implications for the year to come] is

frankly not possible using simple reason, scientific objectivity, or even human instinct. The irrational and hallucinatory music of *Götterdämmerung* confuse the songs that ordinarily make up our end-of-year rounds and rob us of all confidence and assurance. The Alberich of today has more power at his disposal than the former Gods of light. [. . .] In wishing to guess what may be in store, we can only grope blindly forward, trying to make out shapes in the dim light of a sun losing its warmth. We must free ourselves of everything we've ever believed – horror is the only emotion allowed. However, if we wish to divine the fate of humanity, we have no choice but to remain objective. Without objectivity, we're unable to place all that is hateful into its true alignment with our present condition. [. . .] Yet this year's greatest outrage has been the dehumanising of humanity – the indifference to the fate of others, the greedy grasping of uncontrolled power and the idolisation of vulgar bigotry which is spreading like an intellectual epidemic more deadly than any variant of mediaeval mysticism. [. . .] European culture itself as a spiritual entity has been destroyed. The intellectual traditions of generations have been wrecked. The dictators of recent times are uncannily adept at using the double edge of their swords: they position themselves at home as military absolutists on the one hand, while on the other, they make outward declarations of peace. [. . .] Hitler has risen to the very top and has managed uncontested to rub out all political opposition like smudges on a chalkboard. [. . .] He brought on elections that resulted in a monopoly in the Reichstag, which he has nevertheless succeeded in excluding from all political and economic decisions. He's turned theories of race into an anti-gospel that stands in stark contrast to the true gospels of mercy and charity towards one's neighbour. He has forced tens of thousands to flee, and many more have been ejected from their places of work. He ignores Frederick the Great's view that 'misplaced zeal results in a tyranny that leaves the country barren – tolerance on the other hand is a gentle mother which nurtures and yields forth fruit'. The National Socialists have been able to carry out these brutalities by going out of their way to avoid conflict with the world's most important powers. They have spoken words of peace to all who chose to listen, expressed their desire to strike deals and negotiate the unresolvable. Nobody seems to recall their previous statements regarding Poland. [Hitler's government] has even been able to make a reasonable impression in Britain by acknowledging the mistakes made in previous disarmament conferences, counting on the desire of peace by the majority of the British people along with their sickness of war and their abject reluctance to start another arms-race. It is from precisely this point that we witness a new era in European politics: a shift away from the recent axiom of all western nations aligned against Germany. From now on, we witness concessions as the basis of all negotiations.[7]

The writer goes on to despair of the League of Nations, oblivious to the vulnerability of Austria which was being placed under intolerable financial pressure as a result of restrictions imposed by Nazi Germany. He ends after brief excursions into global economic and political matters, expressing hope in Dollfuß and his plans for a hybrid state of democracy and corporatism. And in a plea that must have been uttered for the first time since the end of the First World War, he implores all to show charity towards the many refugees who now live amongst them.

Exit from Chaos: Dictatorship

It is worth remembering how fragile democracy was in the turbulent interwar years: even Britain, at the time of entering the First World War, had less enfranchisement than the Germany of Kaiser Wilhelm II. The new democracies that emerged at the end of the First World War fell again just as quickly: Hungary was turned into a monarchy from 1920 by the brutal Miklós Horthy, who made himself 'regent' in place of a king. His secret police terrorised and tortured Socialists, Communists and any other 'ungodly' political opposition. Bulgaria never really had a chance to try democracy as it moved to the dictatorship of Tsar Boris III. Italy went fascist in 1922, Lithuania and Poland in 1926, and as the 1930s progressed, Latvia, Estonia, Spain and Portugal also fell to various forms of dictatorships. In March 1933, only a month after Hitler's assumption of absolute power in Germany, Austria suspended parliament and joined Italy in its very specific form of 'corporatist' non-democratic government.

To speak of fascists as a single block is misleading. The corporatist Mussolini and the National Socialist Hitler loathed each other until circumstances and national greed pushed them together (as would also be the case with Hitler and Stalin in 1939). Up to this point, Italian and even Austrian Jews who feared Hitler saw Mussolini as a bulwark against the racist National Socialism of Germany.

On 20 January 1927, Winston Churchill made a statement in Rome praising Mussolini's brand of Fascism.[8] 'I will, however, say a word on the international aspect of Fascismo. Externally, your movement has rendered a service to the whole world.'[9] Reading what was reported in Austria's still free press offers an independent view from Germany's nearest neighbour: according to the *Neue Freie Presse*, Churchill praised fascism's ability to order the state's finances. The paper goes on to report that Churchill seemed to enjoy siding with Italy to score points against France – by calling for sensible expectations on the question of war reparations. He admired Mussolini's ability to galvanise his country in the fight against Bolshevism and believed that this authority also taught Italians the responsibilities of citizenship, demonstrating how honourable it was to defend themselves 'against the social sores that were festering all around'.[10]

In reporting Churchill's statement, the *Neue Freie Presse* is just as fascinated that Churchill was the first British statesman of his time to comment in public on another country's form of government. In fact, this is far more significant to the Austrian observers than Churchill's admiration for Mussolini. The paper also expresses surprise at Churchill's endorsement of fascist policies as an 'antidote to the virus coming from Russia'. The article ends with the observation 'that no democrat can truly share Churchill's views, interesting though they are'.[11]

The *Manchester Guardian* was also circumspect in its coverage of Churchill and Mussolini. It informs us that the *Corriere d'Italia* had praised Churchill as having a better understanding of fascism than most fascists. It quotes much of the statement, including the parts described by the Austrian journalist:

> If I had been an Italian I am sure I should have been entirely with you from the beginning to the end of your victorious struggle against the bestial appetites and passions of Leninism. [. . .] It has been said that a continual movement to the Left, a kind of fatal landslide towards the abyss, has been the character of all revolutions. Italy has shown that there is a way to combat subversive forces. This way can recall the mass of the people to co-operation that is loyal to the honour and interests of the State. Italy has demonstrated that the great mass of the people, when it is well led, appreciates and is ready to defend the honour and stability of civil society. It provides the necessary antidote to the Russian poison. Henceforth no nation will be able to imagine that it is deprived of a last measure of protection against malignant tumours and every Socialist leader in each country ought to feel more confident in resisting rash and levelling doctrines.[12]

Austria itself represented one of the more intriguing models of these varieties of fascism. A technicality in Austria's parliamentary voting system led to the chambers being suspended in March 1933 by its Christian Social Party Chancellor, the 40-year-old Engelbert Dollfuß. His assumption of absolute power was intended to combat encroaching National Socialism. He saw in

Hitler's methods little difference from the other great European dictator of the day, Joseph Stalin, conjuring up the spectre of godless Russian Bolshevism. Mussolini agreed with him and treaties were made between the two states in which Italy guaranteed Austria's sovereignty. Dollfuß initially banned the Austrian Nazi Party and soon followed this with bans on Communist and Socialist parties as well. The state took Italy as its model, with an even greater role accorded to Austria's Roman Catholic Church. Conservative and centralist parties were merged into the single Fatherland Front, with a symbolic rump of the disenfranchised Social Democratic Party being side-lined as the only potential voice of opposition. In his memoirs, Ernst Krenek reluctantly welcomed the new government as it confirmed each Austrian's place within the body of the state, with the Catholic Church's central position being the aspect that appealed to him most.[13] This centrality of the church offered Krenek some compensation for the suspension of democracy, which he had most certainly not welcomed.[14] Egon Wellesz was only slightly more circumspect and admits in his own memoirs that he joined 'the general Catholic renewal movements taking place in Austria at the time'.[15]

As noted in Chapter 7, there was endemic anti-Semitism within the Austrian Catholic Church – hence Krenek's shocking conversation regarding Jewish atonal composers with the Church's head of music Josef Lechthaler. However, social and religious tolerance was strongly endorsed by the church as well. On 23 December 1933, only nine months after Dollfuß's suspension of Parliament, the bishops and archbishops of Austria published a lengthy pastoral letter against National Socialism and the 'Insanity of Racism'. It stated unequivocally that humanity was founded on justice, and the love that bound all to live as a single family.[16] It was a fearless attack on National Socialism. It deplored the violence witnessed in Germany and specifically mentioned the racial hygiene laws, such as the 'Law Preventing Inherited Diseases' (passed on 14 July 1933) that forced sterilisation on those deemed to be anti-social, congenitally ill or mentally deficient. It was a law that Germany's Catholic clergy had also protested against. The law and the response of the church served as a reminder of the extreme secular nature of National Socialism, reinforcing the view of Austrofascists that there was little difference between Hitler and Stalin. The church deplored nationalism built on hatred and went so far as to denounce the extremism that could lead to a state church, forcing a break with the Catholic centre in Rome.[17] This point is made to counter the view of many pan-German Austrians, expressed at the end of the nineteenth century by Ritter von Schönerer, that 'true Germans' must free themselves from Rome and convert to Protestantism. Schönerer's movement fell apart precisely because pan-German Austrians would not abandon

Catholicism. Austria remained resolutely bound to its Roman confession, with Judaism its second largest denomination.

The Catholic Church went on to maintain a questionable and equivocal stance during the Nazi years; Cardinal Theodor Innitzer, who had drawn up the denunciation against National Socialism, welcomed Hitler in 1938, then told his flock at St Stephen's Cathedral that the only true 'Führer' was Jesus Christ, leading to the ransacking of his palace by Nazi youths. The first Nazi resistance movement originated at the Augustinian monastery in Klosterneuburg, led by one of the monks, Roman Karl Scholz, who was executed in 1944 despite direct pleas to Hitler for clemency from Cardinal Innitzer.

Felix Austria

For Austrian Jews living and working in Germany, a return to Austria was not an ideal solution, but it was preferable to emigration. Max Brand, Hans Gál, Max Reinhardt and Alexander Zemlinsky returned, while Arnold Schoenberg and Ernst Toch went to France before emigrating to the USA. Hanns Eisler also returned to Vienna, but left again almost immediately to mobilise the left into a 'Unity Front' coalition against fascism. His wife Charlotte and infant son Georg remained to act as secret conduits for communists coming in and out of the country via nearby Bratislava until they were forced to flee persecution by the Austrofascist dictatorship, settling in Moscow until their visas expired in 1938. Their subsequent move to Manchester in England most likely saved them from Stalin's paranoid purge of German and Austrian left-wing refugees.

Contemporary Austrian historians remain unclear on the ultimate legacy of Austrofascism. To some, it was a bulwark against Nazism; to others, it has been judged a 'Nazi ante-chamber'. In fact, it provided simultaneously both an anti-Nazi safeguard as well as a hot-house where Nazism could flourish as nowhere else. The five years under Austrofascist rule, from 1933 to 1938, were tolerant of other faiths while remaining officially Catholic. Apart from those private organisations and societies in sympathy with the Nazi Germany which enacted their own 'Aryan Paragraphs', Austria's Jews enjoyed relative security under the authoritarian regimes of both Dollfuß and his successor, Schusschnigg. With the failed Nazi coup of 1934 leading to a bloody civil war and Dollfuß's assassination, order was restored only with the threat of intervention by Mussolini. Dollfuß's successor, Kurt Schusschnigg, came down even harder on National Socialists until, in 1936, Realpolitik forced him to begin a period of appeasement, leading to Austria's eventual annexation –

resisted by Schusschnigg, but by now unstoppable. The Austrofascists' draconian ban on the Nazi Party, which most certainly would have enjoyed the sympathy, if not outright support, of just under half the population, forced it under ground, meaning that by March 1938 it erupted with explosive ferocity. In a repeat of the pogroms following the fall of the House of Habsburg in 1918, the overthrow of the Austrofascist regime led to anti-Semitic mobs unleashing terror on the streets of Austrian cities and towns. Even in Hitler's Germany such spontaneous public violence against Jews had not been seen. It shocked the world. The 'bulwark' against Nazism had unwittingly turned Austria into National Socialism's most fertile breeding ground.

Nazi Germany's anti-Semitism had until then been tolerated by the outside world as an unwholesome consequence of the injustices of the Versailles Treaty and the ensuing economic chaos in which Jews, deplorably, had been made the scapegoats. However, once the murderous racism of Austria's Nazis was allowed full rein, a shocked Britain, along with other democracies, including the United States, immediately enacted strict visa requirements and quotas in order to stem the tide of refugees desperate to flee. Austrian Jews knew that it would be sheer folly to assume that things would return to normal once their new masters realised what upstanding citizens they were. This had been a common fallacy among German Jews following Hitler's appointment as Chancellor in 1933. Those who already knew what to expect had secured their tickets and, if necessary, their visas. Hans Gál and his family, for instance, left for England within days of Hitler's arrival in Vienna. Julius Korngold described his family's escape as follows:

I have my oft-ridiculed pessimism to thank for our rescue. It was always my intention, should there be an outbreak of war, to get ourselves and one of Erich's sons, who was left in our care [while Erich, his wife Luzi and their other son were in America], out of Vienna. And I was always thinking about the outbreak of war. What I hadn't anticipated, however, was a conquest of Austria without so much as a single shot in the country's defence being fired. Thus, on the day when German troops marched into Vienna for their 'friendship visit' as the lie on the radio would have had us believe, I simply purchased ordinary train tickets and took my wife and grandchild over the border. I discovered later that it was one of the last trains for which this was still possible. I remember that it was a quiet Sunday and a normal train with the only deviation being our unexpected removal from our carriage in Innsbruck. But then, after a lengthy delay, an even more unexpected instruction followed that we could re-board. [. . .] It was 'a miracle', we were later told, though at the time we were not in a position to put much value in 'miracles'. What dangers we endured over the next days I shall pass over. Ultimately, with the rescue of my son's son, I rescued myself [and wife]. From Switzerland, Erich phoned and arranged for us to join them in Hollywood.[18]

Vienna, once the imperial capital, had been reduced to the provincial seat of Ostmark, a region within greater Germany. Embassies were required to relocate to Berlin as one country after another protested but then recognised the legality of the annexation. The consulates remaining in Vienna were woefully inadequate for dealing with the thousands of 'Ostmarkers' desperate for visas. Queues formed around blocks as applications were made and interviews held to determine who would be allowed to emigrate and who would not. Many escaped to Czechoslovakia not realising how temporary that refuge would be. Switzerland, too, would soon start to round up refugees and place them in internment camps for eventual repatriation should visas and affidavits not be forthcoming. In 1938 the Swiss insisted that German officials place a 'J' in the passports of Jewish Germans to differentiate between political and 'racial' refugees. All countries, including Great Britain and the United States, accorded the former a higher status.

The German Tragedy

In his chillingly realistic novel *The Oppermanns*, published in 1933, the novelist Lion Feuchtwanger deals with the dashing of the illusions of liberal-minded democrats in Germany as the Nazis seized power. He reminds us that initially it was not racial bigotry that shaped anti-Semitic purges but the far more 'reasonably' argued position that Jews, like Socialists and Communists, represented political opposition to the strong economic and political agenda the Nazis felt had been mandated by the German electorate. In Feuchtwanger's narrative we encounter a metaphor for the insidious infiltration of progressive educational institutions by German Nationalists: a new professor of literature arrives at a liberal school for bright boys preparing for university entrance a year before Hitler is made Chancellor. He has been imposed on the school by the local educational board, which has been taken over by members of anti-Semitic nationalist groups. The new teacher comes into his class with a proud and arrogant rejection of every 'rationalist' value that the Enlightenment has bequeathed since Immanuel Kant. He declares that actions must be based on feelings and inner instincts, which to him constitute the only moral compass any German needs. The use of 'reason' is to be rejected as 'un-German'. Culturally and politically, this amounted to a denunciation of the unemotional New Objectivity that flourished after the First World War. It confirms Ludwig Stein's view that revolutions were fundamentally 'Romantic' in nature and brought periods of sober Classicism to an end.

It is surprising to discover that the violinist Gustav Havemann shared a similar view. As leader of the Havemann Quartet, he had made a name for himself as an exponent of the composers associated with New Objectivity. In 1925, he had joined the radical 'November Group',[19] which also included such figures as H. H. Stuckenschmidt, Max Butting, Heinz Tiessen, Kurt Weill, Wladimir Vogel, Stefan Wolpe, Hanns Eisler and Jascha Horenstein, along with the artists George Grosz, John Heartfield, Otto Dix, Lyonel Feininger, Wassily Kandinsky and other prominent cultural figures within the Weimar Republic. At the same time, however, Havemann was a secret supporter of National Socialism and would become a member of the Nazi *Action League for German Culture*.[20] As such, he objected to the half-Jewish Franz Schreker as Director of the Berlin Hochschule für Musik. Since his appointment in 1920, Schreker had assembled an impressive faculty with illustrious names including Paul Hindemith, Georg Szell and Heinz Tiessen for composition; Edwin Fischer and Artur Schnabel for piano; Carl Flesch (and Havemann) for violin; and Emanuel Feuermann for cello, along with a host of wind players from the Berlin Philharmonic.

In 1931, Carl Flesch, who had joined the Hochschule faculty in 1928 at a time when Havemann's star was thought to be on the wane, published a book on tone production entitled *Das Klangproblem im Geigenspiel*.[21] A comment in the book on the innate musicality of the Jewish 'ghetto fiddler' led to an attack by Havemann in the *Allgemeine Musikzeitung*, in which he asserted that 'the presumption of Jewish racial advantages in violin playing' offended him 'as a German'. He further accused Flesch of wanting to impose the Jewish violin tone onto Germans: 'This is a tone that our race rejects, as it is too soft and sensuous.'[22] A heated debate then ran from 4 December to 18 December 1931 before the two teachers were persuaded to end their public argument with a statement of mutual respect.[23] Much of this bickering was politically motivated and was specifically directed against Leo Kestenberg, who, as a Jew, was also adviser to the Prussian Cultural Ministry. More generally, the attack was directed against the entire Prussian Social Democratic Government's cultural policy-making, an area that happened to include Schreker's faculty appointments at the Hochschule.[24]

In 1932, Flesch appointed his former pupil Stefan Frenkel, a Polish Jew, to cover his violin class during the periods he was away on tour. In light of the previous year's debate, the appointment proved explosive. It resulted in a storm of indignation from Havemann and his 'Action League' colleagues, including the composer Max Trapp, and less illustrious teachers such as

Romuald Wikarski and Valeska Burgstaller.[25] Their tedious machinations, full of anti-Semitic innuendo, ultimately forced Schreker's resignation as the school's Director in June 1932.

As compensation, Schreker was offered a composition master class at the Prussian Academy of Arts, where Schoenberg had taken over a similar position in 1926. They both found themselves beholden to the new President of the Prussian Academy of Arts, the composer Max von Schillings, who joined the National Socialist Party on 1 April 1933. Schillings began the systematic removal of all members and faculty who were either Jewish or unsympathetic to the new regime. On 18 March, both Schoenberg and Schreker attended their last meeting at the Academy, where they were informed that they could not expect to keep their positions. The official dismissal was to take effect from 31 December.[26]

Schreker's appeal to the composer Joseph Marx to help find him a position in Vienna was met with seeming callousness by his friend and former colleague, who replied in a letter dated 2 July 1933: 'The developments in Germany followed a clear inner logic of its own; it was to be expected that this enormously gifted and industrious people would not submit to being shackled forever by every conceivable and inconceivable kind of political trick. And as far as the Jewish matter is concerned, I explained to a Jew just a short time ago that they themselves are the ones who encouraged all manner of anti-Semitism with their absolutely indescribable actions.'[27]

At his holiday home in Estoril in Portugal, Schreker worked on the monumental overture to his unfinished opera *Memnon* which he entitled *Vorspiel zu einer großen Oper*. In October he returned to Berlin, where he completed its composition in preparation for a concert in Vienna while continuing to search for projects or opportunities that would enable him and his family to leave the country. Removal of his works from performance (the *Vorspiel* would not be played until 1958), his inability to appear as a conductor, and a forced retirement from teaching with the knowledge that his pension was barely above subsistence level, most likely brought on the stroke in late December that eventually killed him on 21 March 1934. Not surprisingly, the 'New Germany' did not heap him with posthumous praise and honours. In the case of the unapologetically Nazi house magazine, the once moderate *Die Musik*, he received only the vilest opprobrium – indeed, it extended to well beyond his death. In May 1938, *Die Musik* ran a retrospective article on music since 1933:

> No less destructive was the foreign Jewish spirit which was accompanied by the bastardisation within German musical life. Heading the Central Institution of

Education and Culture within the Prussian Ministry sat Leo Kestenberg, the son of a Jewish cantor. That he should appoint and promote his racial comrades will not surprise those who know the mentality, ways and means of Jews. The Directorship of the Music Academy was in the hands of the racial half-breed Franz Schreker, who poisoned the spirit of the people with his over-wrought and perverted operas.[28]

Christopher Hailey reminds us that the German press offered only two sympathetic obituaries. It must be counted an unexpected stroke of good fortune that only a month before Schreker's death, Julius Korngold retired from the *Neue Freie Presse*, meaning that Schreker's obituary was written by the more sympathetic Josef Reitler. A condolence letter to Schreker's wife from Anton Webern reminds us of Schreker's importance within twentieth-century Viennese music. If Webern's appreciation reminds us of Schreker's contribution to the shaping of the Second Viennese School, Reitler reminds us that, with his early libretto-writing instruction coming from the Austrian novelist and playwright Ferdinand von Saar, Schreker was equally part of 'Old Vienna' (an important differentiation from 'Young Vienna', the group of writers who congregated at Café Griensteidl, such as Hermann Bahr, Arthur Schnitzler, Peter Altenberg and Hugo von Hofmannsthal). Reitler goes on to write:

So much is made of the distant and near sounds to be heard in Schreker's opera texts that one starts to believe them just as one believes in the beauty of the Queen of Sheba or the invincibility of Walter's prize song in *Meistersinger*. It's impossible to deny his mastery or his ability to create extraordinary orchestral sounds and particularly his genius for producing colours with his extravagant orchestrations. It may be argued that the price he paid for this, however, would be a loss of the melodic and dramatic narrative, which may explain why certain works now seem pale and others were not successful at all. He once said, 'I actually don't have a music-dramatic idea. I simply write without any plan at all and what I write is simply there.' This ability to call up the shadows of his subconscious has been mentioned critically in these pages before [...] yet the specific genius of Schreker is beyond question. If Schreker had to fight as a composer, he was revered as a teacher. His students represent an entire generation of Vienna's talent, which he replicated with his move in 1920 to Berlin. They all held on to his every word and action. He took whoever represented independence of spirit and originality and he was no pedant. [...] It is a tragic coincidence that this obituary appears on what would have been his 56th birthday.[29]

Hailey also reminds us of a view expressed by the musicologist Károly Csipák that Schreker's 'persecution complex' made him unaware of the scale of what was happening around him.[30] Unlike Gál, Erich Korngold or even Schoenberg, Schreker did not identify himself as a Jew, was never raised as a Jew, and was unversed in any Jewish traditions, even if other non-Jewish composers saw him as displaying Jewish musical characteristics. Ernst Krenek's recognition of Schreker's 'Jewishness' has already been mentioned, and as early as 1915 the composer Hermann Wolfgang von Waltershausen had sensed features in Schreker's music which, though praiseworthy, could never be considered native to 'German' composers. Be that as it may, it's worth recalling that Schreker's Jewish father had converted before his second marriage, and so before the birth of the children that came from this union. He died when his son Franz was only nine years old. Schreker therefore never developed the antennae of his colleagues from Jewish or partially Jewish households. Yet even among Jewish colleagues, he was hardly alone: Hans Gál, as we have seen, also refused to recognise the seriousness of the changes that were taking place around him.

Schreker's attitude may have been naïve, but his situation vis-à-vis the Nazis was similar to that of Walter Braunfels, whose father Ludwig had been baptised as an infant by his converted Jewish father. Like Gál and Schreker, Braunfels was also head of a leading music institution, the Cologne Music Academy, a school that during the nineteenth century had once been headed by the Jewish composer and pianist Ferdinand Hiller. Braunfels was married to the daughter of a notable German sculptor, Adolf von Hildebrand. He was thus partially immune from the loss of social status that threatened Schreker with financial ruin. Braunfels even felt that his removal from the directorship in Cologne following a denunciation by one of his faculty members, Hermann Unger (who replaced Braunfels in the next Dortmund Tonkünstlerfest), was responsible for his new-found creative vigour. Despite these injustices, and his ejection from musical life under similar circumstance to Schreker, Braunfels seems to have been confident that he would remain unharmed and moved first to Godesberg and, from 1937, to a modest home near Überlingen on Lake Constance, where he remained in near total anonymity writing some of his most important and searching music.

The works that came out of this period in Braunfels's life included a powerful String Quintet, three string quartets, a number of church cantatas and three large-scale stage works: *Die Verkündigung* (1933–5), *Der Traum ein Leben* (1937), and *Szenen aus dem Leben der heiligen Johanna* (1939–43).[31] The reason he gave later for not choosing emigration was 'the conviction that, merely through my continued presence, I was a stone in the dam that was keeping evil from flooding everything; but also I realised that should I decide to leave my homeland, I would be ripping out the most important roots to my own creativity. I was well rewarded for keeping to this position [...] the source of inspiration welled up.'[32]

For his part, he refused any participation in German musical life on the rare occasions it was offered, initiating an internal boycott of his own. With the outbreak of war in 1939, he relocated to Florence, where he continued to work on his opera *Heilige Johanna* before returning to Lake Constance in the spring of 1940 eking out a living teaching local children. It is miraculous that in the course of the war he was neither denounced nor deported, but kept himself safe and anonymous among the villagers of Überlingen – coincidentally the same village where Winifred Wagner died in 1980 at the age of 82.

If the professional circumstances of Schreker and Braunfels appeared to be almost identical, Schreker spent his adult life in fear of having to return to the horrors of the genteel poverty of his youth, an insecurity that did not trouble Braunfels.[33] Schreker's most successful years were during the period of Germany's hyper-inflation, meaning that he never achieved true financial security despite immense popularity. The shock of losing all sources of income at the age of 55 was more than his nervous state could bear. Braunfels, with a far larger family, followed a deeply devotional life as an observant Catholic. Schreker kept no such faith, and with his death in 1934 he can be counted as the first important musical victim to fall to Nazi persecution.

The Mechanics of the Purge

Scholars of National Socialism's music policies relate a never-ending tug-of-war for the cultural soul of the Nazi Party and, by extension, the German nation between the ministers Joseph Goebbels and Alfred Rosenberg concerning questions of party dogma versus image and propaganda. Rosenberg, along with members of the younger Wagner clan, the virulently anti-Semitic editor of the *Zeitschrift für Musik* Alfred Heuß, and the editor of the Bayreuth newsletter, Hans von Wolzogen, formed the Kampfbund für Deutsche Kultur in 1929. Rosenberg remained its director and gave the appearance of having the upper hand in musical matters prior to 1933. Goebbels, perhaps owing to his hate-inspired rhetoric, gained Hitler's confidence and was permitted to incorporate music policy within his own Ministry of Propaganda. He was certainly the cleverer and more sophisticated of the two. There are even indications, such as the supervision of his doctorate by Jewish professors, that his anti-Semitism was an opportunistic add-on.

Goebbels was amenable towards new trends in the arts and he wanted to find a means of keeping Hindemith in Germany as the standard-bearer for contemporary music under National Socialism. For the purposes of selling Germany's image – especially abroad – it was important for Goebbels to challenge the perception that National Socialism, in common with other European Fascist regimes, was culturally backward-looking.

Rosenberg, despite what many took to be a Jewish-sounding name and his rather un-Teutonic appearance, took Nordic imagery as his reference for political dogma. Hitler told Rosenberg on 24 January 1934 that he expected him to act as his personal representative in all educational matters relating to National Socialist culture and the interpretation of its 'world view'. In 1936–7, Rosenberg fused his money-losing Action League with Kraft durch Freude,[34] an organisation that provided education and entertainment for the masses. Bundled together, they became known as the 'Reich's Supervision Bureau',[35] colloquially referred to as 'The Rosenberg Office'. This was subdivided into the various disciplines of Education, 'The Cultivation of Literature', 'The Cultivation of the Arts', 'The Department of Early and Pre-History', as well as an archive of 'Clerical, [church]-Political Issues', and the more general field of the sciences. The Department for Music, a subdivision of the Arts section, was under the responsibility of the musicologist Herbert Gerigk, later the co-author of the notorious *Lexikon der Juden in der Musik*.[36] With this increase of influence, Rosenberg's department became a counter-balance to Goebbels's Ministry of Propaganda.

A Contemporary Account of Rosenberg in London

On 10 May 1933, the *Neue Freie Presse* gleefully recounted a story reported in a 'London Telegram' of the right-wing, anti-Nazi German paper, *Deutsche Allgemeine Zeitung*, regarding the intellectual drubbing Rosenberg received at the hands of Margot Asquith, 'Countess of Oxford and Asquith' and widow of the former Prime Minister Herbert Henry Asquith. Rosenberg was in England in his capacity as Head of the National Socialist Party's Foreign Affairs Office. His stay had not been a success, and when Rosenberg laid a wreath on the Cenotaph, one of the monument's guards later tossed it into the River Thames. As related in the 'London Telegram', the encounter with Margot Asquith was even more humiliating:

> Lady Oxford [Margot Asquith] told Rosenberg that he was a brave man to come to a country where there was only one opinion to be heard on the horrors and stupidities emanating from the new regime in Germany. She asked if Hitler had no God, and assuming he hadn't, 'couldn't he at least leave

those who had one in peace?' Rosenberg explained that there was a huge job ahead and that she had misunderstood the nature of the miracles that Hitler had already brought forth. 'They were not fighting against religion as such, but against various people, particularly the Jews, who everyone knows are opposed to the new regime.' He told her of the hunger, the desperation and the despair of Germany before Hitler and how now, everyone was filled with hope and new ideals. Lady Oxford countered that these things did not apply to Germany's great men, but to Germany's sheep. She asked Rosenberg what was happening to the country's many scholars, the doctors, the lawyers, the musicians and writers – all the people who had made Germany a country of cultural greatness. Rosenberg explained: 'These things will settle down again. There can be no revolution on this scale without some injustices being committed. But these are minor in comparison with the great act of unity currently under way.' Lady Oxford replied that 'Creating fear is not the same as creating unity' and that she 'would shudder' should she find herself in Germany today. Rosenberg retorted that the National Socialists know that the German people are on their side; but the Jews are against them. 'After the previous war, the Jews managed to secure all of the best positions for themselves. They are corrupt, easy to bribe and have promoted Communism.' Lady Oxford again: 'It is intelligence that makes a country great, and if Germany expels all of its most capable intellects amidst shouts of "Heil Hitler", they make themselves a laughing-stock.' Rosenberg's response was that 'no revolution as large as the National Socialist Revolution has been carried out with so little loss of life. Had the NS Revolution come only a month later, Germany would have descended into even greater bloodshed. The network of intrigues and Communism was only waiting for the right moment.' He ended by stating that he hoped she would live long enough to see how Germany would be saved by the acts of this one great man, Adolf Hitler.[37]

Margot Asquith died in July 1945, only two months after the fall of the Third Reich.

A Confused Beginning

The Wagnerian tendency to write new stage works on ancient Germanic themes in the late 1920s and early 1930s has already been mentioned in the context of the diminishing popularity of *Zeitoper*. This trend was accorded a more sinister meaning by the youthful head of Universal Edition's opera department, Hans Heinsheimer, who saw a continued 'Teutonisation' of the repertoire being conceded by conservatives as a means of tossing a bone to the rowdy Nazi opposition.[38] One of these works would have been *Friedemann Bach*, by Paul Graener, who would become very much a Nazi favourite. As it happened, Graener would eventually take over one of the positions left vacant by the enforced retirements of Schoenberg and Schreker at the Prussian Academy in 1933. He also took on one of the positions at the *Allgemeiner deutsche Musikverein* (ADMV) left vacant after the removal of Berg, Gál and Toch, two of whom were Jewish and one of whom was tainted by association with Schoenberg. Not only were all three Austrian citizens, but their works were deemed to be inappropriate to the 'new' Germany. Graener would also head the composer's division at the Reich's Musikkammer, the Nazi office for musical affairs. *Friedemann Bach* shares its Jewish librettist Rudolf Lothar with Eugen d'Albert's *Tiefland* – another popular work among National Socialists and reputed to be one of Hitler's favourites. Despite conflicting messages coming from those close to Hitler's inner circle, Viktor Zuckerkandl's review of *Friedemann Bach*'s 1932 Berlin performance reveals the direction in which the politico-musical wind would ultimately blow:

> Paul Graener, the composer of many successful orchestral and chamber works, along with his opera *Don Juans letztes Abenteuer* [*Don Juan's Last Adventure*], which has been seen on most stages throughout Germany, is also director of the Sternschen Conservatory in Berlin and has only recently celebrated his 60th birthday. A few days following this event, the Städtische Oper [in Berlin-Charlottenburg] mounted its first performance of his new work, *Friedemann Bach*. It was an occasion for friends and pupils to join in the celebratory festivities.

There follows a summary of the plot, which is loosely based on fictitious events in the novel of the same name by Albert Emil Brachvogel. Zuckerkandl continues:

> This is, as we see, an opera about an artist. It's also, as Graener would have us understand, an opera of avowal: it is an opera that is pure music. [Graener explains:] 'I have attempted to express Friedemann Bach's essential humanity and experience by using simple musical means. The libretto is merely an excuse to write music; in fact this is an opera that only exists thanks to its music!' With this, we have Graener's avowal to pure music. [. . .] And as such his music is undoubtedly pleasant sounding with lots of melody, harmonic consonance – it is music that exists well beyond any awkward complications.

Its artistic qualities are immediately apparent. It is the work of an honest and masterful craftsman. The small forms which shape most of the acts create a formal, yet lyrical structure and are easily linked together and pleasingly executed. It is filled with melody. [. . .] What this music lacks, however, is dramatic power and originality. The libretto is conventional – and the music doesn't permit us to forget this fact. As a result, there can be no talk of a great dramatic success. The artistic avowals lack profundity as the voice that expresses them simply doesn't carry. It is without question 'pure music', but less pure and bit more substantial would have been preferable.[39]

The conflicting messages and the subsequent difficulty of establishing any consensus for what music should be in the New Germany of Goebbels and Rosenberg is reflected in H. H. Stuckenschmidt's review for *Anbruch* of Paul von Klenau's opera *Michael Kohlhaas*, based on Heinrich von Kleist's novella, premiered in Stuttgart in 1933, a year after *Friedemann Bach*:

Modern Music is in a difficult situation in today's Germany. The few who have held their ground are battling against a majority whose enthusiasm is matched by their lack of theoretical substance. Neither side seems to be in the position of addressing the question of what, exactly, within our artistic lives is 'corrupting' and what is meant by 'Cultural Bolshevism'. The opinions are even varied amongst the different departments within our arts' bureaucracy. The very same Stravinsky who is called a cultural Bolshevist by the journalists of the *Zeitschrift für Musik* is loudly applauded by the radical leader of the 'Action League for German Culture', Hans Hinkel. The same [Fritz] Jöde [Music pedagogue: 1887–1970] who is fought against as a separatist and anti-nationalist by 'Action League' musicians, led by Dr Fritz Stein, has thousands of supporters in the [NS] party. The same Max v. Schillings, who couldn't possibly be more covered with honours, certificates and medals bestowing him with the full confidence of the new regime, is defamed by the leader of the Saxon committee of music critics, Dr Alfred Heuß, as an arch-protagonist in Germany's fall during the last war and as composer of the un-German, 'sadistic' opera *Mona Lisa*. Is there even such a thing as 'corrupting manifestations' in music? Perhaps it's the departure from tonality, the robust basis of which is so highly praised from all sides, as a point of permanence. Is tinkering with it an obvious artistic taboo? Or is tonality, as Arnold Schoenberg writes in his book on Harmony, only one of many creative means? The official view of the music-politicians, as far as they have been able to address such detailed issues, is basically that they are against atonality. Only a few months ago, the Jury of the Dortmund

Tonkünstler Festival forced the composer Peter Schacht to forgo performance of his String Quartet once it was established that the work had been
composed using the twelve-tone technique.

And it is in this confusion that Stuttgart's premiere of Paul von Klenau's
opera *Michael Kohlhaas* clarifies like a blaze of light. As here we have a work
that is supported by the highest powers in the land as a 'national work', yet is
undeniably modern, a score which is largely twelve-tone and shows a disregard, with few exceptions, of standard harmonic modulatory rules.[40]

Music Policies in Hitler's Germany

Sorting out such confusion, and with an eye towards the not yet enacted racial
purges, demanded some sort of organisation and planning. There are extensive and detailed accounts by historians including Fred Priberg, Michael
Kater, Erik Levi and, most recently, Amaury du Closel[41] regarding the Nazi
machinations which sought to isolate those composers who were not part of
the 'New Germany' while promoting the Nazis' own musical ideals.

The obvious rallying point for the National Socialists was Wagner. Indeed,
he was very much the Ur-National Socialist, having been, at different stages in
his life, both a nationalist *and* a Socialist. Hitler's devotion to the music and
philosophy of Wagner was reciprocated by two British members of the
Wagner family.

Houston Stewart Chamberlain, husband of Wagner's daughter Eva, died
six years before Hitler's rise to power while providing the Nazis with a quasi-
scientific basis for their racist policies in his *Foundations of the Nineteenth
Century* published in 1899. His feelings for Hitler personally were nearly
devotional, as correspondence from 1923 indicates:

> You are not at all, as you have been described to me, a fanatic, rather I would
> like to describe you as the direct opposite of a fanatic. The fanatic heats
> heads, you warm hearts. [. . .] That Germany in the hour of its deepest need
> has raised up a Hitler attests to its vitality; likewise the effects emanating
> from him; for these two things – personality and its effect – belong together.
> That the great Ludendorff openly allies himself with you and joins the
> movement emanating from you: what a splendid confirmation! I can now
> safely fall asleep at night and not even need to wake up again. May God
> protect you![42]

Wagner's daughter-in-law, Winifred (née Winifred Marjorie Williams), the
wife of Wagner's son Siegfried, was to become Hitler's most devoted muse and

disciple. From 1925, Bayreuth started to publish a newsletter which, by 1933, had become an instrument of virulent racist propaganda. Hitler himself proposed marriage to Winifred, widowed since the death of her older, homosexual husband, the composer Siegfried Wagner in 1930. Despite providing the paper on which Hitler wrote *Mein Kampf* while he was in prison after the 1923 aborted beer-hall coup in Munich, she rejected his proposal on the grounds that he did not have an 'official position'. By the time he was appointed Germany's Reich Chancellor, he no longer needed the status of a link with the Wagner clan, though he remained a Bayreuth devotee and an extremely close friend of Winifred and at least three of her four children. Rumours of the intimacy between them were such that during her war-crime hearings, she was forced to deny that they had had sexual relations.

Despite her daughter Friedelind denouncing the family's association with Hitler and going into American exile from where she broadcast anti-Nazi propaganda in German, the rest of the Wagner family, headed by Winifred, continued to have warm feelings for the private Hitler, whom they called 'Uncle Wolf'.[43] Winifred never expressed anything other than total devotion for him. In television interviews from 1975, she called him 'unser seliger Adolf' (Our blessed Adolf), abbreviated in the postwar years to 'USA'. Winifred's grandson Gottfried has recounted how his grandmother greeted other dedicated postwar Nazis using the secret number 88: the letter 'H', as the eighth letter in the alphabet, was repeated as 'eighty-eight' to escape postwar detection of fervent Nazis who still wanted to greet each other with 'Heil Hitler!'

In musical matters, Rosenberg's 'Revolution' started off with some slips of policy. Kurt Weill's highly political opera *Der Silbersee* managed a simultaneous premiere in Erfurt, Leipzig and Magdeburg on 18 February 1933 around the same time as the premiere of Hans Gál's Violin Concerto in Dresden with soloist Georg Kulenkampff, conducted by Fritz Busch. Korngold's adaptation of Leo Fall's *Die geschiedene Frau*[44] limped on for a few weeks at Berlin's Theater am Nollendorfplatz immediately following Hitler's appointment – intriguingly, subsequent lawsuits relating to its early closure made no mention of the Jewish authorship of the work, the libretto or the arrangement, but involved the alleged chicanery of various theatre directors.[45]

Even Alexander Zemlinsky had his opera *Der Kreidekreis*[46] performed at the Berlin Staatsoper under Robert Heger in January 1934. Heinz Tietjen, the Director of the Staatsoper, had postponed the premiere from April 1933, having reneged on his contract with Otto Klemperer – who was originally scheduled to conduct it – with the excuse that, as a Jew, Klemperer's safety at the Staatsoper could not be guaranteed. *Der Kreidekreis* went on to enjoy a further twenty performances in Berlin, despite the fact that Zemlinsky's

Kleider machen Leute[47] had been banned as early as March 1933. *Der Kreidekreis* had received its premiere in Zurich on 14 October 1933 with its first performance in Nazi Germany occurring at Stettin on 16 January, followed by another production in Coburg (21 January), before opening in Berlin on 23 January and further stagings in Nuremberg and Cologne. It would be the last work by a high-profile Jewish composer to be presented at such an important venue in the Reich's capital city after January 1934. It counts as a minor miracle that it happened as late as it did, during a period when Goebbels and Rosenberg were squabbling for positions of cultural dominance, thus allowing some flexibility within artistic planning.

Writing of the Berlin performance, H. H. Stuckenschmidt praised the opera as being worthy of the best opera house in the Reich's most important city, highlighting the objections made by the Head of Police following the work's premiere in Stettin, where further performances were banned for reasons of 'public decency' (due to some scenes being set in a 'tea house' which was in fact a brothel). This ban was then taken up by some of Germany's smaller opera houses. Stuckenschmidt applauded the fact that the central government had thwarted locals who had worked themselves into a state of indignant outrage and writes that it is a relief 'to see the limb being sawn off by those from above, upon which small-town protectors of local morality are seated'.[48] It was to be a tragically short-lived false dawn. The Nazi critic Rudolf Bilke called Zemlinsky a 'wolf in sheep's clothing', pointing out that if performances by Zemlinsky were permitted, then nothing could stand in the way of Schoenberg and Schreker also being brought back.[49] Viktor Zuckerkandl writing for a Viennese readership was far more welcoming. For him, it represented exactly what opera managements were looking for: a modern opera with music that didn't frighten the public.[50]

Following Hitler's appointment as Reich Chancellor on 30 January 1933, there had been suggestions that he might abandon some of the anti-Semitic rhetoric of his campaign. In spite of these misplaced expectations, the revolutionary machinery disrupted performances of Ernst Toch's 'capriccio' Zeitoper *Der Fächer*[51] in mid-rehearsal at Cologne, while Berthold Goldschmidt's *Der gewaltige Hahnrei* never made it to the Charlottenburg Städtische Oper in Berlin after a successful Mannheim premiere. *Die beiden Klaas* by Hans Gál was struck off the schedule at Hamburg, and with the open Nazi harassment of Fritz Busch in March 1933 during rehearsals of *Rigoletto*, there was no chance of it being mounted, as planned, in Dresden. Clemens Kraus dropped Egon Wellesz's *Die Bakchantinnen* in Munich; Jascha Horenstein's dismissal from Düsseldorf kicked the premiere of Marcel Rubin's opera *Prinzessin Brambilla* into the long grass; and Karl Böhm's forthcoming performance of Max Brand's

Requiem at the Berlin Staatsoper was also quietly shelved. Even Manfred Gurlitt, a supporter of the Nazi regime and a party member since 1 May 1933, had the Mannheim premiere of his opera *Nana* cancelled as it was wrongly believed that he was Jewish – a position the Nazis maintained at the expense of all of his works including his treatments of *Soldaten* and Büchner's *Wozzeck*.

Jews, such as Bruno Walter and Otto Klemperer, were not allowed to conduct for so-called 'security reasons', spurious excuses made along the lines that the public and musicians would no longer tolerate Jewish conductors, singers and instrumentalists and, therefore, 'their safety could not be guaranteed'. It was just an extension of Nazi double-speak – similar excuses were made for the official boycott of Jewish shops and professional services on 1 April 1933, when it was claimed that if the boycott had not been officially sanctioned, it would have been carried out by a mob and public safety would have been at risk.

Mass resignations of conductors were demanded: Josef Rosenstock in Mannheim, Jascha Horenstein in Düsseldorf, and Fritz Stiedry in Berlin; Otto Klemperer's Staatsoper contract was torn up by the same man who had made Hans Gál's *Heilige Ente* such a success with Maria Schreker only a few years before – Heinz Tietjen – though it was the same Heinz Tietjen who put on Zemlinsky's *Kreidekreis* the following year. Gustav Brecher, Director of the opera in Leipzig who had premiered both Krenek's *Jonny spielt auf* and Kurt Weill's *Aufstieg und Fall der Stadt Mahagonny*, was forced out of Leipzig after having a performance of Weill's *Der Silbersee* interrupted in March 1933. He and his wife committed suicide in Ostend in 1940 as Belgium fell to the Nazis. Non-Jews also protested, resigned and left the country, including Erich Kleiber, Fritz Busch, Karl Rankl, the opera director Carl Ebert, the theatre director Josef Gielen (father of Michael Gielen), and the composers Robert Stolz and Ralph Benatzky.

It was just as Lady Oxford had predicted to Rosenberg: Germany was haemorrhaging its most important intellects and talents. What was happening in music was being replicated in academia, the law and medicine. Jewish doctors were rounded up and thrown out of hospitals, and patients who allowed themselves to be operated on by Jewish surgeons were themselves subject to persecution. These were not the 'minor injustices' that Rosenberg spoke of, but major outrages that would damage the country for generations. What this meant in practical terms for music is explained by Viktor Zuckerkandl, writing from Berlin in July 1933:

It is a remarkable phenomenon, that the general movement that is currently sweeping across Germany and is the fruit of a younger generation of politicians has not succeeded in establishing equivalent young voices to achieve similar breakthroughs in music. After all, when all is said and done, music must ultimately be considered the most characteristic means of national self-expression. But, in fact, it appears that the opposite is more the case. The men we see coming forward today were all born in the 1890s and hail from older generations, if not perhaps in actual age, then certainly in attitude: stolid bourgeois taste resulting in worthy Romantic expression has been the trend. We're treated to picture-book scenes from the countryside of yore, rich with the naïve joy of kitschy costumes and trite sets. We are reaching back to the times of Richard Strauss and Pfitzner. It's not difficult to understand what drives this counter-revolution against rationalist trends that have dominated music in Germany for the past two decades. Perhaps the criticism that modern German music has too assiduously avoided direct association with its forests and fields, or even its own folk traditions is legitimate, at least if compared with Slavic and Latin cultures. If we recall the many new forms that have resulted from this most recent revolution in the political sphere, it is astonishing that such ambitions for new beginnings are totally missing within music. Of course, the truly 'new' can only come about as an act of genius, and the present trend of reaching into the past is mere compensation for having nothing original to say.[52]

Zuckerkandl's last sentence offers an eerie, if unintentional echo of Wagner's comments on Jewish composers.

Furtwängler

On 12 April, reports appeared in the *Neue Freie Presse* of an appeal to Goebbels made by the conductor Wilhelm Furtwängler with the heading 'There is only good and bad art':

Furtwängler has presented an appeal to the Propaganda Minister Dr Joseph Goebbels in which he places his entire authority upon the belief that in Germany, much that is presently taking place has absolutely nothing to do with the restoration of the nation's cultural heritage. Furtwängler is dismayed that 'lines are being drawn between the confessional persuasions of individuals' – even in circumstances where this must have little or no bearing on professional and state affairs. According to Furtwängler: 'rather than drawing a division between confessions, one should draw it between good and bad art. This is the only line that should not be crossed and should be the only line that we heed. Musical life has been damaged already by both the world financial crisis and the advent of the radio – it cannot bear further social experiments. If nothing worthwhile can be offered in concerts, the public simply turns away. Questions of quality are not just questions of aspirations and ideals, but become questions of our very existence as musicians. Of course one should fight the destructive kitsch that is rootless, dry and soulless; but it can never be in the interest of our cultural life to turn this fight against real artists. It has to be said very clearly that men such as Bruno Walter, Otto Klemperer and Max Reinhardt are necessary for the future cultural life in Germany and must be allowed to continue to have their say.'

Goebbels's response was that 'there is not only the dividing line between good and bad art, but the only art that can be considered good is that which springs from the eternal well deep inside the people and this art must also *mean* something to these people'. Dr Goebbels takes the view that true German artists have been forcibly silenced over the past fourteen years, though he conceded that mistakes had perhaps been made and wrote that 'any true artist need not worry about his position'. It is to be understood that Goebbels is expressing polite respect towards Furtwängler rather than any actual intention of rectifying previous excesses. Reading between the lines, one may, however, sense a hint of an admission that perhaps they have on occasion been over-zealous.[53]

The article goes on to list the many German scientists and doctors who would be without employment under the conditions dictated by the new regime and makes the point that 20 per cent of Germany's Nobel Prize winners would also find themselves unemployed. The journalist then turns to a quote by the Nazi minister Hermann Göring, which he follows with an analysis by the conservative German press:

[Göring:] 'It is impossible to build a Reich that is both large and glorious if groups within our nation are reduced to slavery. With a cowed people, or where millions feel themselves to be excluded, it is not possible to inspire a country to historic deeds.' The *Allgemeine Deutsche Zeitung*, a paper from the political right, expresses the fear that the new Reich is being built on feelings and instincts and not, as with previous governments, on reason: 'It can only lead to intolerable uniformity of Germany's political and intellectual life, a feat that the rest of the world would gaze upon with open mouths. In our opinion,' [the *ADZ*] continues, 'this contributes just as little to the work that still needs to be done during these dangerous times as playing lovey-dovey to Hitler's enemies from earlier days.' [The *ADZ*] goes on to despair of the cowardly resignation, the byzantine lack of tact in all dealings and the total absence of cultivation and civil courage. The appeal of Furtwängler, however, reminds us that there is still to be found within the German people the bravery that does not quake at the foot of the thrones of kings. It would be a true blessing if it were on these foundations of past ideals that a country's history was being inspired.[54]

Goebbels represented a more nuanced and ambivalent view, that the public should decide for itself if it liked atonal, dissonant music, just so long as it was not of Jewish authorship. To this end, Erich Kleiber conducted Alban Berg's *Lulu Suite* at Berlin's Staatsoper in December 1934. During the Nazi years, more stridently modernist music was occasionally tolerated; even more rarely – as with Klenau's opera *Michael Kohlhaas* – it would be promoted as part of Goebbels's propaganda attempts to portray National Socialism as progressive.

Who's a Jew?

The removal of Jews and their works from the repertoire meant breaking countless contracts which would have led to costly court actions. To circumvent this, a law called 'The Re-establishment of the Professional Civil Service' was passed on 7 April 1933 barring Jews from any publicly subsidised position unless they could prove that they had fought on the front in the First World War – an exception that enabled the Jewish composer and conductor Leo Blech to remain in his position as Music Director of the Berlin State Opera Unter den Linden until 1937. This law hit orchestras, opera houses and theatres particularly hard, and it was in direct response to this that Furtwängler addressed his appeal to Goebbels on 12 April. The Städtische Oper in Berlin-Charlottenburg, the venue for many of Berlin's most important premieres such as Schreker's *Der Schmied von Gent*, Weill's *Die Bürgschaft* and Gál's *Die heilige Ente*, lost its founding music director Ignaz Waghalter, its conductor Fritz Stiedry, its assistant conductors and pianists Berthold Goldschmidt and Kurt Sanderling, and its chief administrator, Rudolf Bing. Waghalter fled first to Czechoslovakia, then to the United States. Carl Ebert and Bing resigned and moved to England, where they took on the management of the Glyndebourne Festival Opera. Goldschmidt followed in 1935 in the mistaken belief that Ebert would be able to find him a position, and hopeful that, following a BBC broadcast of Berg's *Wozzeck*, he might find opportunities no longer afforded to modern Jewish composers in Germany. Kurt Sanderling took the courageous decision to go the Soviet Union, where he miraculously avoided the purges of 1938 and later became one of Shostakovich's closest associates.

Much stricter legislation would soon come into force. The notorious 'Nuremberg Laws' were announced at the Nazi Party Conference in Nuremberg in September 1935. The laws were designed to protect German blood and prohibited 'inter-racial' sexual relationships and marriage. Those who could not prove their pure Aryan lineage were stripped of fundamental rights, which would soon progress from the profoundly distressing, such as losing all means of employment, to the petty and mean-spirited, such as not being allowed in public parks or attending entertainments held in public venues. In August 1938, a law was passed that required all men and women of Jewish descent to take a common middle name that would instantly identify them as Jews. For men this name was 'Israel', and for women 'Sarah'. These regulations spread from region to region as each tried to outdo the others in finding new means to isolate and humiliate German Jews.

With the annexation of Austria, the full fury of Austrian Nazi frustration unleashed a blood bath. What had taken five years to carry out in Germany was accomplished in a matter of months in Austria. The extreme brutality caused a wave of suicides among Jews with no foreign connections to help them escape. Even well-known figures were affected, such as the cultural historian and writer Egon Friedell, who leapt to his death from a window when he believed Nazis were storming his apartment building.

Nazi laws would extinguish Austria's literary identity. The annexation would be the last nail in the coffin of the depressive and alcoholic writer Joseph Roth, who died in Paris in 1939. Robert Musil died in Swiss exile in 1942, the same year that Stefan Zweig and his wife jointly committed suicide in Brazil. The works of writers who had died before the annexation, such as Karl Kraus in 1936, Franz Kafka in 1924, Rainer Maria Rilke in 1926, Arthur Schnitzler in 1931 and Hugo von Hofmannsthal in 1929, were taken out of circulation and even burned, though Hofmannsthal, as Strauss's librettist, was treated more lightly than others despite his Jewish ancestry.

On 22 September 1933, the Nazis created the Reichskulturkammer (RKK) or the Reich's Chamber of Culture under Goebbels as a means of foiling the Deutsche Arbeitsfront (DAF) or the German Workers' Front, organised under Robert Ley. The DAF had been set up as a National Socialist umbrella organisation for German workers after the disbanding of all Weimar Republic trade unions in 1933. Under Ley's guidance, it had begun encouraging professionals and employees involved in the arts and culture to join. But this was an area that Goebbels saw as very much his own. Goebbels's RKK consisted of seven subdivisions, represented by the usual artistic disciplines of 'written word', 'music' and the 'visual arts', but also extending to the press and broadcasting. Beneath these were representatives of Germany's 31 districts. The RKK division devoted to music was called the Reichsmusikkammer (RMK – Reich Chamber of Musical Affairs), initially with Richard Strauss as its president and Wilhelm Furtwängler as his deputy. In fact, the 69-year-old Strauss had been appointed without his acceptance even being sought, but believing his new-found influence might help his Jewish in-laws and be useful to other musicians and friends, he complied and took up the post without further question. It looked as if there was a glimmer of hope that some sense of restorative balance might be brought to the racist fanaticism that dominated all other aspects of Nazi cultural policy.

Both appointments proved to be short-lived. Strauss was replaced by the more hard-line Peter Raabe in 1935 following Strauss's collaboration with Stefan Zweig on *Die schweigsame Frau*. The ubiquitous Paul Graener took over from Furtwängler as early as 1934 after Furtwängler publicly expressed support for Hindemith's opera *Mathis der Maler* and resigned from the RMK in protest at its banning. The purpose of the RMK was to provide support for composers and performers, protect their interests and offer a minimum of social security. Under Strauss's short presidency, the one position that was markedly improved was, unsurprisingly, that of copyright protection, which was extended to fifty years after a composer's death.

Despite the relatively early arrival of the RMK within the political apparatus, its removal of Jews from musical life was initially fairly half-hearted owing to Strauss's insistence on following the word, rather than the spirit, of the regulations. As the statutes of the RMK did not specifically prohibit Jews, Strauss was inclined to include them. This was despite a vague RKK statement from 9 November 1933 with the implication that Jews should be excluded. It took a specific instruction from Goebbels in March 1934, stating unequivocally that Jews were inappropriate stewards of German culture, before they were officially excluded. This position was reconfirmed the following month in an internal document of the RMK.[55]

Establishing whether a person was an Aryan or not, was to be based on information provided by applicants to the RMK on a questionnaire that was otherwise meant to establish the professional suitability of musicians. As the RMK had become *de facto* a closed trade union, it was impossible to work without membership, and this was only offered on the basis of the questionnaire. Surprisingly, it was almost a year after Goebbels's instruction that Jews be removed from musical life before the legal mechanism was put into place to dismiss the remaining 8,000 Jewish musicians still in employment in February 1935.[56] Nevertheless, according to several entries in Goebbels's diaries, the RMK even under Raabe was not purging Jews efficiently enough. The problem lay in defining exactly who should be classed as a Jew.[57] The

Nazi answer was to count the number of Jewish grandparents. This was straightforward if the grandparents were Jews, but more complicated if the grandparents came from mixed marriages. This hair-splitting became endemic at the RMK. For example, racially pure Germans, without any Jewish grandparents, were treated as Jewish if they converted to Judaism or if conversions to Judaism had taken place in previous generations. If an Aryan musician was married to a Jew, he or she was to be classified as 'half-Jew'. Unsurprisingly, full Jews could not be classified as 'half-Aryan' under similar circumstances.

The Music Business

The Aryanisation of music publishers was a much slower process. Nevertheless, the voluntary organisation of publishers and music sellers (Deutsche Musikalien Verleger Verein – DMVV) was incorporated into the RMK in January 1934. Before that, as early as April 1933, the DMVV had declared itself supportive of the new government, and although it initially did not explicitly ban Jews, Viktor Albertis, Wilhelm Zimmermann, Henri Hinrichsen, Gustav Bock and Kurt Eulenburg found themselves removed from the executive committee of the DMVV and replaced with supporters of the new regime.[58] Once incorporated into the RMK, membership of the DMVV became compulsory for all music dealers and publishers. Between 1933 and 1938, about forty publishers were run by Jewish owners or employed Jews in key executive positions. This amounted to a mere 10 per cent of music publishers, but had a severe impact on publishers of serious music. Peters, Benjamin, Bote & Bock, Eulenburg, Fürstner and Alrobi were the leading German publishers most severely affected, and with the annexation of Austria, a further 24 publishers were added including such prestigious houses as Universal Edition, Doblinger and Weinberger.[59] Though there were no direct anti-Semitic attacks aimed specifically against Jews in the various trade magazines that served music publishers, there were clear instructions coming from above that Aryanisation should proceed apace and that under no circumstances should German publishers collaborate with non-Aryan publishers newly relocated abroad.[60]

Hermann Göring, who had been granted dictatorial powers in the implementation of a draconian 'Four Year Plan', started large-scale expropriation of Jewish businesses in 1936. Such powers allowed him to justify this as an 'economic necessity', and the removal of the last legal obstacles before the total economic disenfranchisement of all German Jews. Following the Austrian annexation, publishing houses such as Josef Weinberger – Mahler's first publisher, and the publisher of many important operetta composers – managed to relocate to London. Peters, Universal Edition, Bote & Bock and others were Aryanised, with many of their former employees moving to G. Schirmer in New York, or Boosey & Hawkes in London. GEMA,[61] the rights management agency charged with collecting royalties from performances and broadcasting, was disbanded in March 1933 and replaced in September by the Nazi company STAGMA.[62] The Austrian AKM (Autoren, Komponisten, Musikverleger) was folded into STAGMA after the annexation in 1938, despite protests from such international figures as Béla Bartók.

Logic suggests that Aryanisation would have been internationally sensitive, since publishers based in Germany provided scores and orchestral material for performances around the world. Indeed, a directive from 14 April 1939 stated that works banned in Germany (including annexed Austria) could still be exported, thereby providing much-needed foreign currency and, presumably, encouraging the further 'degeneration' of the world's non-Aryan population.[63] Until 1942, catalogues that featured Jewish composers, along with printed scores by Jewish composers, were either consigned to be pulped, or marked as unavailable for sale or performance. Sales of scores by Jewish composers from antiquarian shops were to be restricted to music historians, and clearly marked with the letter 'J' along with a visible explanation as to its meaning.[64] However, most publishers had taken the precaution of producing multiple copies, so that when some 30,000 printed scores and books were confiscated from Universal Edition, almost everything could be recovered later. Alfred Schlee informed Kurt Weill in 1946 that some works had been destroyed, including *Aufstieg und Fall der Stadt Mahagonny*.[65] Fortunately he was mistaken as most of Schoenberg's and Weill's scores had been hidden behind the organ of a provincial village church.[66] Weinberger suffered the destruction of scores by Leo Fall, which had been specifically moved to safety away from their normal place of storage but were later found by Nazis.[67] However, the same publisher managed to rescue the manuscript of Erich Korngold's opera *Die Kathrin* from the composer's villa. Along with other items in Korngold's library, *Die Kathrin* was being thrown into the furnace of the central heating system by marauding Nazis while Korngold was away in Los Angeles composing the film score to Errol Flynn's *The Adventures of Robin Hood*.[68] Weinberger employees broke into the cellar, recovered what was left of the manuscript, and returned it to Korngold by interleaving sheets between pages of Beethoven, Mozart and other acceptably 'Aryan' composers and posting these to the composer in California. The orchestral material was rescued from the archive of Vienna's Staatsoper, where it had been scheduled to go into rehearsal under Bruno Walter. The opera was given its premiere in October 1939 in Stockholm, where it was met with mixed reviews, some of them confrontationally anti-Semitic.[69] By the time of the officially unleashed overnight pogroms of 9–10 November 1938 (Reichstkristallnacht or Kristallnacht), and the stipulation the following month forbidding non-Aryans from attending any public events, Jews found themselves effectively removed from every means of social, economic or cultural interaction in what had formerly been their native country.

The concert agency Wolff & Sachs in Berlin, formerly the representative for nearly all major performers in Germany and providing day-to-day management for the Berlin Philharmonic since its foundation in 1882, was dissolved in 1935.[70] In Vienna, the publisher Hugo Knepler (brother of the librettist Paul Knepler, who had written texts for Leo Fall and Robert Stolz as well as for Franz Lehár's *Giuditta*) took over Vienna's Gutmann concert agency in 1907 and became the city's most powerful concert promoter, mounting over 2,000 events and managing such important artists as Maria Jeritza, Arthur Nikisch, Pablo Casals, Jascha Heifetz, Bronisław Huberman, Artur Schnabel and many others until the company crashed in 1931. After Austria's annexation, Knepler fled to France but was captured and deported by the Vichy Regime and murdered in Auschwitz in 1944. Smaller Jewish agencies in Germany and Austria were broken up, dissolved, subsumed or Aryanised under the Reichsmusikkammer.

The purging of musical life of all elements not deemed Aryan was fraught with complexities. As late as 1936 and 1937, Berlin Radio had compiled a blacklist of artists who were to be banned from engagement or performance. This included musicians who were not remotely Jewish such as the Austrian composers Julius Bittner and Wilhelm Kienzl, while the Jewish Erich Korngold is conspicuous by his absence.[71] Against such blatant and obvious inconsistencies, the idiosyncratic infringements of other musical Gauleiters, such as those who banned the non-Jewish Manfred Gurlitt while allowing the premiere of *Concertante Musik* by the partially Jewish Boris Blacher by the Berlin Philharmonic under Carl Schuricht in 1937, come across as arbitrary at best, or incompetent at worst.

An acute problem was caused by one of the mainstays of German literature, the Jewish writer Heinrich Heine, who died in 1856. Hardly any other poet had been set so enthusiastically by so many of the great German composers of the nineteenth century. Karl Blessinger in *Judentum und Musik* – one of the most astounding anti-Semitic tracts of the Nazi era – makes the paranoid observation that Jews had camouflaged themselves through a clever use of language to conceal their ambitions for world domination.[72] He even goes so far as to suggest that Schumann was able to stop Jewish subterfuges by setting a sufficient number of Heine texts to nip Jewish plots in the bud.[73] Nazi favourites such as d'Albert's *Tiefland* and Lehár's *Lustige Witwe* were also compromised by librettos by Jewish authors – as Ralph Benatzky pointed out in his diaries, he couldn't recall the name of a single operetta librettist who wasn't Jewish.

Hofmannsthal was another 'difficulty'. The president of the Reichsmusikkammer, Richard Strauss, however, had seen their collaboration as artistically crucial to his own success, though he went too far in engaging Stefan Zweig, another non-Aryan, as librettist for *Die schweigsame Frau* – an act considered so reckless that it cost him his position at the RMK. Lorenzo da Ponte, Mozart's Jewish librettist for *Don Giovanni, Così fan tutte* and *Le Nozze di Figaro*, was yet another headache, as were the German translations of these operas by another Jew, Hermann Levi, the very same Jew who had conducted the premiere of Wagner's *Parsifal*. Even the other Strausses, Johann, Father and Son, had inconveniently turned out not to be of the pure Nordic stock demanded by the new rulers of the Reich. This was stealthily rectified using a pair of scissors on the Registry of Baptisms in St Stephen's Cathedral, where the names of the offending Jewish grandparents were snipped out. These doctored Strauss credentials may have helped Nazi purists save face, but it was already well known that the Strauss family lived in Vienna's Jewish district, locally known as the 'Matzos Island'; and as two of Strauss the younger's three wives indicate, he showed a clear preference for Jewish women. Being the Waltz King's step-child did not save the daughter of his third wife Adele from deportation and the gas chambers. Still, it must have been clear to even the dimmest of wits that German and Jewish culture had become so closely intertwined that it was impossible to disentangle them without significant self-harm.

The various attempts at tabulating who was Jewish and who wasn't, and under what conditions certain works could be performed, resulted in the circulation of alarming quantities of misinformation. Advertisements were taken out by many performers offering to prove their Aryan lineage in order to avoid removal from programmes and schedules. A definitive guide was needed and it was commissioned from two leading musicologists in Rosenberg's Office, Herbert Gerigk and Theo Stengel. It appeared under the very utilitarian title of *Lexikon der Juden in der Musik*[74] and was first published in 1940, with regular updates and amendments until its final edition in 1943. Deplorable in context it surely was, but with its list of some 10,000 names, it offers one of the most useful references for composers and works officially removed from Nazi musical life. As it was meant as a manual for concert promoters, it does not include Jewish performers who died before 1933 but it does include long-dead Jewish composers, librettists and poets. Nevertheless – and perhaps as a tacit admission of the utter futility of such an undertaking – the name of Heinrich Heine is absent. This is a silent acknowledgment that the authorities could not expect singers to forgo such classics as Schubert's *Die Lorelei* or Schumann's *Dichterliebe* and *Liederkreis* – and even Wagner's *Flying Dutchman* was based on a Heine source. In recital programmes featuring Heine settings by the likes of Brahms, Schumann, Schubert and Liszt, the solution chosen by most was not to mention the poet's name at all or, more iniquitously, to use alternative 'Aryanised' texts provided by the Reichsmusikbearbeitungen. Failing this, they simply inserted someone else's name. Heine, more than anyone, proved the futility of trying to disentangle German and Jewish culture, though tragically, this did not stop the Nazis from continuing to try.[75]

Jewish Cultural Leagues

It is no surprise that expelling Jews from musical institutions did little to relieve the problem of the 24,000 German musicians already out of work, or the 50,000 who were earning less than 100 Marks per month.[76] No amount of Nazi legislation could enable inferior Aryans stepping seamlessly into positions left by more competent Jews. As such, the difference made to unemployment among musicians, beyond rank and file orchestral players, was hardly noticeable. If anything, firing such large numbers of Jews merely increased the unemployment statistics, adding to the obligation to pay benefits to individuals whose loss of employment was brought about by the government that claimed to be solving Germany's economic difficulties. This conflict had already been anticipated, however, as had the potential problem of the appearance of Nazi ghettoization of Jews to the outside world.

As early as April 1933, the Nazis had succeeded in bringing various Jewish charitable societies together into a Central Committee for Aid and Development. These included both Zionist and non-Zionist organisations, which had been unwilling to co-operate until pressure from National Socialists left them with no option. From the beginning of June 1933, a Central Office for Jewish Economic Development was initiated,[77] followed by the Reich's Representation of German Jews in September,[78] as a collective body for all regional Jewish societies. The rapid pace of this reorganisation was designed to make it appear to the outside world that Jews themselves were involved in their own exclusion from wider German society. The Central Committee for Aid and Development was also able to raise funds for emigration from sponsors in the United States and elsewhere, freeing the Nazi State from supporting its domestically unemployable Jewish citizens. The idea of a Jewish Culture League grew as a consequence of these developments and was the brain-child

of a 26-year-old theatre director named Kurt Baumann and his cousin, the
critic Julius Bab, along with the conductors Michael Taube, Joseph Rosenstock
and the neurologist who had become Carl Ebert's deputy director at Berlin's
Charlottenburg Opera, Kurt Singer. Singer would become the prime mover
within the organisation and the front man in all of its dealings with Hans
Hinkel, its Nazi partner and ultimately by necessity, its protector. Singer
outlined the purpose of the League as follows:

> Keeping outer politics at bay from our affairs and not mixing in the domestic
> affairs regarding Jewish policies. We nonetheless stand up more boldly than
> ever for our Jewish heritage and believe in drawing from that, all which is
> specifically Jewish in drama, music and various intellectual fields. [This] is
> our uppermost duty and must ultimately be our greatest gain! That we are
> living proof of what has been nurtured by German culture and its great
> masters does not need to be repeated to any German Jew. So, is this a
> compromise? Yes! But it is one that is made in the conviction that there is a
> will to join German Jewry's diverse communities of ideas into a single unit![79]

The League's inception was recounted by Singer in the *Zentral Vereins Zeitung*
on 28 September 1933:

> In those days during which we Jews had to put up with work restrictions, the
> young director Kurt Baumann came to see me at the beginning of April with
> a plan for the foundation of a theatre and members' organisation. I had
> already worked out a similar plan and passed both of them on to Rabbi Dr
> Baeck for his consideration. With his support I invited leading representa-
> tives of Jewish organisations for preliminary consultations. [...] One
> working committee drew up the statutes, while another prepared the organ-
> isational aspects for recruitment evenings and yet another took on the
> artistic planning. I presented official requests for permission to set up the
> 'Cultural League of German Jews' to various government offices. The deci-
> sion on the matter was handed over to the Prime Minister of the Ministry of
> Education and the Arts, under whom was placed the President of the
> Prussian Theatre Committee and the State Commissioner Hinkel, who
> conducted the negotiations in part in person and in part through his repre-
> sentatives. At the same time I continually kept police headquarters and the
> Ministry of Propaganda [...] informed of the progress of discussions.[80]

Kurt Baumann gives a slightly different account of the founding of the
Kulturbund.[81] He begins by mentioning that he had calculated that a city

like Berlin, with 175,000 Jews, would be able to maintain a parallel cultural existence that could go some way towards compensating Jews for their exclusion from mainstream cultural life. Some of the initial difficulties he encountered came from Zionist organisations who wanted plays and readings to be in Yiddish or Hebrew. However, Berlin's Jews were largely unable to speak or understand either language, and many were reluctant to place themselves, seemingly of their own free will, into a ghetto. Baumann points out that Jews had not yet been banned from attending public performances and if they possessed coveted tickets to Philharmonic subscription concerts, they simply closed their eyes and settled down among the surrounding Nazis in the audience. Baumann wrote: 'People later said that we only founded the Kulturbund to provide a few Jewish artists with work and bread, but this is only half true. Of course we were concerned with giving the hundreds of Jewish artists who had been summarily dismissed a modest living until such time as they could leave the country. But for us in those days it was much more important to provide the Jewish public in Germany, which had once stood at the forefront of German cultural life, with a home for as long as possible.'[82]

The resulting creation of the Jewish Cultural League was finalised by Hans Hinkel who, under Göring and Goebbels, was responsible for removing all Jews from Prussian, then national, cultural life. The League was founded, according to its first statute, in order to 'support Jewish cultural and scientific interests and to create work places for Jewish artists and scientists'. Paradoxically, Hinkel had already admitted that 'Jews with their naturally superior intellectual abilities had simply led to a situation in which Germans were no longer masters of their own homes'.[83] With this thought uppermost, it was clear to Hinkel that heading such an organisation with a highly creative workforce would be politically advantageous. He became the Cultural League's defender against future Nazi excesses, while remaining the most wholehearted believer in the removal of Jews from German cultural life.

By May 1933, a Cultural League Orchestra and Chorus, conducted by Michael Taube, had been established in Berlin, and by June, Singer had approached Hinkel with a petition to establish the Cultural League ('Kulturbund') officially, a move disparaged by many in the Jewish Community, not least the philosopher Martin Buber, as a 'ghetto that is called a league'.[84] Singer, however, was of the view that the ghettoization of Jewish culture would become so important that Nazis would soon see the error of their ways. It was a fatal misreading of Nazi intentions. Singer eventually managed to escape to the Netherlands in 1938, but he was captured and murdered in Auschwitz in 1944. From his indefatigable efforts to meet the genuine cultural needs within the remaining German Jewish communities between 1933 and 1938, he managed to establish a network of Cultural League chapters throughout the country. Performances were for Jews and given by Jews, taking place in disused cinemas and theatres.

There remained the irksome and continuing dilemma of who actually counted as a Jew in the eyes of the Nazis – and who was thereby allowed to participate in the Cultural League. Equally complex for a largely secular community was how the various religious communities addressed this question. It was a conflict that would be encountered again by charities working to free Jews from Nazi Europe over the coming years as well. The confederation of German Jewish Cultural Leagues had its headquarters in Berlin, and in April 1935 it was renamed the Reichsverband Jüdischer Kulturbünde (JKB),[85] the word 'German' having been removed. In Hitler's New Germany, German Jews were an obvious contradiction.

One of Hinkel's principal worries was exactly the point that Singer had stated as the League's ultimate goal: that non-Jewish Germans would gravitate towards the Cultural League's events. Baumann mentions that there was even a suspicion that the whole thing could be a Jewish trick to take Germans away from their own, dedicated Nazi events. Enormous hurdles were imposed: tickets could only be sold to members carrying photo identification and it was impossible to buy a ticket for an evening's performance by walking in from the street. Material was censored and the Kulturbund was expected to steer clear of conspicuously German content. In return, the Nazis offered the League and its members protection. The first event, following the placement of an advertisement in both the Jewish and general press, resulted in a midsummer attendance of 2,500 at Berlin's central Prinzregenten Synagogue and subsequent events attracted even larger numbers.

Baumann explains in his essay that the League's scheduling in Berlin meant that a play would run for one month, followed by an opera which also ran for a month. In addition, there were two concert programmes and two lecture series per month: 'Subscribers could choose their own days and were guaranteed two programmes, whatever they selected.'[86] According to Baumann, the orchestra became one of the best in Berlin. When Michael Taube emigrated to Palestine, his position was taken by Joseph Rosenstock, who arrived from Mannheim (where shortly before he had conducted the premiere of Berthold Goldschmidt's *Der gewaltige Hahnrei*). By 1935, the membership figures of the JKB and its affiliates were quite staggering: there were 46 local chapters in all, with a combined membership of 70,000, a number that more than doubled to 153,000 in the course of a single year.[87]

Programming was to become difficult for the organisers; at first the Cultural League was the only place where it was possible to hear music by Mahler and Mendelssohn, or to watch a play by Schnitzler. Though works by non-Jewish German composers and writers were banned from the programmes, this did not keep the JKB affiliates from scheduling works by non-Germans, including Austrians. With the annexation of Austria in March 1938, this would change, and Mozart and Schubert joined the list of composers outlawed from JKB performances. Over time, limitations became even more restrictive, eventually resulting in all non-Jews being excluded from the programmes.[88] Those Jews who had not managed to emigrate tried to fill the void, writing new plays and composing new music. Singer, in retrospect, was starting to cause more harm than good as he attempted to persuade the best musicians against leaving or even to return for important performances. From 1938, venues began to be closed down, while the few that remained had their utilities severely restricted: electricity, lighting, water and heating were often shut off. More and more programming was relocated to private homes, the Josef Lehmann School or the small Kulturbund Saal in Berlin. With the Reichskristallnacht in November 1938, the Cultural League effectively came to an end, though it was not officially disbanded until 1941.

Austrian Leagues

A thesis completed at Vienna Music University in 2000 by Yukiko Sawabe highlights four organisations and ensembles in Austria that shadowed Germany's Kulturbund from 1933, though this is not specifically noted by the author.[89] The relationship with the Kulturbund was not the subject of the thesis, but the repertoire choices and programme development of these institutions seemed to run in tandem with that of the Kulturbund in a way that does not appear to be merely coincidental. The organisations were the Society for the Promotion of Jewish Music, the Hakoah Orchestra, the Jewish Song Society, and the Symphony Orchestra of the League of Jewish Austrian Front Soldiers, which was established later than the others, in 1932.[90]

All four of these ensembles had originally been inspired by the idea of preserving Jewish folk music, as part of an initiative started in St Petersburg in 1908 by the composer Joel Engel. Noted members of his Russian Society of Jewish Folk Music included, Josef Achron, Michael Gnessin and Alexander Krein. The Austrian Zionist and cellist Joachim Stutschewsky pushed for the establishment of several of the Viennese organisations and left an account of their activities in his book *Mein Weg zur jüdischen Musik*.[91]

The Hakoah Orchestra, under the direction of Salomon Braslavsky, had already been established in Vienna in 1919, fourteen years before the founding of the Kulturbund Orchestra in Berlin. Hakoah (Hebrew for 'Strength') was the name of the Viennese Jewish sports club which would produce not only many Olympic medallists but also a football team that won the league championship in the 1924–5 season, having become the first continental club to defeat an English team when they beat London's West Ham 5–1 in 1923. Though the Hakoah concerts started off fairly conventionally with programmes consisting mostly of Mendelssohn and the occasional Russian, they became more specifically Jewish and closely shadowed the repertoire restrictions being imposed on Germany's Jewish Kulturbund. It is unclear if this was an act of solidarity or simply a way of profiting from the greater pool of Jewish musicians available. Concerts were held in either Vienna's Musikverein or the Konzerthaus and were well attended by subscribers. If in 1919 a typical concert programme consisted of Puccini, Liszt, Chopin and Sarasate, with an interpolated monologue from Karl Gutzkow's play *Uriel Acosta* as nearly the only Jewish element, by 1936 this had changed to performances of works by Darius Milhaud, Jacques Offenbach, Joel Engel, Friedrich Bloch and Adolf Fleischer.

Things were slightly different with the Jewish Song Society, which had also been founded in 1919. The material that made up its concerts had been largely liturgical from the outset, though the Society programmed many secular Jewish and Hebrew works as well as more familiar choruses by Mendelssohn, or works by Rubinstein and Handel.

The Society for the Promotion of Jewish Music was established in 1927 with Julius Korngold's arch-enemy, the music critic Max Graf, as its president. A previous organisation operating under the same name had been founded in 1919 with Erwin Felber as president, but this had come to nothing, owing to unresolved arguments over what constituted Jewish music. A concert to launch the new Society by Austria's B'nai Brith was met with ridicule in a review written by Felber in the *Wiener Morgenzeitung* of 13 May 1927:

> The offerings of the second part of the concert showed even more clearly that we have still not succeeded in establishing what a Jewish musical language should actually sound like. A full emancipation from European music has yet to take place. What one hears in Vienna from such long-familiar composers as Achron, Krein and Milner was an enthusiastic avowal of orientalism which is left unfulfilled when it comes to actual implementation. And when these Jewish masters do take up the styles of the east with their free variations and improvisations, they inevitably sink into the mono-

tone, twisted and complex. [. . .] As interesting as the evening was, it proved that only with organic nurturing from the traditions of the homeland can one expect to develop an authentic Jewish musical language. Every national culture demands a landscape from the 'Motherland' in order to develop its own uniqueness. And only the most audacious of souls would suggest that, in the millennia that have elapsed since the days of the Jewish Kings, Jewish musical individuality has in any way truly managed to survive.[92]

Nevertheless, it was this Society that eventually drove the planning and the performances of the other three ensembles. From 1936 onwards, The Society for the Promotion of Jewish Music was forced to start meeting in closed groups in private homes, again mirroring the situation with the Kulturbund, and was finally disbanded in 1939 following Austria's annexation in 1938.

To make a more public declaration of Austrian patriotism, the League of Jewish Front Soldiers was founded in 1932 with a membership of some 4,000. By 1935, this had grown to 20,000, and by the time of Austria's annexation to 24,000.[93] Members of its orchestra undoubtedly doubled up with the Hakoah Orchestra and its repertoire was somewhat similar – but with more emphasis on Jewish composers writing European music rather than on the more 'oriental' music favoured by the Hakoah Orchestra. As such, it made a speciality of promoting Austrian composers with Jewish roots including, intriguingly, a good deal of Johann Strauss, though in truth this was probably due to a desire to present popular programmes. In 1934, for example, the orchestra offered an evening of Mendelssohn and a Chanukah Festival concert, an event repeated every year until the annexation of Austria. Kurt Pahlen was its regular conductor and its events were well attended. Pahlen went on to establish the Opera Studio, the only fruit of which was a single performance of *Der Freischütz*, mounted a couple of weeks before Austria's annexation. The Chanukah concert of 1937 consisted of works by Goldmark and Meyerbeer, an improvisation on *Kol Nidrei* by Josef Sulzer; *Psalm 111* by Salomon Sulzer; the Overture to the *Merry Wives of Windsor* by Nicolai; a selection of Palestinian folk songs, and some of Brahms's *Hungarian Dances*; it ended with Johann Strauss II's *Frühlingsstimmen* and his father's *Radetzky March*.[94]

The Final Solution was still a few years away and, despite the hardships endured by Jewish musicians and composers, what lay in store did not become apparent until the annexation of Austria and its ensuing flood of refugees, sending countries around the world into panic at the thought of the potential consequence of millions of homeless European Jews. In the expanding Reich, wanton arrests, pointless beatings and bully-boy sadism were rife. The Nazis claimed that this was all an attempt to persuade Jews to leave. By this point, most would willingly have done so had they had the connections or the money, or even had they been allowed to take what little money they had with them; punitive taxes imposed by the Nazis meant that emigrating Jews arrived penniless at their eventual destination. The exile that Walter Braunfels rightly identified as ending his creativity as a German composer would do exactly that to most of the others who fled. Those who stayed risked internment, slave labour and, ultimately, horrors that were unimaginably worse.

CHAPTER 11

Exile and Worse

In accordance with the appropriation regulation of 22.01.1041 B.No. 10341/38, all financial holdings of Egon Israel Wellesz and his wife Emilie Sarah née Stross last resident at Vienna, 19th District, Kaasgraben 38, have been confiscated on behalf of the 'German Reich' Arbeitsgruppe 9.

Assets-registry, 03.03.1941

Aryanisation documents housed at Vienna's Widerstandsarchiv relating to Egon and Emmy Wellesz

. . . More than once I envied my Jewish friends who seemed to be able to find relatives at the right time and in the right places. But Jews have two or three thousand years' experience of persecution, whereas we have had to learn about such things quickly and with considerable effort.

Ernst Krenek, *Im Atem der Zeit*

So what should I do as an émigré from 8:00 every morning, other than compose? [. . .] The greatest source of inspiration for an émigré is [. . .] the torturous power of boredom that forces him to gaze at himself for twelve hours. That's productive power.

Hanns Eisler in conversation with Hans Bunge, 5 May 1958

Escape: Destination, Unknown

In a letter to Erich Korngold dated 6 December 1934, Ludwig Strecker of the music publisher Schott confirms that with the new situation in Germany, the firm is not in a position to take on the composer's new opera *Die Kathrin*: 'Only yesterday, Furtwängler, Kleiber and Hindemith have resigned from all of their posts and they stand accused of being "too Jew-friendly". Fall's operettas, even Offenbach and Mendelssohn, are being boycotted these days and not even works by Kreisler are allowed to be broadcast on the radio.'[1] When, four years later, Otto Witrowsky wrote to his brother-in-law Julius Korngold on 15 August 1938 to inform him of their progress in leaving Austria, he made the humorous aside that a new history of the Jews was being written with the title 'From King David to Affidavit'.[2] To the cynical, the Austrian version of this 'history' would have been more accurately and less humorously titled 'From the December Constitution of 1867 to the Affidavit of 1938: 71 Years of Delusion'. The subtitle for the German edition would have read '62 Years of Delusion' as Jewish emancipation arrived four years later (1871) only to be removed five years earlier (1933) than in neighbouring Austria.

By 1938, nearly every Austrian and German Jew was concerned with finding an affidavit somewhere, somehow, from someone. Only with a document guaranteeing that somebody in America would cover financial costs could one obtain one of the coveted 'quota' or 'non-quota' visas to enter the country. Under the so-called quota-scheme, a certain number of immigrants, based on current numbers of any given ethnic community already resident in the United States, were allowed entry. Under the 'non-quota' scheme, a smaller number of immigrants were given permission to stay as a result of political or religious persecution. Entering merely with a common visitor's visa would mean deportation or arrest once the visa had expired or if the visitor had taken up any kind of employment. Despite the offer of a professorship at New York's New School for Social Research, Hanns Eisler and his wife Lou entered the United States with a visitor's visa and found themselves one step away from the police with arrest warrants being issued at one point. They were legally barred from re-entering the US from Mexico where they had to return continually in order to renew their entrance applications. Only after an official at a remote crossing (ignorant of the Eislers' status) issued a visa that permitted them to enter the US and to work were their problems resolved – until Ruth Fischer denounced her two brothers five years later (see Chapter 7).

Gertrude Zeisl, wife of the composer Erich Zeisl, managed to lay her hands on a New York phone book and wrote to every Zeisl or Zeisel she could find, eventually locating a plumber named Morris Zeisel who agreed to provide her family with the necessary documentation. When Morris disappeared, they were helped by an equally unfamiliar and unrelated Arnold Zeissl from Milwaukee. They were lucky but had worked hard to make their luck. In truth, though, every individual had his or her own story. Probably the only generalisation that can be attempted is that by 1938 everyone wanting to leave Europe wanted to end up in America. If they landed in Britain or France, it was viewed as a purely temporary measure. A fair number of unlucky individuals went east to the Soviet Union, where many would fall victim to Stalin's purges in the late thirties and again in the early fifties. By the time of Austria's annexation in 1938, it was clear to the rest of the world that there would be a massive number of refugees to accommodate. How this was handled remains a matter of ethical debate to this day.

The World Braces Itself for a Refugee Crisis

By April 1933, British officials alerted by the Home Secretary Sir John Gilmore – who had raised matters at a cabinet meeting on 5 April – became concerned that though there were numbers of Jews arriving from Nazi-occupied Europe who were well-qualified professionals, there were others who were destitute.[3] At this point, Jewish charities stepped in to cover the expenses incurred by German Jews without the financial means to support themselves. From 1933 to 1938, Jewish refugee organisations in the United Kingdom, alongside the Home Office, managed a controlled entry of Jews from Nazi Germany. The Home Office insisted that refugees register with the police on arrival but that refugee charities, such as the Jewish Temporary Shelter and the Jewish Refugee Committee headed by the stockbroker Otto Schiff, meet the costs of what was assumed to be transit immigration.[4] In contrast to France, there were no visa requirements and the British government left it to Jewish charities to shoulder the immigration costs of refugees. It was assumed that given the restrictions placed on transmigrants, such as leave to stay for only short periods without the right to work, most would soon move on, generally to the USA.[5] A few wished to remain in Europe in the anticipation that the 'Brown Bolshevism'[6] would eventually run out of steam and sanity would return. From April 1933, a new restricted visa policy was set in place that offered refugees a visitor's visa, limited to a single month with a clause that forbade employment of any kind. Estimates of how many Jews could arrive came from British Jewry's weekly newspaper the *Jewish Chronicle*, which reported that of the 4,000 refugees who arrived between March 1933 and October 1934, four-fifths were German and most were doctors, lawyers, academics, accountants and other professionals.[7] It was during this interim period, while refugees were organising further onward travel elsewhere, that Jewish charities guaranteed support.[8]

An additional difficulty emerged, since it was not immediately clear who counted as a Jew. Those who were defined as 'Jews' by Hitler and his regime were by no means Jewish according to the definition understood by the various charities or even the Jewish Refugee Committee. Hitler's view of Jews as a 'foreign race' was thus in stark contrast to the conventional, confessional definition held by charities. Jews who had left the religious community through conversion or conviction, or who were born in mixed marriages where the mother was not Jewish, were technically not Jews according to strict religious definitions. As far as Hitler and his Reich were concerned, someone born of, say, a converted half-Jewish mother and a converted or non-practising Jewish father was still a full Jew with three 'racially' Jewish grand-parents (one from the half-Jewish parent and two from the converted Jewish parent), despite the fact that it was highly improbable that this person, or anyone in his or her immediate family, had ever been near a synagogue. Though Germans who converted to Judaism without any previous Jewish ancestry were counted as full Jews by the Nazis, few orthodox Jews would recognise them as such.

The British central government and the Jewish charities agreed that it was best not to emphasise the fact that the refugees pouring out of Nazi Germany were largely Jewish out of fear of inflaming anti-Semitism, which had briefly got out of control after the First World War, exacerbated by the *Morning Post* and *The Times* publishing articles on the notorious *Protocols of the Elders of Zion*, a mendacious bit of ant-Semitic counter-intelligence 'leaked' by Russia's Tsarist police.[9] The British Union of Fascists (BUF) under Oswald Moseley was growing in popularity and by the mid-1930s had some 16,000 members, though it claimed membership to be as high as 50,000.[10] Authorities were still mindful of the Battle of Cable Street of 4 October 1936, followed by London's East End pogrom along the Mile End Road. The BUF even enjoyed the support of the tabloid *Daily Mail*, with its proprietor, Lord Rothermere, writing an editorial in 8 January 1934 entitled 'Hurrah for the Blackshirts'.

To the British Foreign Office, Jewish persecution was seen as an obstacle to Anglo-German relations and it was wiser not to publicise the problems Jews were having in Germany. Neville Chamberlain, Prime Minister from 1937, accepted German anti-Semitism as 'a fact of life' but was unhappy at its extreme manifestations, and feared that public debate could be damaging to commercial, social and cultural relations between the two countries.[11] He was inclined to believe the official line coming out of Berlin that, by not formally sanctioning the Jewish boycott of 1 April 1933 or the Kristallnacht pogrom in November 1938, far greater bloodshed would have ensued.

Commercial considerations were an important issue and resulted in the British government taking the decision to downplay Nazi brutality towards Jews. In April 1933, the British directors of Anglo-Persian Oil (today known as British Petroleum or simply BP) dismissed all German Jews in its German sales subsidiary; still fearing potential loss of German sales, all non-German Jews were then dismissed, including Jewish Britons.[12] The Foreign Office's determination to cultivate deeper Anglo-German relations with the holding of a football match between the two countries in December 1935 was equally questionable. But the decision that it be held in White Hart Lane, the home stadium of Tottenham Hotspur – a club that was (and is) predominantly supported by Jewish Londoners – was recklessly provocative. With an attendance of 9,500 predicted, tensions rose between the Home Office, concerned that there would be civil disturbances should the game proceed, and the Foreign Office who saw the match as a crucial step towards maintaining good Anglo-German relations. It ultimately took place with only minor incidents. Jewish refugees even stepped in to earn much-needed cash by conducting tours of London in German for visitors from Hitler's Reich. Meanwhile Lyons and Co., branded by the Nazi publication *Der Stürmer* as 'a Jewish enterprise that all good Germans should avoid', provided the catering. The visitors offered the Hitler salute before the anthems and swastikas were waved throughout the game. The home team won 3–0 – a predictable result.[13]

British government policy at this time stands in contrast to the United States, which had its strict quotas. British policy was still undefined and allowed individual officials to make case-by-case decisions. These were largely sympathetic, as can be deduced from the relatively small number of entry refusals. From 30 March 1933, Harwich officials enforced certain refusals, but reversed them as soon as support guarantees could be obtained.[14] Such policies allowed for a greater degree of flexibility than America's quota system. Nevertheless, by 1938, officials were considering new measures that would go against prevailing public opinion – still largely sympathetic to the plight of Germany's Jews. With the annexation of Austria, visa requirements were enforced, and with Vienna operating as a provincial capital rather than a national seat of government, its embassies had been turned into much smaller consulates with reduced staff. As a result, desperate Austrians, now considered Germans, often had to queue for days for an appointment, while Nazi hooligans openly harassed them on the street. This method, though painfully slow, allowed British officials to preselect Austrians for immigration before their arrival in Britain. With the recognition of the legality of Austria's annexation in April 1938, only well-connected Austrians with excellent qualifications and access to foreign funds were being accepted, accounting for the high profile of émigré Austrians in Great Britain – especially in music, the arts and sciences – despite their proportionately small number.

The British government continued even after 1938 to have Jewish charities deal with refugees in order to avoid the appearance of public money being spent on foreigners immigrating at a time of financial austerity, international uncertainty and an increasingly shrill tone in the tabloid press. Though the *Daily Mail* had dropped its open support of the BUF by 1934, it was still suggesting that Jewish refugees were economic migrants. Meanwhile, Lord Rothermere remained friendly with both Hitler and Mussolini. As MI5 papers released in 2005 show, Rothermere congratulated Hitler on his invasion of the Sudetenland and encouraged him to march into Romania.[15]

The musicologist Alfred Einstein writing to Hans Gál from America in April 1940 explained how he viewed international reaction at the time: 'I certainly share your wish to see Hitler and his accomplices hanged, but I fear we shall have to wait quite a while as England has made its own job all the more difficult by spending the last six-and-a-half years filling its soup bowl so full that it now has to try carefully to spoon it out again. We just finished reading the book by Sir Neville Henderson [British Ambassador to Germany, 1937–9] regarding the failure of his mission in Berlin, and what comes across most strongly is that he and others truly believed the words of the Führer. If the entire world had not been morally paralysed, things may have turned out differently. I simply hope that the censor who is no doubt reading these lines agrees with me, since I just happen to *be* one of the many victims of this moral paralysis. Especially as America is afflicted by the same condition and hasn't yet realised . . . how high the stakes are for this country.'[16]

The Évian Conference

Nevertheless, it was the Americans who proposed setting up an Intergovernmental Committee on Refugees (IGC) to coordinate refugee policies. This was established in what became known as the Évian Conference, held at Évian-les-Bains on Lake Geneva, 6–15 July 1938, and involving 32 different nations. The establishment of the IGC was not particularly well received by the Chamberlain government as it was wary of potentially unwelcome consequences. Indeed, it was thought that the use of public money for the Jewish refugee crisis would ultimately exacerbate the situation. However, the British wanted to work with the Americans and welcomed this as an initiative towards closer cooperation.[17] Even at this late stage – after the annexation of Austria and with the impending annexation of Czechoslovakia's Sudetenland – Jewish refugees, who vastly outnumbered all others fleeing Nazi Germany, were not being identified specifically as Jews for fear of anti-Semitism in host countries. This was even the case with the 'Kindertransport', officially the Refugee Children Movement (RCM), which saw many Jewish children brought up as Christians by well-meaning adoptive parents, unaware of the true nature of Nazi persecution. As long as refugee work was carried out by Jewish charities, the scale of the crisis could remain helpfully vague. Should official agencies, especially international agencies, become involved, this could make the problem more complex, and more perilous.

The League of Nations remained sensitive to the danger of violent anti-Semitism erupting in countries with large Jewish populations such as Poland, Hungary and Romania. As it was, these countries had already approached the Council of the League of Nations asking for aid in relocating their own Jewish populations. The countries of the IGC would be vulnerable to such requests, since Poland, Hungary and Romania would not be receptive to help being made available for the relocation German and Austrian Jews when they saw their domestic Jewish 'crisis' as being equally severe. Sir John Hope Simpson, Director of the Royal Institute of International Affairs' Refugee Survey, argued that the threats of violence against Jewish populations were potentially greater in these countries than in Germany and Austria.[18] It was therefore decided at the Évian Conference that Poland, Romania and Hungary should be persuaded against making petitions for IGC funding. Britain, however, was concerned that the USA would manipulate the situation so that government spending would eventually become necessary, indeed unavoidable. The view of Sir Warren Fisher – Permanent Secretary to the Treasury – was more proactive:

> The principal element is of course the Jews who are exposed to unspeakable horrors. It is clear that, however much we may sympathise, we cannot provide a solution of the terrible problem (which is not confined to Germany). [. . .] (On a wholly lower plane of thought I may mention that this country has frequently been the gainer by providing refuge to foreigners highly qualified in various walks of life.) While, therefore, I would start in at the conference apparently square-toed about the American exclusion of Government Finance from any scheme of help, I think we should be well advised from every point of view – if not for reasons of humanity – to keep open minds (without avowing it) and be on the look-out for any opportunity of intelligent assistance (this of course won't help the majority of these poor people).

The Chancellor of the Exchequer, Sir John Simon, initialled Fisher's memo without comment.[19] In general, and in stark contrast to other Whitehall departments, the Treasury was receptive to the idea of providing public aid for humanitarian support.

The initial plan of the IGC was to use diplomatic means to persuade the German government to subsidise the removal of Jews by allowing refugees to retain some of their capital on leaving the country. Ultimately, the IGC provided a useful smokescreen, making it appear that governments were more involved than was actually the case. These often undermined private initiatives that would have provided more immediate aid to refugees. Official British policy clung to the idea of using diplomatic pressure to encourage other countries, especially the USA, to take more Austro-German Jewish refugees. The Americans avoided every one of these diplomatic booby-traps while Chamberlain remained paralysed by indecision.

On the one hand, he was appalled by German policy against the Jews, while on the other, he was nervous about damaging relations, which might make matters even worse. One moment he was refusing an honorary presidency of the German Shakespeare Cooperative because it had expelled its Jewish members, while the next he was writing the following letter to his sister Hilda, dated 30 July 1939: 'I believe that the persecution arose out of two motives, a desire to rob the Jews of their money and a jealousy of their superior cleverness. No doubt Jews aren't a lovable people; I don't care about them myself; but that is not sufficient to explain the pogrom.'[20] Ultimately, it must be to Chamberlain's credit that despite his vacillation, he expanded a policy of offering temporary refuge to Jews, in the teeth of opposition from his Home Secretary, Sir Samuel Hoare.[21]

With the annexation of the Sudetenland in September 1938, and Hitler's declaration of the Moravian and Bohemian Protectorate on 15 March 1939 effectively placing the largest Czech regions within the Nazi Reich, British reluctance to accept Jews became more pronounced. In this context, it needs to be noted that, with the break-up of the Austrian Empire in 1919, German speakers who lived within the borders of the new state of Czechoslovakia were offered the choice of becoming Czechs or remaining Austrians. Many German speakers who had lived in Vienna but who continued to maintain business or family interests in the newly founded republic of Czechoslovakia chose to become Czech citizens, a status that did not alter their rights to remain in Austria. Meanwhile, many German speakers who lived in Czechoslovakia chose to remain Austrians. The two countries were socially and culturally intertwined. Ernst Krenek chose to remain Austrian (he had always lived in Vienna and spoke only rudimentary Czech), much to the annoyance of his fellow Schreker pupil and Czech nationalist, Alois Hába. Viktor Ullmann was studying with Zemlinsky in Prague in 1919, but chose to remain Austrian – as did Zemlinsky himself, who continued working at the German Theatre in Prague until 1927. Czechoslovakia was not the ethnically homogenous country that emerged after 1945; there were pockets of Hungarians, Ukrainians, Poles and many German communities. The German-speaking Sudetenland community was the crux of the problem. Sudetenlanders saw themselves disadvantaged by the majority Czechs and appealed to Nazi Germany for annexation which was agreed after lengthy negotiations between major European powers (excluding the Czechs) on 30 September 1938. Since independence, the Czechs had indeed become more openly anti-German after centuries of anti-Slav attitudes emanating from their rulers in Austria. The Czech response to the Munich Agreement was to become even more antagonistic to its German speakers, and in September 1938 the German Theatre – one of the most prestigious German stages in Europe – was closed. Indeed, the Austrian-German equivalent of 'Oxford English' or 'Tuscan Italian' was *Pragerdeutsch*, the German spoken in Prague. Zemlinsky took over the music directorship of the German Theatre from the well-known entrepreneur Angelo Neumann, and he was followed by the conductors Wilhelm Steinberg and Georg Szell. Not only was this the theatre where Zemlinsky had conducted the premiere of Schoenberg's *Erwartung* in 1924, but also where Krenek's anti-fascist opera *Karl V* was first performed in June 1938 under Karl Rankl, after Clemens Kraus's decision not to mount it at Vienna's State Opera following the Nazi ban on Krenek's music, in place since 1933.

As it was largely British negotiations that had precipitated the fall of Czechoslovakia, it is surprising that British policy towards Czech Jews would be so unsympathetic. They placed refugees into three distinct categories. The first were the Sudeten Germans who supported the anti-Nazi 'German Social Democratic Party'. They were seen as principal collateral damage from the Munich Agreement; though they were also German speakers, they obviously did not support the aims of Hitler. But as German speakers, they now belonged to the group that Czech speakers believed to have undermined national sovereignty, leading to the Czech central government revoking their citizenship. As anti-Nazis, they were unhappy with the outcome of the Munich Agreement and were rightly seen by the British as highly vulnerable. Politically active Jews and even Communists, along with other anti-Nazi activists, also belonged to this group.

The second group was the mix of Austrians and Czechs who had fled to Czechoslovakia following the annexation of Austria in March 1938. British officials referred to this class of refugees as 'Old Reich', meaning citizens of the old Habsburg Empire, and further divided this group into 'political refugees' and 'Jewish refugees'.[22]

The third group were the Jews who had, until the Munich Agreement, lived without difficulties in the Sudetenland. These numbered approximately 22,000 and began relocating to the still independent regions of Moravia and Bohemia. Slovakia, as a consequence of the Munich Agreement, would be partially folded back into Hungary between November 1938 and March 1939. Confusion reigned. As nearly all the Jews from these Czech regions were German speakers, they were not welcomed by the Czechs, and bureaucratic shenanigans made their continued presence dangerous. As it was, Moravia and Bohemia already had a total Jewish population numbering some 300,000, making a refugee tsunami inevitable. Britain, which had pushed for the outcome of the Munich Agreement, was caught between shoring up what remained of the Czech state and officially recognising Germany's sovereignty over the Sudetenland. It offered the Czech government huge funding, much of it private, but also a good deal of public money to deal with the refugee problem in the hope that this would somehow ease pressure on the United Kingdom.[23]

It was the opinion of British officials that the Munich Agreement had left anti-Nazi Sudeten Germans and former 'Reich-refugees' exposed to the most danger. They felt that they had an obligation to resettle these groups at the expense of the Sudetenland Jews. As the British government, the Intergovernmental Committee on Refugees, and the British committee for Refugees from Czechoslovakia were all agreed that that they should in principle be against the emigration of Jews, they were accorded the lowest priority. This position was held not only because of fears of anti-Semitism in host countries, but also out of concern that it would encourage Germany's continued persecution of Jews by giving the appearance that they would be resettled elsewhere. From this context, it is possible to understand why Viktor Ullmann's children were evacuated to Britain, even though he and their mother were not. Tragically, nearly all of the Jewish composers living in Czechoslovakia, including such important figures as Ullmann, Pavel Haas, Hans Krása and Erwin Schulhoff, would ultimately end in Nazi camps – as would the exceptional young composer, Gideon Klein.

Of course, America, Britain and France were only three destinations. The Hindemith pupil Hans Joachim Koellreuter went to Brazil where he taught Antonio Carlos Jobim, the prime creator of the bossa nova. Manfred Gurlitt and Klaus Pringsheim ended up in Japan and were in no small measure responsible for fostering the talents of the postwar generation of Japanese performers. The Webern pupil Philipp Herschkowitz ended up in the Soviet

Union and became the influential mentor to the 'Underground' composers
of the post-Shostakovich generation that included Sofia Gubaidulina and
Alfred Schnittke.[24] Herbert Zipper eventually landed in the Philippines and,
of course, there were many musicians who went to Palestine, such as Paul
Ben-Haim, formerly known as Paul Frankenburg, who went on to establish a
national school of the Eastern Mediterranean, a sound world that was an
inspiring mix of Jewish ghetto and sacred music with a touch of Impressionism
and Bauhaus Functionalism. However, the influences to come out of these
far-flung destinations were ultimately marginal on postwar Western European
and American music. The story of Palestine's evolution into Israel and the role
music played in this process is too broad a topic to be covered in this context.

Escape: Great Britain

On 25 March 1938 Georg Szell wrote to his old friend Hans Gál from
Marseille in France:

> I can't tell you how happy I am to know that you are safely in London. I shall
> drop Tovey a quick note, he's a charming but somewhat cranky and unreli-
> able individual who <u>never</u> answers correspondence. I advise you to contact
> (by mentioning my name) Dr Adolf Aber; he was formerly of [the music
> publisher] Hofmeister and critic in Leipzig; he's now a representative of
> many German publishing houses and is partial owner of Novello's. He may
> have something to offer to you in dealing with music publishing – at least he
> can offer advice. In England you must have, above all else, lots of patience![25]

Szell then itemises his schedule for the next six months – divided between
orchestras in The Hague and Glasgow – and provides his temporary addresses
in the Netherlands and Sydney. Szell's future in America looked barely
possible at this time. As the letter is dated less than two weeks after Austria's
annexation, plotting elaborate career moves was less of a priority than getting
friends and family out of Hitler's way. Writing to Gál from California a few
months later, on 15 June 1938, Ernst Toch adds his advice:

> I can only offer at most an introduction to [Alexander] Korda, but I can't
> promise much. It certainly didn't help [Nikolai] Lopatnikoff – but take it
> anyway. You have to put up with everything we've already been through and
> continue to go through. During my time in London, I wrote to every studio
> in town and begged for appointments. 98% were *DIS*-appointments and 2%
> resulted in stumbling a few steps forward by way of a couple of contacts. It's

astonishing that somehow things work as long as you stay patient. Only when I left London was I told that it would have been better had I had an agent. So for good measure, I'll pass this bit of advice on to you. Nevertheless, here I have five agents and not one has ever managed to do anything for me. Ultimately, you have to do everything yourself. From where I am at the moment, I can't do anything for you. I would love to have helped Lopatnikoff, but here I'm simply a kernel of dust being stirred around in a witch's cauldron of intrigues and plotting. [. . .] Louis Greenberg [1883–1964], one of America's most respected composers who had his opera [*The Emperor Jones*] performed at the Metropolitan Opera in New York as well as in Chicago, has been sitting around here for the last two years without work, despite having an agent, while others seem to strike lucky. There seems to be no recipe of how things turn out. [. . .] Emigration has taught me that you need to do everything tirelessly by yourself without losing patience; at some point, you find a small safe hole to slip into and from there, it all continues up-hill. What you need to appreciate is the fact that you're out of there. What would we give – my wife and I – if we could get our relatives and friends out of Vienna. Please don't be too disappointed and don't curse me too much for this idiotic letter. Believe me, it would make me the happiest man alive if I could help everyone who asked me – even if I could help those who *don't* ask me, but who I know need help.[26]

The music historian Jutta Raab Hansen in her seminal work on musical exile in Great Britain explains in detail the restrictions to which musicians who made it to the United Kingdom were subjected by the Incorporated Society of Musicians (ISM), headed by Sir George Dyson.[27] Essentially, it was designed to protect the interests of British musicians who had been steadily losing employment since the demise of silent films in the late 1920s. Dyson's ISM successfully lobbied for regulations to guard against further threats by the influx of potentially better qualified musicians from the continent. These were controversial measures that were flagrantly broken by the likes of the tenor Richard Tauber, who toured the country without the slightest trace of official hindrance giving popular concerts and recitals. The wartime National Gallery Concerts organised by the pianist Myra Hess were slightly more provocative, since she involved many unknown refugees (such as the aforementioned Lopatnikoff), while numerous refugees took up employment at Glyndebourne, the country house opera company run by Sir John Christie before it closed for the duration of the war in 1939, or at the invitation of Michael Tippett, at London's Morley College. These infringements were more than balanced by the determined harassment of foreign teachers and orchestral players, a practice that relaxed slightly in the early 1940s as refugee organisations such as the German Kulturbund, the Austrian Centre and the Anglo-Austrian Music Society began admitting the public to its concerts. Hitherto, admission had been restricted to fellow refugees, who couldn't in any case pay for tickets.

One area where refugee composers were able to work with some degree of impunity was the film industry. By 1933, motion pictures using recorded sound had been around for some six years, but experiments as to how to position music within films was still quite hit-and-miss. Most film composing simply meant writing a hit song or two that cropped up at an apposite moment during the movie. Though Baden-Baden's new music festival had already focused on the potential uses of music with cinema as early as 1928, the first dedicated original score for a Hollywood film was not until 1933, with *King Kong*, and music by Max Steiner, a Viennese Jew who as a student had been dismissively regarded by Mahler as being 'without talent'.[28] Already recounted in Chapter 7, silent films, such as *Berlin, die Symphonie der Großstadt* (1927) and *Battleship Potemkin* (1925), both with scores by Edmund Meisel, had shown what the combination of music and image could achieve. By 1933, the field of film composition was still so specialised that composers such as Mischa Spoliansky, who arrived in London from Berlin almost as soon as Hitler took power, could start work without raising the suspicions, let alone the hackles, of the ISM. Other composers arriving in Britain for film work included Hanns Eisler with his 1936 adaptation of *Pagliacci* starring Richard Tauber, and his 'anti-Hitler' film *Abdul the Damned* (1935). Ernst Toch wrote scores for two films directed by Alexander Korda, *Catherine the Great* and *The Private Lives of Don Juan*, and a third, *Little Friend*, directed by the Austrian Berthold Viertel; to these composers can be added the Schreker pupils Karol Rathaus and Wilhelm Grosz.

As they were accepting commissions to produce music for films, they were not officially resident in Britain, but only in transit. They therefore did not need to apply for refugee status (though evidence has come to light that the British Secret Service was tailing Hanns Eisler and making it difficult for him to be paid for his work).[29] This gave composers the same advantage as the pianist Artur Schnabel, who decided early on that the only way to continue performing in Great Britain was to be based elsewhere.

One notable exception to this rule was the former Schoenberg pupil Allan Gray who, as Josef Zmigrod (as he was originally known), had written the music for such classics as *Berlin Alexanderplatz* and *Emil and the Detectives*, both from 1931. Though he also arrived in London in 1933, it would be ten years before he wrote another film score with *The Life and Death of Colonel Blimp* in 1943 and, in 1951, John Huston's *The African Queen*. Others who escaped the bans of the ISM by composing for the British film industry were Hans May, whose 1933 film with heartthrob tenor Joseph Schmidt, *Ein Lied geht um die Welt* (and its 1934 English-language remake, *My Song goes Round the World*), would assure him steady employment with a number of British 'B' movies such as *No Monkey Business* (1935) and a further film with Joseph Schmidt, *A Star Fell from Heaven*, in 1936.

Mischa Spoliansky had made a name for himself in Berlin cabaret with the husband and wife team of Marcellus Schiffer and Margo Lion, and the then still unknown Marlene Dietrich, who would be discovered by Josef von Sternberg performing in Spoliansky's *Zwei Kravatten* (*Two Neckties*); von Sternberg was seeking a leading lady for his film *The Blue Angel*. Spoliansky remained Dietrich's regular confidant until his death in 1985, and his daughter, Irmgard or 'Spoli' Mills, recalled first memories of London with Dietrich preparing breakfast for them, a family of freshly arrived, excited, yet insecure, refugees. Spoliansky moved seamlessly into composing for British cinema and provided scores for such films as *The Man Who Could Work Miracles* (1936), *King Solomon's Mines* (1937), *Over the Moon* (1939), continuing through the war and up to retirement. His career ended, appropriately, with the score for *Hitler: The Last Ten Days* (1973), starring Alec Guinness.

Since the beginning of the First World War, Great Britain had lost its enchantment with all things German. The British royal family's name-change from 'Saxe-Coburg-Gotha' to 'Windsor' was symbolic of their specific shift from their Hanoverian roots, and Britain's broader rejection of German cultural influence in general. British music began looking towards Paris rather than Leipzig, Vienna or Berlin. Composers who had once embarked on pilgrimages to absorb the mastery of Mendelssohn and Schumann now immersed themselves in the musical spirit of France, creating a fusion from which grew England's appetite for all things pastoral as a distinctly British take on French Impressionism. Paradoxically, this occurred as Germany was locking itself into its mood of unemotional sobriety, and the French themselves had started to shed Impressionist tendencies in favour of a leaner neo-Classicism.

Ralph Vaughan Williams, writing to the Austrian pianist Ferdinand Rauter, commented on the 'trampling of the tender flower of English music'[30] by insensitive but marvellously trained Austro-German musicians. There was, in general, scant sympathy in Britain for music coming out of Germany and Austria during the interwar years. The critic Ernest Newman disparaged the music of Weill's *Threepenny Opera* as being a conglomeration of the worst traits of numerous styles and the best traits of none.[31] To be fair, he was in good company: Schoenberg had also commented that Weill was the only composer in whom he could find no qualities whatsoever.[32] As if Newman's review of *The Threepenny Opera* wasn't bad enough, the *Times* correspondent declared that 'Weill writes a particularly nauseous kind of jazz', following the short run of his operetta *Kingdom for a Cow* at the Savoy Theatre in 1935. The incomprehension of London's critics contributed to Weill's decision to quit Britain as soon as possible.[33] The British press treated contemporary Austro-German developments with varying degrees of disdain, with only the likes of Edward Dent and Adrian Boult showing any kind of sympathy for recent continental trends.

By contrast, Berthold Goldschmidt saw England as especially welcoming, following the BBC broadcast of Berg's *Wozzeck* conducted by Adrian Boult in 1934. Goldschmidt had been Erich Kleiber's assistant and orchestral keyboard player for the Berlin premiere in 1925. Despite Goldschmidt's hopes placed in the sophistication of the British public, he found that in general they thought the music coming out of Germany clangorous and dissonant with heavy dollops of artless pseudo-jazz. *The Threepenny Opera* would not enjoy the same success in England that it had in Paris, despite the high profile anti-Semitic cat-calls of the French composer Florent Schmitt at the Salle Pleyel during a Kurt Weill concert in 1933: 'We have enough bad composers in France and don't need to add to them by bringing in all of the German Jewish composers as well.'[34] Ultimately, Schmitt was denounced as an extremist by most of the French press. In Great Britain, the press was more inclined to view German composers as the 'extremists'.

With a few exceptions, British music from the interwar years veered towards some form of pastoralism, or found itself aesthetically between the salon and the palm-court, with only rare ventures into the tamer realms of Modernism. Indeed, the British composer most regularly mentioned in the German new-music publications *Anbruch* and *Melos* is Cyril Scott. Progressive British composers from the generation of Weill, Eisler and Goldschmidt were not nearly as domestically established as their German and Austrian colleagues had been. By 1940 the BBC had compiled a list of composers it had decided could not be broadcast, including many refugees who had fled to Britain. The influence of the Austro-Germanic tradition would thus have to be applied vicariously via teaching: Egon Wellesz arrived at Lincoln College, Oxford, in 1939, and Hans Gál was appointed Lecturer at Edinburgh University immediately after the end of the war, though neither was engaged to teach composition. Hans Ferdinand Redlich lectured first at the Workers' Education Association as well as extramural departments of the Universities of Cambridge and Birmingham before accepting a professorship in Manchester. Walter Goehr and the Hungarian composer Mátyás Seiber found positions at

London's Morley College. The Webern pupil Leopold Spinner and Arthur Willner, a former composition teacher from Berlin's Stern'schen Conservatory, worked as copyeditors or arrangers for music publishers, while the Schoenberg pupil Erwin Stein became the musical midwife to the young Benjamin Britten. Britten had hoped to study with Berg in Vienna, but was persuaded against the idea by his teachers at the Royal College of Music, who were suspicious of musical developments in central Europe. Erwin Stein's influence served as an aesthetic link to the Second Viennese School, arguably aiding the projection of Britten's work beyond the insular world of British music.

The Academic Assistance Council of Great Britain (AAC) was set up in 1933 by William Beveridge, Director of the London School of Economics. It was meant to help place reputable academics, but the reality was quite different. Of the 2,200 academics leaving Nazi Germany and Austria by 1938, half went first to Britain, but the AAC dealt only with what it considered the 'elite', so that many ordinary teachers and researchers were never allowed to stay. By 1935, only 60 permanent university posts had been found for fleeing academics, including a small number of scientists. The AAC was under pressure from the Ministry of Labour to encourage academics to find employment in the USA, with only 31 refugee academics ultimately ending up in British universities.[35]

Internment

It was in 1940 that Churchill gave his infamous instruction to 'collar the lot', meaning that 'enemy aliens' were to be interned.[36] These included male (and in some cases female) Germans and Austrians, but not the so-called 'Old Reich' Austrians who held Czech, Polish or Hungarian citizenship. It also included Britons of German and Austrian origin, so that in a few instances Britons found themselves interned (or indeed deported) because their parents or even grandparents had settled in Britain. Until May 1940, 'enemy aliens' had been classified in one of the three categories listed as A, B and C. Those in category A were deemed an obvious threat and were already detained. Most able-bodied Jewish and political refugees fell into category B and were subject to employment and movement restrictions, while those in category C were exempt. Churchill's order resulted in 27,000 category B aliens, and many from category C being added to the category A aliens, already detained,

Hans Gál's internment memoirs *Musik hinter Stacheldraht* or *Music behind Barbed Wire* offers a vivid first-hand account of life in British internment camps, recalling his five months surrounded by despair, death and frequent suicides.[37] His own family was ripped apart: in 1942, his youngest son, unable to cope with the new life forced upon him, committed suicide, and his oldest son was deported to unknown shores during the months in which Gál was detained on the Isle of Man.

Jewish asylum-seekers, businessmen with Nazi sympathies working in Britain when war broke out, first- and second-generation Austro-German Britons, along with political refugees, were all thrown into camps together (Italians were placed in separate camps). As Gál explained, the cynical view among refugees was that Britain was preparing to present Hitler with all of his escaped Jews on a silver platter, once the country fell to Germany.[38] The music that Gál composed in camps at Huyton (outside Liverpool) and Douglas (Isle of Man) does not reflect his mood of desperation. On the contrary, he wrote pieces to take people's minds away from the situation. He composed for whatever instruments were available, and when performers were released, transferred to other camps or simply deported, he rescored his pieces for new arrivals, or transposed them as the situation demanded. He described the guards as obtuse and often sadistic. The frequently cited 'camp universities' with lectures held by Nobel Prize-winning scientists and concerts by some of the greatest performers of the day, all of whom were interned together, reflect only a partial truth that belongs mostly to postwar British mythology. The lectures and concerts, the art classes offered by the likes of Kurt Schwitters and plays mounted by refugee actors and directors were, according to Gál's memoirs, far less of a feature of daily life than the unremitting tedium. Wellesz's Oxford University diary is empty from the moment he is interned until the week of 8 July 1940, with two consecutive entries that read 'Schöne Müllerin – Zusammenbruch', referring to a performance of Schubert's *Die Schöne Müllerin,* and the total mental breakdown which led to his being released after the personal interventions of Myra Hess, Vaughan Williams and others.

The Austrian pianist Ferdinand Rauter campaigned tirelessly after his own release from internment for freeing musicians who clearly posed no threat to the British public and who were sometimes young enough to be in danger of suffering permanent psychological scarring. Among this group were several young Austrians including Norbert Brainin, Siegmund Nissel and Peter Schidlof, whom Rauter managed to have released and placed with the Viennese violinist Max Rostal for instruction. Rostal was impressed enough by the youngsters to teach them without charge, and in 1947 he introduced them to the English cellist Martin Lovett, with whom they formed the Amadeus Quartet. Gál was also lucky enough to be released early and returned to Edinburgh in late September 1940 after suffering from an inexplicable skin disease.

During his internment, Gál worked with a group of writers and performers to put on an internment-camp revue entitled *What a Life!* for which Gál wrote the music, and among the humorous writers was the Schubert scholar, Otto Erich Deutsch. The first performance was such a success with both prisoners and camp personnel that Gál was persuaded to delay his release by one day so that a second performance could take place. Songs were bilingual and a taste of a verse in English translated by Gál himself from an original text by someone he identified only as 'Hutter' certainly implies a baffled incomprehension at locking up 'Hitler's best enemies'.[39]

The seagulls are in a curious mood
Maybe they are getting too much food.
One thing they all very much deplore,
Is the ugly barbed-wire that grows up the shore.
So in the seagulls' parliament
There was a great debate on that end
And many of them did then enquire:
'Why are human-beings behind barbed-wire?'

In truth, internment was standard in times of war and carried out by all sides, often with tragic consequences. Roosevelt's order for the internment of Japanese-Americans is copiously documented and the United States has been quicker than other countries in dealing with this dark chapter of its domestic history. Documentation concerning British internment that should have been released after 30 years remains embargoed to this day. But the Nazis also operated internment camps in addition to their many concentration camps. It was in such a camp, in the small Bavarian town of Wülzburg, that the Jewish, Prague-born composer Erwin Schulhoff died. He had been imprisoned, not as a Jew, but as a naturalised Soviet citizen, even though the camp in Wülzburg separated Jewish prisoners from other internees. His death from tuberculosis in 1942 was in the same year that the film star and opera tenor Joseph Schmidt died in a Swiss internment camp at the age of 38, proving that even the internationally famous matinee idol was not spared unsanitary and crowded conditions. There were also many deaths and suicides in French and British camps. Jewish inmates of French internment camps were regularly deported to the death camps in the East after the fall of France in 1940. The twelve-tone composer and protégé of Theodor Adorno, Erich Itor Kahn, and his wife, the Russian pianist Frida Rabinovitch, were relatively lucky. Having been shipped from one camp to another in France, they eventually managed, with help from the American Refugee Committee, to reach Casablanca and find safe passage to the United

States in 1941. If his music remains largely unfamiliar today, his view of the dilemmas presented to a German Jewish composer at that time is revealing:

> I believe that during such a time of profound world crises even art must be affected. In such periods as these, there is no stability of stylistic or expressive means and anything that is completed appears short-lived. The ultimate recognition of the limitations of recognised truth, treated also as a dialectical argument regarding material, is fundamentally shattering and seen as a point of departure. In the midst of such an age, the composer has only one means of guaranteeing his artistry: to yield to the rights and duties that have grown from an historic musical inheritance while at the same time yielding to the spiritual and intellectual vision demanded by its expression. The first and most determining question is this: How far can we go without betraying the past, and what do we need to keep without betraying the future?[40]

Less fortunate was the violinist Alma Rosé (niece of Gustav Mahler, and daughter of Arnold Rosé and Mahler's sister Justine), interned in Drancy before being deported to Auschwitz. The librettist Richard Fall, brother of the composer Leo Fall, was also arrested in France before his murder in Nazi gas chambers, sharing the same fate as the composers Szymon Laks and James Simon along with Fritz Löhner-Beda, the librettist for Lehár's *Land of Smiles* and *Giuditta*.

Escape: France

Fleeing from Nazi Germany in 1933 to neighbouring France, Czechoslovakia, Italy or Austria was only a short-term solution. But unlike Czechoslovakia and Austria, there was less apparent sympathy in France for Nazi anti-Semitism. Indeed, France had been helping Jews flee from central and Eastern European pogroms with its Comité central d'assistance aux réfugiés juifs since 1928. There was broad establishment support for aiding German Jewish refugees from 1933, and for Austrian composers such as Toch and Schoenberg, France was felt to be a more secure refuge than a return to Dollfuß's corporatist dictatorship in Austria. French was also the most common second language for German and Austrian refugees, and this fact regularly tipped the balance in favour of Paris over London.

But like Britain, France too was suffering from massive unemployment; its musicians were reeling from the loss of work that came with the arrival of sound films, and as a result, life was especially difficult for fleeing musicians. German music was not appreciated by the broader French public, though young French composers had greater sympathy for German modernist trends than their British counterparts.[41] Refugee musicians did not form self-help leagues or societies such as those formed by German writers in French exile. Nor were they engaged to teach in institutions.[42] If the British were fretful that, by hiring refugees as teachers, they were putting their native musical flower, 'tender' as it was, at risk from being trampled underfoot by better-qualified Huns, the French were sufficiently nationalistic to dismiss the idea of Austro-Germans teaching at their institutions altogether. With the exception of the teutophile, anti-Semitic Florent Schmitt and a small number of others, the French maintained the anti-German stance present since their defeat in the Franco-Prussian War.

As in Britain, official attempts were made to preserve an outward appearance of friendly cultural relations between Germany and France, often leading to excessive concessions being made to avoid harming international relations. In 1936, Hanns Eisler submitted several movements of an oratorio that would eventually become his *Deutsche Sinfonie*, with texts by Bertolt Brecht and Ignazio Silone, to the committee of the ISCM in the hope of having it performed at the 1937 ISCM festival in Paris. The composer Jacques Ibert headed the jury along with the ISCM President Edward Dent. Neither was instinctively sympathetic to Eisler's politics, and both were wary of offending the remaining German delegates (Nazi Germany had officially withdrawn its cooperation and started a rival organisation). In an effort to appear as non-partisan as possible, the ISCM committee suggested to Eisler that the vocal passages be replaced by saxophones – a suggestion that Eisler, unsurprisingly, did not take up.

The film industry provided the easiest means for composers to enter French musical life. The Hungarian pupil of Hanns Eisler, József Kozma, later Joseph Kosma, arrived in Paris from Berlin in 1933. His first score, following the success of his 1936 hit-song 'Au jour, le jour; à la nuit, la nuit' from Jean Renoir's film *Le Crime de Monsieur Lange*, was *La grande illusion* (also directed by Renoir) in 1937, followed by *La Règle du jeu* in 1939. In due course, Kosma became the father of postwar chanson with such hits as *Les feuilles mortes* and *Les enfants qui s'aiment* set to texts by Jacques Prévert. But other composers would also find work in France's film industry, Eisler himself with *Le grand jeu* in 1934 and *La vie est à nous* in 1936. Paul Dessau, another frequent Brecht collaborator, composed scores for *L'or dans la rue* in 1935, *Taras Bulba* in 1936, and *Cargaison Blanche* in 1937, and even the future Hollywood great, Franz Wachsmann, later known as Franz Waxman, worked in Paris on the films *La petite de Parnasse* and *Un peu d'amour* (1932) and *La crise est finie* and *Mauvaise graine* (1934) prior to leaving for America. Of all of the composers seeking refuge in France, only a few, such as the Hungarians Joseph Kosma and Imre Weisshaus (later known as Paul Arma), and the Polish Webern pupil René Leibowitz, remained in France during the years of the Vichy regime, while the Austrian operetta composer Joseph Beer remained in hiding until the end of the war.

Most German and Austrian composers either left France or were deported to the East. Beer remained too damaged through his experience to participate in postwar musical life and any of his prewar operettas that found postwar productions were mounted without his involvement. His family, along with his regular librettist, Fritz Löhner-Beda, had all been murdered. He remained a virtual recluse in the South of France until his death in 1987. During the Occupation, Jacques Prévert was able to feed film work through to Kosma, under house arrest in France's Alpes-Maritimes region, which was then published under the names of other, non-Jewish composers. Arma, also hiding in the South of France, compiled political songs held today at the Musée régionale de la Résistance de Thionville, and composed a song cycle entitled *Les chants du silence* setting poems by Vercors, Éluard and others. In the immediate postwar years, Leibowitz, who would become the teacher of Boulez and Henze (among many others), fostered an interest in Schoenberg among younger composers in both France and Germany.

Escape: The United States

Given the choice, nearly all Jewish refugees would have preferred emigration to the USA, but the quota system made this difficult for those without funds and contacts. Introduced in 1921, the quota system was a convoluted affair: within the total number of annual immigrants set at 350,000, 'quotas' were pegged at no more than 3 per cent of the absolute number of émigrés from any given country living in America since 1910. In 1924, the laws were made even more proscriptive with the capping of levels of existing populations being backdated from 1910 to 1890, and the total number of immigrants was reduced to 150,000. These regulations were brought in to stem the flow of immigrants after the First World War, and to reduce the numbers arriving from Southern and Eastern Europe in order to give an advantage to those from Northern Europe, which already represented the largest of the many ethnic groups.[43]

With many prominent professionals and intellectuals stranded in France in 1940, Roosevelt was able to introduce an Advisory Committee on Political Refugees (known as the 'Refugee Committee') so that visas could be quickly made available to selected individuals who could make their way to neutral

Portugal, possibly via French Morocco. From this pool, over 3,000 special visas were offered to those who were deemed to be able to make a tangible contribution to American cultural, financial or academic life. It was under this system that Heinrich Mann, Lion Feuchtwanger, Franz Werfel and his wife Alma Mahler-Werfel were able to enter the United States after crossing the Pyrenees on foot and making their way from there to Lisbon. Erich Itor Kahn, once released from French internment, travelled to French Morocco and thence to the United States. Refugees waiting for visas in North Africa were immortalised in *Casablanca* (1942) starring Humphrey Bogart and Ingrid Bergman, a film made all the more authentic by the participation of numerous Austro-German refugees working in Hollywood including Paul Henreid, Conrad Veidt, Peter Lorre, Curt Bois, Ilka Grüning and Ludwig Stössel. The music was by the Vienna-born, Hollywood-based Max Steiner.

The composers Eisler and Toch, the director Erwin Piscator, the critic and musicologist Max Graf and other academics were able to enter the USA with offers to take up professorships at New York's New School of Social Research, a specialist college founded in 1919. Graf, Eisler and Toch were only a few of the well-known European intellectuals to be offered positions by one of the School's co-founders, Alvin Johnson. In 1933, Johnson, together with the Austrian economist Emil Lederer, set up a postgraduate division of the New School that he called the University in Exile, supported in part by the Rockefeller Foundation and the Jewish philanthropist Hiram J. Halle. Over the next few years, it would offer permanent positions to refugee-academics including the philosophers Hannah Arendt and Leo Strauss, and the Gestalt psychologist Max Wertheimer. The New School of Social Research, however, was only one of several elite institutions that saved lives by making offers of employment to refugee intellectuals and artists. The neo-Marxist Frankfurt School (of interdisciplinary social theory), formed under the sociologist Max Horkheimer, left Germany and relocated to Columbia University in New York in 1933 where it re-established itself as the Institute for Social Research. From the very beginning, it had attracted leftist scholars, intellectuals and academics such as Walter Benjamin and Paul Tillich.[44] Theodor (Wiesengrund) Adorno was director of a social research project called the Radio Project, which would lead to collaboration with Hanns Eisler on the use of music and film, and was funded by the Rockefeller Foundation, a source of income that must have left many Marxists culturally bemused. Eventually, it resulted in the publication of their co-authored book *Composing for the Films* (1947).[45]

One of the most prestigious locations of all was Princeton, New Jersey, where the generously endowed Institute for Advanced Study established by

Abraham Flexner became the temporary home for the writers Thomas Mann and Hermann Broch, the art historian Erwin Panofsky, and the archaeologist Ernst Herzfeld, with its most significant academic acquisition being the physicist Albert Einstein.[46] America was proving itself enormously resourceful at taking in the brains which were being squeezed out of Hitler's Europe and marginalised in nationalist Britain, though it was a source of endless frustrations and humiliation for many of the émigrés themselves. Salaries for academics in America were not always what Europeans expected, nor did the system appeal to academics from Germany and Austria, where universities had been places for students to learn from professors. In America, students were able to choose the people under whom they wished to study, a change in focus that caused bewilderment. Along with these cultural upheavals came the genuine difficulties of not finding suitable employment at all. Paul Dessau worked on a chicken farm; the satirical writer Walter Mehring was a warehouse foreman; the poet, philosopher and second husband of Hannah Arendt, Heinrich Blücher, was a porter in a chemical factory; the Brechtian actress Ruth Berlau worked in a bar; and Lou Eisler worked as a cleaner.[47]

Ernst Krenek wrote of the 'echolessness' of America's vast expanses,[48] which seems to refer to not only the geographical size of the country but also the inability of a composer to resonate. After countless false dawns and frustrations, some of Europe's finest composers and musicologists found themselves teaching in America's numerous provincial colleges and small universities. Krenek himself taught at Vassar, America's leading college for privileged young women, but left under a cloud, ostensibly for promoting twelve-note composition. He subsequently found a post at Hamlin University in St Paul, Minnesota, which provided him with the introduction to his third wife, the composer Gladys Nordenstrom. Other notable names would also find themselves teaching in colleges: Karol Rathaus at Queens College in New York, Alfred Einstein at Smith College (like Vassar, an outstanding liberal arts college for women), Paul Pisk at the Baptist University of Redlands in California, before he moved to the University of Texas in Austin, Erich Zeisl at Los Angeles City College, while the Austro-Hungarian pianist Lili Kraus took up the position of artist in residence at Texas Christian College in Fort Worth.

There is no question that many were deeply grateful to the United States for the opportunities they were offered. At the time, the American West Coast became such a haven for refugee academics that the musicologist Christopher Hailey told the author that, as a youngster growing up in California, he and other young musicians didn't trust a teacher without a foreign accent. These were known locally as the 'Bei-uns-niks' for their constant prefacing of every conversation with the phrase 'Bei uns . . ', which in this context meant 'Back where we're from . . '. Hailey wrote in his essay 'Émigrés in the Classroom':

> It is possible that the influx of German-speaking émigrés of the 1930s and the '40s served as something of a brake on America's process of self-discovery. Through the introduction of systematic musicology, analytical procedures such as those of Heinrich Schenker, and compositional models such as those of Hindemith and Schoenberg, the émigrés helped establish a set of academic priorities that were heavily dependent upon the precedents of central European repertoire. The émigré presence also introduced or re-enforced certain long-held prejudices, including the notion that German music was superior to that of, say, France or Italy (substance over style), and the belief that instrumental music represented a higher, purer form of musical culture than vocal or theatrical forms, which were among America's strengths.

Hailey concludes, however, that far from transferring the seed of European culture to the fertile soil of California, young American composers such as John Cage and Lou Harrison, both Schoenberg pupils, would react with their own strong musical statements, representing a definitive break with old-world aesthetic principles.[49]

American ensembles and opera companies were just as suspicious of musicians without foreign accents, and probably nowhere were refugees taken up with greater enthusiasm than by American orchestras and the organisers of subscription concert series. Established conductors such as Bruno Walter, Georg (now George) Szell and others soon found first-rate orchestras with much better terms and conditions than the ones they had conducted in Europe. Otto Klemperer may have been frustrated with life in Los Angeles, and its obligatory income-producing Hollywood Bowl season, but there was no denying that he was able to establish a world-class ensemble from what was still a relatively young orchestra at a time of general financial hardship. In addition, he had the freedom to perform a good deal of modern repertoire to an inquisitive, if occasionally puzzled, audience. With so many immigrants arriving, many émigré conductors recognised players in their new ensembles from earlier days in Europe. A few had orchestras founded for them, such as the NBC Orchestra established in 1937 for Arturo Toscanini but also regularly conducted by Bruno Walter, George Szell, Ernest Ansermet and Charles Munch. The Jewish Hungarian Fritz Reiner had been working in the United States since 1922, long before the arrival of Hitler; but Erich Leinsdorf came to New York's Metropolitan Opera in 1937 on the recommendation of the soprano Lotte Lehmann. By the 1950s, he had become a household name throughout America, while remaining largely unknown in his native Vienna. The Hungarian conductor and violinist Jenő Blau, later known as Eugene Ormandy, had, like Fritz Reiner, also come to America before the advent of National Socialism. Like Reiner, he was unable to return to Europe and was plagued by the inability to rescue family and friends after the outbreak of war. He went on to enjoy 44 years as music director of the Philadelphia Orchestra, from 1936 until 1980. Wilhelm, now William, Steinberg and Antal Doráti were other names that started to appear as regular conductors with provincial ensembles, while the Utah Symphony Orchestra in Salt Lake City was able to increase its national profile substantially from 1947 with the help of the Jewish Swiss conductor Maurice Abravanel, who fled Germany in 1933. These were just some of the conductors. There were, if anything, even more instrumentalists who arrived first as refugees in the United States, then stayed as immigrants such as the pianists Rudolf Serkin, Artur Schnabel, Lili Kraus, Eduard Steuermann; Jews from Russia such as Vladimir Horowitz and Arthur Rubinstein from Poland; the Viennese cellist Emanuel Feuermann and the violinists Fritz Kreisler, Rudolf Kolisch, along with the Russian violinists Jascha Heifetz and Nathan Milstein, who as Jews were unwilling to return to Nazi-dominated Europe, having already fled Bolshevik Russia.

American musical life took off as never before, with every school and provincial orchestra boasting its own celebrity émigrés who guaranteed that local standards of performance were as high as they were in Europe. More importantly, they inspired young Americans to meet the exacting standards demanded by their new teachers, conductors and even administrators. George Szell (who remained 'Georg' in correspondence with Austrian friends), wrote to Hans Gál in 1946 to explain his conducting post in Cleveland:

> The position in Cleveland, about which I have been unable to write until now, is truly ideal. The financial foundation of the society is the best that can be found amongst all American orchestras with the possible exception of Boston. The Hall, and indeed the entire building, is splendid and is in due course meant to become our permanent home. The orchestra, which was already one of the best in the country, will soon become one of the very best to be found anywhere as I have succeeded in increasing the personnel to 95 and have all of programmes for the coming season now scheduled. It goes to press in September and I'll have a copy sent to you.
>
> The interest and the participation of the public is enormous. Six weeks ago we had already sold $92,000 worth of subscription concert tickets. Last year at this time the figure stood at $42,000, but we need to remember that

the strongest month for subscription sales is September, meaning it's still to come. Last year the final amount came to $77,000.[50]

The musicologist Alfred Einstein, writing to Gál in early 1940 from Northampton, Mass., offers another picture of émigré life:

> Our larking about at Christmas in New York was repaid with double the normal work-load upon my return. In New York we heard almost only German – and what's more, German with a Viennese accent. Heini Schnitzler [son of Arthur Schnitzler], an evening spent with three conductors: Szell, Stiedry and Breisach, each at varying points put into a bad mood as they switched on the radio to hear a good Belgian conductor. [...] We missed [...] Karl Weigl, but the best of all, the one we most longed to see was of course you. Back in Northampton, one only hears English, but English that is coloured by every imaginable accent these days.[51]

A selection of correspondence gives an impression of the pressures and problems of leaving Germany and Austria, and of obtaining an American visa. Temporary asylum in Switzerland is illustrated by letters of reasonably well-connected refugees trying to get to the United States. Erich Korngold's brother Hanns writing from Zurich on 26 March 1939 (where he had been stuck since the previous year) writes as follows:

> Four weeks ago, I received my deportation orders, against which I have already appealed. I've had numerous meetings at the special police office in charge of aliens. These meetings deal largely with the question of when I am planning to leave and what funds I have for supporting myself. Prospects are worse than ever with the American visa. The latest news from the local consulate is that it's pointless to expect a visa for at least another two years. This is hopeless. That was point one; my second point is that the officials here cannot be duped into thinking that I finance my existence simply by selling jewellery. The only means of deferring my planned deportation is not by showing them the cash I have in hand but by showing them bank statements that prove that I'm being supported from overseas. The longer such funding appears to be guaranteed, the better my position for trying to remain here.[52]

He goes on to request a sum of between $60 and $70 a month – astronomical, he admits, and 'adding unwanted pressure on Erich who already has so many obligations'. With this amount of money, he wrote that he would move out of

Zurich and live in a small provincial bed-and-breakfast somewhere in the country until his visa came through.[53]

Alfred Einstein, writing to Hans Gál in 1939 from Brooklyn, seems to corroborate this sorry state of affairs:

> Sorry to have missed you in London. [. . .] We had to break our necks to get out of Switzerland and on to Naples in order to go through the usual purgatory at the American consulate (trying to organise matters from the Consulate in Zurich would have meant a delay of 2 to 3 years), without having the foggiest notion that we, that is to say, our daughter, was to be detained by Mussolini. In short, we did not return to Zurich where there was a British visa waiting for us. We were instead relieved that under these most dangerous circumstances, we managed to cross the border by boat from Ventimiglia into Cannes.[54]

Hollywood

As with the UK and France, one of the choice positions for a musician in America was with a film studio. For instrumentalists, it was a secure, well-paid job with one of the Hollywood orchestras or as a rehearsal pianist. For composers, it meant making arrangements, checking parts, orchestrating or, for an elite, actually composing film music. The nature and purpose of film scores was still not fully established. During the days of silent films, it was largely left to pianists to improvise as they saw fit. Larger cinemas in metropolitan centres had organs, and even bands and small ensembles. In due course, scores of arrangements were provided, but there was little if any original music included, and films ran to the accompaniment of well-known works such as Rossini's *William Tell* Overture or a Liszt Hungarian Rhapsody, or generic works that could be slotted in for any given love scene or moment of suspense. If there was thought and planning behind the potential of music and film, it seemed to be coming in the main from Russia and Germany.

Everything changed in 1933 when Max Steiner wrote the music for *King Kong* and transformed a gorilla puppet that had raised guffaws from American test-audiences into an object of genuine terror. In their book *Composing for the Films*, Adorno and Eisler lay out the means of achieving the maximum emotional effect by combining music with moving images: either musically to 'replicate' and amplify the visuals, or to set off images with a contrasting musical counterpoint – composing the obverse of what the visuals dictated; if the scene was swift-moving and tense, the music was slow and dreamy, and if the scene was dreamy, the music was tense and fast-paced. In this manner, a 'dramatic dialectic' or a synthesis of emotional responses could be created. The opposite extreme was to emphasise the visuals; for example, a ship on the high seas called for music that accentuated the vastness and majesty of the ocean. In other words, the composer simply replicated the visual image by expanding it musically.[55] Not surprisingly, Hollywood usually opted for the latter solution and left arty intellectual ideas to Soviet and European filmmakers. For a Hollywood blockbuster like *King Kong* to come across as frightening, the music had to exaggerate the visual terror as much as possible. This recipe worked, and few studio composers, apart from Eisler, considered the alternatives.

Steiner composed music for nearly a dozen films a year. The sheer number he worked on (no fewer than 62 from 1930 until *King Kong* in 1933) meant that he is remembered for the themes of such iconic pictures as *Now Voyager*, *Gone with the Wind* and *Casablanca*. Compare this with Erich Korngold, who during the decade he worked in Hollywood provided scores for roughly the same number of films as Steiner in a year. Korngold, who certainly drew on Steiner's methods (and vice versa), arrived in Hollywood as the first composer of film music already established as a successful composer of serious, 'classical' music. Up to this point, film composers had come from vaudeville or cabaret, or had worked as arrangers or bandmasters. Korngold was far classier than anyone Hollywood had encountered before, and everyone was in awe of him. His contract was unique, and he was spared the assembly line methods of other studio composers. He could choose which films he worked on, composed everything himself (with very few exceptions), and orchestrated as much as commitments would allow. His usual editorial and musical assistant was the young American cellist Hugo Friedhofer, who also came from a 'classical background' and had the advantage of speaking German. Korngold, who first went to Hollywood to arrange Mendelssohn's score for Max Reinhardt's *Midsummer Night's Dream* in 1935, left his mark on a series of swashbuckling films with Errol Flynn and Olivia de Havilland along with classics such as *The Prince and the Pauper* (1937), *The Adventures of Robin Hood* (1938), *Anthony Adverse* (1939), *Juarez* (1939), *The Sea Wolf* (1941) and *Kings Row* (1942, starring the young Ronald Reagan).

The many Jewish composers arriving in Hollywood from Vienna could hardly have been more varied. On one hand, there were Steiner and Korngold, who, along with Franz Waxman from Berlin, dominated cinematic, wide-screen sound with extraordinary acoustical effects and romantic, sweeping melodies accompanied by lush harmonies that stirred the passions of the motion-picture-loving public. On the other, there was Dr Ernest Toch (as he insisted on being credited, though he grumbled at being billed as 'Ernest'), who was a child of Germany's New Objectivity and a fearless enemy of the ersatz-Romanticism that Hollywood promoted (though on occasion he could provide generic movie tunes as required, such as, for example, his Oscar-nominated theme for *Peter Ibbetson*). As a modernist, he specialised in tense chromatic sequences, which were perfect for supplying the studios with yards of stock music that could be used for gangster car chases through Chicago, or the sleigh-chase through the Alps in Shirley Temple's *Heidi*. Though he received Oscar nominations for his music to *Peter Ibbetson*, he was normally assigned to comedy horror films (some of the best of which were with the young Bob Hope) and suspense movies.

Hanns Eisler arrived in Hollywood with a decade of composing for European political cinema under his belt. Though he never worked at the same exalted heights as Korngold, Waxman, Steiner or Toch, he did set new standards for music in Hollywood with scores that achieved powerful effects by remaining in the background for much of the time, coming forward as part of the dramatic action, or by having no music at precisely the moment when it was expected. In short, his genius was in doing everything differently from the typical Hollywood film composer. Though studios allowed him less latitude for his dialectical dramatic effects than he enjoyed with his frequent collaborator, the Dutch director Joris Ivens, he still managed to achieve a great deal. His score for Fritz Lang's *Hangmen also Die* (1943, the story partially adapted by Bertolt Brecht) even managed an Oscar nomination. This was a remarkable achievement considering that the use of music in the film is sparse and nearly always operates as an active part of the drama rather than as mere illustration.

After the war, Zeisl, Toch and Korngold left studio work as quickly as they could, sensitive to the harm it would do their reputations and fearful of the damage inflicted on their talent by years of creativity on demand. After 1945, Waxman reduced his studio work to less than one film a year, but Eisler was keen to continue, and slowly but surely he started to demonstrate new directions in film music and to produce convincing cinematic effects with his counter-intuitive ideas and theories. It must remain a matter of speculation whether he could have changed the course of Hollywood film music had he not been forcibly removed from the United States by the House of Un-American activities in 1948.

No Escape

By 1939, just before the Nazi invasion of Poland, German, Austrian and Czech Jews were applying for visas for any country that would take them. Refugee colonies were springing up as far afield as Lima and Shanghai. Britain had started to deport refugees and internment prisoners to Canada, Australia and New Zealand, though Canada notoriously refused to take in more than 5,000 Jewish immigrants, while making it clear that it was happy to take any other highly qualified refugee. The heavy loss of life resulting from the sinking of the SS *Arandora Star* (one of several ships carrying refugees or 'enemy aliens' sunk by German torpedoes during the war) en route to Canada in 1940 along with the case of the transport ship *Dunera* would eventually result in a temporary suspension of this policy.

The case of the *Dunera* would become one of the most notorious accounts of disregard for the rights and wellbeing of 'enemy aliens' held in British detention. On 10 July 1940, 2542 inmates from internment camps, some having already survived the sinking of the *Arandora Star*, were placed on the *Dunera* with the information that they would be deported to Canada. Instead, after they had been rifled, robbed and abused by their British guards, their luggage, including musical instruments, was wantonly thrown overboard. They were taken under unsanitary and inhuman conditions to Australia and arrived malnourished and ill some 60 days later, resulting in the court-marshalling of several senior officers and a severe reprimand to Lieutenant-Colonel William Scott. The refugees were then transported to the middle of the Australian outback to a camp in the town of Hay in New South Wales, where they further suffered from extreme heat while enclosed behind several barriers of barbed wire. Relatives were not informed of their location and eventually objections to their treatment were raised in the British Parliament.[56]

Another tragedy was the MS *St Louis*, which transported over 900 Jewish refugees from Hamburg to Cuba in May 1939, only to have entry refused by Cuban bureaucrats on a contrived technicality. Canadian and American immigration officials also refused entry to the increasingly desperate passengers, and though the nearby Dominican Republic agreed that it would accept 100,000 Jewish refugees at the 1938 Évian Conference, the captain of the *St Louis* decided to return to Europe, docking in Antwerp on 17 June, more than a month after leaving Hamburg. Negotiations resulted in passengers being offered asylum in France, Holland, Belgium and the United Kingdom before the *St Louis* returned to its home port in Germany. With the fall of all of these countries (apart from the United Kingdom), it has been estimated by the United States Holocaust Memorial Museum that 254 of the original 937 passengers were subsequently murdered by the Nazis. The captain of the ship, Gustav Schröder, would not return to Germany until he was certain that every one of his charges had found a safe haven, an act of humanity that postwar was widely recognised in his native Germany as well as in Israel.

There are many published accounts and several websites devoted to the music composed in Nazi concentration camps. For the present writer, it has always seemed a miracle that anyone could find the wherewithal to write anything in an environment that demanded so much in order to survive. Yet the essay by the composer Viktor Ullmann entitled 'Goethe und Ghetto' written in Theresienstadt (or Terezín), the so-called 'model ghetto' north-west of Prague and designed to show visiting dignitaries that Jews were being well looked after, raises important points and sheds light on how creativity could thrive under the most desperate circumstances:

> Theresienstadt was and continues to be for me the school of form. In earlier days, when the magic of civilisation suppressed the weight and fury of material life, it was a simple matter to create beauty in form. Our true master-class in form, however, is to be found within our present situation, where we require form to dominate everything that makes up the material of our daily life, and any inspiration the muses may offer stands in the starkest contrast to our surroundings.[. . .] It's only worth emphasising how much my work as a musician has gained by being in Theresienstadt: in no manner did we just sit on the banks of the rivers of Babylon and weep that our cultural needs were not able to keep pace with our will to live. I am quite convinced that anyone who has ever had to wrestle art from life will confirm how true this is.[57]

This raises a crucial point about how environment can affect creativity. Whether adversity and a stressful environment are themselves the catalysts of creativity must remain a thorny, albeit rhetorical question. The circumstantial evidence offered by many exiled composers suggests that the transplantation of talent is rarely successful unless the artists have the resources to reinvent themselves in ways that are compatible with their new surroundings.

With Thomas Mann (but not his brother Heinrich), there was such a large international public that the change of geographical location made little difference to the nature of his output: *Doktor Faustus*, written in exile, became one of his most significant works. Lion Feuchtwanger was in a similar situation, with his international royalties allowing the purchase of an enormous villa in Pacific Palisades. Thomas Mann, while during this period not as popular as Feuchtwanger, also required his creature comforts, something his highly resourceful wife Katia Pringsheim (sister of the composer Klaus Pringsheim) was evidently able to provide.

Composers, however, are different from writers. Mann's quintessential novel-of-exile *Doktor Faustus* was read by individuals in the original language, or in translation, in the privacy of their homes all over the world. Mann certainly did not depend exclusively on an American public to guarantee readership. But music is an experience shared by an audience in a fixed place. At this time, music was usually only recorded if it had already established its popularity in the concert hall or the opera house. If the public did not respond, a composer's creativity either atrophied, as with Arthur Willner and Leopold Spinner, or went into overdrive in search of reinvention. This was the case with Toch, Rankl and arguably with Wellesz, all of whom embarked on a frenzy of symphonic composition.

The important composers working in Theresienstadt – Pavel Haas, Gideon Klein, Hans Krása and Viktor Ullmann – have become fairly well known, and their works are becoming a regular feature of the concert repertoire. All, with the exception of the younger Klein, were en route to becoming established composers before internment. Klein's genius was one of the many tragic miracles of Theresienstadt, his brilliance not becoming evident until he was imprisoned and long after his death.

In any case, the inhumanity of man and the undeniable creativity that it can generate is demonstrated in one highly symbolic work that came out of the Theresienstadt Ghetto. It can stand without explanation and be counted, regardless of its provenance, as a masterpiece: *Der Kaiser von Atlantis* by Viktor Ullmann and his youthful librettist, the painter and poet, Peter (or Petr) Kien. It is also a work of ethical genius. Its alternative title is *The Abdication of Death* and the plot is simple but powerful: Death has been over-worked by the megalomaniac Emperor Overall and decides to go on strike. It was an obvious and dangerous parody of Hitler's ambitions. Yet what places it beyond the expectations of listeners today is its apparent lack of anger; soldiers who can't kill each other wonder why they're fighting, and a soldier-girl and soldier-boy fall in love after fruitless attempts to annihilate each other. A harlequin figure moves the action along while the Emperor Overall and Death argue. A drummer makes further pronouncements, ordering people to kill until nobody is left standing, while singing parodies of the German national anthem. The main protagonists are portrayed as buffoons while the music veers from the Bergian to cinematic hit-song and cabaret.

Ullmann's message, though, is that the only thing that needs to be feared is an *absence* of death. Its ethical message goes even further with Emperor Overall agreeing to be the first to die in order for Death to end his strike and thereby redeeming the apparently irredeemable. This was an extraordinary idea to present in a situation where death was ever-present – parts of the libretto were written on the backs of deportation lists to Auschwitz. Unsurprisingly, it did not make it to performance, though according to the memoirs of the bass Karel Berman, also interned in Theresienstadt, it did go into rehearsal. It has several alternative endings, and though Ullmann gives the official completion date as 13 January 1944, it is clear that during rehearsals there were disagreements about the ultimate version of the text. Kien was in general more cynical, angry even, while Ullmann comes across as verging on the serene with a view of death closer to that of Felix Salten's *Bambi* or Janáček's *Cunning Little Vixen*. The many variants of the final aria result in very different conclusions, changing the entire character of the work. It must surely be one of the bravest pieces of music-theatre ever written – and a powerful ethical testimony.

Music in Terezín, by the Polish-American music historian Joža Karas, remains the definitive work on music in Theresienstadt. Since its publication in 1984, the composers have become far better known and some, especially Ullmann, have been recognised as major figures. Hans Krása and Pavel Haas were two very distinctive composers who maintained a Czech musical identity that would be carried forward after the war by Martinů. Krása studied with Zemlinsky and Haas with Janáček, and both composers maintained a pronounced aesthetic distance to the New Objectivity, or twelve-tone trends dominant in Germany at the time. So, too, did their teachers, both of whom had already developed distinctive musical styles without conforming to current developments. Though the cultivated Krása employed neo-Classical Stravinskian devices, his music remains essentially Czech, with fewer rugged edges than Pavel Haas. It would be unfair to call their styles eclectic, as they seemed to have come up with something that was individual, though a fusion offering traces of Stravinsky, Janáček and even French Impressionism can be heard in the works of both.

The world inhabited by Czech composers grew from the same surreal environment that produced Franz Kafka: an emotionally defuse world somewhere between dream and awakening. In Krása's Dostoevsky-based opera *Verlobung im Traum*,[58] given its premiere in Prague under Szell in 1933, there's a strong sense of the disparity between reality and the imagined. This blurring of reality and magic is also present in Pavel Haas's folk-opera *Šarlatán*[59] of 1936, and in Erwin Schulhoff's weirdly surreal treatment of the Don Juan story in his only opera, *Flammen* (1929). It is a musical world that survived in Martinů's *Julietta*, given its premiere three days after the annexation of Austria, on 16 March 1938 in Prague, conducted by Václav Talich, the teacher of Karel Ančerl, who conducted much of the music composed in Terezín. Czech music was a product of what Max Brod – journalist, composer,

Janáček translator and Kafka biographer – called 100 per cent Czech, 100 per cent German, and 100 per cent Jewish. It was a description he gave to the Czech capital, Prague, but it also works as a description of Czech composers as well.

There were other composers in Theresienstadt such as the Hindemith and Hába pupil Zikmund (Siegmund) Schul, whose few surviving works, such as the *Two Chassidic Dances*, various Hebrew Choruses and a *Cantata Judaica*, employ explicitly Jewish subjects. There was the bass Karel Berman, who as well as being a singer, also composed songs and piano works; and there was the Austrian-Polish composer Carlo Taube, who composed a *Terezín Symphony*. The score is lost, but a report of a secret performance held in a prayer room in one of the barracks has come down to us from one of the prisoners, an engineer named Arnošt Weiss:

> Not much remains in my memory from the first two movements that characterized the milieu with Jewish and Slavic themes. But the third movement had a shattering effect on the listeners. Mrs Erika Taube, the wife of the composer, recited in a moving way, with a pianissimo obligato from the orchestra, a lullaby of a Jewish mother, which she had composed. There followed a turbulent finale in which the first four bars of *Deutschland, Deutschland* [. . .] did not continue to *über alles*, but died out in a terrible dissonance. Everyone had understood and a storm of applause expressed thanks to Carlo and Erika Taube and all the musicians. Naturally a work of this sort could not be performed officially, and it is distressing that this unique cultural document was not passed on to us.[60]

There were other less important figures composing in Theresienstadt. The 22-year-old Robert Dauber wrote a delightful yet disturbing *Serenade* for violin and piano, in the Palm Court style of his father Adolf 'Dol' Dauber. It remains the only work of this gifted young man who died of typhoid in Dachau at the age of 23. Dauber was the only member of his family to end up in Theresienstadt and even sent occasional post-cards telling his family that he was well. The *Serenade* is best seen as another of Dauber's post-cards: short, sweet and positive. As with the works by Gál composed in Huyton, it has nothing didactic, symbolic or redolent of his experience as a prisoner. On the contrary, it is a work that was no doubt written to help people forget their situation. Perhaps another of these lesser figures who still resonates today is the poet Ilse Weber whose poem *I wander through Theresienstadt / My heart a lump of lead* . . . has become a regular feature at the many concerts in which the music of Theresienstadt is remembered. All of these composers, apart from Berman, were either murdered or died in camps. More recently and astonishingly late in the day, Hungarian composers murdered in the camps are starting to receive scholarly attention. In addition to Ferenc Weisz, murdered in 1944, we are finally able to hear works by Pál Budai, Jenő Deutsch; György Justus; Sándor Kuti; Walter Lajthai-Lazarus; Sándor Vándor; and László Weiner.[61]

It is a bitter irony that the Austro-German music tradition held in such high esteem by the third generation of emancipated, assimilated Jews was last heard wafting across the tundra and barbed wire of Eastern Europe's death camps, played by desperate inmates, most of whom would not survive. Heinrich Heine was surely thinking of the Germany of *Dichter und Denker*, 'poets and philosophers', when he wrote in his forward for *Germany, a Winter's Tale*: 'If we could rescue God from indignities which inhabit mankind here on earth, we would thus become the redeemers of God himself – if we could restore dignity to a people deprived of joy [. . .] then [. . .] the whole of Europe, indeed the whole world, will fall to us! It is this message of universal domination by Germany of which I so often dream when I wander amongst the oaks. This is my patriotism.'

The poems of the Jewish poet Heine, which inspired countless settings by Schubert, Schumann, Brahms, Liszt and Loewe among many others, were banned. Jewish musicians performing Beethoven and Wagner, the strands of which whispered across the moorlands and plains in Central Europe (the very regions being claimed for German *Lebensraum*), had previously, as with Heine, considered themselves ardent defenders of Germany's most humanist values. Yet here they were, their national and cultural identity taken away by neighbours who had convinced themselves that their own entitlement to all that was 'German' could only come at the expense of those whom they could unilaterally declare 'un-German'. Wagner was arguably more accurate in his view that Jews would eventually undermine the essential moral fabric of German culture than he could have known. Nazi anti-Semitism, much of which was inspired by Wagner himself, had driven non-Jewish Germans to perform acts of cultural barbarity that would bankrupt for generations any ethical legacy bestowed by its greatest writers, artists and philosophers.

CHAPTER 12

Restitution

... By the way, we're also in receipt of many letters from [Austria]; amongst others, one from Dr Robert Haas who has lost his position and needs recommendations from people with such dubious sounding names as 'Nettl' (whom he has contacted) and Einstein. Are you aware of the story about how they got rid of Guido Adler's spinster daughter [Melanie]? It seems the rogue Erich Schenk wanted to get his hands on the old man's library. I don't know whether for himself or his institute, but he wouldn't rest until she had landed in one of the gas-ovens in Auschwitz. Just remember these things when arming yourself against calls to hook up with former professional acquaintances 'for old time's sake'.

Alfred Einstein, letter to Hans Gál, 30 May 1947

In today's so-called Fourth Reich, everyone is enthusiastically embracing anything that between 1933 and 1945 would have counted as 'Cultural Bolshevism' as an effective means of justifying their sudden change of heart.

Alfred Einstein, letter to Hans Gál, 29 May 1948

The letters quoted above provide a snapshot of life after Hitler. The first refers to cringing attempts by former Nazi-supporting academics to hold onto their livelihoods during the denazification processes. The plea for positive endorsements from the colleagues they forced into exile (or worse) is made in the context of revelations of extreme ruthlessness carried out by many non-Jewish academics between 1933 and 1945, profiting from the anti-Semitic *tabula rasa* in their institutions. Robert Haas, to whom Einstein refers, was the Nazi-supporting head of the Austrian National Library's Music Collection and principal editor of the Bruckner critical edition. He was removed from his position after the war and replaced by Leopold Nowak. Haas was a cantankerous anti-Semite who maintained that Bruckner had been corrupted by exposure to the 'cosmopolitan influences of Jews'. With denazification underway, he was now trying to persuade various 'Jewish corrupting influences' to come his way as well.

Erich Schenk, also referred to by Einstein, was the controversial rector of Vienna University who from 1957 had, *faute de mieux*, ended up as effective head of the Institute of Musicology founded by Guido Adler. Though Adler had retired in 1927, he was still Editor of *Denkmäler der Tonkunst in Österreich*, the series he had initiated before the Nazis removed him at the age of eighty-one. The former Adler student, Rudolf von Ficker recalled that after Adler's death in 1941, he found his former professor's library stacked in Schenk's study. When von Ficker challenged Schenk about this, Schenk explained that Adler's daughter Melanie had tried to stop his requisitioning the library and had behaved 'like a stupid sow'. Schenk went on to explain that though she had fled (after appealing to him for protection), he was confident that she would soon be found by the Gestapo and then, 'she's off to Poland!' She was murdered in the extermination camp Maly Trostinec near Minsk on 26 May 1942 after her deportation on 20 May.[1]

Haas and Schenk were just two of the musicologists of the same generation as Gál and Einstein who had happily supported the Nazi regime. None of them would have anticipated the posthumous controversy surrounding the noted Schütz and Bach scholar, Hans Heinrich Eggebrecht, who was implicated as a member of the SS Einsatzgruppe D, which, under SS Gruppenführer Otto Ohlendorf, murdered some 5,000 people in the Crimea between 9 and 13 December 1941.[2] In twelve years, Hitler had converted Germans from their centuries-old reputation of 'Dichter und Denker' (Poets and Philosophers) into 'Mörder und Henker' (Murderers and Executioners).

Einstein's second letter reveals the cynical view that self-preservation was being attempted by the postwar German music establishment through feigning revulsion at twelve years of Nazi brain-washing. The consequence was an escape into the arms of whatever appeared to be the diametric opposite of Hitler's national Romanticism. This reaction to the excesses of the past was strangely reminiscent of the early 1920s when writers, painters and composers turned to 'New Objectivity'. Works such as Franz Schreker's *Irrelohe*, first performed in 1924, and Berg's *Wozzeck*, given in Berlin a year later, certainly owed much to Wagnerian Romanticism, turned Expressionist, and were written at the height of artistic detachment that followed the First World War. But if Germans in 1919 were trying to sober up their vision after the intoxicating delusions growing out of Bismarck's short-lived German Empire, the implications post-1939 of criminal behaviour accorded to every German man and woman by Hitler's yet more delusional Third Reich caused an even stronger artistic reaction.

Music in the American, British, French and Soviet Zones

In 1943, the USA, Great Britain and the Soviet Union recognised the illegality of Austria's Nazi annexation and issued the Moscow Declaration which guaranteed a free Austria independent from Germany. This was enforced as early as 27 April 1945 under the new Austrian President Karl Renner, who from 1918 until 1920 had served as Austria's first chancellor and from 1931 to 1933 had taken on the Presidency of Austria's parliament. Paradoxically he had sought the annexation of Austria with Germany as early as 1919 and welcomed it in 1938, deciding that Nazism was just a passing phenomenon and no worse than the Dollfuß-Schuschnigg dictatorship that had removed him from his position in 1933. On 3 June 1945, only five weeks after the founding of Austria's Second Republic, the Vienna Philharmonic under Robert Fanta performed Mahler's *Resurrection* Symphony. The symbolism was powerful, though the reality was more bracing. Austria post-1945 was divided into four different zones, each with local administrations determined by the values and priorities of whichever of the allies was in control: France was stationed in the West, Great Britain in the South, America in the middle, and the Soviet Union in the East. Germany was similarly divided with the Soviets occupying what would become the German Democratic Republic in 1949 in the 'middle' of Germany, reaching into the North East; the British were in the North West, the French in the Rhineland and the United States in the central regions and South East. As with Berlin, Vienna was in the Soviet Sector, but divided between the four victorious powers with each power responsible for rebuilding, restoring utilities, medical treatment, education and the process of 'denazification'.

Music was not the top priority when the Allies took on the responsibilities of occupation and re-education. Much of the documentation related to the restructuring of music in the different zones has been lost. Though there is plenty of information regarding the denazification of high profile individuals such as Furtwängler or Winifred Wagner, there is little on the rank and file, and academics, as we shall see, were treated quite differently. Documentation from the British and American zones is largely lost, while documentation on individual denazification processes in the French zone remains classified.[3]

Nevertheless, music was an important element in re-education, and musical events were started in all sectors almost as soon as Nazi Germany had fallen. All four occupying powers were outwardly respectful of the importance of music in defining German identity, and all went in for varying degrees of undeclared cultural competition with one another. The view in Britain and the US was largely that Austro-German music had come to a standstill in 1933, the position that Adorno took in March 1945 when he spoke of the Nazi destruction of German culture in *What National Socialism Has Done to the Arts*. Certainly, the overwhelming number of important and high-profile musicians who had fled the country added considerable weight to this view.[4]

The French, who had been made to watch their musical heritage subordinated to German occupation from 1940, quickly mounted their own counter-cultural and ideological agendas. René Thimonnier, Head of the Bureau des Spectacles et de la Musique, had initially considered a ban on all music composed after 1933, but abandoned this as impractical when it became apparent that many composers who were not sympathetic to the former regime would also be affected. French music was introduced to the Germans, and the French saw themselves as sharing with their German neighbours a higher regard for music than either the British or the Americans. The French were also quick to recognise the role that music had played in confirming a Nazi belief of racial superiority and brought in concrete measures such as broadcasting guidelines to counter former Nazi propaganda.[5]

Censorship was practised in all the sectors, banning overtly political songs and music associated with the Nazi regime – not just blatant Nazi agitprop but also, at various times, core repertoire including Beethoven's *Eroica*, Siegfried's Funeral March from Wagner's *Götterdämmerung* or Strauss's *Ein Heldenleben*. The French went even further, placing temporary bans on German 'monumentalist' music and adding Bruckner to the list of banned composers alongside Strauss and Wagner.[6]

The Soviets saw music as a tool for shaping society. The Communists made a point of reclaiming high culture for the proletariat and were unwilling to see it exclusively reallocated to the bourgeoisie; as such, there were many musical events scheduled in the Soviet Zone – more so than in the others. Walter Ulbricht, the future First Secretary of the German Democratic Republic Communist Party, headed members of the so-called Ulbricht Group, made up of German political exiles returning from the Soviet Union. They were now employed as agents of the occupying Soviet forces and, having arrived in Berlin several weeks before the other Allies, the Ulbricht Group was able to establish a 'Cultural Federation for German Renewal'[7] (referred to as the

'Kulturbund'), which, though outwardly non-political, was run by the poet
Johannes R. Becher, who later supplied the text to Eisler's music for the
National Anthem of the GDR. Before this point however, music was not an
important feature of the Kulturbund and, indeed, did not even warrant a
mention in its manifesto.[8] As the Ulbricht Group did not have any musicians
among its members, it allowed music a degree of independence not accorded
to the visual arts, theatre and literature.[9] The Soviets were also the first to
reinstate broadcasting and were offering a full programme of music by June
1945. The greater musical dynamism within the Soviet Sector was also a
reflection of the musical pluralism permitted by the USSR during the later
war years: Communist ideologues would have to wait until émigrés such as
Hanns Eisler, Paul Dessau, Georg Knepler and Ernst Hermann Meyer returned
before translating musical policy into broader Marxist doctrine.

A problem encountered by all of the Allies was the high degree of
Nazification among the German musical elite. Most soloists and professors
had been obliged to join the Nazi Party, a situation that would lead to difficulties for a number of pianists, composers and scholars who were not remotely
sympathetic to the Nazi regime. Many had even seen their own compositions
banned as 'cultural Bolshevism' leaving them no option but to join the Nazi
Party in order to earn a living, at least as performers or teachers. Three of the
most intriguing of these were composers with highly individual views of
musical modernism. One was the Baltic German pianist Eduard Erdmann;
another was the Socialist composer Max Butting, who, despite his music being
banned, joined the Party in 1940; a third was the Schreker pupil, Felix Petyrek.
All had previously moved in progressive circles, with Erdmann a close friend
of the notorious anti-Nazi Ernst Krenek, the Jewish pianist Artur Schnabel
and the charismatic Australian violinist Alma Moody who had spent much of
her childhood mentored by Reger and later became Carl Flesch's favourite
pupil. Moody came to prominence as a champion of concertos by Pfitzner and
Krenek, and became the basis for the character Anita in Krenek's opera *Jonny
spielt auf*. These individuals were not only unsympathetic to the Nazi cause,
despite enforced party membership, they did not move in Nazi circles.
However, to overworked re-education officials, membership of the Nazi Party
– for whatever reason – was difficult to justify. Another headache was caused
by the composer Heinz Tiessen. Though he was a vehement anti-Nazi, a
former member of the 'November Group', denounced as a 'cultural Bolshevik',
and had performances of his music banned in 1933, he also served on the
jury of the Olympic Music Competition in 1936. Thiessen had been brought
in as the conspicuous dissenting voice to give an appearance of balance to
international critics. The paradox was that having been removed from various

positions, participation on the jury was one of his only sources of income, leaving him severely compromised following the defeat of Nazism. It goes without saying that he had never considered joining the Nazi Party, though incredibly they allowed him to remain composition professor at the Berlin Music Academy.[10]

In any case, the Americans had confiscated the Nazi membership index and were in a position to enforce the exclusion of all members of the party regardless of their personal sympathies. American blacklists were hastily drawn up and are often illegible. As the historian Toby Thacker writes in his summary of postwar musical life in Germany, *Music after Hitler*, it was 'draconian, inevitably arbitrary, and partial. It left hundreds of professional musicians out of work and facing an uncertain future.'[11] Denazification was accorded higher priority in the American sector than even reconstruction. It was carried out with a breathless zeal and penetrated into even the smallest of villages and communities. This intense denazification reached its peak in April 1946, when the names of 10,000 musicians, some extremely prestigious, were added to the American Information Control Division. They included the performers Wilhelm Kempff and Elisabeth Schwarzkopf, and the composers Johann Nepomuk David, Ernst von Dohnányi (father of the resistance hero Hans von Dohnányi, executed by the Nazis in 1945) and Wolfgang Fortner. The American hard-line policy could not be maintained, as many of the most famous musicians simply carried on performing in the French, British and Soviet Zones.

By January 1947, musicians were being cleared for performance in the American sector, though in March 1947, the composers David, Fortner, Richard Strauss and Carl Orff remained banned. Notwithstanding this American embargo, Strauss was accorded a hero's welcome when he visited London in 1947. It was slowly becoming apparent in all sectors that denazification in general wasn't working. It simply left too few competent and qualified professionals to re-build the devastated infrastructure of the country.[12]

If the Americans were unyielding, they had little to gain. They uniquely held the position that music had been used as a political weapon by Hitler's regime. By sticking to this belief, they forfeited any advantages that a rapid rehabilitation of blacklisted musicians would have brought among the German people and even missed the opportunity of positioning their clemency as an endorsement of their counter-Nazi cultural policies. The British by contrast were cynical and resigned, believing denazification to be largely pointless, while the French joined with the Germans in venerating artists and musicians to the point of forgiving all transgressions. It came down to the Russians as the most accepting of all in recognising the advantages of co-opting important musicians in the physical as well as cultural reconstruction and re-education of the Germans. The notorious Gustav Havemann, who had been responsible for hounding Schreker from his position at the Berlin Music Academy, testified to an 'anti-fascist' past and settled down within the Soviet Sector. As he had been an advocate of progressive, modernist music prior to the arrival of the Nazis, there was perhaps some foundation to this self-delusion. He had been cold-shouldered by the Nazis following his defence of Hindemith, despite years of purging Jews from any and every institution or event with which he was associated. Similarly, defence of Hindemith's opera *Mathis der Maler* in November 1934 had cost Furtwängler his position at the Reichsmusikkammer.

It quickly became apparent to even the most robust denazifier that it would take more than the personal distancing of individual musicians from the previous regime to restore legitimacy. Several additional changes were demanded. The most obvious was a return to programming composers whose works had been central repertoire before their banning from 1933. To these were added composers who had been removed during the course of the 'Totaler Krieg' including French, British and Russian composers who had joined the ranks of those the Nazis had already declared racially or politically 'degenerate'. As a result and following Hitler's downfall, performances of Tchaikovsky or Mahler conveyed to German audiences the same clear anti-Nazi statements. In the case of Mahler, as related by the writer Soma Morgenstern in his memoirs, most of his public had gone into exile or been murdered. Writing in the 1950s, he mentioned that though Mahler performances in Vienna before 1938 were sold out weeks in advance, he was depressed to discover on revisiting the city in 1957 that there was hardly anyone attending a performance of Mahler's 6th Symphony with the Vienna Philharmonic conducted by Dimitri Mitropoulos.[13] As a result, Mendelssohn, rather than Mahler and certainly more than Schoenberg, Zemlinsky or Schreker or indeed more than any other 'degenerate' composer, came to symbolise the newer post-1945 anti-Fascist Germany.

Despite Goebbels's professed belief that the Nazi government should support modernism, National Socialism was fixed in the minds of denazification officials as musically reactionary. As we have seen, this was not always the case: performances of a twelve-tone work such as Paul von Klenau's opera *Michael Kohlhaas* in Stuttgart in 1933, or *Die Windsbraut* by Winfried Zillig at Leipzig in 1941, were officially sanctioned.[14] Less controversial, but welcomed by the critic H. H. Stuckenschmidt, who had previously been a member of the 'November Group' and was close to the Schoenberg circle, was the opera *Die Wirtin von Pinsk* by Richard Mohaupt, first performed in

Dresden in 1938 before Mohaupt left Germany with his Jewish wife in 1939.[15] The pressures of rapid reconstruction and re-education meant that attitudes deemed anti-Fascist by the Allies were sufficient to help the vetting of many composers. This would set the tone for the musical avant-garde for the next two generations, when to call oneself 'modernist', or outwardly to support 'modernist' aims, became synonymous with making a declaration of anti-fascism in general and, more specifically, anti-Nazism.

Promoting modern music, particularly its less audience-friendly varieties, thus became a priority of postwar re-education. The Bavarian government brought back the composer Karl Amadeus Hartmann, who had spent the Hitler years in self-imposed internal exile, to conduct the new *Musica Viva* series at the Prinzregententheater, broadcast by Bavarian Radio. It was not a popular success, as he wrote to Egon Wellesz on 2 January 1948:

> Sadly new music is not much appreciated. The public thinks back with longing to the past twelve years: Art for the people! How nice that was: the tastes of the average-Joe were well catered for. It is because of this that someone with absolutely no artistic qualities such as Carl Orff was heaped with honours. Believe me, observing such things makes one despair of having to live amongst such people. We can only slowly build up circles and groups. At the moment, I have one that consists of only 250 people, but they're loyal and attend all events. It is for this group that I would ask permission to perform your [latest] quartet.[16]

The address that Hartmann gives for receipt of Wellesz's score is revealing: 'Music Control Section; Information Control Division, APO 407; US Army.' Given the fact that *Musica Viva* had been running since October 1945, it must have been frustrating to have taken more than two years to reach a mere 250 subscribers.

Even some of the most respected institutions of the postwar musical avant-garde, the summer courses in Darmstadt and the New Music Festival in Donaueschingen, are examples of modernism being used as an effective 'seal of approval' by the occupying Allies. Donaueschingen was in the French zone, and it was consistent with French cultural policies to leave its Nazi director, the former Schreker pupil Hugo Herrmann, in place when it restarted in the summer of 1946. This was despite the fact that Hermann had published an arrangement of the Nazi anthem, the *Horst Wessel Song*, as early as 1933 (along with various other Nazi songs for male chorus) before joining the party in 1939. The programmes offered during his post-Hitler tenure were hardly challenging. The occasional work by Shostakovich and Walter Piston leavened the fare of more or less the same composers featured since 1937, including forgotten names such as Joseph Haas, Ernst Lothar von Knorr, Ottmar Gerster, as well as Herrmann himself. All were highly compromised, many were party members, and Gerster had even made it onto Hitler's 'Chosen-by-God-List' compiled as a weapon of cultural propaganda in 1944.[17] This was too much for even the culturally tolerant French who closed it down until 1950 when it later reopened with a clear anti-Nazi and avant-garde agenda.[18]

The origins of the Darmstadt summer courses, located in the American Zone, are more obscure. Originally led by two composers on America's black-list, Wolfgang Fortner and Hermann Heiss, both emerged as vocal proponents of twelve-tone music after spending their years under the Third Reich composing propaganda marches and songs for the Hitlerjugend. At least in the case of Heiss, he could claim that before the rise of Hitler he had studied with both Josef Matthias Hauer and Arnold Schoenberg, thereby proving his legitimate entitlement to promote dodecaphony. They were joined by other composers and performers on the American blacklist such as Udo Dammert and Bruno Stürmer. Thacker in *Music after Hitler* speculates that they simply lied about their Nazi pasts when engaged to teach at Darmstadt, while American denazification officials were not really aware of what was being initiated.[19] In any case, by 1948 blacklisting had ended and the most tenacious American denazifiers had returned home. The Soviet Union and its Eastern bloc had been identified as a far more important concern than the remnants of Nazism left scattered across Germany and Austria.

The Beginning of the Cold War and a Change of Policy

It would not take long for it to dawn on American Intelligence officials that former Nazis, particularly those who had fought behind Soviet lines, would be useful in battling the rapidly spreading Soviet empire. The International Committee of the Red Cross, based in Geneva, had been issuing blank refugee passes to various organisations based in Rome and Genoa for legitimate humanitarian reasons. The Vatican's Pontificia Commissione di Assistenza, headed by the future Pope Paul VI, had been operating since 1944, ostensibly aiding refugees from Catholic countries. By the end of the war it was already assisting anti-Communists flee the Soviet Union.[20] Vatican committees were engaged in what they perceived as a re-Christianisation of Europe by providing refuge to fleeing Nazis, many of whom allowed themselves to be baptised or re-baptised into the Catholic faith before shipping off to South America.[21] All escaping Nazi criminals had to do was to reach Italy's ethnically Austro-German region of South Tyrol where they could be placed in safe houses, receive their documentation and new identities before continuing their journey. The Office of Strategic Services (OSS), the forerunner to the CIA, labelled these escape routes 'ratlines' and quickly recognised their intelligence potential, subsequently co-opting many war criminals, certain of their usefulness in the emerging Cold War.

This created a complex scenario: rehabilitated Nazi criminals and sympathisers placed in culturally sensitive positions allowed a shoring up of anti-Communist defences from the right while American intelligence services were co-opting liberal and progressive groups into an anti-Communist block on the left. That the CIA fronted any number of 'foundations' and charitable organisations supporting anti-Communist activities in the arts has been known since the disclosure of documents in 1967; their extent and long-term effects are less clear. Frances Stonor Saunders's *Who Paid the Piper* (1999) contends that artists participated in festivals and events with the express knowledge that they were demonstrating freedoms not enjoyed on the other side of the iron curtain. *The Mighty Wurlitzer* by Hugh Wilford, published in 2008, states that though some administrators in organisations such as the Fairfield Trust, the Ford Foundation and the Congress for Cultural Freedom (CCF) were aware of direct CIA support, most of the artists weren't; indeed, according to Wilford, even some of the senior staff of these organisations were unaware of where their money was coming from. Those who were trusted with information about the source of their funding were referred to in CIA parlance as 'witting'. The classification of 'witting' or 'unwitting' was used internally by the CIA in describing an organisation's head, and various artists.

The exceedingly 'witting' Nicolas Nabokov ran the CCF for some fifteen years and organised propaganda cultural events such as the festival *L'Art du XXe siècle* in Paris in 1952, and later the International Conference of Twentieth-Century Music in Rome, which also included a composition prize. The competition, according to Pierre Boulez, featured a 'folklore of mediocrity' nurtured by an obsession with the number twelve: 'a council of Twelve, a committee of Twelve, and Jury of Twelve' and of course focusing largely on twelve-tone music.[22] Stravinsky, a close Nabokov associate, headed the jury and had only recently taken up dodecaphonic composition himself. Boulez was not far off the mark. Writing in the *New York Herald Tribune* on 8 February 1953, Nabokov informed readers that 'we are going to have a composers' contest that is unlike any other competition ever held. Twelve young and promising but internationally unknown composers are to be invited to Rome, all expenses paid. Each will bring a score and these will be performed. . . . [A] special jury, democratically elected by all those attending the conference, will pick from these twelve a winning work. . . . First, there will be a cash prize; second, there will be a promise of performance by three major orchestras in Europe and three in America; third, the work will be published, and fourth, it will be recorded by a leading company.'[23] The composition prize was won by Lou Harrison.

As with Karl Amadeus Hartmann's plans, convincing the public was more of a challenge. In *The New Yorker*, the writer and feminist Susan Sontag's reaction had by 1987 become more considered: 'We were deferential – we knew we were supposed to appreciate ugly music; we listened devoutly to the Toch, the Krenek, the Hindemith, the Webern, the Schoenberg, whatever (we had strong stomachs).'[24] It was certainly not what was being performed in the USSR or the Communist Bloc, where artists did not have the freedom to perform or write 'ugly music' and it was this essential, but perhaps not so explicitly stated, point that anti-Communist propagandists were eager to make.

Whatever the artistic merits of the music coming out of postwar Rome, Darmstadt and Munich, it was most certainly not the Socialist Realism promoted behind the Iron Curtain. We return to Hanns Eisler's quote from 1950 with which we concluded Chapter 7; perhaps he was even anticipating Sontag's later appraisal: 'If modern – that is – serious art distances itself progressively from the broader masses, then it becomes progressively more cynical, decadent, nihilistic and formalistically isolated; monopoly-capitalism's cultural industry has always understood the masses. . . . "True" art becomes merely "merchandised" art.'[25] The capitalist West was certainly vulnerable on this front. Soviet cinema, ballet, classical music and theatre were not only widely available for the masses to enjoy, they maintained relatively high artistic values while remaining intellectually and artistically accessible to receptive audiences. It goes without saying however, that there was also a diet of bombastic Socialist Realism that the compliant citizens of the Eastern Block had to tolerate with varying degrees of appreciation and desperation, while secretly delighting in whatever light-weight American cinema and television could be accessed through an otherwise impenetrable 'iron curtain'. Assertions such as those made by Eisler that these mass-market offerings dulled the wits of consumers did not appear to dampen Eastern European enthusiasm. Still, one thing the CIA and the West could not really judge was how many creative artists from Communist Europe were longing for the freedom to write music that, according to Sontag, one needed a 'strong stomach' to appreciate.

The American arm of the CCF, known as the American Committee for Cultural Freedom, was aware of this and concentrated on organising tours to

Europe by America's most prestigious cultural organisations such as the Boston Symphony Orchestra and the Metropolitan Opera. They also began welcoming into the United States such tainted artists as Wilhelm Furtwängler and Herbert von Karajan. Wilford in his book on the CIA, and its means of infiltrating leftist non-Communist organisations and the arts, is more measured in his assessment of the CIA and music. He acknowledges that the CIA with its top people coming from Yale had a natural tendency to promote modern art and literature over 'serious' music. Jazz and popular music were supported but the American composers who represented an equivalent aesthetic development to, say, Jackson Pollock – such as John Cage and Milton Babbitt – seem to have been missing from CIA cultural planning.[26] Contradicting this, however, is the view of the German composer Konrad Boehmer in an interview with the *Süddeutsche Zeitung* from 30 November 2008 in which he states that the CIA was 'always in the background', specifically with those composers associated with Adorno's Cologne School. These included Stockhausen, Kagel and Bernd Alois Zimmermann.[27] Wilford's claim that the CIA was less interested in the musical avant-garde is disputed by Boehmer, who not only specifically mentions Cage in Darmstadt, but makes it clear that thanks to Adorno's influence with the CIA, and their specialist in psychological warfare, Michael Josselson, it was an open secret in the summer courses that they were involved to a significant degree.

Adorno's theory, taken much to heart by the CIA, was that 'emancipated art led to an emancipated society'. It was quite clear that neither art nor society behind the Iron Curtain were particularly 'emancipated', but music composed in the Soviet Bloc was still able to attract audiences to a degree that 'serious' composers in the West could not. Extrapolating other Adorno observations on music in modern society may have sat less comfortably with the capitalist West, such as his statement that 'society's resistance to music that represents such abused concepts as "Individualism", "artistry" and "the technically esoteric", are themselves manifestations of society and are to be corrected within society, rather than within music.'[28] Ultimately, Adorno seems to come to the same conclusion as his Communist colleague Eisler, as quoted above: 'Wahre Kunst wird zur Ware Kunst' – 'True art becomes merchandised art', with the German homophones for 'true' and 'merchandised' (*Wahre* and *Ware*) being put to especially effective use.

Consequences for the Banned

For composers who had been thrown out of Germany and Austria, the postwar environment was not very inviting. If former Nazis weren't in charge, then bug-eyed experimentalists were found attempting to rebuild a society amenable to the 'technically esoteric'. Neither was interested in re-establishing the careers of those forced into exile, though Sontag's quote which specifically mentions exiled composers highlights their revival as part of the allies re-education programme in the immediate decade following the war: Egon Wellesz's First Symphony was performed by the Berlin Philharmonic under Sergiu Celibidache in 1948, and the following year, his Second Symphony was given by the Vienna Symphony Orchestra conducted by Karl Rankl before being taken up by Adrian Boult and the BBC Symphony Orchestra in London. Boult and the BBC then commissioned the Third Symphony, which, as we shall see, never reached performance. Hans Gál's oratorio *De Profundis* was first performed in Wiesbaden in 1948; Ernst Toch's first two symphonies were given their premieres by the Vienna Symphony Orchestra in the early 1950s; Korngold's opera *Violanta* was recorded by Austrian Radio (RAVAG) in 1947 and his opera *Die Kathrin* had its premiere – postponed from 1938 – at the still bombed-out Staatsoper in 1949.[29] In 1955, Zemlinsky's *Der Kreidekreis*, the controversial run of which had taken place during the early Nazi years before being banned, was broadcast on Vienna Radio and was staged in Dortmund. Interest in composers banned by Hitler's Reich may have waned after its rapid postwar recovery, but it was maintained in fits and starts until 1960 when Winfried Zillig recorded Schreker's *Die Gezeichneten* for Austrian Radio, after which it more or less vanished altogether from scheduling.

Yet if former colleagues were carrying the torch for those composers they had known and respected from the interwar years, something else was happening with the younger generation and their supporters. A clear discrepancy seemed to be emerging between the positive response to a new work from the public and the vehemence of its subsequent dismissal by the press. Tonal works, especially by composers forced to flee Nazi Europe, were not welcomed by a new generation of critics and composers. As Pierre Boulez observed, 'we wanted everything [during the first years after the war], that was the context. Imagine a young German like Stockhausen discovering new music after twelve years of Nazi time. Can you imagine the desire to get out of that?'[30] It was a generation of angry youngsters who had watched helplessly as their parents' generation brutalised their cultural inheritance. For them, there was every incentive to distance their creative identities from their cultural roots. With the CIA taking Adorno's 'emancipation of culture' as meaning anything that would not be permitted under Communism, the scene was set for a shift away from the past, even if the past included composers who had always seen themselves as progressive. In the words of Berthold Goldschmidt: 'Suddenly, we were out of date!'[31]

Publishers

A practical consideration for many exiled composers was re-establishing ties with former publishers, and, in rarer cases, publishers re-establishing ties with composers. On 24 October 1946 Hans Gál received a letter from the young German composer Günter Raphael. He reminds Gál of having met in 1932, 'before the [Nazi] storm' at the Tonkünstler Festival in Zurich. Revealingly, he defines himself as 'half-Aryan' rather than the preferred Nazi designation of 'half-Jew' and explains that this meant that he was unable to work in Germany.[32] He mentions his connections with various publishers, something that piqued Gál's interest as a couple of weeks later, on 5 November, Raphael responded to inquiries regarding publishers in Leipzig. This is not only a fascinating source of information, but also a veritable time-capsule of feelings, thoughts and responses. Raphael begins with a run-down of publishers in Leipzig:

Breitkopf und Härtel was totally destroyed on 4 December 1943 – that is to say, the main building on Nürnberger Street was bombed right down to its foundations. The so-called fire-proof strong-boxes were strewn across the street and it took over a month and a half before they could be opened as sparks were still spitting out of the rubble. Once they could be opened, all of the valuable manuscripts were nothing but dust and ashes. However a number of their manuscripts along with their archive were evacuated and the publisher found a new location in the small Saxon town of Lausitz. Of the various editions, at least one copy was evacuated, but of course, only of those desirable, that is to say, *Aryan* composers. I wouldn't wish to guess if your violin concerto has by happenstance found its way into one of these piles of aryanised editions. I can only tell you that everything of mine is completely gone. (I had approximately forty-five works with Breitkopf und Härtel). . . . I haven't dared venture into the Russian Zone yet, though my flat with two grand pianos, an upright and a Baroque organ is in Meiningen in Thüringen and therefore in the Soviet Sector. (The Russians seem keen to have me and have offered professorships in Leipzig, Halle and Weimar but as long as they maintain their Zone frontiers, I shan't take a single step towards the East. I wish to remain free to go from one place to another). Well, anyway, that was Breitkopf in Leipzig. Dr [Hellmuth] von Hase has gone to Wiesbaden and is trying to set up an alternative head office of the business. . . . Dr von Hase is

compromised as he was a former member of the Nazi party and his brother
Martin is now supposed to run the company from Wiesbaden. New editions
are to be produced thanks to photo-mechanical means of reproduction. I've
seen what they intend to release in the first year, Classics, Romantics and
more Classics. They wouldn't so much as consider releasing any works by
contemporary composers. In any case, only Germans and Americans were
represented:[33] Pfitzner with his Op. 1 cello sonata, Hindemith with his Op. 8
cello works. Nobody gave Hans Gál, Paul Kletzki or me a single thought.
Now to Leuckart. Sander Junior [Horst Sander: 1904–45] fell in the last days
of the war in one of the battles around Leipzig. *De mortuis nihil nisi bene*[34]
Sander was a big Nazi. The publisher apparently was burnt right to the
ground. Who should now run it is unknown to me. Perhaps it will be merged
with Kistner und Siegel which is presently run by Dr Walter Lott. Perhaps it
will be taken over by Sander's other son [Erich] who is sitting with his family
and mother in Upper Bavaria (in the American Zone) from where he's presently managing their business affairs. I haven't heard anything about Simrock
yet. They have two of my chamber works. Peters Verlag is totally intact
(including the Peters Library). Walter Hinrichsen came back as a young
American lieutenant and reclaimed his father's property with his own hands.
Just as the Russians arrived, he disappeared in the American Sector and put
Dr [Johannes] Petschull (who also has Universal Edition) in charge. It's all
now run from Berlin. Peters doesn't deliver anything – actually, they haven't
for years now. The Russians are now taking all of C. G. Röder's printing
plates to Moscow . . . (along with all of the Peters printing plates and eight
complete local paper factories!). Are you by chance acquainted with Max
Hinrichsen?[35] . . . As we're on the subject of publishers, Schott has been given
a licence by the French – the Americans would never have issued one to
them since they published [one of Hitler's favourite marches] *Baden-Weiler
March*. It's now back in business despite the fact that the Mainz printing
presses are still not working. The offices in Weihergarten were hardly
damaged. There are no paper shortages in the French Sector (the best magazines are published there as well and enjoy huge print-runs). I'm working a
good deal with Willy Müller, a publisher in Heidelberg (Süddeutscher Musik
Verlag) who for years has been taking works by North German composers.
Now to [Karl] Straube and [Günther] Ramin: Straube has been through a lot,
but he's still alive. On the same infamous 4 December, he was bombed to
smithereens. His marvellous library however was stored in the cellar of the
Gewandhaus, which remained undamaged even if the actual building itself
was reduced to rubble (along with half of the Conservatory). Kippenberg's
wonderful collection of Goethe and Rilke etc. was also stored in the cellar.

Everything was saved. Straube who is now seventy-three years old admitted to our amazement that he had been a member of the Party since 1933! . . . Of course he has been relieved of all of his positions by the Russians (the Communists!).[36] Slowly however, he's regaining influence, especially in the field of church music. He's been able to return to giving organ lessons though I feel very sorry for him. It is unfathomable what could have possibly driven him to take the step of joining the Nazi Party. There were of course many exceptionally intelligent and cultivated people such as Straube who did the same. They believed that, by being members, they could raise the level of things. . . . This war had probably to be fought to the bitter end, if only to stop the myth of 'the greatest battle commander of all time being felled as a martyr for a just cause . . .' Ramin runs Leipzig's musical life: he's the Thomascantor (both the Thomaskirche[37] and the Nikolaikirche are still standing), he's conductor of the Bach Society and the Gewandhaus Chorus. Organist, harpsichordist etc. We also have, as of late, a new conductor of the Gewandhaus: Herbert Albert who used to be in Stuttgart. Abendroth left Leipzig in a dreadful sulk and has become an alderman for the Weimar 'Thüringer' local council and head of all music provision. His swastika would not have gone down well in the West! But perhaps he carried the red flag long before it had a swastika in the middle! This is also why I don't return to Middle-Germany [The Soviet Sector]: Everywhere you go, you meet the same old 'good' friends (even still in their same old uniforms) who look down on you.[38]

Gál was anxious about the fate of his works, as were nearly all of the composers of his generation who had signed agreements with German and Austrian publishers prior to 1933 and 1938. As early as 26 December 1946, Gál wrote to Universal Edition with a list of his works, asking what the state of the scores and material might be. He was primarily concerned about works that only existed in manuscript and for which he had no copies. It would have come as a great relief to Gál that UE had thought to take copies of almost everything it possessed which they then deposited in places of safety. The musicologist Thomas Gayda, while rummaging around in the UE Vienna archives in 1994, found scores by Berthold Goldschmidt that even the composer himself had thought to have been irretrievably lost. These included, among other things, his score of the *Passacaglia* for orchestra which won the Mendelssohn Prize in 1925, resulting in performances in 1926 by Erich Kleiber and the Berlin Staatskapelle. Gayda speculated that the location of the material, uncovered among various unrelated files, gave the distinct impression of someone actively hiding manuscripts of UE's non-Aryan composers.[39]

New Homelands, Lost Identities

How music was developing after the war was not only determined by what was still available from the ruins of publishing houses. Nor were developments being shaped only by an 'unwitting' younger generation manipulated by an unscrupulous CIA for propaganda purposes. There were at least two other crucial factors. One was the large number of former Nazis or those with strong Nazi sympathies still occupying senior cultural positions throughout Germany and Austria and deliberately hindering the remigration of former refugees. The other was the regular and frequent reluctance of host countries to accept immigrant-composers as their own.

In the rare instances when previously established composers from Germany and Austria were successful in their newly acquired homelands, it was, as highlighted in the previous chapter, the result of a monumental effort of reinvention such as Kurt Weill's Broadway style with a Berlin edge, Korngold importing Viennese opulence to Hollywood, or Joseph Kosma incorporating echoes of Jewish Budapest into postwar French chanson. Composers who had not managed to establish themselves in Austria or Germany, often because they were too young at the time of their emigration, managed to integrate more easily. Many of these younger immigrants were successful: André Previn and Lukas Foss in the USA, or Joseph Horovitz, Franz Reizenstein, Alexander Goehr and Mátyás Seiber in England. By and large, however, established émigré composers were side-lined and ended up teaching, working for broadcasters and publishers or composing and conducting stock-scores for film, television and radio. Often, as was the case with Ernst Toch, an appearance of acceptance came thanks to performances by fellow émigré conductors and their American orchestras in Cleveland, Boston, Los Angeles and Pittsburgh. Toch's Third Symphony even won the Pulitzer Prize, and its recording with William Steinberg and the Pittsburgh Symphony Orchestra won a Grammy. However, with Toch's death in 1964, performances came to an end. With the death of his generation of performers, no American-born musicians championed him. It was for Toch and many others just as Krenek had written: a sobering confrontation with the utter 'echolessness' that their music generated in the wide, innocent spaces of America.

But if Americans found most European music not to be worth the extra effort, the British closed their minds to German music altogether. Such had been the case since the First World War and no amount of interwar goodwill had changed this view. Adrian Boult's commission of Egon Wellesz's Third Symphony for BBC Symphony Orchestra never saw the light of day. Wellesz wrote to his daughter: 'For the last year, I've had much aggravation surrounding my intended performance at the BBC. The manager of the orchestra who only likes French music has cancelled not only the performance of my Third Symphony, which Boult wished to conduct, but also (!!) that of *Prospero*.'[40] Boult was visibly annoyed, though his letters to BBC officials on the matter are spineless. In May 1952 he wrote first to the BBC's Third Programme scheduler Eric Warr, commenting that Egon Wellesz 'tells me that there are now a number of eminent composers whose work is no longer submitted to the [vetting] Panel [of the BBC] . . . he is now a British subject.'[41] In October he wrote to Leonard Isaacs, head of music for the Third Programme, that Wellesz had informed him that his Third Symphony had been rejected by the BBC panel. He goes on to write: 'I need hardly say I have offered again to do the Second Symphony if at any time you feel you could arrange this. Please do not bother to answer.'[42]

The Arts Council Opera Competition was another reality check for émigré composers. Lewis Foreman has described it as 'a classic British funding cock-up'.[43] The object was to promote the composition of a new opera in English which, despite a short notification period, would be performed during the Festival in Britain starting in May 1951. The Arts Council announced the competition in February 1949 and, as Foreman writes, under a Labour Government it would have been largely expected that such an event sponsored by the public purse would result in performances, especially given that the national jamboree celebrations of the Festival of Britain were in sight. This would have specifically been the expectation of the refugees from pre-Nazi Germany and Austria who wished to participate. In postwar Britain, they saw themselves as some of the most experienced composers in the country. The response to the competition was greater than expected, with 117 anonymous submissions. It's possible today to see that even at this early stage of the competition many of Britain's leading native-born composers had submitted outlines. These included such figures as Malcolm Arnold, Albert Coates, Cyril Scott and Bernard Stevens. Egon Wellesz was one of the many refugee composers who also entered with an opera based on Congreve called *Incognito*. Following these submissions, the judges shortlisted three operas. To their alarm, they discovered that they had chosen three composers who were not native born. These were the Australian Arthur Benjamin with *A Tale of Two Cities*, the German Berthold Goldschmidt with *Beatrice Cenci*, and the Austrian Karl Rankl, with *Deirdre of the Sorrows*. At that time, Rankl was music director at Royal Opera House, Covent Garden, and in charge of rebuilding the orchestra and ensemble of the war-damaged company. Eric Walter White, who had dreamt up the idea of the competition, wrote to the Chairman of the Arts Council, Stewart Wilson: 'In some ways I think it may be desirable for us to give publicity to the commissioned operas as soon as possible; but I realize that if there is to be a fourth commissioned opera and its composer happens to have an English name, it may be preferable to hold up press publicity until we can include him as well as the three composers mentioned above.'[44] As events unfolded, the operas were all behind schedule and were not completed in time for the Festival of Britain, dashing the original hopes of the organisers. The English operas scheduled for the Festival were hardly encouraging. Vaughan Williams's *A Pilgrim's Progress* was mounted at the Royal Opera House in April 1951 and was the only one to have shown any potential durability, thanks in part to the existing reputation of the composer. Even Britten's *Billy Budd*, now considered one of his greatest works, when presented in its original four-act incarnation, was not mounted until December 1951. With its all-male cast and glimmers of homo-eroticism (naïvely un-noticed by contemporary grandee assessors), it was not viewed as mainstream. By 1951 the Labour Government had been toppled and any expectations of publicly funded performances had collapsed with it. With the lack of home-grown talent in the final competition line-up, additional operas were included by Alan Bush with *Wat Tyler* and Lennox Berkeley with *Nelson*.

As productions could not be mounted, the commissioning fee of £300 was paid and attempts were made to secure broadcasts of the winning entries. Rankl and Benjamin were opposed to this as they saw broadcasting as an inadequate means of introducing a new stage work. Bush and Goldschmidt agreed and their scores were passed to the panel headed by Leonard Isaacs at the BBC. The panel consisted of Benjamin Frankel, William Alwyn and Gordon Jacob, all of whom gave fairly negative assessments to Goldschmidt's *Beatrice Cenci*. In general, the panel members objected to the subject matter though they had more positive things to say about the music. Frankel, himself the son of Polish Jewish emigrants, makes the rather bizarre point that 'the implication of the incestuous episode in the prelude to Act II is too obvious and painstakingly German a device to be dramatically effective and remains merely repellent.' Alwyn is, 'dubious whether two hours of unrelieved gloom is suitable for broadcasting.' Gordon Jacob ducks a decision and seconds Alwyn, but admits that there is much within the work that one can admire. Rudolf Bing, general manager of the Metropolitan Opera in New York, while not on the panel, was quite taken with *Beatrice Cenci*. Bing had been manager of Glyndebourne when the company's guest performance of *Macbeth* at the first year of the Edinburgh Festival had been thrown into doubt after George Szell's unexpected departure. Goldschmidt was called in to rescue the performances and was praised by public and press alike. Bing, who probably felt he owed Goldschmidt some support, wrote to John Denison of the Arts Council:

The particular purpose of this letter is to implore you to rack your brains and see if there is anything you can do for Berthold Goldschmidt. I personally think that his *Beatrice Cenci* is really a very fine opera and I would love to do it here, but cannot for the simple reason that a new production of this sort would cost $60,000 and I could not, with the attitude of the New York public towards contemporary works, hope for more than three performances. . . . Even *Peter Grimes*, although by a composer well-known here, had not more than four or five performances with diminishing and shocking box office results.[45]

Sadler's Wells also rejected the work for a similar reason to the BBC panel: its plot about incest and the murder of the sadistic Count Cenci carried out by his daughter Beatrice and her step-mother Lucrezia.

That *Beatrice Cenci* should be a cause for moral concern seems astonishing. The libretto, adapted by the Viennese refugee Martin Esslin, was based on a historic event that Percy Bysshe Shelley had turned into a dramatic poem as long ago as 1819. That Shelley's *The Cenci* was a classic made it no more acceptable to British opera managers who – until 1968 – had to present new works to the Lord Chamberlain for approval before any public performance. It was eventually agreed that a sequence of excerpts could be broadcast as compensation. Whether such muddling was the result of anti-German prejudice, or just a funding 'cock-up' as Foreman believes, is difficult to say. Had time not been wasted expanding the remit to include a native candidate, things may have turned out differently. Following concert performances of the work during the 1994 Berlin Festival, *Beatrice Cenci* was eventually recorded by Sony, finally giving listeners a chance to assess the work. It shows how far Goldschmidt had travelled from his edgy style in prewar Berlin. It's full of counterpoint (a quibble highlighted by William Alwyn in his assessment), but also full of an abundant tunefulness that was clearly meant to appeal to British audiences. Rankl's opera *Deirdre of the Sorrows* was withdrawn, and scores and orchestral material were on the verge of being pulped by Oxford University Press's music department before Foreman rescued enough for a broadcast of excerpts in October 1995. The score and remaining performance material is preserved in the archive of the Music University in Graz.

Some seventy composers landed in the UK and each had an individual story. The only consistent narrative that emerges from all the various host countries is that of the composer trying to recapture the resonance enjoyed prior to the arrival of the Nazis. Some tried as hard as they could to gain local acceptance before giving up composing altogether. In Goldschmidt's case, the silence lasted for a quarter of a century until he was persuaded to compose a

Clarinet Quartet in 1983, at the age of 80. While Toch, following his departure from Hollywood's film studios and a heart attack in 1948, reacted by embarking on a composing binge.

The Austro-German 'Exile Symphony'

Toch, Wellesz and Korngold all felt an inner drive to compose a symphony despite the fact that they had shown scant interest in the medium before. Wellesz was first off the mark and his *Prosperos Beschwörungen*, completed in 1936 and based on Shakespeare's *Tempest*, was an attempt to create a symphony using the Mahlerian means of sequencing tone-poems into a coherent symphonic narrative. The thematic ideas of his First Symphony came exactly ten years later while he was walking in England's Lake District, an area that reminded him of Austria's countryside. He went on to compose nine symphonies along with a monumental *Symphonic Epilogue*.

Toch completed his First Symphony in 1949, first performed in 1950 by the Vienna Symphony Orchestra under Herbert Häfner. His Second Symphony (there would be six altogether) followed the next year. Toch, like Korngold, had left the studios at the first possible opportunity once the war was over. He continued teaching until a heart attack in 1948 reminded him that he was not immortal. The compositional frenzy that he unleashed was unprecedented. Even in his heyday in Weimar Germany Toch had not turned out works at the rate of Krenek, Weill, Milhaud or Hindemith. After his heart attack, music poured out of him. By his own admission, it was more important to write down all that churned up inside, than to evaluate innate quality.[46] As a result, the works from this period often seem both vivid and slapdash. There is a desperation about some of them suggesting an attempt to recapture an elusive prewar brilliance.

Toch's prewar reputation – and the fact that he wasn't the son of the detested Julius Korngold and hadn't made such a conspicuous name for himself in Hollywood – led to support from the same refugee conductors who went to great lengths to distance themselves from Erich Korngold.

Yet Korngold's Symphony in F Sharp Op. 40, completed in 1952, was by any measure a strong work. It was given its premiere by Harold Byrns and the Vienna Symphony Orchestra in an under-rehearsed broadcast for Austrian Radio in 1954 that left Korngold so depressed that he requested that the tapes be wiped. The sloppiness of the performance was felt by Korngold to be overt belligerence aimed at himself and his musical values, and he was probably right. Though it does include quotations from some of his film scores, the Symphony also distances Korngold from his Hollywood years. Critics and public were baffled and ultimately left cold. This was not the nostalgic Korngold they knew before the war that since the early 1930s had remained preserved in a jar of Hollywood schmaltz. For the musical press on the other hand, it simply wasn't an appropriate reaction to the harder-edged, postwar world. Korngold's Hollywood past had tainted any objective appraisal of his work. Attempts to have it performed by colleagues who had worked with him before the Nazi years, were met with polite but chilly dismissals. The letters from the offices of Bruno Walter, Fritz Reiner, William Steinberg and others make depressing reading. This would be Korngold's only symphony and was his last work of note.[47]

Why did so many of these refugee composers even chose to write something as apparently outmoded as a symphony? The form was redolent of the 'Old German' school of Leipzig, and the composers who ended up as refugees though sympathetic with 'Old German' values, were not visibly drawn to its classical models. Mahler had changed the entire symphonic ideal, and Shostakovich was showing that the episodic model of symphonic writing was something that was exportable and not uniquely bound to the German tradition. Despite the symphonies of such important émigré composers as Korngold, Toch, Gál, Wellesz, Rathaus, Weigl, Karl Rankl[48] and many others, Germany and Austria had essentially abdicated the symphony in favour of the Slavs, the Scandinavians and even the Americans and British. Franz Schmidt was the last of the traditional Austrian symphonists from the years before Austria's annexation by Germany. Émigré composers on the other hand appeared duty-bound to reassert their native entitlement to a form that had emerged from the same cultural environment as themselves. The Austro-German 'exile symphony' deserves a special place in twentieth-century musical history: its content cannot be disassociated from the circumstances under which it was composed.

Nazi Resistance

New musical developments in Europe were not simply the result of a reaction to Nazi atrocities, or covert indoctrination meted out to a group of intellectuals and artists too international to be susceptible to jingoistic anti-Communist propaganda. Equally potent – and equally frustrating for once prominent composers and academics living in exile – was the haphazard denazification process in the music business and academic institutions. The letter from Einstein to Gál (quoted at the head of this chapter) relating Robert Haas's desperate search for recommendations from former Jewish colleagues followed an earlier letter of 1 January 1946 in which he wrote the following:

Have you heard that Robert Haas, *the man of many smells* [written in English] has either returned, or is still sitting with all the dignity and honour that befits his former position, and today is now one of the mightiest beasts in the jungle? The 'three Kings from the East' (or the West) made one of their biggest ever mistakes when they decided not leave 'Ostmark' as part of the Third Reich.[49] The Austrians would certainly have earned such treatment![50]

That Haas was later removed from his position as Director of the Music Collection at the Austrian National Library and editor of the Bruckner Edition was some consolation, but it was hardly a significant step forward. Nowak, unlike Haas, had not been a vocal supporter of the Nazi Regime but was made to carry out Haas's bidding as necessary. This certainly did not look promising as a return to the central position Berlin and Vienna once held in musical scholarship. Wellesz had been removed from the University of Vienna after 1938, and though he was able to maintain a respectable profile with a lectureship at Lincoln College Oxford, he wanted to return to his former professorship in Vienna. With the death of Adler in 1941, he would certainly have been a leading candidate to take over Adler's Institute. Since Adler's death occurred while Austria was annexed, this meant that his Jewish pupils were unable to participate in the development of one of the most respected musicological institutions in the world. Instead, Erich Schenk, the Salzburg-born head of the musicological institute in Rostock, was brought to Vienna in 1940 by Robert Lach, another Adler pupil who had taken over Adler's professorship of comparative musicology in 1927. Schenk moved in quickly. He maintained that he protected the elderly Adler and his daughter from deportation by the Nazis until Adler Sr's death in 1941. He fooled no one: Wellesz sent an open letter in English to a number of important musicologists and members of the ISCM. It is undated but presumably sent sometime in 1946. The correspondence from Rudolf von Ficker to which it refers is dated 28 May 1945:

More than a year ago a letter from an old friend of mind, and former colleague at the University of Vienna, Professor Rudolf von Ficker, brought me news of Miss Melanie (Mely) Adler, daughter of our former teacher, Hofrat Professor Dr. Guido Adler, Honorary President of the International Musicological Society. Professor Ficker occupied the Chair of Musicology in Munich from about 1930. He was known as a strong anti-Nazi. Miss Adler had also lived in Munich and was an intimate friend of Professor Ficker and his wife. [Professor Ficker's account follows] When Professor Adler, who was a Jew, was dying at the age of eighty-six in 1941 in Vienna the Gestapo wanted to turn him out of his house. His daughter, who nursed him, appealed to Professor Schenk, *Ordinarius der Musikgeschichte*, for help. Whether through his intervention or not, the Gestapo stopped their proceedings, and Adler died in his house. Miss Adler wrote a letter to Schenk thanking him for his help and asking him if he could help her to get to Italy to her relations. . . . The next evidence comes from letters which she wrote to Professor Ficker asking him to help her. As the price for his help Schenk demanded Adler's library. Miss Adler refused to part with it. At this point the Gestapo summoned her, threatening her with deportation, and members of the Musikhistorische Institute of the University of Vienna [Robert Haas and Leopold Nowak[51]] searched the library for autographs. Professor Ficker acted quickly and got the Public Library of Munich to offer Miss Adler a good price for the library and the guarantee of personal safety. The sale was prevented by Schenk, who said that such a valuable collection ought not to leave Austria.[52] His intervention did not affect the library alone. It deprived Miss Adler of the opportunity of obtaining the guarantee of safety. The key of the library was taken away, and the threats of the Gestapo increased. Professor Ficker got no further letters from Miss Adler, and at last went to Vienna and saw Professor Schenk. He saw Adler's library, stored at the Institute.[53]

The denazification hearing of Schenk – a result of von Ficker's efforts – was farcical. Schenk produced the letter from Melanie Adler thanking him for saving her father from the Nazis. Ficker, who was close to Adler's daughter wrote to Wellesz on 1 September 1947 explaining how she showed him the letter she had obtained from Schenk: 'A copy of the statement given by Schenk was shown to me by Mely sometime during the early part of March 1941. How it began will stay with me forever, it started: "Though it disgusts me having to deal with a Jew . . ."'[54] Ficker went on to explain to Wellesz that the guarantee of Adler's safety was given by Baldur von Schirach, Gauleiter of Vienna, at the request of his cultural advisor Dr Thomas who had been beset by pleas from former Adler pupils. All of this information was of no consequence. Schenk remained in his position until 1971, and Wellesz was not invited to return to his former post in Vienna. Schenk was supported by a network of former Nazi supporters and in a relatively small country such as Austria, this kind of protection was easily acquired and reciprocated. But Schenk's influence reduced Vienna's reputation for musicology to a trace of what it had once been. He had made a name for himself with a popular Mozart biography and furiously denied young musicologists any chance of researching the contributions of Jewish composers prior to the Nazi arrival in Austria in 1938. Accounts of his refusal to countenance doctorates on Mahler were legion, and even made it into the local papers with one relating the thwarted attempts by the Canadian Timothy Vernon. Schenk told him 'to forget the idea. He was a Jew'.[55] Schenk's comment to the young composer Gösta Neuwirth, when he expressed his intention to write a dissertation on Schreker, is now notorious: 'There's no chance of anyone writing a dissertation about Jews under my supervision!'[56] Charges continued to be brought against him until 1967, all of which he saw off with the disdain – and the confidence, of someone who knew where skeletons were buried. All this was grossly disheartening to Austrian musicians and composers still living in exile.

Einstein summed up the situation to Gál in another letter from 15 February 1947: 'It's perfectly understandable to me that you should dismiss tempting invitations from Salzburg and Vienna – such siren songs have lost all appeal to those such as us. Even I wouldn't wish to find myself in the position of not offering my hand or greetings to colleagues who tell me that at the time they "never really believed any of that nonsense".'[57] Einstein was as good as his word. In 1949 he refused an invitation by the Freie Universität in West Berlin and rejected the Golden Mozart Medal awarded by the Mozarteum Foundation in Salzburg.

Einstein's remarks about not wanting to greet or shake the hands of former Nazis who later claimed not really to have 'believed any of it', finds an echo in an experience Gál had when he received a letter from Heinz Tietjen, dated 23 August 1951. Tietjen was the man who had mounted *Die Heilige Ente* in Berlin and Breslau in the 1920s. Under the Nazi dictatorship he became one of the most influential managers in theatre and opera, when Göring appointed him – along with Gustaf Gründgens (on whom Klaus Mann based his novel *Mephisto*) –as cultural advisor on the Prussian State Council in 1936, and general director of the Prussian State Theatre. This was followed by taking over effective management, with Winifred Wagner, of the Bayreuth Festival until 1944. Even as the most powerful theatre manager in pre-Nazi Germany, he approved of the closure of Berlin's bankrupt Kroll Opera in 1931, which the Nazis had branded a 'cultural institution of Reds and Jews.' Upon his appointment by Göring he promptly dismissed 27 non-Aryan employees and tore up contracts with Jewish performers. As with Gründgens, he was reprimanded after the war for 'behaving opportunistically' and yet was also allowed to take on the directorship of Berlin's Municipal Opera, the renamed Deutsche Oper. In 1951, he was made head of the Berlin Festival and from 1954, director of the Hamburg Opera. In his friendly letter to Gál, Tietjen reminds him that he's just been in London directing *Parsifal* and *Meistersinger* at Covent Garden, conducted by his 'old friend from former Berlin days', Sir Thomas Beecham.[58] Beecham's position vis-à-vis the Nazis has long been contentious. He continued to conduct in Nazi Germany until virtually the declaration of war, whereupon he quit England and did not return until 1944.[59] It must have been deeply disillusioning for someone like Gál, living in exile in Edinburgh seeing a slippery operator like Tietjen carrying on as if nothing had changed.

Georg Szell wrote to Gál (in English) on 15 October 1942: 'All the relatives of Lene including her old mother have been deported to Poland as far as we know, her two sons are living with their father in occupied France – of course we have had no news from them for years and can only hope they have not been deported. All the people we used to know in Prague have been deported, including women of eighty years – isn't it a beautiful world we live in? No matter what happens after the war, no punishment can be equal to these crimes.'[60] Then again on 30 May 1946 (this time in German), Szell wrote: 'My parents were deported from Nice in the autumn of 1943, first into the notorious camp at Drancy. From there, we lost track. I hope they didn't have to suffer too much.'[61] This is followed by another letter on 14 July 1946:

We are in receipt of much news from Europe but every letter is so filled with gruesome things that both Lene and I start to shake the moment we spot a European postmark. In addition, I've been able to speak with friends who in recent weeks have been travelling in Europe and what they report *is not too pretty* [in English]. In addition to all of these things, I've received invitations to conduct in Salzburg in August and in September to conduct concerts in Vienna. Naturally I've refused without giving it so much as a second thought. Also ... I have quite enough to do here. I've just had eight concerts in Chicago, and next week I have three further performances in Philadelphia. . . . I haven't the slightest sense of nostalgia for my former corner of the world.[62]

If Germany dealt with its denazification more efficiently than Austria, Austria had specific problems of its own. The anti-Nazi, clerical, Austro-Fascist government from 1933 to 1938 was essentially a right-wing dictatorship. Despite the leading role the Catholic Church played within this government, it had many Jewish supporters. Today, we are inclined to see Hitler and Stalin as the embodiment of either a right-wing or left-wing dictatorship. But to many who lived through this period, their regimes seemed identical. The National Socialism of Hitler and the Communism of Stalin were both centralist-authoritarian and invested heavily in their respective domestic economies. They could only afford to carry out such policies by confiscating the personal wealth of easily isolated groups. To the Soviets, it was middle-class professionals and land-owning farmers; and to the Nazis, it was the Jews. Both were essentially anti-social forms of Socialism, and their political capital was guaranteed by the support of the disenfranchised class of the working poor, the unemployed and the unemployable, duped by endless streams of mendacious propaganda. To anyone who saw the individual as the building block of society, there was virtually no difference between the two ideologies.

What this meant to Austrians after 1945 was a return of many right-wing political refugees who had gone into exile as supporters of the Austro-Fascist state. Competition for positions in institutions after 1945 was often between returning Jews and returning political exiles of either the extreme anti-Nazi right or the extreme left. As Germany did not have a period of anti-Nazi fascist government prior to Hitler, it did not experience the remigration of returning anti-Nazi fascist-supporters after 1945. Despite highly placed Communists and Social Democrats in the post-1945 Viennese municipal government, the Republic of Austria was less sympathetic to returning left-wing refugees than it was to those from the right. Its sympathy for returning Jews of any political persuasion was altogether more erratic. The new president of Austria, Karl Renner, had declared that claims by Jews against the state should be kicked as far as possible into the long grass.[63]

Hanns Eisler would have preferred to find work in Vienna rather than relocating to East Germany; but he was further handicapped by his close Schoenbergian connections. Affiliations among returning refugee musicians were not easy to untangle. The Jewish composer Marcel Rubin was a pupil of Franz Schmidt and thus no supporter of Schoenberg. He escaped to France before finding refuge in Mexico. He returned to Austria in 1947. As an anti-Schoenberg Communist, he found himself more welcome in Vienna than two Jewish Schoenberg disciples from different ends of the political spectrum: Wellesz, who had supported the Austro-fascist regime, and Eisler, who was Communist.

Schoenberg's near-fatal heart attack in 1946 was an additional reason for him not to return to Vienna. The new family he had started with his second wife Gertude Kolisch had settled in and gone native in California. Children born in America had no desire to leave friends and return to the ruins of the country that had thrown out their parents. It no doubt suited Vienna's musical establishment, led by Joseph Marx (who from 1938 to 1945 had enjoyed the status of being the Ostmark's most frequently performed living composer), not to give any encouragement to Schoenberg or his followers.[64]

Egon Kornauth was a Schreker pupil, who, together with Marx, led the committee that awarded the postwar Austrian State Prize for Music. Kornauth wrote to Marx on 4 May 1957: 'I completely agree with you and . . . wish to confirm that with full conviction, I would propose Dr Hans Gál so that we make sure that people who receive this prize write genuine music with imagination and skill which a normal listener with normal ears can appreciate – someone who can show a true lifetime's work – all of which is the case [with Dr Gál] (otherwise, we'll soon be swamped by masses of twelve-tone tinkerers).'[65] Marx's only conceivable objection to Gál receiving the prize had been expressed in a statement he had made regarding the prize in 1953, when he suggested that being in exile (or 'living abroad' as he put it) was grounds for being denied the prize, should it be deemed that a composer had 'lost their sense of being Austrian while profiting from all of the advantages and opportunities that working in foreign countries provided'.[66] Korngold was not proposed for this reason – 'He's earned enough money in Hollywood already!' as Kornauth wrote to Marx on 9 May1956.[67] Gál, on the other hand, was praised by both Marx and Kornauth as being an Austrian composer 'living abroad' who did not give a false impression of musical life in Austria with 'all of that atonal and twelve-tone fiddling about'. Kornauth went on to hope that the following year they could award the prize to someone who actually lived in Austria.[68] It would take Kornauth's death in 1959 before Krenek, Wellesz and other, more progressive voices would be recognised. Obviously, Schoenberg and anyone connected with his school were unwelcome.

The political jostling between former Nazis who refused to budge from the positions bestowed upon them with the departure of Jewish colleagues made life both stressful and traumatic for returning composers, performers and academics. But duplicity and mendacity were not limited to the men and women encountered in the course of trying to return to a pre-Hitler existence. Korngold's publisher Schott had earned enormous sums from composers banned by the Third Reich and had every motivation to resist Nazi efforts and intervene in cultural policy. Instead, Schott went over to the other side – while writing cringing letters to its 'non-Aryan' composers such as Korngold, Toch and Gál. Both the Strecker brothers were sympathetic to National Socialism, and Ludwig was assumed to be a member of the party,[69] while his brother Willy had written to Stravinsky in April 1933: 'This movement has so much that is healthy and positive about it . . . a welcome cleaning-up has been undertaken . . . in an attempt to restore decency and order.'[70]

It was a perfect storm that now raged against Jewish composers, who, having been banned by Hitler and his odious Thousand-Year Reich, found themselves unwelcome in their former homes, and only reluctantly accepted in their new ones. The ravages of war left Germany needing every capable pair of hands available to rebuild its devastated infrastructure and to establish stability in the middle of a very unsettled Europe. Apart from efforts by the Americans, the removal of former Nazis from cultural positions was not a high priority for any of the occupying forces. The other three occupying powers had decided that music was so close to the German psyche that it was important to guarantee its seamless continuity, which they saw as extending from 1945 rather than 1933. It appeared a harmless trade-off against ridding the country of Nazis in more sensitive positions.

The Cold War polarised matters even further. The continuity of tradition and craftsmanship that had been so important to Jewish composers in their journey to becoming German composers had been cut off, and this isolated them even further. As the decades rolled past, it became ever more apparent that the gratitude felt by refugee musicians and composers was not reciprocated by their host countries. Britain was no more inclined to view Goldschmidt and Wellesz as British composers than America was to treat Hindemith and Toch as Americans. With many managers, directors, conductors, and performers sharing the refugee experience with émigré composers, their works continued to enjoy performances for as long as this generation remained active. But as these individuals began to die out, performances became rarer. They were no longer seen as former refugees but as dinosaurs from Germany's age of Utilitarianism, composing reams of *Gebrauchsmusik*, as all German and Austrian interwar music was disingenuously classified. They were considered as having nothing of interest to say compared with the daring experiments of younger composers. New music in the West was intellectually challenging and was meant to discomfort listeners. Not to embrace it was to be aligned with the reactionary forces of the past. As Adorno wrote: 'It doesn't even occur to anyone to compose music like [Dietrich von] Bausznern and [Siegmund von] Hausegger, or like Georg Schumann and Max Trapp – even less does it occur to anyone to play these monstrosities in concert. The conviction of such musical rhetoric doesn't merit opposition and even their natural habitats have not remained unaffected.'[71] For a generation of angry young European composers, it was too easy to see any and every composer from the previous generation as tainted.

The final dilemma facing émigré musicians was whether to return to their former homes in Austria and Germany. It was far from certain that they would be allowed to make a worthwhile contribution. In Austria, at least, little or no effort was made to restore returning musicians to their previous posts. Over the intervening twelve years, lives had moved on, and there was a legitimate suspicion that even if they returned, they would not be wanted – and even the chilling realisation that they had perhaps never been wanted. This pain was not just the result of injustices and deep personal losses, but grew out of the recognition that generations of German and Austrian Jewish musicians and composers had imagined themselves to be equal celebrants in the greater Germanic cultural pageant. The composer Erich Zeisl writing to his old friend, the author Hilde Spiel, expressed this frustrated anger succinctly in a letter dated 17 May 1946:

Dear Hilde! I can't tell you how excited Trude and I were upon receiving your letter. To be back in Vienna, yet wearing the uniform of a British soldier! I simply can't imagine how you could bare it – I'm sure I would shake with such a force that I would simply topple over dead. It will take a long time before we've managed to come around to things . . . [and] it will be ages before we can bring ourselves to return to Vienna: both parents gone! Those slimy Viennese! *Pfui*! They can all go to hell![72]

Erich Korngold's response is more intriguing. Few composers would have felt themselves to have been so defeated by postwar developments. Following his heart attack in 1947, Korngold escaped into the world of Viennese melancholy with an operetta somewhat appropriately called *Die Stumme Serenade* or *The Silent Serenade*, completed in 1950. Like his earlier opera *Das Wunder der Heliane*, it was wholesale retreat into the past, but Korngold didn't seem to care. If Toch's heart attack had generated an outpouring of compositional energy, in Korngold's case it resulted in an increasingly sullen isolation. Following Korngold's death in 1957, the letters of rejection sent to his wife are both moving and coldly dismissive. Hal Wallace, a producer at Warner Bros, offered 20 dollars to a Korngold Foundation, in a dictated letter typed on internal memo paper. RCA rejected a memorial recording; Rudolf Bing twisted himself into knots to explain why he could not mount *Die Kathrin* at the Metropolitan opera; and conductor after conductor rejected the Symphony in F sharp. Most of the letters are from the offices of former friends, now prominent musicians, and are often signed by secretaries sending dictated replies in English. Even letters from such formerly close colleagues as Paul Wittgenstein spoke only vaguely of their collaboration, and 'how long ago it all was' with more than a whiff of embarrassment.[73]

Yet one of the most surprising items among the Korngold papers at the Library of Congress is a letter dated 14 January 1942 from the Assembly for a Democratic Austria, which is incensed to find that Korngold had been donating money to a monarchist committee supported by Otto von Habsburg. As it happened, they could not have known that Korngold was also giving money to Socialists, Communists, Christian Democrats, organisations founded to help feed Austria's starving children, and another that had sent him a self-important proclamation from Zurich in dense legal German (which he most certainly did not bother to read) regarding the obligations of artists and intellectuals in Austria's approaching post-Hitler era. Every organisation claiming to be anti-Nazi that asked Korngold for money was sent a cheque for 200 dollars. The terrible ambivalence of his love for Austria – the only place he truly felt at home – drove him to want the best for its people. Yet following the accounts of Nazi atrocities, many were initially unable to face any thought of returning. This was hardly an unsurprising position for Jewish exiles, yet resulted in much mutual suspicion between former refugees and Germans and Austrians who would have genuinely welcomed them back. In 1949, Korngold returned to Höselberg, the family estate in Austria's picturesque Salzkammergut, where he discovered that the house was in ruins, overrun by desperate refugees and operating as a centre for displaced people. The police arrested the former caretaker when it was discovered that some of Korngold's possessions had found their way into his lodge. Korngold sold the estate to the local mayor for nearly the price of a pepper-corn and told the police not to press charges against the caretaker, explaining that he had given everything away upon leaving Austria.

Such mutually felt paranoia, distrust and pain could only cause an emotional, indeed a very practical, paralysis that would make a reconcilable future together nearly impossible. Such debilitating mistrust was ultimately demonstrated by a telling anecdote related by Korngold's family upon their postwar return to their Villa in Vienna's up-market Cottageviertel. Upon their unexpectedly meeting the neighbour's wife outside their former home, she blurted out: 'Jesus, Mary and Joseph! Professor Korngold! I don't believe my eyes! You're in Vienna! – When are you going back home?'

Epilogue

In the introduction to this book, I write that it would chalk up a cultural victory to the Nazis to accept the belief that the pre-Hitler contributions made by Jewish composers to German music were delusional; however, I end the book paradoxically with Korngold's sobering encounter with this very same delusion upon his return to post-war Vienna. The 2003 Viennese and New York exhibition on Jews and German musical identity, 'Quasi una fantasia', maintained the default setting since the end of the Third Reich that Jewish contributions to German music were never recognised, acknowledged or valued by the societies so valued, acknowledged and recognised by Jewish composers and musicians. Their children and grandchildren inherited this sense of rejection and as generations passed on, estates were handed over to local universities and libraries in the belief that returning them to former homelands would be an act of treachery. To the offspring of musical refugees, themselves now completely assimilated within the societies that had provided safe havens to their parents, former homelands had no right to any claim of cultural ownership. The bitterness and resentment ran understandably deep. Yet it was only with the passage of time that our historic sightlines would become more focused. This meant that London/Decca's recording series 'Entartete Musik' would resonate in the early 1990s in a way that would have been unthinkable before. The angry protagonists on both sides had largely died out and the rest of us were left with a bewildered and bewildering legacy.

Did one value Ernst Toch as a central musical figure during the years of the Weimar Republic or 'Ernest' Toch, the Hollywood composer of comedy horror-films starring Bob Hope? His estate landed in UCLA on the basis that the latter was more relevant than the former. In very few instances could the post-exile contributions of anyone old enough to have already made a name in Germany and Austria amount to the same degree of importance during their pre-exile years. The exceptions are rare yet often mentioned: Kurt Weill on Broadway and Erich Korngold in Hollywood. Yet for every Weill and Korngold there are dozens of Ernst Tochs. As music curator at the Jewish Museum in Vienna, I found unsettling the oft-made confession by even the most helpful archives in distant lands that they had no German speakers and therefore remained unable to identify pre-emigration documentation; especially as the documentation in question was often falling apart and just as frequently, incorrectly catalogued. Yet those children and grandchildren who have taken the leap of faith and offered to return musical estates to the cultural homelands of their parents and grandparents are confronted with the equally baffling situation of insufficient funding and personnel being available to provide what justice demands. As a result, many important musical estates remain stored in private lofts, under beds, in garden sheds or basements. Only within the last years have refugee-composers started to return to the historic consciousness of a younger, more inquisitive generation of Austrian and German musicians and scholars. It is these same young German and Austrian musicians who discover that scores and orchestral parts, even of those works rescued by publishers, are often in a state of editorial disarray, making contemporary performances reliant on guess work.

In our global society, culture is no longer the sole property of a single nation. It is the property of all with the interest and ambition to ask awkward questions and make new discoveries about themselves and the musical environment they inhabit. In a digital world, the need for digital preservation of musical émigré estates is self-evident. Just as important is the editorial input that addresses the issues that make contemporary performances challenging. If the purpose of this book was to demonstrate that the Jewish contribution to German music was not delusional, this epilogue attests to the urgency needed to preserve the widely strewn documentation, and restore the music itself, on which much of this book was based.

Notes

Introduction

1. '. . . ja, nicht bloß Elsaß und Lothringen, sondern ganz Frankreich wird uns alsdann zufallen, ganz Europa, die ganze Welt – die ganze Welt wird deutsch werden! Von dieser Sendung und Universalherrschaft Deutschlands träume ich oft, wenn ich unter Eichen wandle. Das ist mein Patriotismus'; Heine: *Deutschland: Ein Wintermärchen* (digital edition, vol. 7).
2. *The Treasure Hunter*.
3. Alfred Heuß: 'Über Franz Schrekers Oper Der Schatzgräber, seine Geschäftspraxis, die Schreker-Presse und Anderes', *Zeitschrift für Musik*, 1921, 2. Novemberheft, pp. 567–70.
4. Hilmes 2003, p. 119.

Chapter 1. German and Jewish

1. Schreker dropped the č in his name presumably because the now Germanized form 'Schrecker' meant 'frightener', which had potentially negative connotations for a budding composer.
2. *The Treasure Hunter*.
3. The translation of *Juden auf Wanderschaft* is not really the invitingly obvious *Wandering Jews* but more accurately *Jews on a Journey* – or even conceivably, *Jews in Transit*.
4. Roth 2006, p. 112.
5. Ibid., p. 13.
6. Ibid., p. 47.
7. Pedro de Arbués (1441–85), an official of the Spanish Inquisition who tried to eradicate crypto-Judaism in Spain.
8. Hanslick: *Aus meinem Leben* (Berlin: Directmedia), p. 22.
9. 'Das Civil-Ehegesetz', *Die Neue Freie Presse*, 4 May 1869.
10. Dürhammer 2006, pp. 62–70.
11. 'Oh Herr, lass dich herbei und macht die Deutschen frei, daß endlich das Geschrei danach zu Ende sei.'
12. 'Der Weg der neuen Bildung geht, Von Humanität, Durch Nationalität, Zur Bestialität.'
13. Bismarck: *Gedanken* (Berlin: Directmedia), pp. 280–2.
14. Hobsbawm refers to 'Ausgleich' as meaning 'compromise'. It obviously was a compromise for the Austrians to offer parity to the Hungarian half of the empire; however, it came about as the completion of negotiations that had begun before the expulsion of Austria from the German Federation.
15. Krenek 1998, p. 25.
16. Lohrmann 2000, p. 211.
17. 'Das Civilehegesetz', *Neue Freie Presse*, 4 May 1869.
18. Known simply as 'The December Constitution' in Hungary, it was passed the next day on 22 December 1867.
19. Pauley1992, pp. 22–3.
20. Quoted in Scholz 2000, p. 76.
21. Ibid., pp. 76–7.
22. Ibid., p. 77.

23. *Neue Freie Presse*, 23 December 1867
24. Krenek 1998, pp. 808–9.
25. 'Ein großer Tag des Liberalismus', *Neue Freie Presse*, 20 December 1928.
26. Zweig 1970, p. 122.
27. 'Ein großer Tag des Liberalismus', *Neue Freie Presse*, 20 December 1928.

Chapter 2. Wagner and German Jewish Composers in the Nineteenth Century

1. Barry Millington translates the title in English as *Jewishness in Music* – also appropriate and closer than 'Jews in Music' – a translation that would only cover a small part of Wagner's essay.
2. The implication is that Hanslick was not circumcised.
3. Wagner's 'Judenthum in der Musik', *Neue Freie Presse*, 9 March 1869.
4. In the digital edition of the complete writings of Richard and Cosima Wagner, the name Mendelssohn is mentioned 459 times.
5. Wagner: *Oper und Drama*: 'Die Oper und das Wesen der Musik' (Berlin: Directmedia), p. 249.
6. Wagner: *Das Judenthum in der Musik (1850)* (Berlin: Directmedia), p. 81.
7. Ibid., p. 79.
8. By 'expressive effect' Wagner refers to the inner emotional turmoil, both erotic and febrile, that his own music was uniquely capable of eliciting; a shameless invasion of the listener's emotional privacy in the view of aesthetes such as Hanslick.
9. Wagner: *Über das Dirigieren* (Berlin: Directmedia), p. 317.
10. Wagner: *Das Judenthum* (Berlin: Directmedia), p. 80.
11. Wagner: *Oper und Drama*, 'Die Oper und das Wesen der Musik', p. 230.
12. Heine: *Lutetia* (Berlin: Directmedia), vol. 6, p. 424 .
13. Scholz 2000, pp. 78–9.
14. Reproduced in the 1959 Bayreuth *Parsifal* programme, quoted in Scholz 2000, pp. 78–9.
15. Wagner: letter to Tausig, April 1869.
16. Lucian O. Meysels: *In meinem Salon ist Österreich: Berta Zuckerkandl und ihre Zeit* (Vienna: Herold, 1984).
17. Wagner: *Religion und Kunst*, 'Erkenne dich selbst'

18. Ibid.
19. This is ironic when one considers Nietzsche's own chapter on 'Redemption' in *Thus Spoke Zarathustra*. His comments on Wagner's view of redemption come from *Der Fall Wagner* (Berlin: Directmedia, vol. 2, pp. 908–9).
20. Malte Fischer 2000, pp. 177–88.
21. Leon Botstein: 'Unter Wunderkindern' (pp. 145–60) from *Lorenzo da Ponte, Aufbruch in die neue Welt* (Vienna: JMW, 2006).
22. In the digital edition of Richard and Cosima Wagner's writings, Meyerbeer's name appears 615 times.
23. Wagner: *Sämtliche Schriften und Dichtungen* (Berlin: Directmedia), vol. 1, p. 15.
24. Botstein 2006, pp. 145–60.
25. Wagner: *Das Kunstwerk der Zukunft*.
26. Richter: *Aus Leipzigs musikalischer Glanzzeit* (Berlin: Digitalmedia), p. 96.
27. Viereck 2007, pp. 90–126.

Chapter 3. An Age of Liberalism, Brahms and the Chronicler Hanslick

1. *The World of Yesterday*.
2. Zweig 1970, p. 79.
3. Ibid., p. 81.
4. Botstein, Leon: 'German Jews and Wagner', in *Richard Wagner and his World*, ed. Thomas Pleasants (Princeton, NJ: Princeton University Press, 2009), p. 158.
5. *The Path into the Open*.
6. Schnitzler 1908, p. 76.
7. Goldmark 2006 (Berlin: Directmedia), p. 86.
8. 'Zur Erinnerung an Robert Franz', *Neue Freie Presse*, 1 November 1892.
9. *On Musical Beauty*.
10. Hanslick 1950, p, 27.
11. *The History of Concert Life in Vienna*.
12. Hanslick 1869–70, vol. 2, pp. 117–21.
13. 'Concerte', *Neue Freie Presse*, 28 November 1882.
14. Hanslick 1869–70, vol. 2, p. 292.
15. *Pester Lloyd*: the German language newspaper in Budapest.
16. 'Feuilleton: Musik', *Neue Freie Presse*, 22 November 1881.
17. 'Franz Liszt', *Neue Freie Presse*, 8 August 1886.
18. Hanslick 1869–70, vol. 2, p. 227.

19. Ibid., p. 295.
20. Ibid., p. 291.
21. Hanslick 1950, p. 83.
22. Hanslick 1869–70, vol. 2, p. 428.
23. Ibid., p. 340.
24. Ibid., p. 437.
25. Ibid., pp. 437–8.
26. Ibid., p. 439.
27. 'Hofoperntheater (Bianca, Komische Oper in zwei Akten von Ignaz Brüll)', *Neue Freie Presse*, 17 December 1880.
28. Ibid.
29. Hanslick: *Aus meinem Leben* (Berlin: Directmedia), p. 164.
30. *The Destruction of Jerusalem.*
31. *The Catacombs.*
32. 'Zur Biographie Ferdinand Hiller', *Neue Freie Presse*, 18 and 19 August 1885.
33. 'Hofoperntheater (Die Drei Pintos, Komische Oper von C.M. Weber bearbeitet und ergänzt von G. Mahler)', *Neue Freie Presse*, 20. January 1889.
34. 'Die Königsbraut, Romantische, Komische Oper', *Neue Freie Presse*, 31 March 1889.
35. 'Marffa', *Neue Freie Presse*, 7 October, 1886.
36. 'Der Trompetter von Säkkingen', *Neue Freie Presse*, 2 February 1886.
37. 'Andreasfest', *Neue Freie Presse*, 4 February 1885.
38. 'Hofoperntheater: Fata Morgana', *Neue Freie Presse*, 1 April 1886.
39. 'Concerte', *Neue Freie Presse*, 24 January 1882.
40. 'Musik', *Neue Freie Presse*, 20 February 1883.
41. 'J. Offenbach', *Neue Freie Presse*, 10 October 1880.
42. Goldmark: Erinnerungen (Berlin: Directmedia), p. 55.
43. Hanslick: *Aus meinem Leben* (Berlin: Directmedia), pp. 181–2).
44. Goldmark: *Erinnerungen* (Berlin: Directmedia), pp. 84–8).
45. Ibid., p. 88.
46. *Rustic Wedding Symphony.*
47. *The Queen of Sheba.*
48. 'Die Königin von Saba', *Neue Freie Presse*, 13 March 1875.
49. 'Merlin', *Neue Freie Presse*, 21 November 1886.
50. 'Von Johannes Brahms' letzten Tagen', *Neue Freie Presse*, 4 April 1897.

51. Julius Korngold: 'Internationales Kammermusikfest in Venedig II', *Neue Freie Presse*, 29 September 1925.
52. Korngold 1991, p. 33.

Chapter 4. Mahler and His Chronicler Julius Korngold

1. Jüdisches Museum Wien: 'Continental Britons: Hans Gál and Egon Wellesz', Audio guide nos 703–4.
2. Adolf Weissmann: *Der Dirigent im 20. Jahrhundert* (Berlin, 1925), as quoted by Julius Korngold in *Neue Freie Presse*, 19 December 1925.
3. Arnold Schoenberg Center Vienna, Digital Archive: *Gustav Mahler*, T60_10_A.
4. Arnold Schoenberg Center Vienna, Digital Archive: *Gustav Mahler ist tot*, T60_03.
5. Alma Mahler: *Tagebuch-Suiten 1898–1902*, ed. Anthony Beaumont (Frankfurt: Fischer, 1997), p. 639; other journals of the day included Gretl Gallia's as quoted in Bonyhady 2011, p. 178.
6. Bonyhady 2011, p. 118.
7. Haber 2009, pp. 11–15,
8. Ibid., pp. 24–7.
9. Ibid., p. 31.
10. Stourzh 1989, pp. 239–58.
11. Korngold 1991, p. 78.
12. *The Final Days of Mankind.*
13. *The Torch.*
14. *Die Fackel*, 30 May 1913.
15. *Die Fackel*, No. 5, May 1899.
16. David Lloyd George published articles in the *Neue Freie Presse* on 3 January 1914, 14 September 1918, and 2 December 1918.
17. Winston Churchill published an article in the *Neue Freie Presse* on 5 October 1917.
18. Korngold 1991, p. 275.
19. Alexander Moszkowski: 'Feuilleton, Ein Genie', *Neue Freie Presse*, 12 February 1892.
20. *Song of Zion.*
21. Leon Botstein: Exhibition Catalogue *Quasi una fantasia: Vienna Jews and the City of Music 1870–1938*, Bard College, Annandale-on-Hudson, and Wolke Verlag, 2004, p. 43
22. *Scope, Methodology und Purpose of Musicology.*

23. *Monuments of Austrian Composition.*
24. Theodor Haase: 'Antisemitismus: Kleine Studien', *Neue Freie Presse*, 6, 7 and 8 April 1887.
25. Anatole France: 'Über den Antisemitismus', *Neue Freie Presse*, 3 April 1904.
26. Malte Fischer 2000, pp. 134–5.
27. Taruskin uses the term 'Maximalist' to define works such as Arnold Schoenberg's *Gurrelieder* and Mahler's *Symphony of a Thousand.* See Taruskin 2010, vol. 5, p. 5.
28. Korngold: 'Orchester und Kammerkonzerte', *Neue Freie Presse*, 6 May 1914.
29. Letter from Erich Wolfgang Korngold to Arnold Rosé, 3 January 1918 (Internationale Gustav Mahler Gesellschaft, 20–7).
30. Letter from Gustav Mahler to Julius Korngold, 12 June 1908 (Internationale Gustav Mahler Gesellschaft, 1/113).
31. Korngold 1991, p. 123.
32. Korngold: 'Gustav Mahler', *Neue Freie Presse*, 4 June 1907.
33. Korngold 1991, p. 115.
34. Richard Robert: 'Der Fall Korngold', *Wiener Sonn- und Montags-Zeitung*, 11 May 1914.
35. Korngold: 'Musik', *Neue Freie Presse*, 8 January 1907.
36. Korngold: 'Musik', *Neue Freie Presse*, 17 December 1904.
37. Ibid.
38. Arendt 2007, p. 64.
39. Malte Fischer 2000, p. 156.
40. Taruskin 2010, vol. 5, p. 6.

Chapter 5. The Jugendstil School of Schoenberg, Schreker, Zemlinsky and Weigl

1. Zuckerkandl 1970, p. 97.
2. Johnston 1972, p. 71.
3. Hilmar 1974, pp. 20–36.
4. Anon,: 'Fin de siècle', *Neue Freie Presse*, 5 June 1890.
5. Franz Servaes: 'Decadence Romane', *Neue Freie Presse*, 17 August 1899.
6. Anon.: 'Fin de siècle', *Neue Freie Presse*, 30 December 1900.
7. Max Burckhard: 'Der Begriff des Modernen in der Kunst', *Neue Freie Presse*, 19 and 20 November 1900.

8. Max Nordau: 'Socialistische Kunst', *Neue Freie Presse*, 3 March 1896.
9. Alfred Freiherr von Berger: 'Wahnsinn auf der Bühne', *Neue Freie Presse*, 31 December 1906.
10. Hugo Ganz: 'Kranke Kunst', *Neue Freie Presse*, 21 April 1900.
11. Zuckerkandl 1908, p. 47.
12. *Escape into Mediocrity.*
13. Graf 1983, p. 374.
14. Wittgenstein *Tractatus*, Proposition 7.
15. Wellesz 1981, p. 40.
16. 'Musik der Gegenwart, Eine Flugblätterfolge no. 1: von neuer Musik aus Arnold Schoenberg Harmonielehre', *Musikblätter des Anbruch*, issue1-2, 1922, p. 2.
17. Ibid.
18. Botstein 1991, p.129,
19. Bartók was one of the non-Jewish composers who shared Schoenberg's highly developed sense of ethical and artistic ideals.
20. BBC Interview: Deryck Cooke and Egon Wellesz, 1962; 'Continental Britons' exhibition, Jüdisches Museum Wien: Audio guide, no. 723.
21. Wellesz 1985, pp. 32–5.
22. Wellesz 1981, p. 96.
23. Hanns Eisler: speech at International Congress of Composers and Music Critics in Prague, May 1948. Eisler 1982, vol. 2, pp. 17–18.
24. Hans Eisler: *Aufbau*, v (1949), vol. 11, pp. 1035–6.
25. Jürgen Schebera: *Hanns Eisler* (Mainz: Schott, 1998), p. 25
26. 'Schoenberg: der Musikalische Reaktionär', Document, Arnold Schoenberg Center.
27. Society of Creative Musicians.
28. *Once Upon a Time.*
29. Korngold 1991, p. 123.
30. 'Musik aus neuer und neuster Zeit', *Neue Freie Presse*, 4 January 1901.
31. 'Neue Orchester- und Liedmusik', *Neue Freie Presse*, 3 February 1905.
32. Ibid.
33. Ibid.
34. Ibid.
35. 'Festaufführungen Wiener Musik', *Neue Freie Presse*, 5 June 1920.
36. 'Neue Orchester- und Liedmusik'.
37. Ibid.
38. *Neue Freie Presse*, 12 July 1910.

39. *Neue Freie Presse*, 28 April 1917.
40. *Neue Freie Presse*, 25 November 1923.
41. *Neue Freie Presse*, 29 November 1910.
42. Ibid.
43. 'Festaufführungen Wiener Musik'.
44. Arnold Schoenberg to Rudolf Ganz, 1 June 1938, subsequently paraphrased by Weigl in a brochure of composer recommendations.
45. Krenek 1999, p. 140.
46. 'Hofoperntheater', *Neue Freie Presse*, 18 March 1913.
47. *The Birthday of the Infanta*.
48. Wellesz 1981, p. 63.
49. In fact, Berg's reduction proved too difficult, so a simplified version by Ferdinand Rebay was commissioned by Universal Edition.
50. Wellesz 1981, p. 63
51. Ibid.
52. *The Branded*.
53. Hailey 1993, p. 298.
54. Adorno 1986, vol. 16, *Quasi una fantasia*, p. 265.
55. Ibid: *Vergegenwärtigungen*, p. 368.

Chapter 6. A Musical Migration

1. Hamann 1997, p. 398.
2. *Neue Freie Presse*, 21 July 1914.
3. *Die Fackel*, 10 July 1914, p. 2.
4. *Neue Freie Presse*, 25 May 1915.
5. Guido Adler: 'Weltkrieg und Musik', *Neue Freie Presse*, 2 July 1917.
6. Ibid.
7. 'Wo ist Österreich', *Neue Freie Presse*, 3 September 1918.
8. 'Die Verkündigung des Anschlusses an die deutsche Republik', *Neue Freie Presse*, 13 November 1918.
9. 'Angebliche Verhinderung des Anschlussseszwischen Deutschösterreich und Deutschland', *Neue Freie Presse*, 16 March 1919.
10. Zweig 1970, p. 324.
11. Ibid., p. 136.
12. Anton Kuh: *Luftlinien. Feuilletons, Essays und Publizistik*, ed. Ruth Greuner (Vienna: Löcker, 1981), p. 191.
13. *The Word*.
14. Raoul Auernheimer: 'Expressionistische Bewegung', *Neue Freie Presse*, 4 July 1918.
15. Ibid.
16. Ibid.
17. Ibid.
18. Ibid.

19. James Simon: 'Expressionismus in der Musik', *Musikblätter des Anbruch*, June 1920, pp. 408–11.
20. Letter from Kandinsky to Schoenberg, 18 January 1911.
21. Stuckenschmidt 1964, p. 35.
22. *The Singing Devil*.
23. *St Cecilia or the Power of Music*.
24. Hailey 1993, p. 249, and Haas and Hailey 2004, p.104.
25. Hailey 1993, p. 247.
26. *The Blacksmith of Ghent*.
27. *Unknown World*.
28. *The Magnificent Cuckold*.
29. Julius Korngold: 'Novitäten', *Neue Freie Presse*, 10 April 1924.
30. *Murder, the Hope of Women*.
31. Krenek 1998, p. 1015.
32. Ibid.
33. Ibid., pp. 941.
34. *Anbruch*, 1931, no. 1, contents (unpaginated).
35. Walter Braunfels, Berthold Goldschmidt and Hans Krása in *Anbruch*, 1931, nos 6–7, pp. 145–6.
36. Alois Hába in *Anbruch*, 1931, no. 4, p. 91.
37. Paul Stefan in *Anbruch*, 1931, nos 8–9, p. 208.
38. *Anbruch*, 1931, no. 1, p. 16.
39. *Anbruch*, 1931, nos 2–3, p. 52.
40. *The One Who Said 'Yes'*.
41. Harry Stangenberg: 'Krenek's *Leben des Orest* in der Stuttgarter Inszenierung', *Anbruch*, 1931, no. 5, p. 124.
42. Franz Schreker: '*Smee und die sieben Jahre*, große Zauberoper in 3 Aufzügen', *Anbruch*, 1931, nos 6–7, pp. 150–2.
43. Herbert Windt: '*Andromache*', *Anbruch*, 1931, nos 6–7, pp. 152–3.
44. Viktor Zuckerkandl: 'Der Schmied von Gent', *Neue Freie Presse*, 19. November 1932.
45. Ibid.
46. Wellesz 1981, p. 92.
47. *I and Thou*.
48. Wellesz 1981, p. 94.
49. Ibid., pp. 97.
50. Ibid., p. 99.
51. Hans Müller: 'Die Angst vor dem Gefühl', *Neue Freie Presse*, 20 December 1905.
52. Krenek 1999, p. 222.
53. Bek 1994, p. 50.
54. 'New Music at Frankfurt', *New York Times*, 24 July 1927.

55. 'Berlin's New Music', *New York Times*, 10 August 1930.
56. 'Viennese Pianist soloist at League of Composers' Concert', *New York Times*, 4 April 1932.
57. *News of the Day*.
58. Eduard Beninger: 'Pianistiche Probleme, im Anschluss an die Klavierwerke von Ernst Toch', *Melos* VII, 1928, p. 68.
59. The *Genesis Suite* was conceived by the American composer Nathaniel Shilkret in 1945 as a musical setting of the first 11 chapters of the Book of Genesis in a seven-movement suite composed by seven different composers: Shilkret, Schoenberg, Stravinsky, Tansman, Milhaud, Castelnuovo-Tedesco and Toch.
60. Ernst Toch: 'Glaubensbekenntnis eines Komponisten', *Deutsche Blätter*, March–April 1945, pp. 13–15. Ernst Toch Collection: Performing Arts Archive, UCLA. Box 106, item 22
61. Ernst Toch Collection: Performing Arts Archive, UCLA, unclassified correspondence.

Chapter 7. Hey! We're Alive!

1. *The Fall of the Anti-Christ* and *The Emperor of Atlantis*.
2. Max Nordau: 'Das Jahr 1900 in der Weltgeschichte', *Neue Freie Presse*, 1 January 1901.
3. Nordau: 'Das Jahr 1901 in der Weltgeschichte', *Neue Freie Presse*, 1 January 1902.
4. Nordau: 'Das Jahr 1913 in der Weltgeschichte', *Neue Freie Presse*, 1 January 1914.
5. Interview published by *Sinn und Form* in 1964. See Jürgen Schebera: *Hanns Eisler* (Mainz: Schott, 1998), p. 282.
6. Hanns Eisler rarely mentioned his Jewish parentage. In his estate there is little reference beyond an intriguing reminder from an East Berlin synagogue requesting his (continued?) financial support.
7. *The Threepenny Opera* and and *The Rise and Fall of the City of Mahagonny*.
8. Otto Ernst: 'Von der sexuellen Aufklärung', *Neue Freie Presse*, 14 February 1908.
9. Felix Salten: 'Sexuelle Aufklärung in der Schule', *Neue Freie Presse*, 31 December 1919.
10. Zweig 1970, pp. 343–5
11. Jelavich 1993, p. 2.
12. Ibid.
13. Paul Goldman: 'Das Überbrettl', *Neue Freie Presse*, 24 January 1901.
14. Appignanesi 2004, p. 37.
15. 'Café in the West', in this context the western district of Berlin.
16. Stephan Grossmann: 'Nachruf für C.d.W', *Neue Freie Presse*, 20 August 1921.
17. Goldman: 'Das Überbrettl'.
18. Antheil 1949, p. 27.
19. The Kaiser Wilhelm Memorial church on Berlin's Breitscheidsplatz.
20. Hanns Eisler 1982, vol. 1, p. 54.
21. Ibid.
22. Felix Salten: 'Ernst Toller: Hoppla, Wir Leben! im Raimundtheater', *Neue Freie Presse*, 12 November 1927.
23. Ibid.
24. Eisenstein 1983, pp. 87–8.
25. Ibid.
26. Hinton, Schebera and Juchem 2000, p. 438.
27. Benatzky was the principal composer and writer of *Im weißen Rößl*, with individual numbers provided by Robert Stolz, Bruno Granichstaedten and Robert Gilbert.
28. Benatzky 2002, p. 64.
29. See Kevin Clarke's 'Judische Dudelei' in Arnbom, Clarke and Trabitsch 2012, pp. 146–165.
30. Hanns Eisler 1986, p. 67.
31. Hanns Eisler 1982, vol. 1, p. 260.
32. Hanns Eisler 1982, vol. 2, p. 79.

Chapter 8. A Question of Musical Potency

1. Paul Bekker: *Franz Schreker: Studie zur Kritik der modernen Oper* (Berlin: Schuster and Loeffler, 1919).
2. Bekker 1919, and Hailey 1994.
3. Hans Pfitzner: *Die neue Aesthetik der musikalischen Impotenz. Ein Verwesungssymptom?* (Munich: Verlag der Süddeutschen Monatshefte, 1920), p. 124.
4. Paul Bekker: 'Offener Brief an Julius Korngold', *Anbruch*, 1924, no. 9, p. 379.
5. Krenek 1999, pp. 718–19.

6. Stengel and Gerigk 1943, p. 28.
7. *Beethoven and Moderinism.*
8. Julius Korngold: 'Hans Pfitzner über die verunreinigung der Musik', *Neue Freie Presse*, 9 January 1926.
9. *Of the German Soul.*
10. Thomas Mann's *Betrachtungen eines Unpolitischen* (Frankfurt: Fischer, 1918), p. 427.
11. Alfred Einstein: 'The Position of Modern Music in Germany', *The Sackbut*, vol. 4 (1924), p. 194.
12. Ibid., p. 196.
13. Alban Berg: 'Die musikalische Impotenz der "neuen Ästhetik" Hans Pfitzners', *Anbruch*, 1920 nos 11–12, pp. 399–408.
14. Ibid.
15. Ibid.
16. Ibid.
17. Julius Korngold: 'Musik', *Neue Freie Presse*, 31 January 1920.
18. Ibid.
19. Jürgen Schebera: *Hanns Eisler*, Schott 1998, p. 182.
20. *The Sacred Duck.*
21. Waldstein 1965, p. 41.
22. Julius Korngold: 'Epilog zum Spieljahr', *Neue Freie Presse*, 1 July 1925.
23. Josef Reitler: 'Musik', *Neue Freie Presse*, 29 April 1929.
24. Haas and Patka 2004, pp. 37–8.
25. Hanns Gutman: 'Gáls *Heilige Ente* in Berlin', *Anbruch*, 1925, no. 8, p. 467.
26. Ibid.
27. Undated photocopy, Hans Gál estate.
28. Hans Gál: 'Zum Problem der komischen Oper', *Anbruch*, 1927 nos 1–2, p. 91.
29. *The Birds.*
30. Alfred Einstein: 'Walter Braunfels und *Don Gil von den Grünen Hosen*', *Anbruch*, 1924, no. 10, pp. 417–22.
31. *Don Gil of the Green Trousers.*
32. *Rich Claus, Poor Claus.*
33. Letter from Ludwig Strecker to Hans Gál, 19 October 1934 (Gál family collection).
34. Kim Kowalke: 'Dancing with the Devil: Publishing Modern Music in the Third Reich', *Modernism/Modernity*, vol. 8, no. 1 (2001), p. 14.
35. Letter from Willi Strecker to Erich Korngold, 11 October 1933 (Korngold family collection, Portland, Oregon).
36. Krenek 1999, p. 902.
37. Atmospheric Picture, entitled *Early Spring.*

38. *The Miracle of Diana.*
39. Wellesz 1981, pp. 13–14.
40. Julius Korngold: 'Musik: Feste und Jubiläen', *Neue Freie Presse*, 10 May 1919.
41. Julius Korngold: 'Musik', *Neue Freie Presse*, 14 November 1919.
42. Julius Korngold 1991, p. 276.
43. Réti was born in Serbia in 1885 and though he spelled his name 'Reti', his 15 published articles in *Anbruch* are under the name 'Réti', as are references to him in contemporary accounts. It is the spelling I have maintained.
44. Haefeli 1982, p. 37.
45. Wellesz 1981, p. 151.
46. Clipping found in the Wellesz Archive, Austrian National Library, annotated 'The Times, London 1934'.
47. Julius Korngold, 'Atonale Wirren', *Neue Freie Presse*, 9 August 1924.
48. *The Austrian Cultural League.*
49. Haefeli 1982, p. 69.
50. *Festliches Präludium* Op. 100 for chorus and organ (1966) and *Mirabile Mysterium* Op. 101 for two sopranos, two baritones, speaking chorus and orchestra (1967).
51. BBC Third Programme, Hans Gál, interval talk: 'What is Music', BBC Third Programme, 4 March 1971, Jüdisches Museum exhibition Audio Guide no. 571.
52. Unidentified interview reprinted in *Hans Gál Newsletter*, July 2010.
53. Wellesz 1981, p. 165.
54. *Pranks, Intrigue and Revenge.*
55. *The Bacchantes.*
56. *Vagadus's Downfall Through Vanity.*
57. Julius Korngold: 'Die Bakchantinnen von Egon Wellesz', *Neue Freie Presse*, 21 June 1931.
58. Ibid.
59. Ibid.
60. Julius Korngold: 'Wozzeck: Oper nach Georg Büchner von Alban Berg', *Neue Freie Presse*, 1 April 1930.
61. Krenek 1999, p. 1087.

Chapter 9. The Resolute Romantics

1. Klemperer 1998, p. 111.
2. Ludwig Stein: 'Der Rassenimperialismus Chamberlains', *Neue Freie Presse*, 29 January, 19 February, and 12 March 1905.

3. Ibid., 29 January 1905.
4. Ibid.
5. Ibid.
6. Ibid.
7. Ibid.
8. Ibid.
9. Ibid.
10. Ibid.
11. Ibid.
12. Ibid.
13. Ibid.
14. *Music in the World Crisis.*
15. Weißmann 1922, p. 232.
16. Ibid., pp. 232–3.
17. Ibid., p. 243.
18. Ibid, p. 244.
19. Ibid., p. 245.
20. Ibid., pp. 104–6.
21. Julius Korngold: 'Die Musik in der Weltkrise', *Neue Freie Presse*, 25 August 1922.
22. Ibid.
23. Wilhelm Altmann: 'Opern Statistik', *Anbruch*, 1928 nos 9–10, pp. 424–34.
24. Hans Heinsheimer: 'Der geheime Terror', *Anbruch*, 1931, no. 1, pp. 1–4.
25. Ibid.
26. *Schwanda the Bagpiper.*
27. Wilhelm Altmann: 'Opernstatistik', *Anbruch*, 1930, nos 9–10, p. 298.
28. *The Silent Serenade.*
29. Rudolf Réti, letter to Erich Korngold, 1923. Handschriftensammlung, Vienna State Library: no. 942/65 1.
30. Hanns Eisler: *Die rote Fahne am Montag* (Berlin), vol. 6, no. 15, 10 April 1928, printed in Eisler 1982, vol. 2, pp. 72–3.
31. Hanns Eisler: *Die Rote Fahne* (Berlin), vol. 10, no. 246, 19 October 1927, printed in Eisler 1982, vol. 2, pp. 35–6.
32. Korngold 1991, p. 290.
33. Ibid., p. 281.
34. 'Konzert des flüsternden Baritons', *Neue Freie Presse*, 10 November 1928.
35. Anon.: 'Aus dem Kunstleben: Jonny spielt auf', *Deutsch-Österreichische Tageszeitung*, 30 December 1927.
36. Krenek 1998, p. 901.
37. Ibid., p. 852.
38. Korngold 1991, p. 205.
39. Ibid., p. 287.
40. Vienna's Bürgertheater, an operetta house in the Third District, is not to be confused with the classical Burg

Theater in the First District. The Bürgertheater was torn down in 1960 after unsuccessful attempts to turn it into a postwar Broadway venue.
41. Carroll 1997, p. 215.

Chapter 10: Between Hell and Purgatory

1. Berthold Molden: 'Spinoza zum 300. Geburtstag', *Neue Freie Presse*, 24 November 1932.
2. Jakob Fromer: 'Spinoza (zum 250. Todestag)', *Neue Freie Presse*, 22 February 1927.
3. 'Richard Wagner, sein Schicksal und sein Gedanke. Das Verhältnis zur Politik (zum 50. Todestag)', *Neue Freie Presse*, 12 February 1933.
4. A. F. Seligmann and Felix Weingartner: 'Der hundertste Geburtstag von Johannes Brahms', *Neue Freie Presse*, 7 May 1933.
5. Gesetz zur Behebung der Not von Volk und Reich.
6. 'Zwischen Hölle und Fegefeuer', *Neue Freie Presse*, 31 December 1933.
7. Ibid.
8. 'Eine sensationelle Rede Churchills – Der englischer Schatzkantzler über den Faschismus', *Neue Freie Presse*, 21 January 1927.
9. 'Mr Churchill on Fascism', *The Times*, 21 June 1927, p. 14.
10. My re-translation of a German rendering of the lost English original text.
11. Ibid.
12. 'The Non-Englishness of Mr. Churchill', *Manchester Guardian*, 22 January 1927.
13. Krenek 1998, p. 966.
14. Ibid., pp. 944–6.
15. Wellesz 1981, p. 236.
16. 'Hirtenbrief gegen den Rassenwahn', *Neue Freie Presse*, 23 December 1933.
17. Ibid.
18. Korngold 1991, p. 336.
19. See Chapter 6.
20. Kampfbund Deutscher Kultur.
21. *The Problem of Tone in Playing the Violin.*
22. Schenk 2004, pp. 118–19.
23. In the issues of the *Allgemeine Musikzeitung* for 4, 11 and 18 December 1931, pp. 834–5, 839–40 and 850.
24. Hailey 1993, p. 265.

25. Schenk 2004, p. 101.

26. Hailey 1993, pp. 286–7.

27. Hailey 1993, p. 290.

28. Wulf 1966, p. 414.

29. Josef Reitler: 'Franz Schreker', *Neue Freie Presse*, 23 March 1934.

30. Hailey 1993, p. 286.

31. *The Annunciation*, 1933–5; *A Dream, a Life*, 1937; *Scenes from the Life of Saint Joan*, 1939–43.

32. Jung 1980, p. 289, quoting from *Lebensabschnitte* for the *Bodensee-Zeitschrift*, February 1954.

33. Hailey 1993, p. 294.

34. *Strength through Joy*.

35. Reichsüberwachungsamt.

36. Closel 2010, p. 139.

37. 'Die Unterredung Lady Oxfords mit Rosenberg', *Neue Freie Presse*, 10 May 1933.

38. Hans Heinsheimer: *Modern Music*, Jan–Feb 1933, pp. 116–7.

39. Viktor Zuckerkandl: 'Berliner Oper', *Neue Freie Presse*, 15 February 1932.

40. H. H. Stuckenschmidt: 'Paul von Klenau: Michael Kohlhaas, UA in Stuttgart', *Anbruch*, 1933, nos 9–10, pp. 141–3.

41. Priberg 1982, Kater 1997, Levi 1996, Closel 2010.

42. Houston Stewart Chamberlain, letter to Adolf Hitler, 8 October 1923, quoted in Wagner 2000, pp. 68–9.

43. Wagner 2002.

44. *The Divorced Woman*.

45. 'Gerichtliches Nachspiel einer Operetten Aufführung', *Neue Freie Presse*, 14 June 1935.

46. *The Chalk Circle*.

47. *Clothes Maketh the Man*.

48. H. H. Stuckenschmidt: 'Der anstössige Kreidekreis', *Anbruch*, 1934, nos 1–2, p. 32.

49. Beaumont 2000, p. 575.

50. Viktor Zuckerkandl: 'Berliner Musik', *Neue Freie Presse*, 11 May 1934.

51. *The Fan*.

52. 'Neue Musik im neuen deutschen Reich', *Neue Freie Presse*, 14 July 1933.

53. 'Es gibt nur gute und schlechte Kunst! Der Appell Furtwänglers', *Neue Freie Presse*, 12 April 1933.

54. Ibid.

55. Closel 2010, p. 158.

56. Gerhard Splitt: 'Die "Säuberung" der Reichsmusikkammer: Vorgeschichte – Planung – Durchführung', in Weber 1994, p. 49.

57. Closel 2010, p. 168.

58. Fetthauer: 2004, pp. 24–5.

59. Ibid., pp. 60–62.

60. Ibid., p. 62.

61. Gesellschaft für musikalische Aufführungs- und mechanische Vervielfältigungsrechte.

62. Staatlich genehmigten Gesellschaft zur Verwertung musikalischer Urheberrechte.

63. Kim Kowalke: 'Dancing with the Devil: Publishing Modern Music in the Third Reich', *Modernism/Modernity*, vol. 8, no. 1 (2001), p. 20.

64. Fetthauer 2004, p. 239,

65. Kowalke 2001, p. 10.

66. Ibid., p. 25.

67. Michel and Toeman 1985, pp. 57–8.

68. *Josef Weinberger Ltd: 100 Years Remembered*, pp. 30–1.

69. Carroll 1997, pp. 273–4.

70. Aster 2007, p. 186.

71. Rathkolb 1991, pp. 25–7.

72. Blessinger 1944, pp. 51–2.

73. Ibid., p. 99.

74. *Lexicon of Jews in Music*.

75. Stengel and Gerigk 1943, p. 113 ('Heindl, Toni–Heinemann, Amely').

76. Closel 2010, p. 157.

77. Zentralstelle für jüdische Wirtschaftshilfe.

78. Reichsvertretung der deutschen Juden.

79. Weissweiler 1999, p. 414.

80. *Central Vereins Zeitung*, 28 September 1933. German original quoted in Eisler, Bergmeier and Greve 2001, p. 56.

81. Baumann 2006, pp. 118–29.

82. Ibid., p. 120.

83. Closel 2010, p.188.

84. Eisler, Bergmeier and Greve 2001, p. 58.

85. Reich Federation of Jewish Cultural Leagues.

86. Baumann 2006, p. 123.

87. Closel 2010, p. 191.

88. *Geschlossene Vorstellung* 1992 includes programmes from the various organisations throughout Germany.

89. See Sawabe 2000.

90. Verein Förderung jüdischer Musik, the Hakoah Orchestra, the Jewish Song

Society, and the Symphony Orchestra of the League of Jewish Austrian Front Soldiers.
91. *My Path to Jewish Music.*
92. Sawabe 2000, p. 59.
93. Ibid., p. 77.
94. Ibid., appendix with concert programmes.

Chapter 11. Exile and Worse

1. 12 December 1934 letter from Ludwig Strecker to Erich Korngold, 12 December 1934 (Helen Korngold Family Collection, Portland, Oregon).
2. 13 August 1938 Letter from Otto Witrowsky to Julius Korngold, 13 August 1938 (Korngold Collection, Library of Congress, Washington DC).
3. London 2000, p. 26.
4. Ibid., pp. 27–9.
5. Ibid.
6. A reference made by Otto Witrowsky in correspondence from 13 August 1938 to Julius Korngold referring to the apparent contradiction of Nazi Brown-Shirts carrying out Bolshevist policies (Korngold Collection, Library of Congress, Washington DC).
7. 'Refugees in London: The Work of the Jews Temporary Shelter', *Jewish Chronicle*, 14 April 1933 (quoted in London 2000, p. 31).
8. London 2000, pp. 30–32.
9. Endelman 2002, p. 202.
10. Cameron 1979, p. 52.
11. Letter from Neville Chamberlain to his sister Hilda, 30 July 1939, quoted in London 2000, p. 106.
12. London 2000, pp. 33–4.
13. Ibid., pp. 36–7.
14. Ibid., p. 27.
15. Richard Norton-Taylor: 'Months before war, Rothermere said Hitler's work was superhuman', *The Guardian* (1 April 2005); Neil Tweedie and Peter Day: 'When Rothermere urged Hitler to invade Romania', *The Daily Telegraph* (1 March 2005).
16. Letter from Alfred Einstein to Hans Gál, 21 April 1940 (Bayerische Staatsbibliothek, ANA 414).
17. London 2000, p. 86.
18. Ibid., p. 87.
19. Ibid., p. 89.
20. Ibid., p. 106.

21. Ibid., p. 107.
22. Ibid., p. 144: the memorandum 'Emigration of refugees from Czechoslovakia' by Sir Neill Malcolm, 10–12 October 1939.
23. Ibid., pp. 143–5.
24. *Tempo* (Boosey & Hawkes), New Series, No. 173, Soviet Issue (June 1990), *Herschkowitz Encountered*, pp. 39–43.
25. Letter from Georg Szell to Hans Gál, 25 March 1938 (Bayerische Staatsbibliothek, ANA 414).
26. Letter from Ernst Toch to Hans Gál, 15 June 1938 (Bayerische Staatsbibliothek, ANA 414).
27. Raab-Hansen 1995, pp. 100–17.
28. William Malloch: *I Remember Mahler*, broadcast (1964). Copy at Internationale Gustav Mahler Gesellschaft, Vienna.
29. I am grateful to Erik Levi for providing this information which will appear in a chapter on Eisler reception in England to be published in *Eisler Studien*.
30. Letter from Vaughan Williams to Ferdinand Rauter, 29 September 1942 (University Music Archive, Vienna).
31. *Sunday Times*, 10 September 1935.
32. Kowalke 2001, p. 26.
33. Taylor 1991, p. 209.
34. *Berliner Zeitung*, 14 January 2005.
35. London 2000, p. 49.
36. François Lafitte: *The Internment of Aliens* (London: Libris, 1988), p. xiv.
37. Gál 2003.
38. Hans Gál in an interview with Bernard Pfau, Südwestfunk, 4 August 1986 (Gál Family Collection, York).
39. Hans Gál in an interview with Martin Anderson, *Journal of the British Music Society*, vol. 9 (1987), pp. 33–44.
40. Erich Itor Kahn in the Introduction to his *Actus Tragicus* for 10 Instruments, 1946–7.
41. Amaury du Closel: *Les voix étouffées du Troisième Reich* (Arles: Actes Sud, 2005), especially 'Exile en France' pp. 295–337.
42. Ibid.
43. Closel 2010, p. 367.
44. Heilbut 1983, p. 84.
45. The First publication of *Composing for the Films* omits the name of Adorno, who preferred not to be associated with Hanns Eisler during Eisler's

incriminating hearings at the House of Un-American Activities in 1947.

46. Heilbut 1983, p. 80.
47. Ibid., p. 73.
48. Ernst Krenek: 'Amerikas Einfluss auf eingewanderte Komponisten', *Musica XIII* (1959), pp. 757–61.
49. Jüdisches Museum Wien, 2005; Christopher Hailey: 'Émigrés in the Classroom' from Exhibition Catalogue: *Endstation Schein-Heiligenstadt, Eric Zeisls Flucht nach Hollywood*, pp. 86–7.
50. Letter from Georg Szell to Hans Gál, 13 July 1946 (Bayerische Staatsbibliothek ANA 414).
51. Letter from Alfred Einstein to Hans Gál, 9 February 1940 (Bayerische Staatsbibliothek ANA 414).
52. Letter from Hans Korngold to his family in California, 26 March 1939 (Korngold Collection, Library of Congress, Washington DC).
53. Ibid.
54. Letter from Alfred Einstein to Hans Gál, 9 January 1939 (Bayerische Staatsbibliothek ANA 414).
55. Eisler and Adorno 1996, pp. 28–30.
56. Dümling 2011, pp. 188–91
57. Osnabrücker Jahrbuch Frieden und Wissenschaft VIII/2001; Konrad Richter: 'Viktor Ullmann, die Wiederentdeckung eines Verschollenen', p. 121.
58. *Betrothal in a Dream.*
59. *The Charlatan.*
60. Karas 1985, pp. 126–7.
61. Agnes Kory: 'Remembering Seven Murdered Hungarian Composers': http://orelfoundation.org

Chapter 12. Restitution

1. Detailed information regarding the Adler library is contained in documentation held at the Austrian National Library in its Wellesz Collection (Wellesz Fond). It includes correspondence between von Ficker, Edward Dent and Wellesz along with various sworn statements. The above information can be found in file no. 1240.
2. Boris von Haken: 'Spalier am Mördergraben', *Die Zeit*, 20 December 2009.
3. Thacker 2007, pp. 10–11.
4. Theodor Adorno: *Vermischte Schriften I/ II, What National Socialism Has Done to the Arts*, Berlin: Suhrkamp, 1986 p. 413

5. Thacker 2007, p. 28.
6. Ibid., p.24.
7. Kulturbund zur demokratischen Erneuerung Deutschlands.
8. Ibid., pp. 34–5.
9. Ibid., p. 25.
10. Priberg 2004, p. 7195 (interview with Heinz Tiessen, 16 November 1963).
11. Ibid., p. 48.
12. Ibid., p. 63.
13. Morgenstern 1999, pp. 48–9.
14. Klenau's daughter was the wife of Soma Morgenstern.
15. H. H. Stuckenschmidt: 'Die Uraufführung von Wirtin von Pinsk in Dresden', *Neue Freie Presse*, 19 February 1938.
16. Letter from Hartmann to Wellesz, 2 January 1948 (Austrian National Library, Wellesz Fond no. 2208).
17. Gottbegnadeten-Liste.
18. Thacker 2007, pp. 77–8.
19. Ibid., pp. 78–9.
20. Steinacher 2011, p. 95.
21. Ibid., pp. 143–9.
22. Stonor Saunders 1999, p. 224.
23. Ibid., p. 221.
24. Ibid., p. 223.
25. Hanns Eisler: from his unpublished essay 'Comments on the Crisis of Culture in Monopoly Capitalism and to the duties of the Germany Academy of Arts', 1950, printed in Eisler 1982, vol. 3, p. 79.
26. Wilford 2008, pp. 108–9.
27. 'Konrad Boehmer über das Chaos', *Süddeutschen Zeitung*, 29/30 November 2008.
28. Theodor Adorno, vol 18, Musikalische Schriften V, *Zur gesellschaftlichen Lage der Musik*, Berlin: Suhrkamp, 1986, p. 730.
29. Actually *Die Kathrin* was performed at Vienna's Volksoper as the bombed-out Staatsoper's temporary auditorium during reconstruction was the Theater an der Wien, considered too small for Korngold's opera.
30. Pierre Boulez, interview, *Wall Street Journal*, 27 January 2010.
31. Berthold Goldschmidt, during one of many conversations with the author between 1990 and 1996.
32. Letter from Günter Raphael to Hans Gál, 24 October 1946 (Bayerische Staatsbibliothek Munich, ANA 414).

33. Wiesbaden was in the American Sector.

34. 'One should not speak ill of the dead.'

35. Max Hinrichsen (1901–1965) was eldest son of the music publisher Henri Hinrichsen (1868–1942).

36. Straube was the conductor and organist at the Thomaskirche and had taken anti-Nazi stands since 1931. He joined the party in 1933 to keep another party member from ousting him but was relieved of his position in 1939 because of his continued anti-Nazi actions, including maintaining open relationships with Jewish friends and colleagues.

37. The Thomaskirche was the church in which J. S. Bach was organist and music director.

38. Letter from Günter Raphael to Hans Gál, 5 November 1946 (Bayerische Staatsbibliothek Munich, ANA 414).

39. Dr Thomas Gayda in an undated conversation in 1994 with the author and Berthold Goldschmidt.

40. Letter from Egon Wellesz to Elisabeth Wellesz-Kessler, 16 November 1952 (Austrian National Library, Wellesz Fond no. 13).

41. Letter from Adrian Boult to Eric Warr (Austrian National Library, Wellesz Fond no. 1102).

42. Letter from Adrian Boult to Leonard Issacs, 2 October 1952 (Austrian National Library, Wellesz Fond no. 1102).

43. Lewis Foreman: 'Alan Bush, Arthur Benjamin, Berthold Goldschmidt, Karl Rankl, Lennox Berkeley and the Arts Council's 1951 Opera Competition', British Music Society [special number] (2004).

44. Ibid.

45. Ibid.

46. Ernst Toch: 'Der Einfall ist Alles', UCLA Toch Collection, box 106, no. 7.

47. The Dresden-born conductor Rudolf Kempe, who had never worked with Korngold, made a landmark recording of the Symphony (slightly cut) with the Munich Philharmonic for RCA, produced by Korngold's son, George, 15 years after his father's death.

48. The Austrian composer and Schoenberg pupil Karl Rankl (1898–1968) was not Jewish, though his wife was. He wrote eight Symphonies during his exile years.

49. A reference to the Moscow Accord which stated that Austria was the first victim of Nazism and would therefore not be subject to the same war reparations and conditions as Germany.

50. Letter from Albert Einstein to Hans Gál, 1 January 1946 (Bayerische Staatsbibliothek ANA 414).

51. According to the written testimony of von Ficker, 28 May 1945, Wellesz Collection, Austrian National Library F-13 Wellesz 1240

52. An interesting claim as Austria no longer existed and was part of Germany at this point. Schenk himself had arrived from Rostock, though he was born in Salzburg. It throws a fascinating light on the self-identification of even such avid Nazi-supporting Austrians as Schenk.

53. Austrian National Library, Music Collection, Wellesz Collection, no. 1240.

54. Ibid.

55. The Wellesz Collection at Austria's National Library contains correspondence from Hans Keller to Wellesz with an accompanying clipping from Kurier, 27 June 1967.

56. Gerhard Scheit/Wilhelm Svoboda: Feindbild Gustav Mahler, Sonderzahl, Wien, 2002, p. 157.

57. Letter from Albert Einstein to Hans Gál 15 February 1947 (Bayerische Staatsbibliothek ANA 414).

58. Letter from Heinz Tietjen to Hans Gál, 23 August 1951 (Bayerische Staatsbibliothek ANA 414).

59. Beecham's defence was that he had conducting contracts in Australia and America which were not completed until after the declaration of war. He subsequently employed Furtwängler's Jewish secretary, Dr Berta Geissmar.

60. Letter from Georg Szell to Hans Gál, 15 October 194[?] (Bayerische Staatsbibliothek ANA 414). Correspondence in Britain and America during the war was carried out between German-speaking exiles in English to get past the censors.

61. Letter from Georg Szell to Hans Gál, 30 May 1946 (Bayerische Staatsbibliothek ANA 414).

62. Letter from Georg Szell to Hans Gál, 14 July 1946 (Bayerische Staatsbibliothek ANA 414).

63. Cabinet meeting minutes (Robert Knight, ed.) on the matter of restitution to the Jews, from 'Transcripts from the Austrian Federal Republic governments from 1945–52', Frankfurt am Main, 1988, p. 114. Taken from the essay by Karl Pfeifer: *Geschichtsmanipulation im österreichischen Schulbuch*, Linz: Veritas, 2003

64. Monika Kropfl: *Preise und ihre Vergabepolitik im Österreich der Nachkriegszeit am Beispiel von Hans Gál und Egon Wellesz* (Vienna: Mandelbaum, 2004), pp. 119–24

65. Austrian National Library, Handschriftensammlung 833/26-5.

66. Austrian State Archives, Bundesministerium für Unterricht, Akt 86.693/53 GZ7C/ 1948–1955.

67. Austrian National Library, Handschriftensammlung 833/26-4.

68. Letter from Egon Kornauth to Joseph Marx, 16 December 1956 (Austrian National Library, Handschriftensammlung 833/26-4).

69. Thacker 2007, p. 64.

70. Cited in Robert Craft: *Stravinsky: Selected Correspondence* (London and Boston: Faber, 1985), vol. 3, p. 218.

71. Theodor Adorno: *Musik und Neue Musik*, Musikalische Schriften I-III Finale. Berlin: Suhrkamp, 1986 GS 16 p. 477.

72. Wagner 2008, p. 205.

73. Letter from Paul Wittgenstein to Luzi Korngold, 24 February 1958 (Korngold collection, Portland, Oregon).

Bibliography

Adler, Tom, and Anika Scott: *Lost to the World* (Philadelphia: Xlibris, 2002)

Adorno, Theodor W.: *Gesammelte Schriften*, ed. Rolf Tiedemann, Gretel Adorno, Susan Buck-Morss and Klaus Schlutz (Berlin: Suhrkamp, 1986)

Aigner, Thomas, Sylvia Mattl-Wurm, et al., ed.: *Hugo Wolf Biographisches, Netzwerk, Rezeption* (Vienna: Metroverlag, 2020)

Allende-Blin, Juan, ed.: *Musiktradition im Exil* (Cologne: Bundverlag, 1993)

Altenberg, Peter: *Mein Lebensabend Erinnerungen* (Frankfurt: Fischer, 1919)

Aly, Götz: *Warum die Deutschen? Warum die Juden?* (Frankfurt: Fischer, 2011)

Antheil, George: *Bad Boy of Music* (London: National Book Association, 1949)

Appignanesi, Lisa: *The Cabaret* (New Haven and London: Yale University Press, 2004)

Applegate, Celia, and Pamela Potter, ed.: *Music and German National Identity* (Chicago, IL: University of Chicago, 2002)

Arbeitsgruppe Exilmusik Hamburg: *Lebenswege von Musikerinnen im 'Dritten Reich' und im Exil* (Hamburg: von Bockel, 2000)

Arendt, Hannah: *Vor Antisemitismus ist man nur noch auf dem Monde sicher* (Munich: Piper, 2004)

Arendt, Hannah: *Macht und Gewalt* (Munich: Piper, 2005)

Arendt, Hannah: *Verborgene Tradition* (Oldenburg: Akademieverlag, 2007)

Arnbom, Marie-Theres: *Friedmann, Gutmann, Lieben, Mandl, Strakosch–Fünf Familienporträts aus Wien vor 1938* (Vienna: Böhlau 2002)

Arnbom, Marie-Theres, and Christoph Wagner-Trinkwitz, ed.: *Grüß mich Gott! Fritz Grünbaum, eine Biographie 1880–1941* (Vienna: Christian Brandstätter, 2005)

Arnbom, Marie-Theres: *War'n Sie schon mal in mich verliebt? Filmstars, Operettenlieblinge und Kabarettgrößen zwischen Wien und Berlin* (Vienna: Böhlau, 2006)

Arnbom, Marie-Theres, Kevin Clarke, and Thomas Trabitsch: *Die Welt der Operette* (Vienna: Österreichisches Theater Museum, 2012)

Art, David: *The Politics of the Nazi Past in Germany and Austria* (Cambridge: Cambridge University Press, 2006)

Aster, Micha: *'Das Reichsorchester': Die Berliner Philharmoniker und der Nationalsozialismus* (Munich: Siedler, 2007)

Auner, Joseph, ed.: *A Schoenberg Reader: Documents of a Life* (New Haven and London: Yale University Press, 2003)

Barron, Stephanie: *Exiles and Émigrés: The Flight of European Artists from Hitler* (Pittsburgh, PA: Harry N. Abrams, 1997)

Baumann, Kurt: 'The Kulturbund: Ghetto and Home', in *Germans no More: Accounts of Jewish Everyday Life, 1933–1938*, ed. Margarete Limberg and Hubert Rübsaat (Oxford and New York: Berghahn, 2006), pp. 118–29

Bearmann, Marietta, Charmian Brinson, Richard Dove, Anthony Grenville, Jennifer Taylor: *Wien-London, Hin und Retour: Das Austrian Centre in London 1939 bis 1947* (Vienna: Czernin, 2004)

Beaumont, Antony: *Zemlinsky* (Ithaca, NY: Cornell University Press, 2000)

Beevor, Antony: *The Battle for Spain: The Spanish Civil War, 1936-1939* (London: Phoenix, 2006)

Beevor, Antony: *The Spanish Civil War* (London: Cassell, 1999)

Behrens, Roger: *Adorno–ABC* (Leipzig: Reclam, 2003)

Behschnitt, Rüdiger: *'Die Zeiten sein so wunderlich . . .': Karl Amadeus Hartmanns Oper Simplicius Simplicissimus* (Hamburg: von Bockel, 1998)

Bek, Josef: *Erwin Schulhoff, Leben und Werk* (Hamburg: von Bockel, 1994)

Bekh, Wolfgang Johannes: *Gustav Mahler oder die letzten Dinge* (Vienna: Amalthea 2005)

Bekker, Paul: *Franz Schreker: Studie zur Kritik der modernen Oper* (Berlin: Schuster and Loeffler, 1919)

Beller, Steven, ed.: *Rethinking Vienna 1900* (Oxford and New York: Berghahn Books 2001)

Beller, Steven: *Vienna and the Jews 1867-1938: A Cultural History* (Cambridge: Cambridge University Press, 1990)

Benatzky, Ralph: *Triumph und Tristesse: Aus den Tagebüchern von 1919 bis 1946*, ed. Inge Jens and Christiane Niklew (Berlin: Parthas, 2002)

Beniston, Judith, Geoffrey Chew, and Robert Vilain, ed.: *Austrian Studies: Words and Music* (London: Modern Humanities Research Association, 2009)

Benz, Richard: *Vom Erden-Schicksal Ewiger Musik* (Leipzig: Eugen Diederich, 1936)

Berg, Alban: 'Die musikalische Impotenz der "neuen Ästhetik" Hans Pfitzners', *Anbruch*, 1920 nos 11–12

Berthram, Mathias, ed.: *Friedreich Engels und Karl Marx: Ausgewählte Werke* (Berlin: Directmedia, 2004)

Berthram, Mathias, ed.: *Heinrich Heine, Leben und Werk* (Berlin: Directmedia, 2005)

Bilski, Emily D., and Emily Braun, ed.: *Jewish Women and Their Salons: The Power of Conversation* (New Haven and Lonon: Yale University Press, 2005)

Bismarck, Otto von: *Gedanken und Erinnerungen* (Berlin: Directmedia, 2006)

Blanning, Tim: *The Pursuit of Glory, Europe 1648-1815* (London: Allen Lane, 2007)

Blannning, Tim: *The Romantic Revolution* (London: Weidenfeld and Nicolson, 2010)

Blessinger, Karl: *Judentum und Musik* (Berlin: Bernhard Hahnfeld, 1944)

Blom, Philipp: *The Vertigo Years* (London: Phoenix, 2008)

Bonyhady, Tim: *Good Living Street: Portrait of a Patron* Family, *Vienna 1900* (New York: Pantheon, 2011)

Botstein, Leon: *Judentum und Modernität* (Vienna: Böhlau, 1991)

Botstein, Leon, ed.: *The Complete Brahms: A Guide to the Musical Works* (New York: Norton, 1999)

Botstein, Leon, and Werner Hanak, ed.: *Quasi una fantasia: Juden und die Musikstadt Wien* (Vienna: JMW, 2003)

Botstein, Leon: Exhibition Catalogue *Quasi una fantasia: Vienna Jews and the City of Music, 1870 - 1938* (Annandale-on-Hudson, NY: Bard College; Berlin: Wolke, 2004)

Botstein, Leon: 'Unter Wunderkindern', in *Lorenzo da Ponte Aufbruch in die neue Welt* (Vienna: JMW, 2006), pp. 145–60.

Botstein, Leon: 'German Jews and Wagner', in *Richard Wagner and his World*, ed. Thomas Pleasants (Princeton, NJ: Princeton University Press, 2009)

Brand, Juliane, and Christopher Hailey, ed.: *Constructive Dissonance: Arnold Schoenberg and the Transformations of Twentieth-Century Culture* (Berkeley: University of California Press, 1997)

Brand, Juliane, Christopher Hailey, and Andreas Meyer, ed.: *Briefwechsel Arnold Schönberg–Alban Berg* (Mainz: Schott, 2007)

Brezinka, Thomas: *Max Brand (1896–1980) Leben und Werk* (Zirnberg: Katzbichler, 1995)

Brezinka, Thomas: *Erwin Stein: Ein Musiker in Wien und London* (Vienna: Böhlau, 2005)

Broder, H. M., and Erika Geisel, ed.: *Premiere und Pogrom: Der Jüdische Kulturbund, 1933–1941*, (Munich: Siedler, 1992)

Brugger, Eveline, Martha Keil, Albert Lichtblau, Christophe Lind, and Barbara Staudinger, ed.: *Geschichte der Juden in Österreich* (Vienna: Ueberreuter, 2006)

Burleigh, Michael and Wolfgang Wippermann: *The Racial State: Germany, 1933–1945* (Cambridge, Cambridge University Press, 1991)

Busch, Fritz: *Aus dem Leben eines Musikers* (Frankfurt: Fischer, 1982)

Cameron, James: *Yesterday's Witness* (London: BBC Publications, 1979)

Canetti, Elias: *Das Augenspiel: Lebensgeschichte, 1931–1937* (Munich: Carl Hanser, 1985)

Carroll, Brendan G.: *The Last Prodigy: A Biography of Erich Wolfgang Korngold* (Portland, OR: Amadeus Press, 1997)

Clarke, Kevin: *Im Himmel spielt auch schon die Jazzband: Emmerich Kálmán und die transatlantische Operette, 1928–1932* (Hamburg: von Bockel, 2007)

Closel, Amaury du: *Les voix étouffées du Troisième Reich* (Arles: Actes Sud, 2005)

Closel, Amaury du: *Erstickte Stimmen: 'Entartete Musik' im dritten Reich* (Vienna: Böhlau, 2010)

Conway, David: *Jewry in Music: Entry to the Profession from the Enlightenment to Richard Wagner* (Cambridge: Cambridge University Press, 2012)

Craft, Robert: *Stravinsky: Chronicle of a Friendship, 1948–1971* (New York: Vintage, 1971)

Crawford, Dorothy Lamb: *A Windfall of Musicians: Hitler's Émigrés and Exiles in Southern California* (New Haven and London: Yale University Press, 2009)

Cullin, Michel; Primavera Driessen-Gruber, ed.: *Douce France? Musik-Exil in Frankreich* (Vienna: Böhlau, 2008)

Czada, Peter, and Günter Große: *Comedian Harmonists: ein Vokalensemble erobert die Welt* (Berlin: Hentrich, 1993)

Dachs, Robert, ed.: *Sag beim Abschied* (Vienna: Verlag der Apfel, 1997)

Dalinger, Brigitte: *Verloschene Sterne: Geschichte des jüdischen Theaters in Wien* (Vienna: Picus, 1998)

Davies, Norman, and Roger Moorhouse: *Microcosm: Portrait of a Central European City – Breslau/Wrocław* (London: Cape, 2002)

Denscher, Barbara, and Helmut Peschina: *Kein Land des Lächelns Fritz Löhner-Beda, 1883–1942* (Vienna: Residenz, 2002)

Dompke, Christoph: *Unterhaltungsmusik im Exil* (Diss., Hamburg University, 1998)

Downes, Stephen: *Music and Decadence in European Modernism: The Case of Central and Eastern Europe* (Cambridge: Cambridge University Press, 2010)

Drew, David, ed. *Über Kurt Weill* (Berlin: Suhrkamp, 1975)

Drew, David: *Kurt Weill: A Handbook* (London: Faber, 1987)

Dümling, Albrecht: *Die verweigerte Heimat: Léon Jessel, der Komponist des 'Schwarzwaldmädel'* (Munich: DTV, 1992)

Dümling, Albrecht, ed.: *Querstand: Hanns Eisler* (Frankfurt: Stroemfeld, 2010)

Dümling, Albrecht: *Die Verschwundenen Musiker: Jüdische Flüchtlinge in Australien* (Vienna: Böhlau, 2011)

Dümling, Albrecht, and Peter Girth, ed.: *Entartete Musik: Dokumentation und Kommentar* (Düsseldorf: Der kleine Verlag, 1988)

Dürhammer, Ilija: *Geheime Botschaften: Homoerotischen Subkulturen im Schubertkreis, bis Hugo von Hofmannsthal und Thomas Berhnard* (Vienna: Böhlau, 2006)

Eberle, Gottfried: *Erwin Schulhoff: Die Referate des Kolloquiums in Köln 7. Okt. 1992* (Hamburg: von Bockel, 1993)

Einstein, Alfred: 'The Position of Modern Music in Germany', *The Sackbut*, vol. 4 (London: 1924)

Eisenstein, Sergei: *Immortal Memories: An Autobiography*, trans. Herbert Marshall (London: Peter Owen, 1983)

Eisler, Hanns: *Musik und Politik: 1921–1962*, 3 vols, with Addendum (Leipzig: VEB, 1982)

Eisler, Hanns: *Fragen Sie mehr über Brecht: Gespräche mit Hans Bunge* (Munich: Sammlung Luchterhand, 1986)

Eisler, Hanns: *Johann Faustus*, ed. Peter Schweinhardt (Wiesbaden: Breitkopf & Härtel, 2005)

Eisler, Hanns, and Theodor W. Adorno: *Komposition für den Film* (Hamburg: Europäische Verlagsanstalt, 1996)

Eisler, Jakob, Horst J. P. Bergmeier, and Bettina Greve: *Vorbei: Dokumentation jüdischen Musiklebens in Berlin, 1933–1938* (Hambergen: Bear Family Records, 2001)

Eisler, Rudolf: *Philosophenlexikon: Leben, Werke und Lehren der Denker* (Berlin: Directmedia, 2007)

Eisler-Fischer, Louise: *Es war nicht immer Liebe: Texte und Briefe*, ed. Jürgen Schebera, Maren Köster, and Friederike Weßmann (Vienna: Sonderzahl, 2006)

Elon, Amos: *The Pity of it All: A History of Jews in Germany 1743–1933* (London: Metropolitan, 2002)

Endelman, Todd M.: *The Jews of Britain, 1656 to 2000* (Berkeley, CA: University of California Press, 2002)

Enzyklopädie der DDR (Berlin: Directmedia, 2004)

Erben, Tino, ed.: *Traum und Wirklichkeit: Wien 1870–1930* (Vienna: Museen der Stadt Wien, 1985)

Europa Almanach (Leipzig: Gustav Keipenheuer, 1925, repr. Leipzig, 1993)

Exhibition Catalogue: Akademie der Künste, *Geschlossene Vorstellung, Der jüdische Kulturbund in Deutschland, 1933–1941* (Berlin: Hentrich, 1992)

Exhibition Catalogue: Stiftung Archiv der Akademie der *Künste: Hanns Eisler: 's müßt dem Himmel Höllenangst werden* (Berlin: Wolke, 1998)

Exhibition Catalogue: Akademie der Künste, ed.: *Ein Freund, ein gute Freund, Der Komponist Werner Richard Heymann* (Berlin: Stiftung Akademie der Künste, 1999)

Exhibition Catalogue: Stiftung Jüdisches Museum Berlin: *Heimat und Exil – Emigration der deutschen Juden nach 1933* (Berlin: Suhrkamp, 2006)

Exhibition Catalogue: Stiftung, Scholoss Neuhardenberg: *Das 'Dritte Reich' und die Musik* (Berlin: Nicolai, 2006)

Farneth, David, Elmar Juchem and Dave Stein, ed.: *Kurt Weill: Ein Leben in Bildern und Dokumenten* (Berlin: Ullstein, 2000)

Fechner, Eberhard: *Die Comedian Harmonists: Sechs Lebensläufe* (Berlin: Beltz, 1988)

Feisst, Sabine: *Schoenberg's New World: The American Years* (New York: Oxford University Press, 2011)

Fetthauer, Sophie: *Musikverlage im Dritten Reich und im Exil* (Hamburg: von Bockel, 2004)

Feuchtwanger, Lion: *Exil* (Frankfurt: Fischer, 1991)

Feuchtwanger, Lion: *Die Geschwister Oppermann* (Berlin: Aufbau, 1993)

Feurstein, Michaela, and Gerhard Milchram: *Jüdisches Wien: Stadtspaziergänge* (Vienna: Böhlau, 2001)

Fischer-Karwin, Heinz: *Das teuerste Vergnügen der Welt: Die Wiener Staatsoper seit 1945* (Salzburg: Bergland, 1979)

Flanner, Janet: *Paris, Germany . . . Reportagen aus Europa, 1931–1950* (Munich: Antje Kunstmann, 1992)

Flesch, Carl: *Erinnerungen eines Geigers* (Zurich: Atlantis, 1960)

Frankel, Jonathan, ed.: *Dark Times, Dire Decisions: Jews and Communism* (Oxford: Oxford University Press, 2004)

Frey, Stefan: *Franz Lehár und die Unterhaltungsmusik im 20. Jahrhundert* (Berlin: Insel, 1999)

Friedmann, Ronald: *Ulbrichts Rundfunkmann: Eine Gerhart Eisler Biographie* (Berlin: Edition Ost, 2007)

Friedrich, Otto: *Before the Deluge: Berlin in the 1920s* (New York: Harper, 1995)

Friedrich, Otto: *City of Nets: A Portrait of Hollywood in the 1940s* (Berkeley, CA: University of California Press, 1997)

Frischauf, Maria: *Der graue Mann: Roman und Gedichte für Arnold Schönberg* (Vienna: Theodor Kramer Gesellschaft, 2000)

Fuhrich, Edda, Ulrike Dembski, and Angela Eder, ed.: *Ambivalenzen: Max Reinhardt und Österreich* (Vienna: Brandstätter, 2004)

Fulbrook, Mary: *The People's State: East German Society from Hitler to Honecker* (New Haven and London: Yale University Press, 2008)

Fulfs, Ingo: *Musiktheater im Nationalsozialismus* (Marburg: Tectum, 1995)

Gál, Hans, ed.: *Brahms Briefe* (Frankfurt: Fischer, 1979)

Gál, Hans: *Musik hinter Stacheldraht: Tageblätter aus dem Sommer 1940* (Pieterlen: Lang, 2003)

Ganglmair, Siegwald, ed.: *Wien 1938* (Vienna: Österreichischer Bundesverlag, 1988)

Gay, Peter: *Modernism: The Lure of Heresy* (New York: Vintage, 2007)

Gay, Peter: *Weimar Culture: The Outsider as Insider* (New York: Norton, 2001)

Gehring, Melina: *Alfred Einstein: Ein Musikwissenschaftler im Exil* (Hamburg: von Bockel, 2007)

Geiger, Friedrich: *Die Drama-Oratorien von Wladimir Vogel, 1896–1984* (Hamburg: von Bockel, 1998)

Geiger, Friedrich, and Thomas Schäfer, ed.: *Exilmusik: Komposition während der NS Zeit* (Hamburg: von Bockel, 1999)

Geiringer, Karl: *Johannes Brahms: Sein Leben und Schaffen* (Kassel: Bärenreiter, 1974)

Geiringer, Karl: *On Brahms and his Circle: Essays and Documentary Studies*, ed. George S. Bozarth (Stirling Heights, MI: Harmonie Park Press, 2006)

Geissmar, Berta: *Musik im Schatten der Politik* (Zurich: Atlantis, 1985)

Gilliam, Bryan: *Music and Performance during the Weimar Republic* (Cambridge: Cambridge University Press, 1994)

Giroud, Françoise: *Alma Mahler, or the Art of Being Loved*, trans. R. M. Stock (Oxford: Oxford University Press, 1991)

Glanz, Christian: *Hanns Eisler, Werk und Leben* (Vienna: Steinbauer, 2008)

Goldhagen, Daniel Jonah: *Die katholische Kirche und der Holocaust* (Munich: Siedler, 2002)

Goldmark, Karl: *Erinnerungen aus meinem Leben* (Berlin: Directmedia, 2006)

Goldsmith, Martin: *The Inextinguishable Symphony* (Hoboken, NJ: John Wiley, 2000)

Goll, Yvan: *Sodom Berlin* (Frankfurt: Fischer, 1985)

Gordon, Eric A.: *Marc the Music: The Life and Work of Marc Blitzstein* (London: St Martin's Press, 1989)

Gradenwitz, Peter: *Arnold Schönberg und seine Meisterschüler Berlin, 1925–1933* (Vienna: Zsolnay, 1998)

Graetz, Heinrich: *Geschichte der Juden* (Berlin: Arani, 1998)

Graf, Max: *Die Wiener Oper* (Vienna: Humboldt, 1955)

Graf, Oskar Maria: *Die Flucht ins Mittelmäßige: ein New Yorker Roman* (Munich: DTV, 1983)

Grenville, Anthony: *Continental Britons: Jewish Refugees from Nazi Europe* (London: Jewish Museum, 2002)

Grünwald, Rolf, and Rainer Höynck: *Der Titania-Palast: Berliner Kino- und Kulturgeschichte* (Berlin: Hentrich, 1992)

Grünzweig, Werner, et al.: *Artur Schnabel Musiker, 1882–1951* (Berlin: Akademie der Künste, 2001)

Haas, Michael, and Christopher Hailey, ed.: *Franz Schreker: Grenzgänger/Grenzklänge* (Vienna: Mandelbaum, 2004)

Haas, Michael, and Marcus G. Patka, ed.: *Hans Gál und Egon Wellesz: Continental Britons* (Vienna: Mandelbaum, 2004)

Haas, Michael, Werner Hanak, and Karin Wagner, ed.: *Endstation Schein–Heiligenstadt: Eric Zeisls Flucht nach Hollywood* (Vienna: JMW, 2006)

Haas, Michael, Feurstein Michaele, and Brendan Carroll, ed.: *Die Korngolds* (Vienna: JMW, 2008)

Haas, Michael, Wiebke Krohn, and Marcus G. Patka, ed.: *Hanns Eisler: Mensch und Masse* (Vienna: JMW, 2009)

Haas, Michael, and Werner Hanak-Lettner, ed.: *Ernst Toch: Das leben als Geographische Fuge* (Vienna: JMW, 2010)

Haber, Michael: *Das Jüdische bei Gustav Mahler* (Pieterlen: Lang, 2009)

Haefeli, Anton: *Die Internationale Gesellschaft für Neue Musik: Ihre Geschichte von 1922 bis zur Gegenwart* (Zurich: Atlantis, 1982)

Hailey, Christopher: *Franz Schreker, 1878–1934: A Cultural Biography* (Cambridge: Cambridge University Press, 1993)

Hailey, Christopher: *Briefwechsel Paul Bekker/Franz Schreker* (Aachen: Rimbaud, 1994)

Hailey, Christopher, ed.: *Alban Berg and His World* (Princeton, NJ: Princeton University Press, 2010)

Hamann, Brigitte: *Hitlers Wien: Lehrjahre eines Diktators* (Munich: Piper, 1997)

Hamann, Brigitte: *Winifred Wagner oder Hitlers Bayreuth* (Munich: Piper, 2002)

Hanslick, Eduard: *Geschichte des Konzertwesens in Wien*, 2 vols (Vienna: Müller, 1869–70)

Hanslick, Eduard: *Music Criticisms, 1846–1899*, trans. and ed. Henry Pleasants (London: Penguin, 1950)

Hanslick, Eduard: *Aus meinem Leben* (Berlin: Directmedia, 2006)

Hanslick, Eduard: *Vom Musikalisch-Schönen* (Darmstadt: WBG, 2010)

Hase, Hellmuth von: *Jahrbuch der deutschen Musik, 1943* (Leipzig: Breitkopf & Härtel, 1943)

Hauschild, Jan-Christoph, and Michael Werner: *Heinrich Heine* (Berlin: DTV, 2002)

Hayman, Ronald: *Bertolt Brecht: Der unbequeme Klassiker*, trans. Alexandra von Reinhardt (Munich: Heyne, 1983)

Heer, Hannes, Jürgen Kesting, and Peter Schmidt, ed.: *Verstummte Stimmen: Die Vertreibung der 'Juden' aus der Oper 1933 bis 1945* (Berlin: Metropol, 2008)

Heilbut, Anthony: *Exiled in Paradise: German Refugee Artists and Intellectuals in America from 1930 to the Present* (Boston: Beacon Press, 1983)

Heindl, Christian, Michael Publig, and Walter Weidringer, ed.: *125 Jahre Musikverlag Doblinger* (Vienna: Doblinger, 2001)

Heine, Heinrich: *Geständnisse* (Berlin: Directmedia, 2006)

Heister, Hanns-Werner, ed.: *Johannes Brahms oder Die Relativierung der 'absoluten' Musik* (Hamburg: von Bockel, 1997)

Heister, Hanns-Werner: *Musik/Revolution: Festschrift für Georg Knepler zum 90. Geburtstag* (Hamburg: von Bockel, 1997)

Heister, Hanns-Werner, Claudia Maurer-Zenck, and Peter Petersen, ed.: *Musik im Exil* (Frankfurt: Fischer, 1993)

Heister, Hanns-Werner, and Hans-Günter Klein, ed.: *Musik und Musikpolitik im Faschistischen Deutschland* (Frankfurt: Fischer, 1984)

Helmit, Martina: *Ruth Schönthal: ein kompositorischer Werdegang im Exil* (Hildesheim: Olms, 1994)

Henke, Matthias: *Ich hab' von dem fahrenden Zuge geräumt: Die Lebensreise des Komponisten Ernst Krenek* (Stein in Krems: Ernst Krenek Forum, 2008)

Hennenberg, Fritz: *Er muß was Wunderbares sein . . . Ralph Benatzky, zwischen 'Weißem Rößl' und Hollywood* (Vienna: Zsolnay, 1998)

Hennenberg, Fritz: *Hanns Eisler* (Reinbek: Rororo, 1998)

Hermand, Jost, and Frank Trommler: *Die Kultur der Weimarer Republik* (Frankfurt: Fischer, 1988)

Herz, Henriette: *Ihr Leben und ihre Erinnerungen* (Berlin: Directmedia, 2006)

Herz, Peter: *Gestern war ein schöner Tag: Liebeserklärung eines Librettisten an die Vergangenheit* (Vienna: Österreichischer Bundesverlag, 1985)

Heymann, Werner Richard: *'Liebling, mein Herz lässt dich grüßen'*, ed. Hubert Ortkemper (Berlin: Henschel, 2001)

Hiller, Ferdinand: *Erinnerungsblätter* (Berlin: Directmedia, 2006)

Hilmar, Ernst, ed.: *Arnold Schönberg: Gedenk Ausstellung* (Vienna: Universal, 1974)

Hilmes, Oliver: *Der Streit ums Deutsche: Alfred Heuß und die Zeitschrift für Musik* (Hamburg: von Bockel, 2003)

Hilmes, Oliver: *Herrin des Hügels: Das Leben der Cosima Wagner* (Munich: Siedler, 2007)

Hindemith, Paul: *Unterweisung im Tonsatz* (Mainz: Schott, 1937)

Hindemith, Paul: *Aufsätze, Vorträge, Reden* (Zurich: Atlantis, 1994)

Hindemith, Paul: *Komponist in seiner Welt* (Zurich: Atlantis, 1994)

Hinton, Stephen, Jürgen Schebera, and Elmar Juchem, ed.: *Kurt Weill Musik und musikalisches Theater: Gesammelte Schriften* (Mainz: Schott, 2000)

Hobsbawn, Eric: *The Age of Empire: 1875–1914* (New York: Vintage, 1987)

Hobsbawn, Eric: *Age of Extremes: The Short Twentieth Century, 1914–991* (London: Abacus, 1994)

Hobsbawn, Eric: *Interesting Times* (London: Allen Lane, 2002)

Hobsbawn, Eric: *The Age of Revolution* (London: Orion, 2010)

Hobsbawn, Eric: *The Age of Capital: 1848–1875* (London: Orion, 2010)

Hoffmann, Rudolf Stefan: *Franz Schreker* (Vienna: E.P. Tal, 1921)

Hollaender, Friedrich: *Menschliches Treibgut* (Bonn: Weidle, 1995)

Horowitz, Joseph: *Artists in Exile* (New York: Harper Collins, 2008)

Illiano, Roberto, and Massimiliano Sala, ed.: *Music and Dictatorship in Europe and Latin America* (Tournhout: Brepols, 2009)

Janik, Allan and Toulmin Stephen: *Wittgensteins Wien* (Munich: Piper, 1987)

Jansen, Wolfgang: *Das Variété* (Berlin: Hentrich, 1990)

Jelavich, Peter: *Berlin Cabaret* (Cambridge, MA: Harvard University Press, 1993)

Jelinek-Heimann, Felicitas, ed.: *Judenfragen: Jüdische Positionen von Assimilation bis Zionismus* (Vienna: JMW, 1996)

John, Eckhard: *Musikbolschewismus: Die Politisierung der Musik in Deutschland, 1918–1939* (Stuttgart: Metzler, 1993)

John, Eckhard, and Heidy Zimmermann, ed.: *Jüdische Musik?* (Vienna: Böhlau, 2004)

Johnston, William M.: *The Austrian Mind* (Berkeley, CA: University of California Press, 1972)

Josef Weinberger Ltd: 100 Years Remembered, 1885–1985 (London: Weinberger, 1985)

Jüdisches Museum der Stadt Wien: *Die Macht der Bilder: Antisemitische Vorurteile und Mythen* (Vienna: Picus, 1995)

Judt, Tony: *Postwar: A History of Europe Since 1945* (London: Pimlico, 2007)

Jung, Hermann, ed.: *Spurensicherung: Der Komponist Ernst Toch: Mannheimer Emigrantenschicksale* (Pieterlen: Lang, 2007)

Jung, Ute: *Walter Braunfels* (Regensburg: Bosse, 1980)

Jürges, Michael: *Gern hab' ich die Frau'n geküßt: die Richard Tauber Biographie* (Munich: List, 2000)

Kafka, Hans: *Hollywood Calling: Die Aufbau Kolumne zum Film-Exil* (Hamburg: Conference Point, 2002)

Kapp, Juilius: *Franz Schreker* (Munich: Dreimasken Verlag, 1921)

Karas, Joža: *Music in Terezín, 1941–1945* (Hillsdale, NY: Pendragon, 1985)

Karnes, Kevin C.: *Music, Criticism, and the Challenge of History: Shaping Modern Musical Thought in Late Nineteenth-Century Vienna* (Oxford: Oxford University Press, 2008)

Kater, Michael H.: *The Twisted Muse: Musicians and their Music in the Third Reich* (Oxford: Oxford University Press, 1997)

Keiser-Hayne, Helga, ed.: *Beteiligt euch, es geht um eure Erde: Erika Mann und ihr politisches Kabarett die 'Pfeffermühle' 1933–1937* (Munich: Spangenberg, 1990)

Kienzl, Heinz, and Susanne Kirchner, ed.: *Ein neuer Frühling wird in der Heimat blühen* (Vienna: Deuticke, 2002)

Kirk, Timothy: *Nazism and the Working Class in Austria* (Cambridge: Cambridge University Press, 1996)

Klein, Hans-Günter, ed.: *Gideon Klein Materialien* (Hamburg: von Bockel, 1995)

Klein, Hans-Günter, ed.: *Viktor Ullmann Materialien* (Hamburg: von Bockel, 1995)

Klein, Hans-Günter, ed.: *Viktor Ullmann: Referate des Symposions anlässlich des 50. Todestags* (Hamburg: von Bockel, 1996)

Kleinlercher, Alexandra: *Zwischen Wahrheit und Dichtung: Antisemitismus und Nationalsozialismus bei Heimito von Doderer* (Vienna: Böhlau, 2011)

Klein-Primavesi, Claudia: *Die Familie Primavesi und die Künstler Hanak, Hoffmann, Klimt: 100 Jahre Wiener Werkstätte* (Vienna: Claudia Klein-Primavesi, 2004)

Kleinschmidt, Sebastian, ed.: *Stimme und Spiegel: Fünf Jahrzehnte 'Sinn und Form' eine Auswahl* (Berlin: Aufbau, 1998)

Klemperer, Viktor: *LTI Notizbuch eines Philologen* (Berlin, Aufbau, 1947)

Klemperer, Viktor: *Die Tagebücher 1933–1945* (Berlin: Aufbau, 1998)

Klotz, Volker: *Operette – Porträt und Handbuch einer unerhörten Kunst* (Kassel: Bärenreiter, 2004)

Knaus, Herwig, and Thomas Leibnitz, ed.: *Altenberg bis Zuckerkandl: Briefe an Alban Berg – Liebesbriefe von Alban Berg* (Vienna: Löcker 2009)

Knepler, Hugo: *O Diese Künstler: Indiskretionen eines Managers* (Vienna: FIBA, 1931)

Knessl, Lothar: *Ernst Krenek* (Vienna: Lafite, 1967)

Koestler, Arthur: *Als Zeuge der Zeit* (Frankfurt: Fischer, 2005)

Kohlbauer-Fritz, Gabriele, ed.: *Zwischen Ost und West: Galizische Juden und Wien* (Vienna: JMW, 2000)

Korngold, Julius: *Deutsches Opernschaffen der Gegenwart* (Vienna: Leonhardt, 1921)

Korngold, Julius: *Die Korngolds in Wien* (Zurich: M&T Verlag, 1991)

Korngold, Luzi: *Erich Wolfgang Korngold* (Vienna: Lafite, 1967)

Kowalke, Kim, ed.: *A New Orpheus: Essays on Kurt Weill* (New Haven and London: Yale University Press, 1986)

Kowalke, Kim: 'Dancing with the Devil: Publishing Modern Music in the Third Reich', *Modernism/Modernity*, vol. 8, no. 1 (2001), pp. 1–41.

Kraus, Karl: *Schriften*, ed. Christian Wagenknecht (Berlin: Directmedia, 2007)

Krenek, Ernst: *Im Atem der Zeit: Erinnerungen an die Moderne* (Munich; Diana, 1998)

Krones, Hartmut: *Marcel Rubin* (Vienna: Lafite, 1975)

Krones, Hartmut: *Arnold Schönberg, Werk und Leben* (Vienna: Steinbauer, 2005)

Krug, Hartmut, and Michael Nungesser, ed.: *Kunst im Exil in Großbritannien, 1933–1945* (Berlin: Fröhlich & Kaufmann, 1986)

Kubik, Reinhold, and Thomas Trabitsch, ed.: *Gustav Mahler und Wien* (Vienna: Brandstätter, 2010)

Kuh, Anton: *Luftlinien: Feuilletons, Essays und Publizistik*, ed. Ruth Greuner (Vienna: Löcker, 1991)

Kuh, Anton: *Der Unsterbliche Österreicher*, ed. Ulrich Schulenburg (Vienna: Löcker, 2001)

Kunst und Literatur im antifaschistischen Exil, 1933–1945, 6 vols (Leipzig: Reclam, 1981)

Lafitte, François: *The Internment of Aliens* (London: Libris 1988)

Levi, Erik: *Music in the Third Reich* (London: St Martin's, 1996)

Lohrmann, Klaus: *Zwischen Finanz und Toleranz: Das Haus Habsburg und die Juden* (Graz: Styria, 2000)

London, Louise: *Whitehall and the Jews 1933–1948* (Cambridge: Cambridge University Press, 2000)

Lucchesi, Joachim, and Ronald K. Shull: *Musik bei Brecht* (Berlin: Suhrkamp, 1986)

Lunzer, Heinz, and Victoria Lunzer-Talos: *Joseph Roth, 1894–1939* (Vienna: Zirkular, 1994)

Lustiger, Arno: *Rotbuch: Stalin und die Juden* (Berlin: Aufbau, 2002)

Magris, Claudio: *Danube*, trans. Patrick Creagh (London: Collins Harvill, 1990)

Mahler, Alma: *Tagebuch-Suiten, 1898–1902*, ed. Anthony Beamont (Frankfurt: Fischer, 1997)

Mahler, Gustav: *Briefe*, ed. Mathias Hansen (Leipzig: Reclam, 1981)

Malet, Marian, and Anthony Grenville, ed.: *Changing Countries: The Experience and Achievement of German-Speaking Exiles from Hitler in Britain from 1933 to Today* (London: Libris, 2002)

Malte Fischer, Jens: *Jahrhundertdämmerung: Ansichten eines anderen Fin de siècle* (Vienna: Zsolnay, 2000)

Malte Fischer, Jens: *Gustav Mahler* (Vienna: Zsolnay, 2003)

Mann, Golo: *Deutsche Geschichte des 19. und 20. Jahrhundert* (Frankfurt: Fischer, 2008)

Mann, Klaus: *Mephisto: Roman einer Karriere* (Reinbek: Rororo, 1982)

Mann, Thomas: *Betrachtungen eines Unpolitischen* (Berlin: Fischer, 1918)

Mann, Thomas: *Doktor Faustus* (Frankfurt: Fischer, 1947)

Maurer-Zenck, Claudia: *Ernst Krenek: Ein Komponist im Exil* (Vienna: Lafite, 1980)

Mayer, Hans: *Gelebte Musik: Erinnerungen* (Berlin: Suhrkamp, 1999)

McCredie, Andrew D.: *Karl Amadeus Hartmann: Sein Leben und Werk* (Wilhelmshaven: Heinrichshofen, 1980)

Meder, Iris, and Evi Fuks, ed.: *Oskar Strnad, 1879–1935* (Vienna: Anton Pustet, 2007)

Metzger, Rainer, and Christian Brandstätter, ed.: *Berlin: The Twenties* (New York: Abrams, 2007)

Meyer, Christian, ed.: *Schönberg Kandinsky: Blauer Reiter und die Russische Avantgarde* (Vienna: Arnold Schoenberg Center, 2000)

Meysels, Lucian O., *In meinem Salon ist Österreich: Berta Zuckerkandl und ihre Zeit* (Vienna: Herold, 1984)

Michel, Johann, and Richard Toeman: *100 Jahre Bühnen- und Musikalienverlag Josef Weinberger, 1885–1985* (Vienna: Weinberger, 1985)

Morgenstern, Soma: *Alban Berg und seine Idole: Erinnerungen und Briefe* (Berlin: Aufbau, 1999)

Morgenstern, Soma: *Flucht in Frankreich* (Berlin: Aufbau, 2000)

Morgenstern, Soma: *Joseph Roths Flucht und Ende* (Springe: zu Klampen Verlag, 1994)

Morreau, Annette: *Emanuel Feuermann* (New Haven and London: Yale University Press, 2002)

Mösch, Stephan: *Weihe Werkstatt Wirklichkeit: Wagners Parsifal in Bayreuth, 1882–1933* (Kassel: Bärenreiter, 2009)

Moskovitz, Marc D.: *Alexander Zemlinsky: A Lyric Symphony* (Woodbridge: Boydell, 2010)

Müller, Hans-Peter: *Ein Genie bin ich selber! Hanns Eisler in Anekdoten, Aphorismen und Aussprüchen* (Berlin: Verlag neuer Musik, 1984)

Musgrave, Michael, ed.: *A Brahms Reader* (New Haven and London: Yale University Press, 2000)

Mysels, Lucian O.: *In meinem Salon ist Österreich: Berta Zuckerkandl und ihre Zeit* (Vienna: Herold, 1984)

Naegele, Verena: *Viktor Ullmann: Komponieren in verlorener Zeit* (Munich: Dittrich, 2002)

Niekerk, Carl: *Reading Mahler: German Culture and Jewish Identity in Fin-de-Siècle Vienna* (Rochester, NY: Camden House, 2010)

Notley, Margaret: *Lateness and Brahms: Music and Culture in the Twilight of Viennese Liberalism* (Oxford: Oxford University Press, 2007)

Obermaier, Walter: *Johann Strauss ent-arisiert: die Sammlung Strauss-Meyszner* (Vienna: Wiener Stadt- und Landesbibliothek, 2003)

Österreicher, Rudolf: *Emmerich Kálmán das Leben eines Operettenfürsten* (Vienna: Amalthea, 1988)

Österreichische Musikzeitschrift 2/2010: 'Egon Wellesz' [special number] (2010)

Overesch, Manfred, and Friedrich Wilhelm Saal: *Deutsche Geschichte von Tag zu Tag 1918–1949* (Berlin: Directmedia, 2004)

Pahlen, Kurt: *The Magic World of Music*, trans. Oliver Coburn (London: White Lion, 1948)

Palmer, Christopher: *The Composers of Hollywood* (London: Marion Boyars, 1990)

Pass, Walter, Gerhard Scheit, and Wilhelm Svoboda, ed.: *Orpheus im Exil: die Vertreibung der österreichischen Musik von 1938 bis 1945* (Vienna: Verlag für Gesellschaftskritik, 1995)

Pauley, Bruce F.: *From Prejudice to Persecution: A History of Austrian Anti-Semitism* (Chapel Hill, NC: University of North Carolina Press, 1992)

Peacock-Jezic, Diane: *The Musical Migration and Ernst Toch* (Ames, IA: Iowa State University Press, 1989)

Peduzzi, Lubomír: *Pavel Haas: Leben und Werk*, trans. Thomas Mandl (Hamburg: von Bockel, 1996)

Pells, Richard: *Not like Us: How Europeans have loved, hated, and transformed American Culture since World War II* (New York: Basic Books, 1997)

Petersen, Peter (ed.): *Berthold Goldschmidt, Komponist und Dirigent: Ein Musiker-Leben zwischen Hamburg, Berlin und London* (Hamburg: von Bockel, 1994)

Pirker, Peter: *Subversion deutscher Herrschaft, der britische Kriegsgeheimdienst SOE und Österreich* Vienna: Vienna University Press, 2012)

Pollak, Michael: *Wien 1900: Eine verletzte Identität*, trans. Andreas Pfeuffer (Freiburg: UVK, 1997)

Pöllmann, Helmut: *Erich Korngold: Aspekte seines Schaffens* (Mainz: Schott, 1998)

Potter, Pamela M.: *Most German of the Arts* (New Haven and London: Yale University Press, 1998)

Potter, Tully: *Adolf Busch: The Life of an Honest Musician* (London: Toccata Press, 2010)

Preston, Paul: *¡Comrades! Portraits from the Spanish Civil War* (New York: Fontana, 2000)

Priberg, Fred K.: *Musik im NS Staat* (Frankfurt: Fischer, 1982)

Priberg, Fred K.: *Kraftprobe: Wilhelm Furtwängler im Dritten Reich* (Gütersloh: Brockhaus, 1986)

Priberg, Fred K: *Handbuch deutscher Musiker, 1933–1945* (Kiel: Fred K.Priberg, 2004)

Prosl, Robert Maria: *Edmund Eysler: Aus Wiens zweiter klassischer Operettenzeit* (Vienna: Kühne, 1947)

Pross, Steffen: *In London treffen wir uns wieder* (Frankfurt: Eichborn, 2000)

Publig, Maria: *Richard Strauss: Bürger, Künstler, Rebell: Eine historische Annäherung* (Graz: Styria, 1999)

Purin, Bernhard: *Salomon Sulzer: Kantor, Komponist, Reformer* (Bregenz: Land Voralberg, 1991)

Pynsent, Robert, ed.: *Decadence and Innovation: Austro-Hungarian Life and Art at the Turn of the Century* (London: Weidenfeld & Nicolson, 1989)

Raab-Hansen, Jutta: *NS-Verfolgte Musiker in England* (Hamburg: von Bockel, 1996)

Rathkolb, Oliver: *Führertreu und gottbegnadet: Künstlereliten im Dritten Reich* (Vienna: ÖVB, 1991)

Reich-Ranicki, Marcel: *Über Hilde Spiel* (Munich: DTV, 1998)

Reich-Ranicki, Marcel: *Über Ruhestörer Juden in der deutschen Literatur* (Munich: DTV, 2000)

Reilly, Edward R.: *Gustav Mahler und Guido Adler* (Vienna: Universal, 1978)

Richter, Alfred: *Aus Leipzigs musikalischer Glanzzeit* (Berlin: Directmedia, 2006)

Riding, Alan: *And the Show Went On: Cultural Life in Nazi-Occupied Paris* (New York: Knopf, 2010)

Riedl, Joachim, ed.: *Wien, Stadt der Juden: Die Welt der Tante Jolesch* (Vienna: Zsolnay, 2004)

Ross, Alex: *The Rest is Noise: Listening to the Twentieth Century* (London: Fourth Estate, 2008)

Rosteck, Jens: *Zwei auf einer Insel: Lotte Lenya und Kurt Weill* (Berlin: Propyläen, 1999)

Roth, Joseph: *Hiob* (Munich: DTV, 2002)

Roth, Joseph: *Die Kapuzinergruft* (Munich: DTV, 2003)

Roth, Joseph: *Radetzkymarsch* (Munich, DTV, 2004)

Roth, Joseph: *Das Spinnennetz* (Munich: DTV, 2004)

Roth, Joseph: *Juden auf Wanderschaft* (Munich: DTV, 2006)

Rotthaler, Viktor: *Friedrich Hollaender* (Hambergen: Bear Family Records, 1996)

Russell, John: *Erich Kleiber: A Memoir* (London: Deutsch, 1957)

Ryding, Eric, and Rebecca Pechefsky: *Bruno Walter: A World Elsewhere* (New Haven and London: Yale University Press, 2001)

Sachs, Harvey: *Music in Fascist Italy* (New York: Norton, 1987)

Sawabe, Yukiko: 'Das Schaffen jüdischer nationaler Musik und dessen Problematik in Zusammenhang mit Veranstaltungen jüdischer Musikvereine in Wien 1918–1938' (Diss., University of Vienna, 2000)

Schebera, Jürgen: *Gustav Brecher und die Leipziger Oper 1923–1933* (Peters, 1990)

Schebera, Jürgen: *Hanns Eisler: Eine Bildbiographie* (Berlin: Henschel, 1981)

Schebera, Jürgen: *Hanns Eisler im USA – Exil 1938–1948* (Weimar: Hain, 1978)

Schebera, Jürgen: *Kurt Weill: Leben und Werk* (Königstein: Atenäum, 1984)

Schebera, Jürgen: *Hanns Eisler* (Mainz: Schott, 1998)

Scheit, Gerhard, and Wilhelm Svoboda: *Feindbild Gustav Mahler: Zur antisemitischen Abwehr der Moderne in Österreich* (Vienna: Sonderzahl, 2002)

Scheit, Gerhard, and Wilhelm Svoboda: *Treffpunkt der Moderne: Gustav Mahler, Theodor W. Adorno, Wiener Traditionen* (Vienna: Sonderzahl, 2010)

Schenk, Dietmar: *Die Hochschule für Musik zu Berlin* (Wiesbaden: Franz Steiner, 2004)

Schenker, Heinrich: *The Art of Performance*, ed. Heribert Esser, trans. Irene Schreier Scott (Oxford: Oxford University Press, 2000)

Schinköth, Thomas: *Musik: das Ende einer Illusion? Günter Raphael im NS-Staat* (Hamburg: von Bockel, 2010)

Schmidt, Matthias, ed.: *Ernst Krenek Zeitgenosse des 20. Jahrhunderts* (Vienna: Stadt- und Landesbibliothek, 2000)

Schnabel, Artur: *Aus dir wird nie ein Pianist* (Hofheim am Taunus: Wolke, 1991)

Schnauber, Cornelius: *Spaziergänge durch das Hollywood der Emigranten* (Hamburg: Arche, 2000)

Schneider, Heiko: *Wahrhaftigkeit und Fortschritt: Ernst Toch in Deutschland, 1919–1933* (Mainz: Schott, 2007)

Schnitzler, Artur: *Der Weg ins Freie* (Hamburg: Spiegel, 1908)

Schnitzler, Artur: *Jugend in Wien* (Frankfurt: Fischer, 2006)

Schnitzler, Heinrich, and Therese Nickl: *Liebe die Starb vor der Zeit: Arthur Schnitzler und Olga Waissnix – Ein Briefwechsel* (Graz: Molden, 1981)

Schoenberg, Arnold: *Harmonielehre* (Vienna: Universal, 1949)

Schoenberg, Arnold, and Wassily Kandinsky: *Briefe, Dokumente einer außergewöhnlichen Begegnung*, ed. Jelena Hahl-Koch (Munich: DTV, 1983)

Schoenberg, Randol, ed.: *Apropos Doktor Faustus: Briefwechsel Arnold Schönberg–Thomas Mann, 1930–1951* (Vienna: Czernin, 2009)

Schoeps, Julius H., ed.: *Juden als Träger Bürgerlicher Kultur in Deutschland* (Stuttgart and Bonn: Burg, 1989)

Scholz, Dieter David: *Richard Wagners Antisemitismus. Jahrhundertgenie im Zwielicht: Eine Korrektur* (Berlin: Parthas, 2000)

Schoolfield, George C.: *A Baedeker of Decadence. Charting a Literary Fashion, 1884–1927* (New Haven and London: Yale University Press, 2003)

Schorske, Carl E.: *Fin de Siècle Vienna: Politics and Culture* (New York: Vintage, 1981)

Schubert, Kurt: *Die Geschichte des Österreichischen Judentums* (Vienna: Böhlau, 2008)

Schüler der Wiener Schule (Vienna: Internationale Musikforschungsgesellschaft, 1995)

Schulte, Michael: *Berta Zuckerkandl: Salonnière, Journalistin, Geheimdiplomatin* (Zurich: Atrium, 2006)

Schultz, Ingo: *Verlorene Werke Viktor Ullmanns im Spiegel zeitgenössischer Presseberichte* (Hamburg: von Bockel, 1994)

Schumann, Otto: *Geschichte der deutschen Musik* (Leipzig; Bibliographisches Institut, 1940)

Schuster, Peter-Klaus, ed.: *Die Kunststadt München 1937: Nationalsozialismus und 'Entartete Kunst'*, (Munich: Prestel, 1988)

Schwaiger, Michael, ed.: *Bertolt Brecht und Erwin Piscator: Experimentelles Theater im Berlin der Zwanzigerjahre* (Vienna: Brandstätter, 2004)

Schwaner, Birgit: *Die Wittgensteins: Kunst und Klakül* (Vienna: Metroverlag, 2008)

Schwarz, Otto: *Marcel Prawy: ein großes Leben neu erzählt* (Vienna: Amalthea, 2006)

Schweinhardt, Peter: *Fluchtpunkt Wien: Hanns Eisler Wiener Arbeiten nach der Rückkehr aus dem Exil* (Wiesbaden: Breitkopf & Härtel, 2006)

Schweitzer, Eva: *Amerika und der Holocaust: die verschwiegene Geschichte* (Munich: Knaur, 2004)

Sebestyén, György: *Paul Abraham: Aus dem Leben eines Operettenkomponisten* (Vienna: Verlag der Österreichischen Staatsdruckerei, 1987)

Service, Robert: *Comrades – Communism: A World History* (London: Pan, 2007)

Sinkovicz, Wilhelm: *Mehr als zwölf Töne: Arnold Schönberg* (Vienna: Zsolnay, 1998)

Slavický, Milan: *Gideon Klein: A Fragment of Life and Work*, trans. Dagmar Steinová (Prague: Helvetica–Tempora, 1995)

Snowman, Daniel: *The Hitler Émigrés: The Cultural Impact on Britain of Refugees from Nazism* (London: Chatto & Windus, 2002)

Sperber, Manès: *Wie eine Träne im Ozean* (Munich: DTV, 1980)

Spiel, Hilde: *Englische Ansichten: Berichte aus Kultur, Geschichte und Politik* (Munich: DVA, 1984)

Spiel, Hilde: *Glanz und Untergang: Wien 1866 bis 1938* (Munich: DTV, 1994)

Spiel, Hilde: *Rückkehr nach Wien: Ein Tagebuch, 1946* (Vienna: Milena, 1968)

Spiel, Hilde: *Welche Welt ist meine Welt? Erinnerungen, 1946–1989* (Munich: List, 1990)

Spohr, Louis: *Lebenserinnerungen* (Berlin: Directmedia, 2006)

Spoto, Donald: *Dietrich* (New York; Bantam, 1992)

Spoto, Donald: *Lenya: A Life* (New York: Viking, 1989)

Sprengel, Peter, ed.: *Schall und Rauch: Erlaubtes und Verbotenes Spieltexte des ersten Max-Reinhardt-Kabaretts (Berlin 1901/2)* (Berlin: Nicolai, 1991)

Sprengel, Peter: *Scheunenvierteltheater Jüdische Schauspieltruppen und Jiddische Dramatik in Berlin 1900–1918* (Berlin: Fannei & Walz, 1995)

Stefan, Paul: *Das neue Haus* (Vienna: Strache, 1919)

Steinacher, Gerald: *Nazis on the Run: How Hitler's Henchmen Fled Justice* (Oxford: Oxford University Press, 2011)

Steinberg, Michael P.: *Judaism Musical and Unmusical* (Chicago, IL: University of Chicago Press, 2007)

Steinberg, Michael P.: *Listening to Reason: Culture, Subjectivity and Nineteenth-Century Music* (Princeton, NJ: Princeton University Press, 2004)

Steinberg, Michael P.: *The Meaning of the Salzburg Festival: Austria as Theater and Ideology, 1890–1938* (Ithaca, NY: Cornell University Press, 1990)

Steinweis, Alan E.: *Art, Ideology and Economics in Nazi Germany: The Reichs Chambers of Music, Theater, and the Visual Arts* (Chapel Hill, NC: University of North Carolina Press, 1993)

Stengel, Theo, and Herbert Gerigk: *Lexikon der Juden in der Musik* (Berlin: Hahnfeld, 1943)

Stern, Hellmut: *Saitensprünge: Erinnerungen eines Kosmopoliten wider Willen* (Berlin: Aufbau, 2001)

Stevens, Lewis: *Composers of Classical Music of Jewish Descent* (Edgware: Vallentine Mitchell, 2003)

Stoetzler, Marcel: *The State, the Nation and the Jews: Liberalism and the Anti-Semitism Dispute in Bismarck's Germany* (Lincoln, NE: University of Nebraska Press, 2008)

Stonor Saunders, Frances: *Who Paid the Piper? The CIA and the Cultural Cold War* (London: Granta, 1999)

Stourzh, Gerald: *Wege zur Grundrechtsdemokratie* (Vienna: Böhlau, 1989)

Strauss, Richard, and Hugo von Hofmannsthal: *A Working Friendship: Correspondence*, trans. Hans Hammelmann and Ewald Osers (New York: Vienna House, 1961)

Streibel, Robert, ed.: *Eugenie Schwarzwald und ihr Kreis* (Vienna: Picus, 1996)

Stuckenschmidt, H. H.: *Arnold Schoenberg*, trans. Edith Temple Roberts and Humphrey Searle (London: John Calder, 1964)

Stuckenschmidt, H. H., Heidi Schreker-Bures, and W. Öhlmann: *Franz Schreker* (Vienna: Lafite, 1970)

Suchy, Irene, Allan Janik, and Georg Predota, ed.: *Empty Sleeve: Der Musiker und Mäzen Paul Wittgenstein* (Innsbruck: Studienverlag, 2006)

Symons, David: *Egon Wellesz: Composer* (Wilhelmshaven: Heinrichshofen, 1996)

Taruskin, Richard: *The Oxford History of Western Music*, 5 vols (Oxford: Oxford University Press, 2010)

Tausky, Vilém and Margaret: *Vilém Tausky Tells His Story* (London: Stainer and Bell, 1979)

Taylor, Ronald: *Kurt Weill: Composer in a Divided World* (New York: Simon and Schuster, 1991)

Thacker, Toby: *Music after Hitler, 1945-1955* (Farnham: Ashgate, 2007)

Tietze Hans: *Die Juden Wiens* (Vienna: Mandelbaum, 2007)

Toch, Ernst: *The Shaping Forces of Music* (Mineola, NY: Dover, 1977)

Toller, Ernst: *Eine Jugend in Deutschland* (Reinbek: Rororo, 1990)

Torberg, Friedrich: *Die Tante Jolesch, oder Der Untergang des Abendlands in Anekdoten* (Munich: DTV, 1977)

Traber, Habakuk, and Elmar Weingarten: *Verdrängte Musik: Berliner Komponisten im Exil* (Berlin: Argon, 1987)

Tucholsky, Kurt: *Deutsches Tempo: Texte 1911 bis 1932* (Reinbek: Rowohlt, 1990)

Ullmann, Viktor: *26 Kritiken über Musikalische Veranstaltungen in Terezín*, ed. Ingo Schultz (Hamburg: von Bockel, 1993)

Universal Edition 1901-2001 (Vienna: Universal, 2001)

Vaget, Hans Rudolf: *Seelenzauber: Thomas Mann und die Musik* (Frankfurt: Fischer, 2006)

Viereck, Peter: *Metapolitics: From Wagner and the German Romantics to Hitler* (New Brunswick, NJ: Transaction, 2007)

Viertel, Salka: The Kindness of Strangers: A Theatrical Life (Austin, TX: Holt, Rinehart, and Winston, 1969)

Vogelsang, Konrad: *Filmmusik im Dritten Reich: Eine Dokumentation* (Freiburg: Centaurus, 1993)

Vogg, Herbert: *Am Beispiel Egon Wellesz: Briefwechsel mit Doblinger* (Vienna: Doblinger, 1996)

Voit, Jochen: *Er rührte an den Schlaf der Welt: Ernst Busch* (Berlin: Aufbau, 2010)

Völker, Klaus: *Max Herrmann-Neisse: Künstler, Kneipen, Kabaretts* (Berlin: Hentrich, 1991)

Vries, Willem de: *Sonderstab Musik: Organisierte Plünderungen in Westeurope, 1940-45* (Munich: Dittrich, 1998)

Wacks, Georg: *Die Budapester Orpheumgesellschaft: Ein Variété in Wien, 1889-1919* (Vienna: Holzhausen, 2002)

Wagner, Cosima: *Tagebücher* (Berlin: Directmedia, 2004)

Wagner, Friedelind: *Nacht über Bayreuth* (Munich: List, 2002)

Wagner, Gottried: *Twilight of the Wagners: The Unveiling of a Family's Legacy* (London: Picador, 2000)

Wagner, Guy: *Korngold: Musik ist Musik* (Berlin: Matthes & Seitz, 2002)

Wagner, Karin, ed.: *Es grüßt Dich Erichisrael: Briefe von und an Eric Zeisl* (Vienna: Czernin, 2008)

Wagner, Karin: *Fremd bin ich ausgezogen: Eric Zeisl* (Vienna: Czernin, 2005)

Wagner, Renata: *Karl Amadeus Hartmann und die Musica Viva* (Munich: Piper, 1980)

Wagner, Richard: *Mein Leben* (Berlin: Directmedia, 2006)

Wagner, Richard: *Werke, Schriften und Briefe*, ed. Sven Friedrich (Berlin: Directmedia, 2004)

Wagner-Trenkwitz, Christoph: *Durch die Hand der Schönheit: Richard Strauss und Wien* (Vienna: Kremayr & Scheriau, 1999)

Waissenberger, Robert, ed.: Vienna 1890-1920 (New York: Rizzoli, 1985)

Waissenberger, Robert, ed.: *Vienna in the Biedermeier Age* (New York: Rizzoli, 1986)

Waldstein, Wilhelm: *Hans Gál* (Vienna: Lafite, 1965)

Walser-Smith, Helmut: *The Continuities of German History* (Cambridge: Cambridge University Press, 2008)

Walter, Bruno: *Gustav Mahler: Ein Porträt* (Wilhelmshaven: Noetzel/Heinrichshofen, 1989)

Walter, Michael: *Hitler in der Oper Deutsches Musikleben, 1919-1945* (Stuttgart: Metzler, 2000)

Wassermann, Jakob: *Mein Weg als Deutscher und Jude* (Munich: DTV, 2005)

Watson, Peter: *The German Genius* (New York: Simon and Schuster, 2010)

Waugh, Alexander: *The House of Wittgenstein: A Family at War* (London: Bloomsbury, 2008)

Weber, Horst, ed.: *Musik in der Emigration, 1933–1945: Verfolgung, Vertreibung, Rückwirkung* (Stuttgart: Metzler, 1994)

Weber, Horst, ed.: *Zemlinskys Briefwechsel mit Schönberg, Webern, Berg und Schreker* (Mainz: Schott, 1995)

Weber, Horst, and Manuela Schwartz, ed.: *Quellen zur Geschichte emigrierter Musiker 1933–1950: Kalifornien* (Munich: Saur, 2003)

Weber, Horst, and Manuela Schwartz, ed.: *Sources Relating to the History of Emigré Musicians, 1933–1950. Vol. 1: California* (Munich: Saur, 2003)

Wegele, Peter: *Der Filmkomponist Max Steiner* (Vienna: Böhlau, 2012)

Weill, Kurt: *Musik und Theater: Gesammelte Schriften mit einer Auswahl von Gesprächen und Interviews*, ed. Jürgen Schebera and Stephen Hinton (Berlin: Henschel, 1990)

Weill, Kurt: *Speak Low (when you speak love): The Letters of Kurt Weill and Lotte Lenya*, trans. and ed. Kim Kowalke and Lys Symonette (Berkeley, CA: University of California Press, 1996)

Weinberger, Peter: *Nanopolis: Geschichten über Menschen entlang der Wiener Straßenbahnlinie D* (Weißenkirchen in der Wachau: Österreichisches Literaturforum, 2011)

Weiner, Marc A.: *Antisemitische Fantasien: Die Musikdramen Richard Wagners* (Berlin: Henschel, 2000)

Weiss, John: *The Politics of Hate: Anti-Semitism, History, and the Holocaust in Modern Europe* (Chicago: Dee, 2003)

Weißmann, Adolf: *Die Musik in der Weltkrise* (Munich: DVA, 1922)

Weissweiler, Eva: *Ausgemerzt! Das Lexikon der Juden in der Musik und seine mörderischen Folgen* (Munich: Dittrich, 1999)

Wellesz, Egon: *A History of Byzantine Music and Hymnography* (Oxford: Oxford University Press, 1961)

Wellesz, Egon: *Arnold Schönberg* (Wilhelmshaven: Heinrichshofen, 1985)

Wellesz, Egon and Emmy: *Memoiren*, ed. Franz Endler (Vienna: Zsolnay, 1981)

Weniger, Kay: *Zwischen Bühne und Baracke: Lexikon der verfolgten Theater-, Film- und Musikkünstler, 1933–1945* (Berlin: Metropol, 2008)

Weyr, Thomas: *The Setting of the Pearl: Vienna under Hitler* (Oxford: Oxford University Press, 2005)

Wheatcroft, Andrew: *The Enemy at the Gate: Habsburgs, Ottomans and the Battle for Europe* (London: Bodley Head, 2008)

Widmaier, Tobias, ed.: *Zum Einschlafen gibt's genügend Musiken: Die Referate des Erwin Schulhoff-Kolloquiums, Düsseldorf 1994* (Hamburg: von Bockel, 1996)

Wilford, Hugh: *The Mighty Wurlitzer: How the CIA Played America* (Cambridge, MA: Harvard University Press, 2008)

Willett, John: *The Weimar Years: A Culture Cut Short* (London: Thames and Hudson, 1984)

Willitt, John: *The New Sobriety – Art and Politics in the Weimar Period, 1917–1933* (London: Thames and Hudson, 1982)

Wiser, William: *The Crazy Years: Paris in the Twenties* (London: Thames and Hudson, 1983)

Wißmann, Friederike: *Hanns Eisler: Komponist, Weltbürger, Revolutionär* (Gütersloh: Bertelsmann, 2011)

Wladika, Michael: *Hitlers Vätergeneration: Die Ursprünge des Nationalsozialismus in der K.u.K. Monarchie* (Vienna: Böhlau, 2005)

Wolffram, Knud: *Tanzdielen und Vergnügungspaläste* (Berlin: Hentrich, 1992)

Wörner, Karl H.: *Schönberg's Moses and Aaron*, trans. Paul Hamburger (London: Faber, 1959)

Wulf, Joseph: *Musik im Dritten Reich: Eine Dokumentation, Zeitgeschichte* (Reinbek: Rowohlt, 1966)

Wunberg, Gotthart, and Johannes J. Braakenburg: *Die Wiener Modern Literatur, Kunst und Musik zwischen 1890 und 1910* (Leipzig: Reclam, 1981)

Zamoyski, Adam: *Rites of Peace: The Fall of Napoleon and the Congress of Vienna* (New York: Harper, 2007)

Zuckerkandl, Berta: *Österreich Intim: Erinnerungen 1892–1942* (Vienna: Amalthea, 1970)

Zuckerkandl, Berta: 'George Minne', in *Bertha Zuckerkandl, Zeitkunst Wien, 1901–1907* (Vienna: Heller, 1908)

Zühlsdorff, Vokmar: *Hitler's Exile: The German Cultural Resistance in America and Europe*, trans. Martin H. Bott (London: Continuum, 2004)

Zweig, Stefan: *Die Welt von Gestern: Erinnerungen eines Europäers* (Frankfurt: Fischer, 1970)

Index